THE DISCOURSE ON

THE ALL-EMBRACING NET OF VIEWS

THE DISCOURSE ON

THE ALL-EMBRACING NET OF VIEWS

THE BRAHMAJĀLA SUTTA AND ITS COMMENTARIES

TRANSLATED FROM THE PĀLI BY

BHIKKHU BODHI

BUDDHIST PUBLICATION SOCIETY
KANDY • SRI LANKA

Buddhist Publication Society
P.O. Box. 61
54, Sangharaja Mawatha
Kandy, Sri Lanka

First published 1978
Second printing 1990
Second edition 2007

Library of Congress Cataloging-in-Publication Data

Bodhi, Bhikkhu
The Discourse on the All - Embracing Net of Views: The Brahmajala sutta and its commentaries / Bhikkhu Bodhi. - Kandy : Buddhist Publication Society Inc., 2007. - p 370; 22cm.

ISBN : 955-24-0052-X

i. 294.382 3 DDC 21 ii. Title
1. Suttapitaka – Deega nikaya 2. Buddhism

ISBN 10: 955-24-0052-X
ISBN 13: 978-955-24-0052-0

Printed in Sri Lanka by Ajith Printers
85/4, Old Kesbewa Road, Gangodawila, Nugegoda. Tel: 2517269

TRANSLATOR'S PREFACE

The Brahmajāla Sutta is one of the most important discourses spoken by the Buddha, as is evident from the uniquely honoured position it holds as the first sutta in the entire collection of the Buddha's discourses contained in the Pāli Tipiṭaka. The importance of the sutta stems from its primary purpose, the exposition of a scheme of sixty-two cases designed to include all possible speculative views on the two central concerns of speculative thought, the nature of the self and of the world. The exposition of these views is an essential step in the overall structure of the Buddha's teaching. It is a preliminary measure necessary to clear the ground for the establishment of right view, the first factor of the Noble Eightfold Path, which is the way leading to the ceasing of suffering, the goal of the entire doctrine. The net of cases woven by the discourse provides a ready tool for assessing any proffered philosophical proposition to determine its compatibility with the Dhamma. For any proposition which agrees with the positions set forth in the discourse can be immediately recognized as an erroneous standpoint leading away from the path to emancipation.

For this reason, the Brahmajāla's scheme has been readily appropriated by the entire subsequent Buddhist heritage as a precision-made instrument for marking the dividing line between the Buddhist point of departure and the standpoints of other systems of belief. The sixty-two views which are already mentioned as a group elsewhere in the Sutta Piṭaka, become a standard category of the commentaries, and continue on through the philosophical treatises of the later periods of Buddhist thought as a convenient means for classifying the diversity of outside creeds.

In recognition of the cardinal importance of the Brahmajāla a bulky exegetical literature has built up around it, including a lengthy and fuller revised subcommentary. The commentary to the sutta is included in the *Sumaṅgalavilāsiṇī,* the complete commentary or *aṭṭhakathā* to the Dīgha Nikāya. This was composed by the great Indian commentator, Bhadantācariya Buddhaghosa (early fifth century C.E.), on the basis of the ancient commentaries, no longer extant, which he edited and fused into the single uniform text that has come down to us in the present day. The commentary has been provided with a subcommentary or *ṭīkā* by Ācariya Dhammapāla of Badaratittha (perhaps 6th century). The purpose of this latter work is twofold: first, to explicate the difficult terms and knotty points occurring in the commentary; and second, to examine in greater detail the positions set forth in the sutta, investigating their rationale, implications, possible objections, etc. In fact, the most valuable and interesting part of the *ṭīkā* is its "examinations" or *vicāraṇa*, which are usually set out in the form of a question or objection followed by a lengthy reply or defense. But the original subcommentary is often rather terse in its manner of expression, or excessively complex in its chains of argumentation, which makes the exact meaning of the passage sometimes difficult to discern. To rectify this defect, a new subcommentary (*abhinavaṭīkā*) to the first part of the Dīgha Nikāya was composed in the late eighteenth century by the Burmese Mahāthera Ñāṇābhivaṃsa. This revised work, named *Sādhuvilāsinī*, largely reproduces the content of the standard subcommentary, but expands and elaborates it for the sake of greater clarity, adding elucidating remarks where required.

The present project is an attempt to make the Brahmajāla Sutta and its exegetical equipment available in English in as complete a form as is compatible with reader-interest and intelligibility. The sutta has been previously translated, most eloquently by T.W. Rhys Davids, but never before presented together with its commentaries, which are necessary to understand the import of the many passages occurring in the original whose meaning has become obscured. In Part One I present the sutta first without comment and with only minimal notes. In Part Two, this is followed by the commentarial exegesis of the sutta, which has been composed after the fashion of a montage, drawing selectively from all three exegetical works so as to focus upon the exposition of the sixty-two views, and setting the remarks down in an intersecting pattern to accord with the order they follow in the explication of the original text.

The explanation for any particular sutta passage receiving comment can be found by consulting the umber of the exegetical section corresponding to that of the sutta. Though I have been selective, and therefore to some extent subjective, in my choice of exegetical material to include in this part of the work, I do not think I have been arbitrary. I have tried to incorporate all passages of doctrinal and philosophical importance, especially those crucial to an understanding of the sixty-two views. I have omitted the greater part of the commentary on the earlier portions of the sutta, as being of only limited interest, as well as the numerous instances of terminological analysis, grammatical inquiries, minor digressions, and other matters that detract from the main thrust of the discussion. In taking this approach I find myself justified in the light of the fact that a similar approach was adopted by Bhadantācariya Buddhaghosa himself when he rendered the Sinhala commentaries back into their original Pāli. Some measure of personal discretion is necessary to maintain interest and intelligibility.

The exegetical literature on the Brahmajāla Sutta contains three tracts which, though tangential to the main movement of the exposition, are of sufficient value to merit inclusion in the present work. One is a detailed analysis of the Brahmajāla Sutta according to the methodology of the *Nettippakaraṇa*, a technical exegetical treatise peculiar to the Theravāda school; this disquisition, included in both sub-commentaries, has been presented in translation in Part Three. The second supplement is a lengthy digression in the sub-commentaries, on the ten pāramīs (first mentioned in the commentary), giving the fullest account in a classical style Pāli text of the Theravāda conception of the Bodhisattva ideal and the practice of the *pāramitās*. I have presented as a separate treatise in Part Four, substituting, however, the full-length version of the commentary (*aṭṭhakathā*) to the Cariyāpiṭaka (which is also the version used in the new subcommentary) for the abridged version of the old subcommentary to the Dīgha Nikāya. And the third is a detailed explanation, found in the commentary, of the meaning of the word "Tathāgata," the most significant and suggestive of the Buddha's epithets. In the original, these last two essays occur in the body of their respective texts, but because they digress from the main trend of the discussion I have extracted them and set them out as supplementary sections following the sutta's exegesis.

An original translation of many passages in the commentary and sub-commentaries was undertaken by Venerable Nyāṇaponika Mahāthera in the years 1949–50. This had remained in manuscript form for twenty-five years. When he showed it to me, I suggested that I might mould it into shape for publication. This I took up with the constant help and encouragement of the Mahāthera—using the Mahāthera's original translation as a model for translating those passages it already covered (a number of which required little revision), adding numerous sections especially from the sub-commentaries, and furnishing in full the two supplementary sections of the *pāramīs* and the word "Tathāgata." For any mistakes I might have made in revising the original translation, I myself take full responsibility.

The style of Pāli in the *ṭīkās* is difficult and complex, the texts replete with telescoped explanations, arguments and allusions. Since the present work is the first attempt at a full-scale translation from the *ṭīkās*, I fear errors may have crept in. For stylistic reasons I have naturally had to take liberties in completing phrases and references understood in the original, in re-arranging the involved structure of the Pāli sentences, in supplying the logical transitions in arguments, etc. To aid students of Pāli in grasping the *ṭīkās* style, I have included an appendix giving a selection of important arguments from the sub-commentaries. It is to be hoped that future generations of Pāli scholars will continue to investigate the *ṭīkās* and render more of this philosophically and psychologically acute phase of Pāli literature into English.

The title of the complete work, *The Discourse on the All-Embracing Net of Views*, is the result of a free treatment of the several alternative titles given at the sutta's close.

Bhikkhu Bodhi

GENERAL CONTENTS

DETAILED CONTENTS OF THE INTRODUCTION AND PARTS ONE, TWO, AND THREE

INTRODUCTION

PART ONE — THE BRAHMAJĀLA SUTTA

PART TWO — THE COMMENTARIAL EXEGESIS OF THE BRAHMAJĀLA SUTTA

PART THREE —THE METHOD OF THE EXEGETICAL TREATISES

TEXTS USED

Primary Sources

1 Dīghanikāya: Sīlakkhandhavagga; Burmese-script Chaṭṭha-saṅgāyana (Sixth Great Council) edition; Rangoon, 1956.

2 *Dīghanikāya-aṭṭhakathā* (*Sumaṅgalavilāsinī*): *Sīlakkhandha-vagga-Aṭṭhakathā*; Chaṭṭhasaṅgāyana edition; Rangoon, 1956.

3 *Dīghanikāya-ṭīkā*: *Sīlakkhandhavagga-ṭīkā* by Bhadantācariya Dhammapāla; Chaṭṭhasaṅgāyana edition; Rangoon, 1961.

4 *Dīghanikāyaṭṭhakathā-ṭīkā*, Vol. I, edited by Lily de Silva; Pali Text Society edition; London, Luzac & Co., 1970.

5. *Sīlakkhandhavagga-Abhinavaṭīkā* (*Sādhuvilāsinī*) by Ācariya Ñāṇābhivaṃsa Mahāthera; Chaṭṭhasangāyana edition; Rangoon, 1961.

Previous Translations Consulted

1 *Dialogues of the Buddha,* Part 1, T.W. Rhys Davids, trans. (Oxford University Press, 1899).

2 *Brahmajāla Sutta: Discourse on the Supreme net,* Union Buddha Sāsana Council (Burma), (Rangoon, no date).

LIST OF ABBREVIATIONS

All editions Burmese-script Chaṭṭhasaṅgāyana, unless otherwise noted.

AN	Aṅguttara Nikāya (Sutta)
Bv	Buddhavaṃsa
Cp-a	*Cariyāpiṭaka-Aṭṭhakathā*
CY.	*Dīghanikāya-Aṭṭhakathā* (commentary)
DN	Dīgha Nikāya (Sutta)
Dhp	Dhammapada
Dhs	Dhammasaṅgaṇī
Dp	*A Dictionary of Pali*, M. Cone, Oxford, 2001
It	Itivuttaka
MN	Majjhima Nikāya (Sutta)
Nidd	Mahāniddesa
N.Sub.Cy.	*Sīlakkhandhavagga-Abhinavaṭīkā* (new subcommentary)
Paṭis	Paṭisambhidāmagga
SN	Saṃyutta Nikāya (Sutta)
Sn	Suttanipāta (Pali Text Society)
Sub.Cy.	*Dīghanikāya-ṭīkā* (subcommentary)
Th	Theragāthā
Ud	Udāna
Vibh	Vibhaṅga
Vin	Vinaya (I = Pārājika)
Vism	*Visuddhimagga*

References to DN and MN give the number of the sutta; those to SN give in turn the number of the major *vagga* (in Roman numerals), Saṃyutta, minor *vagga* (when present), and sutta; those to AN and It give *nipāta*, *vagga*, and sutta; to Ud, *vagga* and sutta; to Paṭis, *vagga*, *kathā*, and section; and to Vin, volume and *kaṇḍa*. References to Dhp, Sn and Th, give verse numbers. The references to Bv follow the chapter and verse numbers in I.B. Horner's translation of the work as *Chronicle of Buddhas* in *Minor Anthologies of the Pāli Canon,* III, (London: Pali Text Society, 1975). References to Vism are followed by the section number and page number of Bhikkhu Ñāṇamoli's translation of the work as *The Path of Purification,* 3rd ed., (Kandy: Buddhist Publication Society, 1975).

INTRODUCTION

I. The Place of the Brahmajāla Sutta in Buddhist Thought

The Brahmajāla Sutta is the first sutta of the Dīgha Nikāya, the first of the five *nikāyas* or collections of the Buddha's discourses making up the Sutta Piṭaka of the Pāḷi Canon. That the Brahmajāla was assigned to this strategic position—that of the first discourse of the first collection—was probably not a matter of chance or haphazard arrangement, but of deliberate design on the part of the Elders who compiled the canon and set it in its present form. Its placement reflects a choice, a far-sighted and carefully considered choice, stemming from a keen awareness of the significance of the discourse, both intrinsically and in relation to the Buddha's teaching as a whole. For just as our sutta, in terms of its position, stands at the entrance to the total collection of discourses preached by the Buddha, so does its principal message provide a prolegomenon to the entire Dispensation itself. It is, so to speak, the sentry at the gateway to the Doctrine, whose seal of approval must be obtained in order to cross the border that separates the Buddha's understanding of reality from all other attempts at a reflective interpretation of man's existential situation.

The paramount importance of the Brahmajāla in the context of Buddhist thought springs from the very nature of the Buddha's teaching—from its aim and from the methodology it employs to actualize that aim. The aim of the teaching is the attainment of nibbāna, the unconditioned state beyond the succession of repeated births and deaths constituting *saṃsāra*, the round of existence. The attainment of nibbāna brings emancipation from the round with all its attendant sufferings, stilling the process of conditioning that leads to a constant renewal of the cycle. Now what holds beings in bondage are their defilements (*kilesa*). So long as their defilements, their passions and delusions, remain unabandoned in the underlying stratum of consciousness, the event of death will only be followed by new birth and the round of becoming made to revolve for still another turn. The only way to bring the round to an end is by removing the springs that keep it in motion, by penetrating to the bottom of its originative chain. The most fundamental cause for the defilements, in the Buddhas's teaching, is ignorance (*avijjā*). Ignorance is the source from which they issue forth, and the root which holds them in place. For this reason, the key to destroying the defilements, and thereby to gaining emancipation from the round, is the destruction of ignorance.

Ignorance is the non-understanding of realities, a spiritual blindness covering over the "true nature of dhammas" that prevents us from seeing things as they really are. Its antidote is wisdom (*paññā*), a way of understanding things free from the distortions and inversions of subjective predispositions, clearly, correctly, precisely. As the opposite to ignorance, wisdom is the primary instrument in the quest for enlightenment and the attainment of deliverance. In classical Buddhist iconography, it is the flaming sword whose light dispels the darkness of delusion and whose blade severs the fetters of the passions.

At its highest level of development, wisdom takes the form of an act of understanding that crosses the bounds of mundane experience to realize nibbāna, the supramundane reality. This realization occurs in the four transcendental stages of the path—the paths of stream-entry, of the once returner, of the non-returner and of arahatship. In the peak-experience of these path-moments, wisdom cuts off the defilements that fetter the individual to the round, until with the attainment of the fourth path all are eradicated without residue. This consummation, however, does not arise fortuitously. Like every other event, it is built into the universal process of conditionality, and thus can only occur as the culmination of a long course of preparatory development that provides it with a groundwork of supporting conditions. This course begins in the same way it ends, with an act of understanding.

It is the experience of suffering that impels a person to seek for the teaching of the Buddha, but it is wisdom or understanding that leads one to accept the teaching and set foot on the path. For, in order to enter the path one must come to understand that suffering is not a mere accidental encroachment on life that can be relieved by simple palliatives, but something inherent in sentient existence itself; and one must come to realize that its cause is not some set of avoidable circumstances, but one's own delusions and desires, which one can set right by following the prescribed path. This is the first essential step without which the great march to liberation could never begin. And just as the last step of a lengthy journey does not differ in nature from the first, but only in its position in the series, so the final breakthrough of wisdom by which ignorance is shattered and enlightenment gained does not differ in essence, but only in strength, clarity, and power of penetration, from the first stirring of wisdom that led a person to begin that long and trying march.

In its rudimentary form, as an intellectual acceptance of the doctrine taught by the Buddha, wisdom provides the impetus for an evolving process of meditative cultivation that will transmute this intellectual view into direct vision. Thus, in the exposition of the Noble Eightfold Path, right view (*sammādiṭṭhi*) comes first. From right view spring all the remaining factors of the path, culminating in right knowledge and right emancipation. But in order that this embryo of correct understanding might come to proper growth it is necessary at the outset to clear away the host of wrong views, false beliefs, and dogmatic convictions that threaten its development at every turn. Therefore, as the forerunner of the path, the first task of right view, which must be accomplished before it can even begin its more demanding chores, is to discriminate between right and wrong views. As the Buddha explains: "Right view, bhikkhus, is the forerunner (*pubbaṅgama*). And how is right view the forerunner? If one understands wrong view as wrong view and understands right view as right view, that is right view" (MN 117.4).

Right view and wrong view each operates on two levels, one regarding the nature of actuality and the other regarding doctrines about the nature of actuality. Right view is able both to understand the nature of actuality and to discriminate between right and wrong doctrines about the nature of actuality. Wrong view both confuses the nature of actuality and cannot distinguish between right and wrong doctrines about the nature of actuality. Only when right view prevails will the correct discrimination between right and wrong view be made. So long as wrong view prevails, their distinction will remain unseen, right view will be unable to exercise its higher functions, and the development of the remaining path factors will be impaired.

In order to develop right view, wrong views must be eliminated, and in order to eliminate them it is necessary to know what they are. For this purpose, throughout the suttas the Buddha has taken special care to explain the different guises wrong view may assume and to point out its dangers. The wrong views mentioned by the Buddha can be classified into three general categories: wrong views with fixed consequences (*niyatamicchādiṭṭhi*), speculative views (*diṭṭhigata*), and personality view (*sakkāyadiṭṭhi*).

Wrong views with fixed consequences are doctrines that tend to undermine the basic principles of morality by denying the framework which gives meaning and validity to ethical notions. They include kinds of ethical nihilism that reject the law of kamma, the reality of moral qualities, or the efficacy of effort. Their consequences are said to be "fixed" because the firm adherence to these views is an unwholesome course of kamma obstructing the paths both to the heavenly worlds and to liberation; in some cases, where such adherence is especially rabid and dogmatic, the kamma generated is sufficient to bring a fall from the human world down to the planes of misery.

Speculative views include all metaphysical theories, religious creeds, and philosophical tenets concerning issues that lie beyond the reach of possible experiential verification. These views are not necessarily an obstacle to rebirth in the higher worlds, but in every case act as impediments to the path to liberation. All such views arise out of the personality view, the fundamental belief in a self or ego-entity which, as the root of its more sophisticated philosophical elaborations, is reckoned separately.

The Brahmajāla Sutta is an attempt at a methodical survey of the most populous of these three classes, the class of speculative views. The other two classes are not specifically mentioned in the sutta, yet they too are drawn in by implication. For the first class, wrong views with fixed consequences, rests its ethically disruptive tenets upon doctrinal presuppositions coming into the purview of the Brahmajāla's project, while the third, personality view, is the seed out of which all speculations evolve. The examination of speculative views is not unique to the Brahmajāla Sutta, for similar inquiries into humanity's systems of belief are carried out by the Buddha elsewhere in the suttas. What distinguishes the Brahmajāla and gives it special importance is the thoroughness with which it follows this enterprise through. The Brahmajāla does not deal merely with a few selected topics of current philosophical interest to the Buddha's contemporaries. It proposes to offer something far more complete: an exhaustive classification into sixty-two cases of the entire range of philosophical views concerning the perennial topics of speculative thought, the ultimate nature of the self and the world.

The Brahmajāla's claim to exhaustiveness is thundered out in the refrain that brings each section of the exposition to a close: "Outside of these there is none." The title of the sutta further underscores this claim while the same idea is given concrete shape in the memorable simile with which the discourse ends. The scheme of sixty-two cases is a net cast out by the Buddha upon the ocean of human thought, designed to catch and contain all possible philosophical theories on the nature of the self and the universe. It takes as its target not only those views that were being formulated by thinkers contemporary with the Buddha, or those that have come to expression in the course of humanity's intellectual history, but all that are capable of coming to expression whether they have actually appeared or not. The Brahmajāla is an all-embracing net, a net which contains no loopholes and no portals of escape. Just as a fisherman casting his net over a small pond can be sure that all fish of a certain size will be caught within the net, so, the Buddha declares, whatever thinkers speculate about the past or the future can with certainty be found within the net of his teaching.

Whether the sutta, in its present form, really does succeed in matching this claim is difficult to assess. On reflection it seems that many views from the history of philosophy and theology can be called to mind which resist being neatly classified into the scheme the sutta sets up, while other views can be found which agree in their basic credo with those cited in the sutta but appear to spring from causes other than the limited number that the sutta states they can all be ultimately traced to. Some of these will be noted when we turn to a separate discussion of the individual views. The subcommentary attempts to widen the scope of several views to show that they include more than they appear to at first glance, but even then there are instances not mentioned by the subcommentary which seem to constitute exceptions to the pronouncements of the sutta. Perhaps with greater insight into the range of each view the apparent exceptions could be shown to fit in. Or perhaps the sutta is, after all, only intended to show a selection of instances, and to allow the thoughtful reader to privately fill in the lacuna. The solution to this particular problem, however, is not so pressing, and certainly does not detract from the truth of the central principles the sutta proposes in its project of encompassing the range of humanity's speculative thought.

The question might arise why the Buddha is so concerned to discourage the inclination to speculation. Answers are found in many suttas where the Buddha details the adversities into which the indulgence in speculative views can lead. Views proceed from ignorance and blindness rather than from knowledge. They involve misinterpretations of experience stemming from subjective distortions of the actual experiential data. They proclaim a part of the truth to be the whole, as in the tale of the blind men who take their own limited conceptions of the elephant to represent the animal in its fullness. Views lead to conceit, to extolling oneself and disparaging others who hold different views. They result in dogmatic clinging, when one takes what one believes to be the only truth and declares everything else to be false. Differences in views become a ground for quarrels and disputes, not only among thinkers but also (as is especially the case today) among nations and groups that accept contrary ideologies. And finally, the adherence to views maintains the forward movement of the round of becoming by obstructing the acceptance of the right view that leads to the cessation of the round and by conditioning kammic accumulations that precipitate renewed existence. It is the last-mentioned danger that is especially emphasized in the Brahmajāla Sutta.

All the views dealt with in the Brahmajāla originate from one of two sources, reasoning and meditative experience. The fact that a great number, perhaps the majority, have their source in the experience of meditative attainments has significant implications for our understanding of the genetic process behind the fabrication of views. It suffices to caution us against the hasty generalization that speculative views take rise through a preference for theorization over the more arduous task of practice. As our sutta shows, many of these views make their appearance only at the end of a prolonged course of meditation involving firm renunciation, intense devotion, and keen contemplative zeal. For these views the very basis of their formulation is a higher experience rather than the absence of one.

That views of a metaphysical nature result from such endeavors indicates that they spring from a source more deeply grounded in the human mind even than the disposition to theorization. This source is the clinging to being, the fundamental need to establish and maintain, within the empirical personality, some permanent basis of selfhood or individualized existence. The clinging to being issues in a "personality view" (*sakkāyadiṭṭhi*) affirming the presence of an abiding self in the psychophysical organism in one of twenty ways: as either identical with, possessing, contained within or containing one or another of the five aggregates that constitute the individual personality—material form, feeling, perception, mental formations and consciousness. Arisen already at the pre-reflective level, this view in turn becomes the basis for later reflective interpretations of existence, crystallizing into the sixty-two views of the sutta. As it is explained: "Now, householder, as to those divers views that arise in the world, ... and as to these sixty-two views set forth in the Brahmajāla, it is owing to the personality view that they arise, and if the personality view exists not, they do not exist" (SN 41:3).

Since the notion of selfhood is accepted uncritically at the level of ordinary experience, higher attainments in meditation, as the Brahmajāla shows, will not suffice to eliminate the notion but will only reinforce it by providing apparent verification of the self originally presupposed at the outset of the practice. It is as if one were to lead a man wearing red-tinted glasses from a small room to an open field. The change of scene will not alter the color of his vision, for as long as he is wearing red glasses everything he sees will be colored red. The change will only give him a larger area to see as red, but will not help him to see things in their true color. Analogously, if one begins a practice with a view of self, and persists without changing this view, then whatever develops in the course of practice will go to confirm the initial thesis. The attainments will not themselves alter the view, while the deeper states of consciousness that unfold will be misconstrued in terms of the erroneous notion. Taking the idea of self at its face value, as indicating a real entity, the theorist will proceed to weave around it a web of speculations apparently confirmed by his attainments: as to whether the self is eternal or non-eternal, everlasting or perishable, finite or infinite, universal or individual, etc.

What is essential, therefore, from the Buddhist standpoint, is not simply to practice rather than to theorize, but to practice on the basis of right understanding. Hence in contrast to the speculative systems, the Buddhist system of meditation takes as its foundation the doctrine of egolessness or non-self (*anattā*). Any states of experience arising in the course of practice, whether of the ordinary or exalted level, are to be scrutinized in the light of the three characteristics of impermanence, suffering, and non-self. This deprives of its ground the tendency to identify with these experiences and to appropriate them in terms of the self-concept, thereby dislodging with final certainty all binding notions of subjectivity from their inner haunt.

It is interesting to observe that the Brahmajāla does not actually provide specific criticisms of the doctrinal positions it describes, nor does it even attempt to refute the general principles governing each class of views. Such refutations are taken up to some extent in the subcommentary, but the sutta rests content simply to explain each standpoint and to show the causal situation out of which it arises. A similar line is followed by the Buddha throughout the suttas. Only rarely is the Buddha seen engaging in reasoned argumentation to expose the flaws in other views, and then only when he is directly challenged, as in the cases of Saccaka (MN 35) or Upāli (MN 56). The Buddha's reluctance to engage in argumentation raises the question of the reasons behind his passive approach. To this question several answers may be offered. First, the disposition to argue and find flaws except when pressed betrays an unwholesome state of mind, a tendency towards aversion and hostility. Since an enlightened sage like the Buddha or an arahat has extricated the root of aversion, he has no inclination to quarrel over differences in doctrine.

As a second reason, it might be held that since conflicting opinions on each of the major doctrinal issues already existed, it was unnecessary for the Buddha to devise his own refutations.

All he had to do was to show the contradictory tenets in their mutual opposition to reveal that no satisfactory solution could be obtained within the limits of the instruments available to the contestants. Perhaps too, each of the contending parties had already developed a proof of their own position and a critique of their opponents, so to bring them into the open in the light of their disagreement would have sufficed to reveal that both were on insecure ground. Even the claim that meditative experience is an infallible source of knowledge would have been difficult to maintain, when one party's meditation revealed the world to be infinite and the other's that it is finite, when one finds no beginning to the soul and another claims to see that it is created by God.

While these answers doubtlessly contain an element of truth, another reason can be offered that cuts to a deeper level, taking us to the heart of the Buddha's teaching. The Buddha does not trouble to refute each separate view because the primary focus of his concern is not so much the content of the view as the underlying malady of which the addiction to speculative tenets is a symptom. This is the malady of *dukkha* or suffering. It has often been noted that the Buddha refused to give a definitive reply to any of the standard metaphysical questions circulating among the thinkers of his day on the ground that a solution to these questions was irrelevant to the problem of suffering, which it was the aim of his teaching to cure. When the bhikkhu Māluṅkyapuṭta told the Buddha that unless he received a clear solution to the ten metaphysical questions he would leave the Order, the Master compared him to a man shot by an arrow who refuses the help of a surgeon until he learns all the details concerning his assailant. Whatever answers are given to these questions, "there is birth, there is aging, there is death, there are sorrow, lamentation, pain, grief and despair, and it is the cessation of these that the Tathāgata proclaims here and now" (MN 63.6).

The same principle that lies behind the Buddha's refusal to solve the key metaphysical problems can also be extended to understand why he declines to enter into detailed criticisms of the proposed solutions. The Buddha's concern is with the immediate existential problem of suffering, and his approach is to deal with this problem directly, without evasions and without detours. This observation, however, should not be taken to imply that the Buddha dismisses the propensity to theorization as a phenomenon altogether disconnected from the problem of suffering; rather, he sees the articulation of metaphysical theories as part and parcel of the illness he wishes to cure. To accept any of these speculative views is to fall into "the thicket of views, the wilderness of views, the scuffling of views, the agitation of views, the fetter of views" (MN 72.14). All of these opinions are "attended with suffering, vexation, despair, and fever," and "fettered by them the ignorant worldling is not released from birth, aging and death, from sorrow, lamentation, pain, grief, and despair, he is not released from suffering" (MN 2.8).

Speculative views are a part of the phenomenon of *dukkha* because they represent a misdirected search for security. There is nothing wrong, from the Buddhist standpoint, with the search for security in itself, since it is this that motivates the Buddhist in his spiritual endeavors as well. The error, in the case of speculative views, is twofold: first, in the primary notion in terms of which security is understood; and secondly, in the place where it is sought. In all the tenets of thought dealt with by the Buddha, the notion of security is interpreted in terms of selfhood, which from the Buddhist perspective is a false notion born of ignorance, craving, and clinging. And secondly, once the self-concept makes its appearance, it clamors for a content, which the theorist seeks to fill in from the five aggregates: "Whatever recluses and brahmins regard anything as self in various ways, all of them do so by regarding the five clinging-aggregates as a self, or a certain one of them" (SN 22:47).

But the notion of selfhood has as its principal connotation the notion of permanence, while the five aggregates are all impermanent—bound to arise, fall and pass away. Hence any attempt to adhere to them as a self is destined to futility, and the endeavor to find in them a stand of security will invariably lead to disappointment and suffering. Since speculative views thus tie in with the net of phenomena embraced by the truth of suffering, the proper way to treat them is the same as that appropriate for the more general malady: to seek out their underlying causes and apply the remedy suitable for eliminating these causes. The remedy is the path that replaces the blindness of views with direct insight, the Noble Eightfold Path "making for vision, making for knowledge, which leads to peace, to understanding, to enlightenment, to nibbāna."

II. The Setting and Structure of the Discourse

In what follows I will briefly sketch the setting and structure of the Brahmajāla Sutta and then go on to discuss at greater length the sixty-two views which are its major theme. In my discussion I will try to weave the suttanta statements and exegetical analysis together into a single whole, adding clarifying comments where required.

For a sutta which will, when finished, expose and dispose of the full range of human speculative constructions and cause the ten-thousandfold world system to shake sixty-two times, the Brahmajāla begins simply and innocuously enough with an everyday scene in the life of the Buddha. The Exalted One is travelling along the highway between Rājagaha and Nālandā together with an entourage of bhikkhus. At the same time, a wandering ascetic named Suppiya is following close behind him together with his pupil Brahmadatta and—the commentary informs us—a company of disciple-wanderers.

As they walk along behind the Buddha, Suppiya speaks in dispraise of the Buddha, the Dhamma, and the Saṅgha, while his pupil, in direct opposition, speaks in their praise. The reasons for Suppiya's animosity are given in the commentary. Before the Buddha appeared as a teacher on the Indian religious scene, the wanderers enjoyed abundant gains and honor, but after he appeared the devotion of the populace was transferred to the Buddha and his disciples. Moreover, it seems that Suppiya was a pupil of Sañjaya, who was also the first teacher of Sāriputta and Moggallāna, the Buddha's chief disciples. When these two left Sañjaya to join the Buddha, their departure caused a split in the ranks of the wanderers, for which Suppiya conceived a grudge against the Master. Hence out of jealousy he spoke in dispraise of the Triple Gem, while his pupil spoke in their praise.

The next morning a number of bhikkhus gather in the pavilion of the resthouse where they passed the night, and discuss with wonder and amazement the precision of the Buddha's "penetration of the diversity in the dispositions of beings," one of his unique types of knowledge. The Buddha learns of this, approaches the bhikkhus, and admonishes them to maintain an attitude of equanimity in the face of the blame and praise of others, giving way neither to resentment in the former case, nor to jubilation in the latter. Both these modes of reaction spring from defilements, and to yield to them would create an obstacle to one's spiritual progress as well as to clear judgment. The correct procedure, the Buddha explains, is to correct the errors of those who level unjust criticism, and to acknowledge the sound words of those who speak praise. But in the case of crude abuse, the commentary adds, one should just remain silent, practicing patience and forbearance.

These two terms, praise and dispraise, provide the "strings" that bind together the different sections of the sutta. Dispraise is handled by the first part of the discourse, the Buddha's instruction on the proper way to behave in the case of dispraise. The remainder of the sutta is concerned with praise, specifically the "praise of the Tathāgata." Such praise is of two kinds: that spoken by a worldling like Brahmadatta, who judges the Buddha by his outward behavior and hence can make favorable pronouncements only in terms of superficial factors; and that spoken by wise disciples like the bhikkhus, who have penetrated the truth of the Dhamma and thus can appreciate the loftier, more profound qualities of the Master.

The first type of praise is made the basis for the second part of the sutta, the analysis of virtue, which enumerates in detail all the moral qualities on account of which the worldling might praise the Buddha. These are called, however, "trifling and insignificant," because they are inferior to the more exalted qualities of concentration and wisdom which elude the perception of the worldling. Following this the Buddha takes up the second kind of praise, that based on an appreciation of his more distinguished qualities, to show the true basis for "praise of the Tathāgata": his ability to analyze and classify the variety of speculative views on the self and the world, to understand them by way of their causes and future destinations, and to comprehend what lies beyond all these views—the state of emancipation without clinging.

This, the major part of the discourse, works through the sixty-two views in their distinct groups, dividing them by way of the period of time with which they are concerned, i.e., whether the past or the future, their general principle, and their particular thesis or mode of origin. It ends with a summary treatment of all the views together. After the views have been classified and explained, a number of sections follow showing how these speculations arise through a complex set of conditions governed by ignorance and craving. This genetic account is then subsumed under the more general principle of dependent origination (*paṭiccasamuppāda*), thereby revealing the predilection for speculation as a contributing factor in perpetuating the round of existence. As the counterpart to the "exposition of the round" there follows a section that shows the right view of the noble path to have the capacity to lead to deliverance from the round. In this way the Brahmajāla's exhaustive treatment of all views is brought into relation to the central theme of the Buddha's teaching: "It is only suffering that I teach, and the cessation of suffering." The sutta then concludes with two memorable similes and five alternative titles, to the shaking of the ten-thousandfold world system.

Before passing on to discuss the sixty-two views, two points in the preliminary exegetical sections call for brief comments. First, in the exegetical section on virtue, the subcommentary raises an interesting discussion on the justification of a precept prohibiting killing in the context of the Buddhist doctrine of non-self (*anattā*). When there is no self to be killed, and no self to kill, what grounds can be advanced for prohibiting the act of killing? A similar question is raised in the Hindu classic, the Bhagavadgītā, and the subcommentator might have had this passage in mind in his own discussion, since certain phrases he employs are reminiscent of the Gītā. The Gītā asks: if the one self is eternal and imperishable, the same in all beings, beyond action and involvement, why should one refrain from warfare? The answer it gives is that one need not refrain, that one can participate, can even kill, provided one follows a righteous course, performs one's duties in a spirit of detachment, and recognizes the reality of the all-pervasive self. But the Buddhist thinker must answer in a way that maintains the validity of the precept forbidding killing, yet does not concede the existence of a self to kill or to be killed.

From the Buddhist standpoint there can be no metaphysical justification for moral antinomianism. The subcommentator establishes his case by defining both the killer and the victim in terms of the "assemblage of formations" (*saṅkhārānaṃ puñjo*), the continuum of material and immaterial phenomena bound together by laws of coordination and transmitted influence. Though there is no self that kills, there is an assemblage of aggregates containing the volition of killing, which motivates and actualizes the murderous act. The victim, again, is not a self, but an aggregation of dhammas that would have continued to arise in the unified sequence of a singe life if the means of killing had not been applied by the killer, but which, because of the application of the means, is deprived of the vital material basis needed to continue in the same single life form. Thus the three notions of the killer, killing, and killed can all be defined in a way that does not require reference to an existing self, and the precept against killing is spared its validity.

The second point calling for explanation is the remark in the commentary that the "dhammas that are deep, difficult to understand" mentioned by the Buddha in the preamble to the classification of views (§28) denote his knowledge of omniscience (*sabbaññutañāṇa*). Two questions arise out of this: first, how this statement can be construed to indicate the knowledge of omniscience; and second, whether the texts actually justify the ascription of omniscience to the Buddha.

The commentary vindicates its position by pointing out that there are four special occasions when the greatness of the "Buddha-knowledge" becomes manifest: (1) the promulgation of the rules of Discipline (*Vinaya*); (2) the classification of dhammas according to plane and category; (3) the exposition of conditionality or dependent origination; and (4) the classification of the diversity of creeds. The Brahmajāla represents the working of the "Buddha-knowledge" in the last-mentioned category. Some hesitancy may be felt over the use of the plural "dhammas" in the Buddha's statement, but the commentary clears this by explaining that the plural is used because the omniscient knowledge occurs in several classes of consciousness and takes a plurality of objects. The first explanation is fanciful, the second has some justification in the present context. The Buddha's statement about "deep dhammas" is repeated after each group of views (§37, etc.), and in this setting it evidently refers to his understanding of the various views by way of their cause and result as well as to his enlightenment and emancipation. Since no one but a Buddha can analyze and classify these views completely, only the knowledge peculiar to a Buddha can be the subject of this refrain.

Nevertheless, while omniscience is commonly ascribed to the Buddha as a matter of course in the commentaries and even in earlier exegetical works such as the *Paṭisambhidāmagga* and the *Niddesa*, it may be questioned whether this ascription receives support from the four main *Nikāyas*. The evidence is ambivalent. In a passage of the Tevijja Vacchagotta Sutta (MN 71.5) the Buddha denies claiming: "Whether I am walking, standing, asleep, or awake, knowledge-and-vision is permanently and continuously before me." Yet to take this statement as a complete denial of all-knowledge would perhaps be to go too far, for in another sutta the Buddha says that to quote him as altogether rejecting the possibility of "all-embracing knowledge-and-vision" is to misrepresent him (MN 90.5). What he asserts is that "there is neither a recluse nor a brahmin who at one and the same time can know all, can see all," and this assertion leaves open the possibility of a non-simultaneous type of all-knowledge that can know whatever it adverts to. This is just the kind of omniscience the Theravāda tradition attributes to the Buddha, as is seen from the discussion in the subcommentary. But from the practical standpoint the question of omniscience is not so pressing for the Buddhist devotee. What is important is that the Buddha has discovered and proclaimed the path to liberation, and this one can verify by one's own practice and experience.

III. Speculations about the Past

The reflective individual finds himself in the world, hurled through time from a past bounded by his capacity for recollection into a future bounded by his imminent death. We may not even understand the actuality of our present existence as it unfolds from moment to moment, but our hopes and anxieties, our impulse toward greater knowledge, as well as simple curiosity, impel us to wonder regarding the mysterious limits to our being—our prenatal past and our future following death. The world also stands before us as an irreducible given, the locus of our being, the range of our action, the field of our enjoyment and suffering. Since the fate of the world is intimately tied up with our own destiny, wonder and psychological necessity again press us to speculate about its origins and ultimate direction. For these reasons the Buddha divides speculative views concerning the self and the world into two broad classes, speculations about the past and speculations about the future.

The commentarial explication of the terms the Buddha uses to express the theorists' adherence to their doctrines (see pp. 127–28) throws an interesting sidelight on the psychology and epistemology behind the fabrication of views. Speculations arise in their nascent stage as vague, groping thoughts (*kappa*) governed by craving and views, *taṇhā* and *diṭṭhi*. Craving reveals its influence in the proclivity to satisfy personal desires, particularly the longing for protection and individual immortality, by the adoption of a certain creed. Views, as a primal genetic psychological factor distinct from the formulated product, shows itself in the theorizing or intellectualizing disposition, which enjoys indulging in speculations merely to satisfy its bent for system-building, postulation, and argumentation. After arising in the nascent stage, these thoughts are reinforced by repetition and diversified considerations until their tenets are apprehended firmly as absolute truth and advanced as formulated doctrines.

The epistemological error is indicated by the comments on the word *adhivutti*. Speculative views are erroneous because they stem from a false apprehension of things. Those who construct such views fail to comprehend realities in their true nature, as impermanent and substanceless events occurring in dependence on conditions; instead they attribute to them a significance they do not possess. They *superimpose* on the concrete actualities an entirely imaginary character such as self, eternity, substance, etc., which originates not in things themselves but in the conceptual interpretive activity of the human mind, operating on the basis of subjective biases rather than on detached observation and clear comprehension.

The Brahmajāla expounds eighteen doctrines regarding the past. These are classified into five general categories: four doctrines of eternalism, four of partial-eternalism, four kinds of "endless equivocation" or "eel-wriggling," and two doctrines of fortuitous origination.

(1) *Eternalism.* Ordinarily in the suttas the term "eternalism" is used indiscriminately to signify any view positing an eternally existent entity without regard for the temporal direction or scope of its reference. But in this scheme of categories the term is used in a more restricted sense to signify only views referring to the past which assert the eternal pre-existence of both the self and the world together. Views affirming eternal perpetuity in the future are here called doctrines of immortality, while those asserting the beginningless existence of only a single entity or a limited number of entities are called doctrines of partial-eternalism.

The four varieties of eternalism are distinguished according to their modes of origin. Three arise from retrocognitive experience of past lives and one from reasoning. The three cases based on recollection of past lives stem from a definite and real spiritual experience. A *yogi*, by means of effort and contemplative devotion, attains to a degree of mental concentration (*samādhi*) of sufficient power to serve as the foundation for the *abhiññā*, or direct knowledge, of recalling past lives. Depending upon the penetrative power of his intellect—whether dull, medium, or keen—he can recall his past lives numbering up to a hundred thousand, throughout a period of up to ten aeons of world contraction and expansion, and throughout a period of up to forty such aeons. This gives the three cases. He then assumes an eternal self persisting through these periods.

The rationalists, regarded as a single type in the sutta, divide into four secondary types according to the commentary. The first reasons from hearsay or tradition; having heard stories of beings who lived through a number of lives, he concludes that there must be an eternal self. The second remembers a small number of past births, perhaps through memories which arise spontaneously without a foundation of meditative experience, and then assumes a self as their basis. The third takes his present fortunes or gains (*lābha*) to be the result of good kamma in the past, and assumes a pre-existent self to perform the kamma and enjoy the results; the third category might also include *yogis* who, without actually recalling past lives, seize upon their blissful meditative experiences as the disclosures of an eternally existent self. And the fourth is the pure rationalist, who posits an eternal self through bare reason in order to uphold the validity of the law of kammic retribution; that the law of kamma can operate in the absence of such a self is to the theorist incomprehensible.

The core of the eternalist position is stated in the thesis: "The self and the world are eternal, barren, steadfast as a mountain peak, standing firm like a pillar." Since two eternal entities are mentioned, the self and the world, two kinds of relationship can obtain between them: one is that they are fundamentally identical, the other that they are distinct. Perhaps with enough subtlety thought can also manufacture the view that they are both identical and distinct, but the two main positions suffice for consideration. The commentary glosses the strange word "barren" (*vañja*) to mean that the self and the world do not produce anything new, i.e., that they do not generate anything not already existent. The implication of this is that change is not real, that its ontological status is subsidiary to that of the eternally existent self and world. A doctrine denying the reality of change seems to clash so violently with the immediate evidence of perception, which uncovers changes taking place internally and externally at every moment, that it is difficult to see how anyone can question its validity. But philosophers are clever people, and have found two devices to reconcile the discrepancy between observed fact and their theoretical postulates. One is by regarding change as mere appearance, a surface illusion wrongly superimposed upon an unchanging reality. The other is by taking change to be the real transformation of a durable substance retaining its identity through the alterations of its adventitious modes.

Combining the two alternative positions on the relations of the self and the world with these two on the status of change, four possible eternalist positions emerge:

(i) The self and the world are identical and change is mere appearance. This is a fundamental tenet of Advaita Vedānta, the Indian philosophy of non-dualism, which advances an illusionist doctrine of change (*vivartavāda*) according to which all phenomena are mere appearances superimposed on the absolute as a result of ignorance.

(ii) The self and the world are identical and change is transformation of state. This position seems to find a place in some of the qualified non-dualistic philosophies of India (*visiṣṭā-dvaita*), arisen after the time of the Buddha, which regarded God, the individual souls, and the world as modes of a single absolute, and their changes as real modifications of the absolute.

(iii) The self and the world are distinct and change is mere appearance. Instances of this position are difficult to think of, since appearance theories generally operate within a monistic metaphysic.

(iv) The self and the world are distinct and change is transformation of state. This tenet, called *pariṇāmavāda*, was held by the Sāṅkhya system, the chief philosophical rival of Vedānta in the Indian orthodox fold. This seems to be the primary target of the Buddhist critique. According to Sāṅkya, the self or spiritual entity (*puruṣa*) and nature (*prakṛti*) are forever distinct. The self, which is particular to each individual being and hence a real plurality, is the pure witness of experience, free from change and alteration. The field of its awareness is nature, which remains self-identical throughout the variety of modifications it undergoes as mere transformations of its substance. All sensory and mental activities, as forms of change, pertain not to the self, which is changeless, but to nature, whose scope is thus mental as well as material.

One particular tenet of the Sāṅkhya, its doctrine of emergent manifestation, is tackled by the subcommentary, which attempts to show the inconsistency in maintaining simultaneously that an effect can pre-exist in its cause and yet come to manifestation at a later time.[1]

The eternalist doctrine is said to originate through a misapplication of the "method of unity" (*ekattanaya*) to the continuum of experience which is the subject of examination. According to the Pāḷi commentaries, to be correctly understood, the continuum must be comprehended through two complementary methods of investigation, the "method of unity" and the "method of diversity" (*nānattanaya*). The method of unity shows the distinct experiential occasions making up the continuum to be interconnected members linked together by the law of conditional dependence. They are "united" in that they are

1. See Surendranath Dasgupta, *A History of Indian Philosophy* (Cambridge University Press, 1922), Vol. I, pp. 254ff., for a more detailed account of this Sāṅkhya tenet.

bound together in a single process of transmission and development. The method of diversity balances this by highlighting the differences between the distinct occasions. Though unified, the current of experience is still a chain made up of distinct links, some of which function as causes, others as effects. Moreover, the onward flow of the continuum is periodically interrupted; the events of death and rebirth break it up into separate life-terms which show marked differences despite the identity of the series.

When these two methods are jointly applied, the current of experience will be correctly understood; but when they are misapplied or applied in a one-sided fashion, it will be misunderstood. If one misapplies the method of unity one will affirm the belief in an identical self and arrive at eternalism. If one misapplies the method of diversity one will take the discontinuous element in experience to be absolute and arrive at a doctrine of annihilationism. The correct application of both will show the continuum to be a causally connected succession of momentary processes, which continues so long as the causes retain their efficacy and ceases when the causes are deactivated. In either case, behind the scenes there is no persisting core to be grasped as a personal self. This is the middle way that avoids the two extremes.

(2) *Partial-Eternalism* (*ekaccasassatavāda*). This set of views differs from the previous set in asserting the eternal existence of only one or a limited number of entities, which may be either living beings or "formations" (*saṅkhārā*). The first three doctrines belong to the former class, the fourth to the latter.

The subcommentary points out that the partial-eternalist views discussed in this section are ontological theories in the full-fledged sense and not epistemological theories like the Jain doctrine of the sevenfold predicable, a relativist position which holds that the same entity can be permanent and impermanent depending on the standpoint from which it is described. According to the Jains, no single mode of describing the nature of reality is adequate to reality in its infinite variability. To compensate for the inadequacy of ordinary modes of conceiving reality they attempted to develop a scheme of predication with seven possible kinds of description, which, they held, was able to do justice to the different angles from which any situation could be viewed. The four basic assertions that could be made about a thing were: that it is, that it is not, that it both is and is not, and that it is unclassifiable. The remaining three are obtained by combining the fourth assertion with each of the preceding three. With regard to the problem of change, the Jains held a doctrine of relativism (*anekāntavāda*) teaching that in everything there is something lasting and something changeable; e.g., in a golden jar, the gold of which it consists is unchangeable, while its shape, color, and other qualities arise and pass away.[2] The subcommentary refutes this view by pointing out that the gold itself is an aggregation of material phenomena that are subject to rise and fall, and hence cannot provide a lasting substantial nature in terms of which the jar could be described as permanent.

The subcommentary also takes care to distinguish the Buddhist position, "the doctrine of analysis" (*vibhajjavāda*), from the doctrines of partial-eternalism. Both assert a dichotomy between eternal and non-eternal dhammas, but the partial-eternalist commits a double error that the Buddhist avoids. First he mistakes non-eternal conditioned dhammas to be eternal and unconditioned; second, he attributes to the things he regards as eternal the property of selfhood. In contrast, the Buddhist draws a correct differentiation between the conditioned dhammas of phenomenal existence, which are invariably impermanent, and the unconditioned dhamma, nibbāna, which is alone permanent; the Buddhist also refuses to attribute selfhood to anything, even nibbāna, since the notion of a self is a fundamental error.

The first form of partial-eternalism is theism, which acknowledges an eternal God as the creator of the universe and holds all other things to originate through the fiat of the omnipotent deity. In the sutta the origin of the God-idea is explained in a myth somewhat reminiscent of the biblical story of man's fall and expulsion from the Garden of Eden. Between these two, however, there is an important difference, in that the biblical story upholds the veracity of the idea communicated by the myth, i.e., the eternity and omnipotence of God and the reality of his creative act, while the Buddhist account is set against an altogether different cosmological background. According to the Buddhist cosmology, no temporal beginning can be found for the universe,

2. For a fuller account of the Buddhist attitude towards theism, see Nyānaponika Thera, *Buddhism and the God Idea*, Wheel Publication No. 47, (Kandy: BPS, 1962)

which consists of an incalculable number of world systems repeatedly evolving and dissolving in patterns governed by an impersonal law.

The belief in God arises through a misinterpretation of the events described in the sutta, a misinterpretation fostered on the one side by "Mahā Brahmā's" wrong understanding of the cosmological story, and on the other, by man's concession to this wrong understanding and subsequently misconstrued yogic experience. Seen in correct perspective the creator comes into being through the same law that governs his creation, and a look into the future would show that he is likewise bound to pass away when the kamma that brought him to his exalted position exhausts its force. He is not the creator and ruler he imagines himself to be, but only a superior being presiding over a higher plane of existence by reason of some good kamma performed in the past. Together with his company and realm, he is just as much subject to the law of impermanence—of becoming, birth, aging and death—as all other beings. It is only the enlightened ones, the Buddhas and the arahats, who have broken the bonds of kamma, escaped from the cycle, and reached the one true permanent state where aging and death reign no more.

It is puzzling that the sutta offers this as the only case for the origin of the God idea. Anthropology and the history of religion cite other causes that can account for the genesis of the idea with perhaps greater plausibility. Most prominent would be the gradual fusion of the animistic spirits posited by primitive man to account for natural phenomena into a single figure, all-powerful and intimately concerned with humanity's welfare. Speculative theology too provides an instance of a rationalistic origin, or at least justification, of the notion of a creator God, but this is not included in the section on the rationalist basis for partial-eternalism. Nevertheless, the sutta does indicate an important source for theism in misconstrued meditative experience, which cautions us against too hastily taking the revelations of supernormal states of consciousness to be conclusive evidence for the ideas they reveal.

The second and third types of partial-eternalism are difficult to identify with certitude in the absence of any clear information as to their historical counterparts. They seem to represent two kinds of polytheism. Both doctrines originate through a misinterpretation of the events recollected in a state of meditative absorption.

The fourth position is the rationalistic dualism of a transient body and an eternal mind. The theorist sees the dissolution of the material body, at least in its grosser forms of decay and death, but does not see the more rapid and subtler momentary dissolution of consciousness (see SN 12:61). Each act of consciousness, in passing away, conditions the arising of its successor, and the process of transition occurs so rapidly that to the theorist the flow of consciousness appears as a self-identical unit rather than as a sequence of discrete states. Hence, neglecting the method of diversity, he misapplies the method of unity, stamps the wrong notion of selfhood on both body and mind, and concludes that the body is an impermanent self and the mind a permanent, eternal self.

It should be noted that, as a doctrine concerning the past, the present rationalist doctrine implies that the mind existed eternally in the past; its main thesis does not concern the future. The doctrine may be interpreted in two ways: (1) as holding that the mind exists eternally and transmigrates through a succession of bodies, as in the Hindu analogy of a man who changes his suits of clothing according to his will, or (2) that the mind pre-exists in a state of isolated self-perfection and subsequently becomes incarcerated in the body through a spiritual fall, as was believed by some of the ancient Greek mystery cults. It remains peculiar why rationalism should be linked up exclusively with a mentalistic eternalism. On the one hand, reasoned demonstration has often been used to prove the existence of a creator God, while on the other, the doctrine of an eternal mind transmigrating through transient bodies might just as well result from the recollection of past lives as a full-fledged eternalist position.

(3) *Doctrines of the Finitude and Infinity of the World* (*antānantavāda*). The present section sets forth a tetrad of doctrines regarding the extension of the world—whether the world is finite, infinite, both, or neither. Where the previous sections expose the errors that originate from misconstrued meditative experience, the present section goes further in demonstrating how the results of such misconstructions can directly contradict one another, even while all claim support from immediate perception. The implication of this contention is the untrustworthiness of perception when not carefully scrutinized in the light of wisdom and comprehended in accordance with the principles of actuality taught by an enlightened teacher.

According to the subcommentary, the "world" spoken of by the theorists signifies the self; thus it is the finitude or infinity of the self that is the real subject of these theories. This interpretation may seem contrived, but other suttas sometimes discuss a set of views on the finitude and infinity of the self and the world, so the word "world" may here be taken as an elliptical designation for both. The objective basis for the formulation of these views, according to the commentary, is the sign (*nimitta*) of the *kasiṇa* functioning as the object of the *jhāna* or meditative absorption. The *kasiṇa* may be a disc representing one of the elements or a colored disc; it is used as a preliminary subject of concentration. Through repeated practice, the original object gives rise to an inner mental replica of itself, which in turn generates a bright and vivid "counterpart sign" (*paṭibhāganimitta*). The counterpart sign, once established clearly, may be gradually extended in circumference until it appears to become all-embracing, as though covering the entire universe (see Vism 4.31 and 4.127). The manifestation of this sign is an experience so exalting, accompanied by such powerful emotions of joy and ecstasy, that if a view of self lies dormant in the meditator's mind, he is likely to seize upon the sign as a manifestation of his "true self," "higher self," or "inner divine nature," which has made its appearance when the clouds of his discursive thinking have been cleared away by the practice of concentration.

If, as the commentary explains, the meditator cannot succeed in extending the sign to the "boundaries of the world-sphere," i.e., to an apparently unbounded area, he will conclude that the world is finite, and advancing this as his view, will claim to know its truth through direct perception. If he succeeds in extending it to an apparently infinite area, he will conclude the world to be infinite, again resting his case on direct perception. If he succeeds in extending the sign without limits along one axis but to a limited extent along the other axis, he will arrive at a synthetic view, that the world is both finite and infinite. The fourth view arises in the case of a rationalist who takes the mutually contradictory reports of the former theorists to annul each other, and thus concludes that the world is neither finite nor infinite. The commentary explains that these views are included among the speculations regarding the past because they occur in consequence of the kasiṇa sign previously seen by the theorist, but this explanation is not very convincing. Perhaps they are included here because the self or the world with which they are concerned is assumed to exist through a beginningless past.

(4) *Doctrines of Endless Equivocation* (*amarāvikkhepavāda*). Despite the use of the word *vāda*, "doctrine," the next four positions are not so much definite standpoints as grounds for refusing to adopt any standpoint. They are therefore called *amarāvikkhepa*, which the commentary explains in two ways. Firstly, taking the word *amarā* to mean "undying," hence unceasing or endless, and the word *vikkhepa* to mean equivocation (literally, "tossing back and forth"), it explains the compound as "endless equivocation," since the theorists who adopt this approach go on hedging without limits, refusing to make a definite assertion. Then, secondly, taking the word *amarā* to signify a kind of fish, perhaps an eel, and the word *vikkhepa* to indicate the movement of this creature, it explains the compound as "eel-wriggling," because this doctrine "roams about here and there, and is impossible to catch hold of."

The four positions given under the heading of endless equivocation all arise in the case of a recluse or brahmin who lacks understanding in regard to the subject of his reflection. In the first three cases this subject is said to be the wholesome and unwholesome courses of kamma, and in the last a questionnaire including a number of the philosophical topics debated in the time of the Buddha. We can assume the problem of the wholesome and unwholesome stated for the first three cases to be just a heading giving the most elementary type of knowledge expected of a respectable thinker, and that the more complex and difficult problems of philosophy should be understood by implication. The line of "endless equivocation" adopted by these recluses and brahmins appears to be similar to skepticism, but differs from the latter in an important respect. The skeptic holds that it is impossible for us to attain certain knowledge in regard to the problems of philosophy, and that any position we may take up can be demonstrated to lead to inner contradictions.

The "eel-wrigglers" represented in the sutta, however, far from denying the human capacity for certain knowledge, actually presuppose it as a very real possibility, only as one beyond reach of their own personal comprehension. Hence their refusal to take a definite stand stems from their anxiety that some item of information may turn up disproving the position they might adopt. But, like the skeptics, the first three equivocators place a special prize on peace of mind. The first two even display a certain degree of moral scrupulousness: one has fear of making a false statement, the other of giving way to desire or aversion. The third does not take a stand because he is afraid of being challenged and refuted by others, while the fourth equivocates out of sheer dullness and stupidity. As in the case of the extensionists, the classification of the equivocators along with the speculators concerned with the past is puzzling. The exegetical explanation is not particularly helpful in clearing up the difficulty.

(5) Doctrines of Fortuitous Origination (*adhiccasamuppanavāda*). The next two views, declaring the self and the world to originate fortuitously, arise in two ways: in the case of a meditator who recalls the seemingly spontaneous arising of consciousness after a period in the non-percipient realm, and in the case of a non-attainer by reasoning. The first calls for some discussion. Buddhist cosmology classifies the various planes of sentient existence in three ways according to the number of aggregates (*khandha*), i.e., psychophysical components, they contain: as five-constituent existence (*pañcavokāra-bhava*), four-constituent existence (*catuvokāra-bhava*), and one-constituent existence (*ekavokāra-bhava*). The first involves the presence of all five aggregates—material form, feeling, perception, mental formations, and consciousness; this is the kind of existence obtained in twenty-six of the thirty-one cosmic planes. But the cosmos contains as well five realms in which the union of mind and matter is sundered. Four are the immaterial planes where the four mental aggregates exist devoid of a material base. The fifth is a purely material plane where the mental current of the "aggregate-continuum" is temporarily shut off and only the aggregate of material form remains. Once the life span in this realm comes to an end, the mental process again arises to continue where it left off, driven by some antecedent kamma.

Whereas life in five-constituent existence is produced both through ordinary kamma and through the attainment of higher states of meditation (as in the Brahma-world), life in the other two modes can only be generated by special meditative attainments. Life in the four immaterial planes comes about only through the four immaterial absorptions, the lowest of which is here called "the development of the fading away of the material" (*rūpavirāgabhāvanā*), as representing the point where materiality is transcended and the purely immaterial sphere entered upon. This attainment, the base of infinite space (*ākāsānañcāyatana*), is realized first by developing the fourth jhāna through any of the nine kasiṇa*s* (omitting the limited space kasiṇa), cultivating dispassion for the subtle materiality of the kasiṇa, and withdrawing the image of the kasiṇa so that infinite space alone remains. This marks the entrance upon the attainment of the base of infinite space (Vism 10.1–10). The other immaterial states are attained by a progressive refinement of each lower attainment in turn. Analogously, by mastering the fourth jhāna based on the wind kasiṇa (chosen because its shapeless character resembles the immaterial factors which must be made to fade away) and by reviewing the danger in consciousness, an attainment called "the development of the fading away of the immaterial" (*arūpavirāgabhāvanā*) can be gained, giving access to the plane of non-percipient beings; in this plane the immaterial factors have been brought to a standstill and only bare materiality remains. Life in this plane endures for a length of time determined by the force of the jhāna that precipitates rebirth.

The belief in the fortuitous origin of the self arises, in the first case, when a meditator recollects a period going back to the first awakening of consciousness following its temporary suspension in the non-percipient plane, but nothing beyond, and on the basis of this recollection concludes that the self and the world are fortuitously originated. The second version of the theory occurs through reasoning, as when an ordinary person, not recollecting anything previous to his birth and not seeing any evidence for pre-existence, infers that before birth he did not exist and only came into existence at birth. It should be noted that the view that the self originates fortuitously does not necessarily imply the same for the world, though the sutta joins them into one. The eternal pre-existence of the world can be recognized even while holding to the spontaneous genesis of the self. This, in fact, has become the dominant outlook of the present-day materialist, which is often assumed to be the dictum conclusively proven by modern science.

The theorist's error is a double one: firstly, he does not realize that other existences preceded his sojourn in the non-percipient realm or that his reasoning is not as cogent as he imagines; and secondly, he attributes to the experience that he does remember the property of being a self.

IV. Speculations about the Future

(1)–(3) *Doctrines of Immortality.* Since human existence is essentially a movement into the future, which gives meaning to the present, it is not surprising that the majority of metaphysical speculations are occupied not with our prenatal past, which is irretrievable, but with our postmortem future, our destiny after death, which always lies before us as an object of conjecture and concern. Thus we find that whereas the sutta lists only eighteen views regarding the past, it discusses forty-four regarding the future.

These views are arranged into five sets. Three assert the immortality of the self in diverse ways; one declares the self's annihilation, and one proclaims "supreme nibbāna here and now." The first three comprise thirty-two varieties of future eternalism, all affirming the self's survival of death. They differ in so far as one declares the self to be percipient, the second that the self is non-percipient, and the third that it is neither percipient nor non-percipient. The differentiating principles that divide each set into its specific members are four: the question of the self's materiality or immateriality, of its finitude or infinity, of the quality of its perception (whether uniform or diverse, limited or unlimited), and the quality of its affective experience (happy, miserable, both or neither). All four apply to the first set, yielding sixteen views of a percipient survival. The last two do not apply to the second and third sets, which therefore only contain eight views each. Though enumerated separately, these views are not mutually exclusive, but simply provide a selection of conceptions of the surviving self that can be combined to form any complete theory. Thus the self might be conceived to be immaterial, finite, of uniform perception, and exclusively happy after death, etc. Instances of some of these views are rarely encountered in the history of thought; nevertheless, any of the immortality beliefs in the world's religions can be readily accommodated within the scheme.

It should be noted that there are two distinct ways in which the postmortem survival of the self can be envisaged, according to whether a reincarnation theory or a one-life theory provides the framework for the conception. If a reincarnation theory is adopted, the surviving self will be seen as transmigrating from existence to existence either *ad infinitum* or (as is more typically the case) until it reaches its final liberation from the cycle, according to the tenets of a particular belief system. If a one-life theory provides the framework, the being will be seen as living a single mortal life on earth, and then, after death, reaping his eternal destiny without further transmigration. Since the sutta does not draw this distinction, we can take its silence as a tacit recognition that both conceptions can be fitted into its scheme. This leads to the interesting result that on the reincarnation theory, the mode in which the self survives in its immediately following existence might differ from the mode of its survival when it reaches final liberation. For example, on the Vedānta doctrine the self will remain immaterial, finite, of diversified and limited perception, and either happy, miserable, both, or neither, so long as it is subject to transmigration. But when it attains liberation it will become, as it always is in essence, infinite, of uniform and boundless perception, and exclusively happy. Christian eschatology also allows some variation in the nature of the self in the postmortem condition. Immediately after death the self is immaterial and may experience happiness in heaven, misery in hell, or both in purgatory. But with the resurrection of the flesh and the reunification of body and spirit, it will become both material and immaterial, while the souls in purgatory who gain admission to heaven will become exclusively happy.

The doctrines of immortality are all stated in the abstract without distinguishing their sources as reasoning and meditative experience. Thus both may be taken as applicable to each case, though rationalists will have a predilection towards some views and meditators towards others. Whereas the recollection of past lives is the higher meditative experience usually responsible for eternalist views referring to the past, the divine eye that perceives the re-arising of deceased beings, as well as speculation based on the absorptions, is the source of eternalist views referring to the future.

(4) *Annihilationism* (*ucchedavāda*). The doctrine of annihilation is the perennial rival to eternalism. In its common form, as the materialist creed that death is the complete end of individual experience, without any continuation of a spiritual or psychic principle of any kind, it is a tenet that has gained a large number of adherents today, especially as humankind's vision turns further from the spiritual heights which held it in the past, to focus instead upon the mere satisfaction of desire as the purpose of our existence. Political and social ideologies which deny that human life has any deeper dimension than economic well-being and social security further

reinforce the appeal of this view by stimulating our desires and blinding us to the subtler facets of our engagement in the world, while the presumptions of scientists who pass beyond the bounds of empirical conclusions have further contributed to the proliferation of annihilationism.

The main thesis of the doctrine is, as given in the sutta, the "annihilation, destruction, and extermination of an existent being." This pronouncement is significant from two angles, indicating the double error at its root. One is suggested by the word "annihilation," the other by the word "existent being." The annihilationist arrives at his notion of annihilation through a wrong application of the "method of diversity". He sees beings dying and passing away, and other beings taking birth, and comes to the conclusion that they are entirely disparate entities, springing up out of nothing with the first moment of life, and passing away into sheer material elements with the extinction of the vital force. He does not see that this diversity occurs within the framework of a unity, that the separate life spans are part of a larger whole, a beginningless life-continuum containing numerous individual "continuities," each marked with a beginning, the event of birth and an end, the event of death. The kammically active factors functioning in any one continuity serve as causes for the factors arising in the succeeding continuities within the series, so that the forward movement of the continuum is maintained by the cause-effect relationship between its members.

By misapplying the method of diversity, which reveals the discreteness of the factors, the theorist wrongly apprehends the causal and resultant elements as absolutely unconnected, and thus supposes that a being is absolutely annihilated at death without any principle of transmission extending into a life beyond. On the other hand, the annihilationist also misapplies the method of unity, wrongly apprehending the discrete interconnected dhammas within a single continuity as an undifferentiated whole and hence as an "existent being." From the conjunction of these two errors arises the view that it is a self-identical being that comes into existence out of nothing at birth, endures as the same being throughout life, and becomes annihilated at death. Correct application of the two complementary methods would show that it is not a being who endures, but a succession of dhammas linked together by bonds of conditioning. So long as the defilements remain intact in the continuum, the succession will pass on through the event of death into a new birth and a consequent existence.

It is revealing that of the seven forms of annihilationism mentioned in the sutta, only one identifies the self with the physical body and proclaims annihilation to follow upon the body's dissolution. The other six identify the self with inner principles corresponding to the heavenly worlds, the fine-material realm, and the four immaterial planes, and hold that it is only with the passing away of this self that final annihilation takes place. This seems to imply that the usual practice of equating annihilationism with materialism is an oversimplification. Only the first form of annihilationism is materialistic; six admit that the doctrine can take on a spiritual garb. It may be that these latter six positions do not regard annihilationism as the inevitable fate of all beings but as the ultimate destiny and highest good of the spiritually perfected saint. They may be formulations of those mystical theologies which speak of the supreme goal of their contemplative disciplines as "the "annihilation of the soul in God," the "descent into the divine abyss," the "merging of the drop into the divine ocean," etc.

On this interpretation, those beings who have not reached the summit will still be subject to continued existence, while those who reach the peak will attain the supreme good of annihilation in the divine essence. The commentary does not offer any direct support for such an interpretation, but does not contradict it. Since such types of mysticism do exist, it is quite possible that the Buddha was referring to them in the exposition given in the sutta. It may be significant in this respect that four of the seven annihilationist doctrines arise out of the experience of the immaterial jhānas; descriptions of the annihilationist-type mystical experience often indicate that it is the immaterial attainments that serve as the basis for their corresponding mystical theologies.

(5) *Doctrines of Nibbāna Here and Now* (*diṭṭhadhamma-nibbānavāda*). The last set of views announces the possibility of a directly visible nibbāna here and now, "for an existent being." A fundamental error is already suggested by the phrase "an existent being," which reveals an implicit adherence to a view of self arising out of the misapplication of the method of unity. Further mistakes arise in the interpretation of nibbāna. For Buddhism, nibbāna means the end of suffering in the sense that it is the termination of the round of existence, which is the essential denotation of the word *dukkha*. Nibbāna itself is

an unconditioned state, unborn, changeless and imperishable, transcendent to all the conditioned, impermanent phenomena of the world. Its attainment occurs in two stages. One is directly visible here and now with the destruction of lust, hatred, and delusion, the forces that maintain the forward movement of saṃsāra. The other is attained with the final cessation of conditioned existence at the passing away of the arahat, the emancipated one. It is this latter that is the final end of the Buddhist path.

The five theories discussed here, however, do not recognize nibbāna in this sense, but conceive it only as the assuagement of pain leading to the experience of supreme happiness in the present life. The first, which proclaims nibbāna here and now through the enjoyment of all sense pleasures, is the position of the hedonist. This doctrine might also apply to the more sophisticated and pernicious school of religious thought, flowing as a dark undercurrent beneath most of the major spiritual movements of the world, which holds that the way to be liberated from passions is to indulge in the passions. The following four positions are held by the attainers of the four jhānas, who mistake the rapture, bliss, and peacefulness of their attainments for the supreme good. From the Buddhist perspective nibbāna can only be realized through the eradication of defilements by insight-wisdom, not by meditative absorptions, which merely suspend the activities of the defilements temporarily but do not eliminate them. In the jhānas the defilements remain latent and can arise again when sufficiently provoked. The absorptions are extremely blissful and tranquil, and when mastered they may issue in supernormal powers, but they are still compounded, conditioned, impermanent states, and thus are still included in *dukkha* or suffering.

According to the commentary, all the five doctrines of nibbāna here and now are comprised within eternalism. But if the first position is a form of hedonism, which sees humankind's highest good to consist in sensual indulgence, it would seem more appropriate to classify it under annihilationism. Perhaps, though, its classification under eternalism indicates that it is the antinomian type of spirituality that is intended. The four doctrines based on the jhānas are all appropriately categorized, for such doctrines invariably recognize a purified self persisting in its own nature following the dissolution of the body.

V. Concluding Sections

Having elaborated each view separately and exhibited its mode of origin, the Buddha next proceeds from the particular to the general, gathering together the specific doctrines under their common denominations in order to reveal the more fundamental matrix of causes from which they all arise. This he does with the pronouncement, simple but profound, that each proclamation of views is "only the feeling of those who do not know and do not see, only the agitation and vacillation of those who are immersed in craving" (V.1). To take this statement too literally would be to confound the words and the sense, for the feeling and the proclamation of views are two distinct things that cannot be identified. The forceful equation of the two is a device, a means for driving home an important point. This point, the central message of the sutta and the key to the whole phenomenon of philosophical speculation, is the fact that views are fabricated and proclaimed because they satisfy the cravings and desires based on the lack of understanding in those "who do not know and do not see." This is the meaning of the proposition: "craving is a condition for clinging," in the formula of dependent origination.

Clinging (*upādāna*) includes both the root error of personality view under the heading of "clinging to a doctrine of self" (*attavādupādāna*) and the more elaborate developments out of this error, the sixty-two speculative theories, under the heading of "clinging to views" (*diṭṭhupādāna*). A person inwardly feels compulsive urges that are manifestations of craving based on his spiritual blindness. In response he formulates views which satisfy these urges and thereby give him pleasure. If he proclaims his views and converts others to his standpoint, his success will reinforce his conviction and thereby enhance his feeling of satisfaction. The sense of pleasure will stimulate more craving, which will generate a still firmer adherence to the views, thus initiating a vicious circle.

The Buddha divides craving into three subsidiary types: craving for sense pleasures (*kāmataṇhā*), craving for existence (*bhavataṇhā*), and craving for non-existence (*vibhavataṇhā*). Since the conditional genesis of views from craving is stated in the sutta only in a general way, it would be interesting to dissect this relationship in order to determine which type of craving gives rise to which type of view. The most potent craving in living beings is the craving for existence, as is evident from the avidity with which they cling to life and endeavors to protect themselves from threats to their survival. But because death is inevitable, to satisfy our yearning for continued existence we fabricate views proclaiming the immortality of the imagined core of our being, our self or soul. Hence the craving for existence lies at the base of doctrines proclaiming eternal existence in a future life. The framework in which this view is set will determine the type of view that is held with regard to the past. If the theorist accepts a doctrine of reincarnation, he will most likely hold to the eternal pre-existence of the self and the world. If he instead works with a one-life frame, he will be more inclined to take up the partial-eternalist position which affirms the creation of the self by God.

When craving for sense pleasures is especially prominent, it may lead to the annihilationist position asserting the extinction of the self following the breakup of the body, for this position gives licence to untrammeled indulgence in sense pleasures. On the other hand, sensual craving, combined with craving for existence, may lead to the adherence to views asserting existence in a paradise of sensual delights after death, sometimes requiring abstinence and ascetic observances in the present life as the price of admission.

The craving for non-existence issues in views proclaiming the annihilation for which the theorist yearns. In its simpler form, this craving, as the outcome of repeated frustration and despair, will express itself in the wish for annihilation immediately after death, and give rise to doctrinal formulations declaring such annihilation to be the imminent destiny of all beings. This view will almost invariably be conjoined with a fortuitous originationist position with regard to the past. On the other hand, in its more spiritual guises, as the wish for annihilation in the "divine essence" or "nameless nothingness," this craving will express itself in one of the annihilationist type theologies following upon mystical attainments. This type of annihilationism can be conjoined with either an eternalist, partial-eternalist, or fortuitous originationist theory concerning the past.

All these views are called "agitation and vacillation." They are "agitation and vacillation" because they are means of gratifying the insatiable impulses of craving, because they cling to things in a manner contrary to their real natures, and because they are grounded in ignorance. Views are an attempt to establish a base of permanence upon a world that is impermanent, to find selfhood in that which is selfless, and to find true happiness in that which is a constant source of suffering—namely, in the five aggregates of clinging. Since views proclaim things to possess a nature that they do not really have, entirely under the dictates of craving, the adherence to them is always accompanied by an inner turmoil or element of anxiety, which vitiates the feeling of pleasure they give with a nagging sense of mental uneasiness. It is this which makes the holding to views a form of suffering.

Views arise in those "who do not know and do not see." While this lack of comprehension can be understood in a general way, the subcommentary points out that it can also be taken to refer specifically to ignorance about the feelings that condition the adherence to views. Not understanding the real causes for their adherence, the theorists delight in the feelings that arise conditioned by the proclamation of their views. This generates more craving and clinging in turn, as attempts to recapture the pleasant feeling, and these maintain the continued revolution of the round of existence. Since craving is the basic root of the round, and the origin of suffering, and craving is conditioned by feeling, the Buddha singles out feeling as the existential factor most in need of examination to bring the round to an end. Feeling is the "bait of the round" (*vaṭṭāmisa*) which will be swallowed when left unexamined, but will be discarded if the hook it conceals is detected. Ignorance of feeling means not seeing its origin, passing away, satisfaction, unsatisfactoriness, and the escape from it—the five angles from which any mundane phenomenon must be inspected to gain insight into its real nature. In order to contrast the ignorance of the theorists with his own wisdom, in the refrain following each of the expositions of views (§36, etc.), the Buddha specifies his own understanding of feelings under these five headings.

In the next two sections (V. 2, 3) the Buddha takes the chain of conditions back one further step, relating feeling to its own causal antecedent, contact. This disclosure of the conditioned arising of feeling provides an inlet for subsuming all the items previously discussed under the law of dependent origination. Contact is the condition for the feeling which arises through the proclamation of views. This feeling conditions craving, which conditions a firmer clinging to the formulated views, which generates kammic accumulations bringing about a descent into renewed birth, followed by inevitable aging and death. In this way the propensity for speculation and doctrinal adherence comes into perspective in its true nature: it is not simply a profitless enterprise or a waste of intellectual energy but a tough fetter which keeps the world in bondage to the cycle of repeated becoming. So long as we are weighed down by the attachment to our opinions, for so long we will remain submerged in the ocean of birth and death, unable to find the path to escape.

It is characteristic of the Buddha's methodology that he does not show a problem without also pointing out the means to its solution. Accordingly, in the following section (V.4), the Buddha reveals the method for cutting through the entangling net of views: the development of wisdom, exemplified by a bhikkhu who understands the origin, passing away, satisfaction, unsatisfactoriness, and escape in regard to the six bases of contact. Since these are the six doors for the origination of all experience, one who understands them from these five angles will no longer be beguiled by craving into forming attachments to views. He sees the entire domain of experience as conditionally arisen, and therefore as impermanent, unsatisfactory, and devoid of an enduring self. With this insight as his instrument, he is able to eradicate ignorance, cut off craving, and arrive in the end at a realization of "that which transcends all these views"—the state of emancipation, the peace of deliverance, which lies beyond the turmoil of the round.

Before closing the discourse, the Buddha gives two monumental similes awesome in their power of expression. The first, comparing the net of the sixty-two cases to a fishing net cast out upon the pool of human thought, we have already discussed. With the second, the Buddha compares his own state of emancipation through the severing of the "leash of existence" to a bunch of mangoes cut off from its tree at the stalk. Just as, by the cutting of the stalk, the bunch of mangoes is separated from the tree, and the tree can never again send forth mangoes from that stalk, so the Buddha has cut off the "leash of existence," i.e., the craving to be, and in cutting off craving he will never again make his appearance in any of the realms of sentient existence. So long as his body endures, gods and men will see him, but with the ending of his life span they will see him no more; for he has torn out the roots of becoming, and with the end of his life will make an end to the round, attaining the element of nibbāna without residue (*anupādisesanibbānadhātu*).

This is the certification of authority for his teaching: it is an emancipating teaching because it is taught by one who has attained emancipation and recognizes his attainment with complete certitude. Then, with five alternative titles, the Master brings the discourse to a close, while the ten-thousandfold world system quakes as a sign of applause.

VI. The Method of the Exegetical Treatises

The subcommentaries, both old and new, add to their elucidation of the commentary a special supplementary section explicating the Brahmajāla Sutta according to the "method of the exegetical treatises" (*pakaraṇanaya*). What is referred to here is a method of analyzing a sutta text developed in a pair of treatises belonging to the Theravāda school, the *Peṭakopadesa* and the *Nettippakaraṇa*. The latter, in particular, being the clearer and more concise of the two, seems to have been the basis for the subcommentarial exposition. The first set of categories in this supplementary section, giving the sutta's origin, purpose, receptacle, and condensed meanings, is not found in the *Netti*, but probably belonged to the standard exegetical equipment of medieval Indian scholasticism. But the rest of the exposition is all taken from the *Netti*.

The *Nettippakaraṇa* is a special exegetical work designed to elicit from the bulk of the Buddha's recorded teachings the unifying principles underlying the variegated expressions of the doctrine. It is founded upon the assumption that beneath the many diverse utterances of the Master, adapted to the temperament and circumstances of the listeners, there runs a single uniform system, which can be extracted from the particular utterance under investigation and displayed in its abstract essence. The *Netti* itself is not a commentary, but a guide for commentators. It presupposes that its reader is already familiar with the Buddha's teachings, and that his purpose is to find a convenient way to explain them to others. Hence it explains, not so much the teachings themselves—though this is done incidentally by way of exemplification—but the techniques that can be used to bring out the structural elements running through and supporting the teachings.

The *Netti* sets out its methodology under two heads, according to the two interwoven elements of the Dhamma, its phrasing (*byañjana*) and its meaning (*attha*). The phrasing is handled by sixteen "modes of conveyance" (*hāra*). These are techniques of verbal and logical analysis that can be applied to any specific passage to bring out the principles entering into the verbal formulation of its ideas; it can also be used to explore the implications of the passage in the context of the doctrine as a whole. The meaning is handled by three methods or "guidelines" (*naya*). Taking the meaning to be the aim or goal of the doctrine (for the word *attha* signifies both), namely, the attainment of nibbāna, these show how the sutta points to this aim by countering the fundamental unwholesome factors—shown by a dyad, a triad and a tetrad—with a corresponding set of wholesome factors, shown by an opposing dyad, a triad, and a tetrad. The *Netti* then reverts to another two methods concerned with phrasing, which handle the sutta's terms in line with the methods explicating the meaning. The work closes with a "pattern of the Dispensation" (*sāsanapaṭṭhāna*) offering a typology into which any given sutta can be classified by way of its principal theme or themes.

The nature of the *Netti* and its place in Buddhist literature have been ably discussed by Bhikkhu Ñāṇamoli in his introduction to his translation of the work under the title *The Guide* (London: Pali Text Society, 1962). Here we confine ourselves only to a brief explanation of the *Netti's* methodology, i.e., its sixteen conveyance-modes and five methods, to facilitate understanding its application to the Brahmajāla Sutta.

THE SIXTEEN MODES OF CONVEYANCE

Mode 1 requires that the text chosen be demonstrated to convey the essence of the Buddha's teaching, given in the *Netti* under six headings: satisfaction, unsatisfactoriness, escape, fruit, means and injunction to devotees. The first three terms are an alternative rendition of the Four Noble Truths: satisfaction (*assāda*) is the truth of origin, unsatisfactoriness (*ādīnava*) the truth of suffering, and escape (*nissaraṇa*) the truths of cessation and of the path. The subcommentary first exhibits how the key terms of the sutta are included by the four truths, and then reduces the truths to the first three headings. Finally, it shows how the text provides instances of the following three headings.

Mode 2 which inquires into the reasons behind the choice of words, is fully intelligible only in the Pāḷi, and hence has been omitted here.

Mode 3 requires the demonstration, from the text's wording, of what may or may not be construed from it. This mode is concerned with rewording the passage chosen in such a way as to bring out its precise signification. Often this will require the help of other modes which show what meanings may legitimately be derived from a selected text.

Mode 4 requires that the dhammas or concrete actualities indicated by the terms of the text be shown to function as proximate causes for other dhammas resulting from them and dependent upon them. This mode brings to the fore the principle of conditionality, the heart of the Buddha's doctrine.

Mode 5 requires that the items mentioned in the text be treated as members of a class governed by a general characteristic, so that when one item of the class is given, the remaining items which share that characteristic may also be brought in under the same principle of interpretation.

Mode 6 requires the specification of four factors: the source, purport, linguistic features, and sequence in regard to the chosen text.

Mode 7 involves two steps: first, extracting from the wording of the text a standard doctrinal concept belonging to one side of the wholesome/unwholesome dichotomy; and then, taking this concept as a proximate cause, showing the implicit factors which may be derived from it, and which therefore "turn up" when the first term is mentioned.

Mode 8 analyzes the dhammas mentioned in the text according to their ethical quality—whether wholesome, unwholesome, or indeterminate; according to their plane of occurrence; and also according to their proximate cause.

Mode 9 requires the "reversal" of wholesome and unwholesome dhammas into their opposites, and a demonstration of what this reversal entails by way of either progress or decline toward the goal of the teaching.

Mode 10 gives synonyms for the key words occurring in the text. Examples are here omitted, as exemplification can be fully appreciated only in the original language.

Mode 11 requires the eliciting of the multitude of items described by each key term employed by the text.

Mode 12 requires that the phrasing of the text be examined for possible entry points into the teaching by way of its major doctrinal categories—dependent origination, the faculties, aggregates, elements and bases.

Mode 13 involves dissecting each passage of the sutta into its starting point, questions raised, clearance of terms, clearance of the starting point and clearance of the questions. Thereby its completeness and fulfilment of its original purpose are demonstrated.

Mode 14 requires the demonstration that each general term in the text includes under itself a number of particulars, so that, without displacing or changing the general term, it can be extended to each of the particular items it covers.

Mode 15 requires the specification of the causes and conditions of the key items mentioned in the text. It is complementary to Mode 4, which shows that the items in the text may be proximate causes for other factors not mentioned but only implied.

Mode 16 requires that the terms occurring in the text be shown to constitute or contribute towards the three training aggregates of virtue, concentration, and wisdom, and that these be co-ordinated with the type of "abandoning" effected by each aggregate.

THE FIVE METHODS

The five methods (*naya*) are moulded upon eighteen root-terms (*mūlapada*) consisting of morally oriented pairs of dyads, triads, and tetrads. The content selected for the root-terms, as defilements and factors of purification, reveals a genetic approach to the central meaning or significance of the Dhamma, the problem of suffering and its cessation. One side of each pair of terms represents the factors which originate suffering and must be relinquished in the course of practice; the other side represents the factors leading to the cessation of suffering, which must be cultivated.

The "method of the conversion of delight" (*nandiyāvattanaya*) works with the dyad. It involves scrutinizing a passage in order to discern its meaning on the side of the unwholesome in terms of craving and ignorance, and to show how these unwholesome factors are countered and overcome by their wholesome opposites, serenity (*samatha*) and insight (*vipassanā*), respectively. These two dyads may be taken as umbrella terms under which the entire host of unwholesome and wholesome qualities can be introduced into the explication of the sutta's meaning.

The "method of the trefoil" (*tipukhalanaya*), as its name suggests, uses the triad, which on the "dark" side of the teaching consists of the three unwholesome roots—greed, hatred, and delusion—and the "bright" side consists of the three wholesome roots—non-greed, non-hatred, and non-delusion.

The "method of the lion's play" (*sīhavikkīḷitanaya*) analyzes the unwholesome side in terms of the four inversions (*vipallāsa*): of conceiving beauty in the impure, pleasure in the unpleasurable, permanence in the impermanent, and selfhood in non-self. It counters them with the four foundations of mindfulness, employing each foundation in a particular mode to rectify a specific inversion. Mindfulness of the body's impurity rectifies the first inversion; mindfulness of all feeling as included in suffering rectifies the second; mindfulness of the changing nature of consciousness corrects the third inversion; and mindfulness of the selflessness of all dhammas corrects the fourth.

Of the two methods concerned with phrasing, the "plotting of the directions" requires that the dhammas mentioned in the sutta be plotted according to the double, triple, or quadruple directional state of the three methods concerned with meaning, deciding under which pair—dyads, triads, or tetrads—the terms found in the text can be fitted. And the next, "the hook," guides together the terms of the sutta along the two sides, the wholesome and the unwholesome.

Once the sutta has been treated in accordance with the modes and methods, it is then classified according to its place in the "pattern of the Dispensation" by way of its dominant themes.

VII. The Treatise on the Pāramīs

In its earliest phase, as represented by the four main collections of the Sutta Piṭaka, the Buddha's teaching focused on the attainment of nibbāna by the practice of the Noble Eightfold Path. In these collections the Buddha teaches his doctrine as a direct path to deliverance, and perhaps no feature of the presentation is so striking as the urgency he enjoins on his disciples in bringing their spiritual work to completion by reaching the final goal. Just as a man who discovers his turban to be in flames would immediately seek to extinguish it, so should the earnest disciple strive to extinguish the flames of craving in order to reach the state of security, the consummate peace of nibbāna.

The oldest *suttas*, however, already mention three types of individuals who attain the consummate state: a sammāsambuddha or perfectly enlightened Buddha, who realizes the goal without the aid of a teacher and teaches the Dhamma to others, founding a "dispensation;" a *paccekabuddha* or solitary enlightened one, who achieves realization unaided but does not teach; and a disciple *arahat*, who realizes the goal through the instruction of a supreme Buddha and then teaches others according to his inclination and capacity. With the passage of time, quite possibly due to a decline in practice and an increasing rarity of higher attainments, these three types came to be viewed as three alternative ideals towards which a disciple could aspire in the hope of some distant future attainment. All were identical in their realization of nibbāna, but each was seen to stand for a distinct aspect of the enlightened personality and to presuppose a distinct *yāna*, a "vehicle" or spiritual career, leading to its actualization.

For the Theravāda, one of the more conservative of the ancient schools, the emphasis was always placed on the ideal prescribed in the Nikāyas, the attainment of arahatship by following the instructions of the historical Buddha; the other ideals remained in the background, acknowledged but not especially attended to. Other early schools, such as the Sarvāstivāda and the Mahāsāṅghika, while upholding the primacy of the disciple's course and the arahat ideal, also gave consideration to the other ideals as possible goals for individuals inclined to pursue them. Thus they came to admit a doctrine of three *yānas* or vehicles to deliverance, all valid but steeply graded in difficulty and accessibility.

Within all the early schools, thinkers and poets alike attempted to fill in the background history to the three enlightened persons, composing stories of their past lives in which they prepared the foundations for their future achievements. Since it was the figure of the Buddha, as the founder of the Dispensation, who commanded the greatest awe and veneration, gradually a literature began to emerge depicting the evolution of the *bodhisattva*[3] or "Buddha-to-be" along the arduous path of his development. In this way the figure of the

3. Here and throughout I use the Sanskrit word in preference to the less familiar Pāḷi "*bodhisatta.*"

bodhisattva, the aspirant to Buddhahood, came to claim an increasingly prominent place in the popular Buddhist religious life. The culmination of these innovations was the appearance, in about the first century B.C., of the Mahāyāna, the self-styled "Great Vehicle," which proclaimed that of the three vehicles to enlightenment the bodhisattva-vehicle was alone ultimate; the other two were only expedients devised by the Buddha to lead his less competent disciples to perfect Buddhahood, from the highest perspective, the only valid spiritual ideal.

Through its conservative bent and relative insulation from the other schools, the Theravāda managed to resist the metamorphic changes taking place elsewhere in the Buddhist world, preserving the teachings as compiled at the early councils without radical alterations of their doctrinal framework. Nevertheless, in this school as well from a period even preceding the rise of the Mahāyāna, the figure of the bodhisattva began to make inroads into both its literature and spiritual atmosphere. Two elements in the early teaching seem to have provided the germs for this development. One was the fact that the Buddha had used the word "bodhisattva" to refer to himself in the period preceding his enlightenment, pushing its scope as far back as his existence in the Tusita heaven before his final descent to earth. The second was the recognition of the multiplicity of Buddhas, which showed the Sakyan Gotama to be, not a unique figure in the cosmic genealogy, but only the most recent member of a series of Buddhas each of whom attains enlightenment, founds a dispensation, and liberates a multitude of beings from the bondage of saṃsāric suffering. The Dīgha Nikāya mentions by name the six most recent predecessors of the Buddha Gotama (DN 1.4), and predicts as well the advent of Metteyya, the Buddha of the future, who will rekindle the lamp of the true Dhamma after it is extinguished in the dark ages that lie ahead (DN 26.25).

These two features in conjunction implied the existence of "germinal Buddhas" or bodhisattvas toiling to perfect themselves through countless lives in order to reach the summit of supreme enlightenment. The trials and triumphs of the being who became our own Buddha were recorded in the Jātaka tales, which relate the bodhisattva's conduct in his previous births. Just when and how the bodhisattva entered upon this course is told in the *Buddhavaṃsa*, a late addition to the Sutta Piṭaka, in a story that has become the paradigm for all subsequent developments of the bodhisattva ideal. According to this story, incalculable aeons ago in the far distant past, our bodhisattva (as the ascetic Sumedha) made an aspiration (*abhinīhāra*) at the feet of the Buddha Dīpaṅkara, the twenty-fourth Buddha of antiquity, in which he renounced the right to enter nibbāna then open to him, in order that he might become a Buddha in the future and provide salvation for the host of gods and humans. He then received a prediction from the Buddha confirming his future success, went off into solitude, and reflected on the qualities that had to be perfected to fulfil his goal. These, the ten *pāramīs*, became the standard constituents of the bodhisattva's practice, the requisites of enlightenment (*bodhisambhāra*) of our present treatise.

But though the existence of a bodhisattva career was thus acknowledged by the Theravāda, the dominant attitude prevailed among the exponents of the school that this path was reserved only for the very rare and exceptional individual. Since it was not recommended in the oldest authorized records of the Buddha's teaching, those who professed to follow the Buddha were advised to comply with the instructions contained in these documents and aim at the attainment of nibbāna by the practice of the Noble Eightfold Path. Thus the bulk of the literature in the Pāḷi school was devoted to explaining the details of this path and its doctrinal ramifications, while the practice of the *pāramīs* was treated only in broad and general terms. As time passed, however, perhaps partly through the influence of the Mahāyāna, the bodhisattva ideal must have come to acquire an increasing appeal for the minds of the Buddhist populace, and the need became felt for a work that would explain, in a practical style, the factors and phases of the *pāramitā* path without deviating from the conservative doctrinal perspective of the Theravāda. Works expounding the bodhisattva career abounded in the Mahāyāna schools, since this was their main concern, but a comparable work was lacking in Theravāda circles. To meet this need, apparently, Ācariya Dhammapāla composed his "Treatise on the Pāramīs," which is found in at least two places in the Pāḷi exegetical literature, in a complete version in the Cariyāpiṭaka Aṭṭhakathā, and in an abridged version in the *ṭīkā* or subcommentary to the Brahmajāla Sutta.

The work introduces itself as a treatise composed "for clansmen following the suttas who are zealously engaged in the practice of the vehicle to the great enlightenment, in order to improve their skillfulness in accumulating the requisites of enlightenment."

Followers of the suttas (*suttantikas*) are specified probably because those who aspired to follow the bodhisattva course had to work selectively from various suttas to determine the practices appropriate for their aim, as the text itself illustrates in filling out its material. The mention of the "vehicle to the great enlightenment" (*mahābodhiyāna,* or possibly "great vehicle to enlightenment") does not signify the historical Mahāyāna, but rather the greatness of the bodhisattva career in the loftiness of its goal and in its capacity to provide for the emancipation of a great number of beings.

The "requisites of enlightenment" are the pāramīs themselves, the main topic of the treatise. The word "*pāramī*" is derived from *parama*, "supreme," and thus suggests the eminence of the qualities that must be fulfilled by a bodhisattva in the long course of his spiritual development. But the cognate "*pāramitā*," the word preferred by the Mahāyāna texts and also used by Pāḷi writers, is sometimes explained as *pāram* + *ita*, "gone to the beyond," thereby indicating the transcendental direction of these qualities. The list of pāramīs in the Pāḷi tradition differs somewhat from the more familiar list given in Sanskrit works, which probably antedates the Mahāyāna and provided a ready set of categories for its use. Our author shows that the two lists can be correlated in section xii, and the coincidence of a number of items points to a central core already forming before the two traditions went their separate ways. The six *pāramitās* of the Sanskrit heritage are: giving, virtue, patience, energy, meditation, and wisdom. Later Mahāyāna texts add four more—resolution, skillful means, power, and knowledge—in order to co-ordinate on a one-to-one basis the list of perfections with the account of the ten stages of the bodhisattva's ascent to Buddhahood. The Pāḷi works, including those composed before the rise of Mahāyāna, give a different though partly overlapping list of ten: giving, virtue, renunciation, wisdom, energy, patience, truthfulness, determination, loving kindness, and equanimity. Unlike the Mahāyāna, the Theravāda never developed a theory of stages, though such may be implicit in the grading of the pāramīs into three degrees as basic, intermediate and ultimate (section xi).

The treatise draws upon various sources for its material, both Theravāda and Mahāyāna, and thus represents a perhaps unique instance of a classical style Theravāda work consciously borrowing from its northern cousin; in matters of philosophical doctrine, however, the work never deviates from the Theravāda perspective.

The set of ten pāramīs itself comes from the *Buddhavaṃsa*, as does the discussion of the great aspiration (*abhinīhāra*) with its eight qualifications. All of this had become part of the standard Theravāda tradition by the time the work was composed and was easily absorbed. Other Pāḷi sources—the suttas, jātakas, later canonical works, the *Visuddhimagga,* etc.—have all contributed to the overall composition of the treatise. The basic methodology of the commentaries is evident in the analysis of the ten pāramīs by way of the fourfold defining device of characteristic, function, manifestation, and proximate cause (section v). The heritage of the oral traditions of various teachers in later Pāḷi scholasticism is seen in the different views expressed on the three grades of practice for each pāramī (section xi), on the correlation of the four foundations with the different stages of the bodhisattva's career (section xii), and on the classification of time required for the completion of the pāramīs (section xiv). Perhaps the influence of another early school, the Sarvāstivāda, lies behind the dyadic treatment of the six *pāramitās* (section xii).

The main Mahāyāna work utilized by the author is the *Bodhisattvabhūmi*, the fifteenth chapter of the *Yogācārabhūmi*, a voluminous text of the Yogācāra school ascribed to Maitreyanātha, the teacher of Asaṅga. The *Bodhisattvabhūmi* provides the model for the four conditions of the great aspiration, the four causes, the traits of the great man adumbrating his future perfections, the characteristics of the good friend and the four powers.[4] The originals, however, have all been divested of their specifically Mahāyāna features to make them fit in with the Theravāda perspective. The *Bodhisattvabhūmi* has also contributed to the sections on the practice of the pāramīs, particularly the first, on the four shackles to giving, and on the special accomplishments resulting from the pāramīs.[5] Mahāyāna influence may further be discernible in the emphasis on compassion and skillful means, in the vows to benefit all beings, in the statement that the bodhisattva causes beings "to enter and reach maturity in the three vehicles," etc.

On points of doctrine, as we have mentioned, the work remains well within the bounds of Theravāda orthodoxy. Its section on the perfection of wisdom has nothing more in common with the

---

4. *Bodhisattvabhūmi*, pp. 4–9, 13–17.
5. *Ibid.*, pp. 114ff., 28–29, etc.

Prajñāpāramitā literature than the core of the Buddhist doctrine shared by all the schools. There is nothing about the identity of nibbāna and saṃsāra, the triple body of the Buddha, the suchness and sameness of all dhammas, mind-only, the provisional nature of the disciple and paccekabuddha vehicles, or any of the other ideas distinctive of the Mahāyāna. Even the mention of emptiness (*suññatā*) is restricted to the absence of a self or an ego-entity and is not carried through to the radical ontology of the Mahāyāna sūtras. The discussion of wisdom draws entirely upon the Pāḷi suttas and the *Visuddhimagga*, but only makes the stipulation that the bodhisattva must balance wisdom with compassion and skillful means and must postpone his entrance upon the supramundane path until his requisites of enlightenment are fully mature.

It should be noted that in the established Theravāda tradition the pāramīs are not regarded as peculiar to candidates for Buddhahood alone but are seen as practices that must be fulfilled by all aspirants to enlightenment and deliverance, whether as Buddhas, paccekabuddhas, or disciples. What distinguishes the supreme bodhisattva from aspirants in the other two vehicles is the degree to which he must cultivate the pāramīs and the length of time during which he must pursue them. The qualities themselves, however, are universal requisites for deliverance, which all must fulfil at least to a minimal degree to merit the fruits of the liberating path.

VIII. The Meaning of the Word "Tathāgata"

The commentary includes a long digression on the derivation of the word "Tathāgata," which I have taken out of its original place in the text and assigned to a separate part of the work. The word "Tathāgata" is probably the deepest and the most suggestive of the many epithets of the Buddha. It is the epithet the Buddha uses with greatest frequency in reference to himself, and it is only rarely used by others, as though its use was a privilege reserved for the Master himself. In recognition of its pre-eminence among the Buddha's epithets, the early Buddhist teachers have evolved an elaborate tradition of exegesis devoted to eliciting the word's multiple implications, which reached its standard form in the detailed account set down by Bhadantācariya

Buddhaghosa in this as well as in several other commentaries to the Canon.

The commentary gives eight basic reasons why the Exalted One is called "Tathāgata." As a glance at these reasons will show, each seeks to relate this term to some aspect of the theory or practice of the Dhamma. Such a procedure, though not strictly etymological, is quite natural to the standpoint taken by the teachers of old, who apprehend the Buddha not merely externally as a historical person but as the concrete embodiment of the Dhamma itself and thus see in his preferred form of self-designation a compendium of the entire Doctrine and Discipline for which he stands. Hence the subcommentary can declare that "the word 'Tathāgata' contains the entire practice of the Dhamma as well as all the qualities of a Buddha."

How this is so, a brief synopsis of each derivation should make plain.

(1) The first, which divides the Pāḷi compound into *tathā* + *āgata*, "thus come," points to the Buddha as the one who comes to the world along the same primordial trail as his predecessors, the Buddhas of the past. The indeclinable *tathā* here indicates conformity to a pattern, the participle *āgata* the arrival at a goal. Together, the two show the advent of a Buddha to be not a chance or unique phenomenon, but a regular outcome of the universal patterning of events. Since our present Buddha arrived at his goal through the same course as the Buddhas of the past, the word "Tathāgata," as the commentary explains, comprises the entire set of practices that constitute that ancient way: the great aspiration, the ten *pāramīs* in their three degrees, the five relinquishments, the thirty-seven constituents of enlightenment, etc.

(2) The second derivation, as *tathā* + *gata*, "thus gone," is elucidated in two ways. The first relates the traditional account of the bodhisattva's deportment at birth, explaining the symbolic significance of each element in the story. The second, like the previous derivation, draws upon the image of a journey, but now viewed from the standpoint of departure and transcendence rather than from that of arrival. Hence the commentary goes on to extract from the term "Tathāgata" the complete practice culminating in final deliverance: the abandoning of the five hindrances, the eight attainments of serenity meditation, the eighteen great insights and the realization of the four

supramundane paths, which sever all the fetters of existence and issue in deliverance from the round.

(3) The third explanation, "come to the real characteristic," hinges upon the tenet that every real *dhamma,* i.e., every concrete actuality, possesses a specific nature (*sabhāva*), characteristic mark (*lakkhaṇa*), or formal essence (*sarūpa*), by way of which it should be understood. Since the discovery of these characteristics is the work of the knowledge of the Buddha, it is appropriate that he be called "Tathāgata."

(4) The next explanation, "awakened to real dhammas," takes us to the heart of the Buddha's doctrine, the Four Noble Truths and dependent origination. Here the prefix *tathā* conveys the sense of reality, actuality, or truth, and the suffix *gata* the sense of knowledge. The compound Tathāgata then implies the awakening to the real, most fundamental facts of life—the truths of suffering, its origin, its cessation, and the path to its cessation, as well as the conditional arising of all phenomena of existence. Since it was the Buddha who first awakened to these truths, and who still awakens other to them through the medium of his teaching, he is called the "Tathāgata."

(5) The account as "a seer of the real" discloses the scope of the Buddha's knowledge: he is a seer of all that is real—whatever can be seen, heard, sensed or cognized by the mind. The commentary goes on to elucidate each category by way of the Abhidhamma scheme of classification, thereby calling attention to the analytical precision of the Buddha's knowledge as well as to its all-encompassing range.

(6) The rendering as "speaker of the real" hinges upon a slight mutation of the hard '*t*' of *gata* into the soft '*d*' of *gada*. *Gada* means speech or enunciation, so *tathāgada* becomes truthful speech or, by extension, one who makes truthful speech—a reference to the unerring veracity of Buddha's words.

(7) The seventh account, as "practicing what he teaches," expresses the perfect consistency between the precept and practice of the Buddha. He does not act in one way and teach his disciples to act otherwise. He does not inspire others with lofty principles while failing to fulfil them himself. Without need for self-justification or excuses, he practices what he teaches and teaches what he has practiced. In his own person he provides the ideal exemplification of his teaching, and he instructs others to emulate his example by rectifying their conduct in accordance with the teaching.

(8) The last rendition, as "surpassing" or "vanquishing," is based on purely fanciful etymology given in the commentary. Of greater value and interest is the following derivation, not separately enumerated, which relates the term "Tathāgata" to the four modes of penetrating the Four Noble Truths. Here the truth of suffering is equated with the world, for the deepest level of suffering or *dukkha* is found in the instability and essencelessness of the five clinging aggregates which comprise the world. The four penetrations are the full understanding (*pariññā*) of the nature of the world, by scrutinizing the impermanence, unsatisfactoriness, and selflessness of the aggregates; the abandoning (*pahāna*) of the origin of the world, the craving which generates the repeated cycles of becoming; the realization (*sacchikiriya*) of the cessation of the world, the unconditioned element, nibbāna, where the aggregates cease; and the development (*bhāvanā*) of the way leading to the cessation of the world, the Noble Eightfold Path.

Because these modes of penetration can each be redefined by a word expressing movement, and the word *gata* signifying movement can come to mean knowledge, the term "Tathāgata," "Thus gone," suggests the penetration of the Four Noble Truths in the mode of penetration peculiar to each truth. In this way once again the word "Tathāgata" implies the entire theory and practice of the Dhamma.

PART ONE

THE BRAHMAJĀLA SUTTA

I. TALK ON WANDERERS
(*Paribbājakakathā*)

1. Thus have I heard. On one occasion the Exalted One was travelling along the highway between Rājagaha and Nālandā together with a great company of bhikkhus, with about five hundred bhikkhus. At the same time the wanderer Suppiya was also travelling along the highway between Rājagaha and Nālandā together with his pupil, the youth Brahmadatta. Along the way, the wanderer Suppiya spoke in many ways in dispraise of the Buddha, the Dhamma, and the Saṅgha. But his pupil, the youth Brahmadatta, spoke in many ways in praise of the Buddha, the Dhamma, and the Saṅgha. Thus these two, teacher and pupil, followed closely behind the Exalted One and the company of bhikkhus, making assertions in direct contradiction to each other.

2. Then the Exalted One together with the company of bhikkhus entered the royal resthouse in the Ambalaṭṭhika garden in order to pass the night. The wanderer Suppiya together with his pupil, the youth Brahmadatta, also entered the royal resthouse in the Ambalaṭṭhika garden in order to pass the night. There, too, the wanderer Suppiya spoke in many ways in dispraise of the Buddha, the Dhamma, and the Saṅgha, while his pupil Brahmadatta spoke in many ways in their praise. Thus these two, teacher and pupil, dwelt together making assertions in direct contradiction to each other.

3. When dawn broke a number of bhikkhus, after rising, assembled in the pavilion. As they sat together, the following conversation sprang up among them: "It is wonderful and marvelous, friends, how the Exalted One, he who knows and sees, the Worthy One, the perfectly enlightened Buddha, has so thoroughly penetrated

the diversity in the dispositions of beings. For this wanderer Suppiya spoke in many ways in dispraise of the Buddha, the Dhamma, and the Saṅgha, while his own pupil, the youth Brahmadatta, spoke in many ways in their praise. These two, teacher and pupil, followed closely behind the Exalted One and the company of bhikkhus, making assertions in direct contradiction to each other."

4. Then the Exalted One, realizing the turn their discussion had taken, entered the pavilion, sat down on the prepared seat, and addressed the bhikkhus: "What kind of discussion were you holding just now, bhikkhus? What was the subject of your conversation?"

The bhikkhus replied: "When dawn had broken, Lord, after rising we assembled in the pavilion. As we sat here, the following conversation sprang up among us: 'It is wonderful and marvellous friends, how the Exalted One, he who knows and sees, the Worthy One, the perfectly enlightened Buddha, has so thoroughly penetrated the diversity in the dispositions of beings. For this wanderer Suppiya spoke in many ways in dispraise of the Buddha, the Dhamma, and the Saṅgha, while his own pupil, the youth Brahmadatta, spoke in many ways in their praise. These two, teacher and pupil, followed closely behind the Exalted One and the company of bhikkhus, making assertions in direct contradiction to each other.' This, Lord, was the conversation we were having when the Exalted One arrived."

5. "If, bhikkhus, others speak in dispraise of me, or in dispraise of the Dhamma, or in dispraise of the Saṅgha, you should not give way to resentment, displeasure, or animosity against them in your heart. For if you were to become angry or upset in such a situation, you would only be creating an obstacle for yourselves. If you were to become angry or upset when others speak in dispraise of us, would you be able to recognize whether their statements are rightly or wrongly spoken?"

"Certainly not, Lord."

"If, bhikkhus, others speak in dispraise of me, or in dispraise of the Dhamma, or in dispraise of the Saṅgha, you should unravel what is false and point it out as false, saying: 'For such and such a reason this is false, this is untrue, there is no such thing in us, this is not found among us.'

6. "And if, bhikkhus, others speak in praise of me, or in praise of the Dhamma, or in praise of the Saṅgha, you should not give way to jubilation, joy, and exultation in your heart. For if you were to become jubilant, joyful, and exultant in such a situation, you would only be

creating an obstacle for yourselves. If others speak in praise of me, or in praise of the Dhamma, or in praise of the Saṅgha, you should acknowledge what is fact as fact, saying: 'For such and such a reason this is a fact, this is true, there is such a thing in us, this is found among us.'

II. The Analysis of Virtue

A. The Short Section on Virtue (*Cūḷasīla*)

7. "It is, bhikkhus, only to trifling and insignificant matters, to the minor details of mere moral virtue, that a worldling would refer when speaking in praise of the Tathāgata. And what are those trifling and insignificant matters, those minor details of mere moral virtue, to which he would refer?

8. "'Having abandoned the destruction of life, the recluse Gotama abstains from the destruction of life. He has laid aside the rod and the sword, and dwells conscientious, full of kindness, compassionate for the welfare of all living beings.' It is in this way, bhikkhus, that the worldling would speak when speaking in praise of the Tathāgata.

"Or he might say: 'Having abandoned taking what is not given, the recluse Gotama abstains from taking what is not given. Accepting and expecting only what is given, he dwells in honesty and rectitude of heart.'

"Or he might say: 'Having abandoned unchaste living, the recluse Gotama lives the life of chastity. He dwells remote (from women), and abstains from the vulgar practice of sexual intercourse.'

9. "Or he might say: 'Having abandoned false speech, the recluse Gotama abstains from falsehood. He speaks only the truth, he lives devoted to truth; trustworthy and reliable, he does not deceive anyone in the world.'

"Or he might say: 'Having abandoned slander, the recluse Gotama abstains from slander. He does not repeat elsewhere what he has heard here in order to divide others from the people here, nor does he repeat here what he has heard elsewhere in order to divide these from the people there. Thus he is a reconciler of those who are divided and a promoter of friendships. Rejoicing, delighting, and exulting in concord, he speaks only words that are conducive to concord.'

"Or he might say: 'Having abandoned harsh speech, the recluse Gotama abstains from harsh speech. He speaks only such words as are gentle, pleasing to the ear, endearing, going to the heart, urbane, amiable, and agreeable to many people.'

"Or he might say: 'Having abandoned idle chatter, the recluse Gotama abstains from idle chatter. He speaks at the right time, speaks what is factual, speaks on the good, on the Dhamma, and on the Discipline. His words are worth treasuring: they are timely, backed by reason, definite, and connected with the good.'

10. "Or he might say:

'The recluse Gotama abstains from damaging seed and plant life.
He eats only in one part of the day, refraining from food at night and from eating at improper times.
He abstains from dancing, singing, instrumental music, and from witnessing unsuitable shows.
He abstains from wearing garlands, embellishing himself with scents, and beautifying himself with unguents.
He abstains from accepting gold and silver.
He abstains from accepting uncooked grain, raw meat, women and girls, male and female slaves, goats and sheep, fowl and swine, elephants, cattle, horses, and mares.
He abstains from accepting fields and lands.
He abstains from running messages and errands.
He abstains from buying and selling, and from dealing with false weights, false metals, and false measures.
He abstains from the crooked ways of bribery, deception, and fraud.
He abstains from mutilating, executing, imprisoning, robbery, plunder, and violence.'

"It is in this way, bhikkhus, that the worldling would speak when speaking in praise of the Tathāgata.

B. The Intermediate Section on Virtue (*Majjhimasīla*)

11. "Or he might say: 'Whereas some honorable recluses and brahmins, while living on food offered by the faithful, continuously cause damage to seed and plant life—to plants propagated from roots,

stems, joints, buddings, and seeds—the recluse Gotama abstains from damaging seed and plant life.'

12. "Or he might say: 'Whereas some honorable recluses and brahmins, while living on food offered by the faithful, enjoy the use of stored up goods such as stored up food, drinks, garments, vehicles, bedding, scents, and comestibles—the recluse Gotama abstains from the use of stored up goods'

13. "Or he might say: 'Whereas some honorable recluses and brahmins, while living on food offered by the faithful, attend unsuitable shows, such as:

shows featuring dancing, singing, or instrumental music;
theatrical performances;
narrations of legends;
music played by hand-clapping, cymbals, and drums;
picture houses;
acrobatic performances;
combats of elephants, horses, buffaloes, bulls, goats, rams, cocks, and quails;
stick-fights, boxing and wrestling, sham-fights, roll-calls, battle-arrays, and regimental reviews—

the recluse Gotama abstains from attending such unsuitable shows.'

14. "Or he might say: "Whereas some honorable recluses and brahmins, while living on food offered by the faithful, indulge in the following games that are a basis for negligence:[6]

aṭṭhapada (a game played on an eight-row chessboard);
dasapada (a game played on a ten-row chessboard);
ākāsa (a game of the same type played by imagining a board in the air);
parihārapatha ("hopscotch," a diagram is drawn on the ground and one has to jump in the allowable spaces avoiding the lines);
santika ("spillikins," assembling the pieces in a pile, removing and returning them without disturbing the pile);
khalika (dice games);
ghaṭika (hitting a short stick with a long stick);

6. The explanations of these games are drawn from the commentary.

salākahattha (a game played by dipping the hand in paint or dye, striking the ground or a wall, and requiring the participants to show the figure of an elephant, a horse etc.);
akkha (ball games);
paṅgacīra (blowing through toy pipes made of leaves);
vaṅkaka (ploughing with miniature ploughs);
mokkhacika (turning somersaults);
ciṅgulika (playing with paper windmills);
pattāḷaka (playing with toy measures);
rathaka (playing with toy chariots);
dhanuka (playing with toy bows);
akkharika (guessing at letters written in the air or on one's back);
manesika (guessing others' thoughts);
yathāvajja (games involving mimicry of deformities)—

the recluse Gotama abstains from such games that are a basis for negligence.'

15. "Or he might say: 'Whereas some recluses and brahmins, while living on food offered by the faithful, enjoy the use of high and luxurious beds and seats, such as:

spacious couches;
thrones with animal figures carved on the supports;
long-haired coverlets;
colored patchwork coverlets;
white woolen coverlets;
woolen coverlets embroidered with flowers;
quilts stuffed with cotton;
woolen coverlets embroidered with animal figures;
woolen coverlets with hair on both sides or on one side;
bedspreads embroidered with gems;
silk coverlets;
dance-hall carpets;
elephant, horse, or chariot rugs;
rugs of antelope skins;
choice spreads made of *kadali*-deer hides;
spreads with red awnings overhead;
couches with red cushions for the head and feet—

the recluse Gotama abstains from the use of such high and luxurious beds and seats.'

16. "Or he might say: 'Whereas some recluses and brahmins, while living on the food offered by the faithful, enjoy the use of such devices for embellishing and beautifying themselves as the following: rubbing scented powders into the body, massaging with oils, bathing in perfumed water, kneading the limbs, mirrors, ointments, garlands, scents, unguents, face powders, makeup, bracelets, headbands, decorated walking sticks, ornamented medicine tubes, rapiers, sunshades, embroidered sandals, turbans, diadems, yak-tail whisks, and long-fringed white robes—the recluse Gotama abstains from the use of such devices for embellishment and beautification.'

17. "Or he might say: 'Whereas some recluses and brahmins, while living on the food offered by the faithful, engage in frivolous chatter, such as: talk about kings, thieves, and ministers of state; talk about armies, dangers, and wars; talk about food, drink, garments, and lodgings; talk about garlands and scents; talk about relatives, vehicles, villages, towns, cities, and countries; talk about women and talk about heroes; street talk and talk by the well; talk about those departed in days gone by; rambling chitchat; speculations about the world and about the sea; talk about gain and loss—the recluse Gotama abstains from such frivolous chatter.'[7]

18. "Or he might say: 'Whereas some recluses and brahmins, while living on the food offered by the faithful, engage in wrangling argumentation, (saying to one another):

> "You don't understand this doctrine and discipline. I am the one who understand this doctrine and discipline."
> "How can you understand this doctrine and discipline?"
> "You're practicing the wrong way. I'm practicing the right way."
> "I'm being consistent. You're inconsistent."
> "What should have been said first you said last, what should have been said last you said first."
> "What you took so long to think out has been confuted."

---

7. *Tiracchānakathā*, often rendered "animal talk"; however, the commentary explains it as "talk which, because it does not lead to emancipation, runs horizontal to the (upward leading) paths to heaven and liberation" (*aniyyānikattā saggamokkhamaggānam tiracchānabhūtā kathā*). An animal, *tiracchānagata*, is called thus because it moves horizontally with the earth, in contrast to man, who walks erect. But talk that moves horizontally is pointless or frivolous talk, not animal talk. Besides, animals cannot speak.

> "Your doctrine has been refuted. You're defeated. Go, try to save your doctrine, or disentangle yourself now if you can"—

the recluse Gotama abstains from such wrangling argumentation.'

19. "Or he might say: 'Whereas some recluses and brahmins, while living on the food offered by the faithful, engage in running messages and errands for kings, ministers of state, *khattiyas*, brahmins, householders, or youths, (who command them): "Go here, go there, take this, bring that from there"—the recluse Gotama abstains from running such messages and errands.'

20. "Or he might say: 'Whereas some recluses and brahmins, while living on the food offered by the faithful, engage in scheming, talking, hinting, belittling others, and pursuing gain with gain—the recluse Gotama abstains from such kinds of scheming and talking.' [8]

"It is in this way, bhikkhus, that a worldling would speak when speaking in praise of the Tathāgata.

C. The Long Section on Virtue (*Mahāsīla*)

21. "Or he might say: 'Whereas some recluses and brahmins, while living on the food offered by the faithful, earn their living by a wrong means of livelihood, by such debased arts as: [9]

- prophesying long life, prosperity etc., or the reverse, from the marks on a person's limbs, hands, feet, etc.;
- divining by means of omens and signs;
- making auguries on the basis of thunderbolts and celestial portents;
- interpreting ominous dreams;
- telling fortunes from marks on the body;
- making auguries from the marks on cloth gnawed by mice;
- offering fire oblations;
- offering oblations from a ladle;
- offering oblations of husks, rice powder, rice grains, ghee, and oil to the gods;

---

8. Improper ways of gaining material support from donors, discussed in detail in Vism 1.61–82.

9. The explanation of these arts, usually indicated by a single obscure word in the text, is drawn from the commentary.

offering oblations from the mouth;
offering blood-sacrifices to the gods;
making predictions based on the fingertips;
determining whether the site for a proposed house or garden is propitious or not;
making predictions for officers of state;
the knowledge of charms to lay demons in a cemetery;
the knowledge of charms to cure one possessed by ghosts;
the knowledge of charms to be pronounced by one living in an earthen house;
the snake craft (for curing snake bites and charming snakes);
the poison craft (for neutralizing or making poison)
the scorpion craft and rat craft (for curing scorpion stings and rat bites, respectively);
the bird craft and crow craft (for understanding the cries of birds and crows);
foretelling the number of years that a man has to live;
the knowledge of charms to give protection from arrows;
reciting charms to understand the language of animals—

the recluse Gotama abstains from such wrong means of livelihood, from such debased arts.'

22. "Or he might say: 'Whereas some recluses and brahmins, while living on the food offered by the faithful, earn their living by a wrong means of livelihood, by such debased arts as interpreting the significance of the color, shape, and other features of the following items to determine whether they portend fortune or misfortune for their owners: gems, garments, staffs, swords, spears, arrows, bows, other weapons, women, men, boys, girls, slaves, slave-women, elephants, horses, buffaloes, bulls, cows, goats, rams, fowl, quails, lizards, rabbits, tortoises, and other animals—the recluse Gotama abstains from such wrong means of livelihood, from such debased arts.'

23. "Or he might say: 'Whereas some recluses and brahmins, while living on the food offered by the faithful, earn their living by a wrong means of livelihood, by such debased arts as making predictions to the effect that:

the king will march forth;
the king will return;

our king will attack and the enemy king will retreat;
the enemy king will attack and our king will retreat;
our king will triumph and the enemy king will be defeated;
the enemy king will triumph and our king will be defeated;
thus there will be victory for one and defeat for the other—

the recluse Gotama abstains from such wrong means of livelihood, from such debased arts.'

24. "Or he might say: 'Whereas some recluses and brahmins, while living on the food offered by the faithful, earn their living by a wrong means of livelihood, by such debased arts as predicting:

there will be an eclipse of the moon, an eclipse of the sun, an eclipse of a constellation;
the sun and the moon will go on their proper courses;
there will be an aberration of the sun and moon;
the constellations will go on their proper courses;
there will be an aberration of a constellation;
there will be a fall of meteors;
there will be a sky-blaze;
there will be an earthquake;
there will be an earth-roar;
there will be a rising and setting, a darkening of the moon, sun, and constellations;
such will be the result of the moon's eclipse, such the result of the sun's eclipse, (and so on down to) such will be the result of the rising and setting, darkening and brightening, of the moon, sun, and constellations—

the recluse Gotama abstains from such wrong means of livelihood, from such debased arts.'

25. "Or he might say: 'Whereas some recluses and brahmins, while living on the food offered by the faithful, earn their living by a wrong means of livelihood, by such debased arts as predicting:

there will be abundant rain;
there will be a drought;
there will be a good harvest;
there will be a famine;
there will be security;
there will be danger;

there will be sickness;
there will be health;
or they earn their living by accounting, computation, calculation, the composing of poetry, and speculations about the world—

the recluse Gotama abstains from such wrong means of livelihood, from such debased arts.'

26. "Or he might say: 'Whereas some recluses and brahmins, while living on the food offered by the faithful, earn their living by a wrong means of livelihood, by such debased arts as:

arranging auspicious dates for marriages, both those in which the bride is brought in (from another family) and those in which she is sent out (to another family);
arranging auspicious dates for betrothals and divorces;
arranging auspicious dates for the accumulation or expenditure of money;
reciting charms to make people lucky or unlucky;
rejuvenating the fetuses of abortive women;
reciting spells to bind a man's tongue, to paralyze his jaws, to make him lose control over his hands, to make him lose control over his jaw, or to bring on deafness;
obtaining oracular answers to questions by means of a mirror, a girl, or a god;
worshipping the sun;
worshipping Mahābrahmā;
bringing forth flames from the mouth;
invoking the goddess of luck—

the recluse Gotama abstains from such wrong means of livelihood, from such debased arts.'

27. "Or he might say: 'Whereas some recluses and brahmins, while living on the food offered by the faithful, earn their living by a wrong means of livelihood, by such debased arts as:

promising gifts to deities in return for favors;
fulfilling such promises;
demonology;
reciting spells after entering an earthen house;
inducing virility and impotence;
preparing and consecrating sites for a house;

giving ceremonial mouthwashes and ceremonial bathing;
offering sacrificial fires;
administering emetics, purgatives, expectorants, and phlegmagogues;
administering medicine through the ear and through the nose;
administering ointments and counter-ointments;
practicing fine surgery on the eyes and ears;
practicing general surgery on the body;
practicing as a children's doctor;
the application of medicinal roots;
the binding on of medicinal herbs—

the recluse Gotama abstains from such wrong means of livelihood, from such debased arts.'

"These, bhikkhus, are those trifling and insignificant matters, those minor details of mere moral virtue, that a worldling would refer to when speaking in praise of the Tathāgata.

III. Speculations about the Past (*Pubbantakappika*)

28. "There are, bhikkhus, other dhammas, deep, difficult to see, difficult to understand, peaceful and sublime, beyond the sphere of reasoning, subtle, comprehensible only to the wise, which the Tathāgata, having realized for himself with direct knowledge, propounds to others; and it is concerning these that those who would rightly praise the Tathāgata in accordance with reality would speak. And what are these dhammas?

29. "There are, bhikkhus, some recluses and brahmins who are speculators about the past, who hold settled views about the past, and who on eighteen grounds assert various conceptual theorems referring to the past. And owing to what, with reference to what, do these honorable recluses and brahmins frame their speculations?

A. Eternalism (*Sassatavāda*): Views 1–4

30. "There are, bhikkhus, some recluses and brahmins who are eternalists, and who on four grounds proclaim the self and the world to

be eternal. And owing to what, with reference to what, do these honorable recluses and brahmins proclaim their views?

31. "In the first case, bhikkhus, some recluse or a brahmin, by means of ardor, endeavor, application, diligence, and right reflection, attains to such a degree of mental concentration that with his mind thus concentrated, [purified, clarified, unblemished, devoid of corruptions],[10] he recollects his numerous past lives: that is, (he recollects) one birth, two, three, four, or five births; ten, twenty, thirty, forty, or fifty births; a hundred, a thousand, or a hundred thousand births; many hundreds of births, many thousands of births, many hundreds of thousands of births. (He recalls:) 'Then I had such a name, belonged to such a clan, had such an appearance; such was my food, such my experience of pleasure and pain, such my span of life. Passing away thence, I re-arose there. There too I had such a name, belonged to such a clan, had such an appearance; such was my food, such my experience of pleasure and pain, such my span of life. Passing away thence, I re-arose here.' Thus he recollects his numerous past lives in their modes and their details.

"He speaks thus: 'The self and the world are eternal, barren, steadfast as a mountain peak, standing firm like a pillar. And though these beings roam and wander (through the round of existence), pass away and re-arise, yet the self and the world remain the same just like eternity itself. What is the reason? Because I, by means of ardor, endeavor, application, diligence, and right reflection, attain to such a degree of mental concentration that with my mind thus concentrated, I recollect my numerous past lives in their modes and their details. For this reason I know this: the self and the world are eternal, barren, steadfast as a mountain peak, standing firm like a pillar. And though these beings roam and wander (through the round of existence), pass away and re-arise, yet the self and the world remain the same just like eternity itself.'

"This, bhikkhus, is the first case.

32. "In the second case, owing to what, with reference to what, are some honorable recluses and brahmins eternalists, who proclaim the self and the world to be eternal?

---

10. Words in square brackets appear in the Burmese, but not in the Roman or the Sinhalese editions of the sutta.

"Herein, bhikkhus, a certain recluse or brahmin, by means of ardor, endeavor, application, diligence, and right reflection, attains to such a degree of mental concentration that with his mind thus concentrated he recollects his numerous past lives: that is, (he recollects his past lives throughout) one aeon of world contraction and expansion, throughout two, three, four, five, or ten aeons of world contraction and expansion.[11] (He recalls:) 'Then I had such a name, belonged to such a clan, had such an appearance; such was my food, such my experience of pleasure and pain, such my span of life. Passing away thence, I re-arose there. There too I had such a name, belonged to such a clan, had such an appearance; such was my food, such my experience of pleasure and pain, such my span of life. Passing away thence, I re-arose here.' Thus he recollects his numerous past lives in their modes and their details.

"He speaks thus: 'The self and the world are eternal, barren, steadfast as a mountain peak, standing firm like a pillar. And though these beings roam and wander (through the round of existence), pass away and re-arise, yet the self and the world remain the same just like eternity itself. What is the reason?

(*The remainder is exactly the same as §31 except for the extent of time recollected.*)

"This, bhikkhus, is the second reason.

33. "In the third case, owing to what, with reference to what, are some honorable recluses and brahmins eternalists, who proclaim the self and the world to be eternal?

"Herein, bhikkhus, some recluse or brahmin, by means of ardor, endeavor, application, diligence, and right reflection, attains to such a degree of mental concentration that with his mind thus concentrated he recollects his numerous past lives: that is, (he recollects his past lives throughout) ten aeons of world contraction and expansion, throughout twenty, thirty, or forty aeons of world contraction and expansion ...

---

11. *Saṃvaṭṭa-vivaṭṭa.* These are the two primary divisions of the great aeon (*mahākappa*). The *saṃvaṭṭa-kappa* is the period between the full evolution of a world system and its complete dissolution, the *vivaṭṭakappa* the period between dissolution and full evolution. The PED definitions should be reversed; see Vism 13.28–30. Since each period contains a phase of incipient development and a phase of stabilization, the two are further divided to yield four *asaṅkheyya-kappas*, "incalculable aeons" in a great aeon. See AN 4:166.

(*As above*). Thus he recollects his numerous past lives in their modes and their details.

"He speaks thus: 'The self and the world are eternal, barren, steadfast as a mountain peak, standing firm like a pillar. And though these beings roam and wander (through the round of existence), pass away and re-arise, yet the self and the world remain the same just like eternity itself. What is the reason?

(*As in §31 except for the extent of time.*)

"This, bhikkhus, is the third case.

34. "In the fourth case, owing to what, with reference to what, are some honorable recluses and brahmins eternalists, who proclaim the self and the world to be eternal?

"Herein, bhikkhus, some recluse or brahmin is a rationalist, an investigator. He declares his view—hammered out by reason, deduced from his investigations, following his own flight of thought—thus: 'The self and the world are eternal, barren, steadfast as a mountain peak, standing firm like a pillar. And though these beings roam and wander (through the round of existence), pass away and re-arise, yet the self and the world remain the same just like eternity itself.'

"This, bhikkhus, is the fourth case.

35. "It is on these four grounds, bhikkhus, that those recluses and brahmins who are eternalists proclaim the self and the world to be eternal. Whatever recluses and brahmins there may be who proclaim the self and the world to be eternal, all of them do so on these four grounds, or on a certain one of them. Outside of these there is none.

36. "This, bhikkhus, the Tathāgata understands. And he understands: 'These standpoints, thus assumed and thus misapprehended, lead to such a future destination, to such a state in the world beyond.' He understands as well what transcends this, yet even that understanding he does not misapprehend. And because he is free from misapprehension, he has realized within himself the state of perfect peace. Having understood as they really are the origin and the passing away of feelings, their satisfaction, their unsatisfactoriness, and the escape from them, the Tathāgata, bhikkhus, is emancipated through non-clinging.

37. "These are those dhammas, bhikkhus, that are deep, difficult to see, difficult to understand, peaceful and sublime, beyond the sphere of reasoning, subtle, comprehensible only to the wise, which the Tathāgata, having realized for himself with direct knowledge,

propounds to others; and it is concerning these that those who would rightly praise the Tathāgata in accordance with reality would speak.

B. Partial-Eternalism (*Ekaccasassatavāda*): Views 5–8

38. "There are, bhikkhus, some recluses and brahmins who are eternalists in regard to some things and non-eternalists in regard to other things, and who on four grounds proclaim the self and the world to be partly eternal and partly non-eternal. And owing to what, with reference to what, do these honorable recluses and brahmins proclaim their views?

39. "There comes a time, bhikkhus, when after the lapse of a long period this world contracts (disintegrates). While the world is contracting, beings for the most part are reborn in the Ābhassara Brahma-world.[12] There they dwell, mind-made, feeding on rapture, self-luminous, moving through the air, abiding in glory. And they continue thus for a long, long period of time.

40. "But sooner or later, bhikkhus, after the lapse of a long period, there comes a time when this world begins to expand once again. While the world is expanding, an empty palace of Brahmā appears. Then a certain being, due to the exhaustion of his life span or the exhaustion of his merit, passes away from the Ābhassara plane and re-arises in the empty palace of Brahmā. There he dwells, mind-made, feeding on rapture, self-luminous, moving through the air, abiding in glory. And he continues thus for a long, long period of time.

41. "Then, as a result of dwelling there all alone for so long a time, there arises in him dissatisfaction and agitation, (and he yearns): 'Oh, that other beings might come to this place!' Just at that moment, due to the exhaustion of their life span or the exhaustion of their merit, certain other beings pass away from the Ābhassara plane and re-arise in the palace of Brahmā, in companionship with him. There they dwell, mind-made, feeding on rapture, self-luminous, moving through the air, abiding in glory. And they continue thus for a long, long period of time.

---

12. The "world of streaming radiance," the sixth of the fifteen planes in the fine-material world (*rūpaloka*), the lowest order to be exempt from the onset of world destruction. The Brahma-world mentioned later is destroyed by the conflagration, but reappears at an early stage.

42. "Thereupon the being who re-arose there first thinks to himself: 'I am Brahmā, the Great Brahmā, the Vanquisher, the Unvanquished, the Universal Seer, the Wielder of Power, the Lord, the Maker and Creator, the Supreme Being, the Ordainer, the Almighty, the Father of all that are and are to be. And these beings have been created by me. What is the reason? Because first I made the wish: "Oh, that other beings might come to this place!" And after I made this resolution, now these beings have come.'

"And the beings who re-arose there after him also think: 'This must be Brahmā, the Great Brahmā, the Vanquisher, the Unvanquished, the Universal Seer, the Wielder of Power, the Lord, the Maker and Creator, the Supreme Being, the Ordainer, the Almighty, the Father of all that are and are to be. And we have been created by him. What is the reason? Because we see that he was here first, and we appeared here after him.'

43. "Herein, bhikkhus, the being who re-arose there first possesses longer life, greater beauty, and greater authority than the beings who re-arose there after him.

44. "Now, bhikkhus, this comes to pass, that a certain being, after passing away from that plane, takes rebirth in this world. Having come to this world, he goes forth from home to homelessness. When he has gone forth, by means of ardor, endeavor, application, diligence, and right reflection, he attains to such a degree of mental concentration that with his mind thus concentrated he recollects his immediately preceding life, but none previous to that. He speaks thus: 'We were created by him, by Brahmā, the Great Brahmā, the Vanquisher, the Unvanquished, the Universal Seer, the Wielder of Power, the Lord, the Maker and Creator, the Supreme Being, the Ordainer, the Almighty, the Father of all that are and are to be. He is permanent, stable, eternal, not subject to change, and he will remain the same just like eternity itself. But we, who have been created by him and have come to this world, are impermanent, unstable, short-lived, doomed to perish.'

"This, bhikkhus, is the first case.

45. "In the second case, owing to what, with reference to what, are some honorable recluses and brahmins eternalists in regard to some things and non-eternalists in regard to other things, proclaiming the self and the world to be partly eternal and partly non-eternal?

"There are, bhikkhus, certain gods called 'corrupted by play.' These gods spend an excessive time indulging in the delights of laughter and play. As a consequence they become forgetful and, when they become forgetful, they pass away from that plane.

46. "Now, bhikkhus, this comes to pass, that a certain being, after passing away from that plane, takes rebirth in this world. Having come to this world, he goes forth from home to homelessness. When he has gone forth, by means of ardor, endeavor, application, diligence, and right reflection, he attains to such a degree of mental concentration that with his mind thus concentrated he recollects his immediately preceding life, but none previous to that. He speaks thus: 'Those honorable gods who are not corrupted by play do not spend an excessive time indulging in the delights of laughter and play. As a consequence they do not become forgetful, and because they do not become forgetful they do not pass away from that plane. Those gods are permanent, stable, eternal, not subject to change, and they will remain the same just like eternity itself. But we were gods corrupted by play. We spent an excessive time indulging in the delights of laughter and play, and as a consequence we became forgetful. When we became forgetful we passed away from that plane. Coming to this world, now we are impermanent, unstable, short-lived, doomed to perish.'

"This bhikkhus, is the second case.

47. "In the third case, owing to what, with reference to what, are some honorable recluses and brahmins eternalists in regard to some things and non-eternalists in regard to other things, proclaiming the self and the world to be partly eternal and partly non-eternal?

"There are, bhikkhus, certain gods called 'corrupted by mind.' These gods contemplate one another with excessive envy. As a consequence their minds become corrupted by anger towards one another. When their minds are corrupted by anger, their bodies and minds become exhausted and, consequently, they pass away from that plane.

48. "Now, bhikkhus, this comes to pass, that a certain being, after passing away from that plane, takes rebirth in this world. Having come to this world, he goes forth from home to homelessness. When he has gone forth, by means of ardor, endeavor, application, diligence, and right reflection, he attains to such a degree of mental concentration that with his mind thus concentrated he recollects his immediately preceding life, but none previous to that. He speaks thus: 'Those honorable gods who are not corrupted by mind do not contemplate

each other with excessive envy. As a result, their minds do not become corrupted by anger towards one another, their bodies and minds do not become exhausted, and they do not pass away from that plane. Those gods are permanent, stable, not subject to change, and they will remain the same just like eternity itself. But we were gods corrupted by mind. We contemplated each other with excessive envy and as a result our minds became corrupted by anger towards one another. When our minds were corrupted by anger, our bodies and minds became exhausted and consequently, we passed away from that plane. Coming to this world, now we are impermanent, unstable, short-lived, doomed to perish.'

"This, bhikkhus, is the third case.

49. "In the fourth case, owing to what, with reference to what, are some honorable recluses and brahmins eternalists in regard to some things and non-eternalists in regard to other things, proclaiming the self and the world to be partly eternal and partly non-eternal?

"Herein, bhikkhus, a certain recluse or brahmin is a rationalist, an investigator. He declares his view—hammered out by reason, deduced from his investigations, following his own flight of thought—thus: 'That which is called "the eye," "the ear," "the nose," "the tongue," and "the body"—that self is impermanent, unstable, non-eternal, subject to change. But that which is called "mind" (*citta*) or "mentality" (*mano*) or "consciousness" (*viññāṇa*)—that self is permanent, stable, eternal, not subject to change, and it will remain the same just like eternity itself.'

"This, bhikkhus, is the fourth case.

50. "It is on these four grounds, bhikkhus, that those recluses and brahmins who are partial-eternalists proclaim the self and the world to be partly eternal and partly non-eternal. Whatever recluses and brahmins there may be who proclaim the self and the world to be partly eternal and partly non-eternal, all of them do so on these four grounds, or on a certain one of them. Outside of these there is none.

51. "This, bhikkhus, the Tathāgata understands. And he understands: 'These standpoints, thus assumed and thus misapprehended, lead to such a future destination, to such a state in the world beyond.' He understands as well what transcends this, yet even that understanding he does not misapprehend. And because he is free from misapprehension, he has realized within himself the state of perfect peace. Having understood as they really are the origin and the passing away of feelings, their

satisfaction, their unsatisfactoriness, and the escape from them, the Tathāgata, bhikkhus, is emancipated through non-clinging.

52. "These are those dhammas, bhikkhus, that are deep, difficult to see, difficult to understand, peaceful and sublime, beyond the sphere of reasoning, subtle, comprehensible only to the wise, which the Tathāgata, having realized for himself with direct knowledge, propounds to others; and it is concerning these that those who would rightly praise the Tathāgata in accordance with reality would speak.

C. Doctrines of the Finitude and Infinity of the World (*Antānantavāda*): Views 9–12

53. "There are, bhikkhus, some recluses and brahmins who are extensionists,[13] and who on four grounds proclaim the world to be finite or infinite. And owing to what, with reference to what, do these honorable recluses and brahmins proclaim their views?

54. "In the first case, bhikkhus, a certain recluse or a brahmin, by means of ardor, endeavor, application, diligence, and right reflection, attains to such a degree of mental concentration that with his mind thus concentrated he abides perceiving the world as finite. He speaks thus: 'The world is finite and bounded. What is the reason? Because I attain to such concentration of mind that I abide perceiving the world as finite. For that reason I know this: the world is finite and bounded.'

"This, bhikkhus, is the first case.

55. "In the second case, owing to what, with reference to what, are some honorable recluses and brahmins extensionists, proclaiming the world to be finite or infinite?

"Herein, bhikkhus, a certain recluse or a brahmin, by means of ardor, endeavor, application, diligence, and right reflection, attains to such a degree of mental concentration that with his mind thus concentrated he abides perceiving the world as infinite. He speaks thus: 'The world is infinite and boundless. Those recluses and brahmins who declare the world to be finite and bounded speak falsely. The world is infinite and boundless. What is the reason? Because I attain to such concentration of mind that I abide perceiving the world as infinite. For this reason I know this: the world is infinite and boundless.'

---

13. *Antānantikā,* lit. "finitizers and infinitizers." The word "extensionists" is borrowed from Rhys-Davids.

"This, bhikkhus, is the second case.

56. "In the third case, owing to what, with reference to what, are some honorable recluses and brahmins extensionists, proclaiming the world to be finite or infinite?

"Herein, bhikkhus, a certain recluse or a brahmin, by means of ardor, endeavor, application, diligence, and right reflection, attains to such a degree of mental concentration that with his mind thus concentrated he abides perceiving the world as finite in the upward and downward directions, but as infinite across. He speaks thus: 'The world is both finite and infinite. Those recluses and brahmins who declare the world to be finite and bounded speak falsely; and those recluses and brahmins who declare the world to be infinite and boundless also speak falsely. The world is both finite and infinite. For what reason? Because I attain to such concentration of mind that I abide perceiving the world as finite in the upward and downward directions, but as infinite across. For this reason I know this: the world is both finite and infinite.'

"This, bhikkhus, is the third case.

57. "In the fourth case, owing to what, with reference to what, are some honorable recluses and brahmins extensionists, proclaiming the world to be finite or infinite?

"Herein, bhikkhus, a certain recluse or a brahmin is a rationalist, an investigator. He declares his view—hammered out by reason, deduced from his investigations, following his own flight of thought—thus: 'The world is neither finite nor infinite. Those recluses and brahmins who declare the world to be finite and bounded, those who declare it to be infinite and boundless, and those who declare it to be both finite and infinite—all these speak falsely. The world is neither finite nor infinite.'

"This, bhikkhus, is the fourth case.

58. "It is on these four grounds, bhikkhus, that those recluses and brahmins who are extensionists proclaim the world to be finite or infinite. Whatever recluses or brahmins there may be who proclaim the world to be finite or infinite, all of them do so on these four grounds, or on a certain one of them. Outside of these there is none.

59–60. "This, bhikkhus, the Tathāgata understands ... *(repeat §§ 51–52 in full)* ... and it is concerning these that those who would praise the Tathāgata in accordance with reality would speak.

D. Doctrines of Endless Equivocation (*Amarāvikkhepavāda*): Views 13–16

61. "There are, bhikkhus, some recluses and brahmins who are endless equivocators.[14] When questioned about this or that point, on four grounds they resort to evasive statements and to endless equivocation. And owing to what, with reference to what, do these honorable recluses and brahmins do so?

62. "Herein, bhikkhus, a certain recluse or a brahmin does not understand as it really is what is wholesome and what is unwholesome. He thinks: 'I do not understand as it really is what is wholesome and what is unwholesome. If, without understanding, I were to declare something to be wholesome or unwholesome, my declaration might be false. If my declaration should be false, that would distress me, and that distress would be an obstacle for me.' Therefore, out of fear and loathing of making a false statement, he does not declare anything to be wholesome or unwholesome. But when he is questioned about this or that point, he resorts to evasive statements and to endless equivocation: 'I do not take it thus, nor do I take it in that way, nor do I take it in some other way. I do not say that it is not, nor do I say that it is neither this nor that.'

"This, bhikkhus, is the first case.

63. "In the second case, owing to what, with reference to what, are some honorable recluses and brahmins endless equivocators, resorting to evasive statements and to endless equivocation?

"Herein, bhikkhus, a certain recluse or a brahmin does not understand as it really is what is wholesome and what is unwholesome. He thinks: 'I do not understand as it really is what is wholesome and what is unwholesome. If, without understanding, I were to declare something to be wholesome or unwholesome, desire and lust or hatred and aversion might arise in me. Should desire and lust or hated and aversion arise in me, that would be clinging on my part. Such clinging would distress me, and that distress would be an obstacle for me.' Therefore, out of fear and loathing of clinging, he does not declare anything to be wholesome or unwholesome. But when questioned about this or that point he resorts to evasive statements and to endless equivocation: 'I do not take it thus, nor do I

---

14. Or "eel-wriggling," as rendered by Rhys-Davids. For the commentarial justification for this rendering, see the commentary section below.

take it in that way, nor do I take it in some other way. I do not say that it is not, nor do I say that it is neither this nor that.'

"This, bhikkhus, is the second case.

64. "In the third case, owing to what, with reference to what, are some honorable recluses and brahmins endless equivocators, resorting to evasive statements and to endless equivocation?

"Herein, bhikkhus, a certain recluse or a brahmin does not understand as it really is what is wholesome and what is unwholesome. He thinks: 'I do not understand as it really is what is wholesome and what is unwholesome. Now, there are recluses and brahmins who are wise, clever, experienced in controversy, who wander about demolishing the views of others with their wisdom. If, without understanding, I were to declare something to be wholesome or unwholesome, they might cross-examine me about my views, press me for reasons, and refute my statements. If they should do so, I might not be able to reply. If I could not reply, that would distress me, and that distress would be an obstacle for me.' Therefore, out of fear and loathing of being cross-examined, he does not declare anything to be wholesome or unwholesome. But, when questioned about this or that point, he resorts to evasive statements and to endless equivocation: 'I do not take it thus, nor do I take it in that way, nor do I take it in some other way. I do not say that it is not, nor do I say that it is neither this nor that.'

"This, bhikkhus, is the third case.

65. "In the fourth case, owing to what, with reference to what, are some honorable recluses and brahmins endless equivocators, resorting to evasive statements and to endless equivocation?

"Herein, bhikkhus, a certain recluse or a brahmin is dull and stupid. Due to his dullness and stupidity, when he is questioned about this or that point, he resorts to evasive statements and to endless equivocation: 'If you ask me whether there is a world beyond—if I thought there is another world, I would declare that there is. But I do not take it thus, nor do I take it in that way, nor do I take it in some other way. I do not say that it is not, nor do I say that is neither this nor that.'

"Similarly, when asked any of the following questions, he resorts to the same evasive statements and to endless equivocation:

A. 1. Is there no world beyond?
   2. Is it that there both is and is not a world beyond?
   3. Is it that there neither is nor is not a world beyond?

B. 1. Are there beings spontaneously reborn?
   2. Are there no beings spontaneously reborn?
   3. Is it that there both are and are not beings spontaneously reborn?
   4. Is it that there neither are nor are not beings spontaneously reborn?

C. 1. Is there fruit and result of good and bad action?
   2. Is there no fruit and result of good and bad action?
   3. Is it that there neither is nor is not fruit and result of good and bad action?
   4. Is it that there neither is nor is not fruit and result of good and bad action?

D. 1. Does the Tathāgata exist after death?
   2. Does the Tathāgata not exist after death?
   3. Does the Tathāgata both exist and not exist after death?
   4. Does the Tathāgata neither exist nor not exist after death?

"This bhikkhus, is the fourth case.

66. "It is on these four grounds, bhikkhus, that those recluses and brahmins who are endless equivocators resort to evasive statements and to endless equivocation when questioned about this or that point. Whatever recluses or brahmins there may be who resort to evasive statements and to endless equivocation, all of them do so on these four grounds, or on a certain one of them. Outside of these there is none.

"This, bhikkhus, the Tathāgata understands … and it is concerning these that those who would rightly praise the Tathāgata in accordance with reality would speak.

E. Doctrines of Fortuitous Origination (*Adhiccasamuppannavāda*): Views 17–18

67. "There are, bhikkhus, some recluses and brahmins who are fortuitous originationists, and who on two grounds proclaim the self and the world to originate fortuitously. And owing to what, with reference to what, do these honorable recluses and brahmins proclaim their views?

68. "There are, bhikkhus, certain gods called 'non-percipient beings.' When perception arises in them, those gods pass away from that plane. Now, bhikkhus, this comes to pass, that a certain being, after passing away from that plane, takes rebirth in this world. Having come to this world, he goes forth from home to homelessness. When he has gone forth, by means of ardor, endeavor, application, diligence, and right reflection, he attains to such a degree of mental concentration that with his mind thus concentrated he recollects the arising of perception, but nothing previous to that. He speaks thus: 'The self and the world originate fortuitously. What is the reason? Because previously I did not exist, but now I am. Not having been, I sprang into being.'

"This, bhikkhus, is the first case.

69. "In the second case, owing to what, with reference to what, are some honorable recluses and brahmins fortuitous originationists, proclaiming the self and the world to originate fortuitously?

"Herein, bhikkhus, a certain recluse or a brahmin is a rationalist, an investigator. He declares his view—hammered out by reason, deduced from his investigations, following his own flight of thought—thus: 'The self and the world originate fortuitously.'

"This, bhikkhus, is the second case.

70. "It is on these two grounds, bhikkhus, that those recluses and brahmins who are fortuitous originationists proclaim the self and the world to originate fortuitously. Whatever recluses or brahmins there may be who proclaim the self and the world to originate fortuitously, all of them do so on these two grounds, or on a certain one of them. Outside of these there is none.

"This, bhikkhus, the Tathāgata understands ... and it is concerning these that those who would rightly praise the Tathāgata in accordance with reality would speak.

71. "It is on these eighteen grounds, bhikkhus, that those recluses and brahmins who are speculators about the past and hold settled views about the past, assert various conceptual theorems referring to the past. Whatever recluses or brahmins are speculators about the past, hold settled views about the past, and assert various conceptual theorems referring to the past, all of them do so on these eighteen grounds, or on a certain one of them. Outside of these there is none.

72. "This, bhikkhus, the Tathāgata understands. And he understands: 'These standpoints, thus assumed and thus misapprehended, lead to such a future destination, to such a state in the world beyond.'

He understands as well what transcends this, yet even that understanding he does not misapprehend. And because he is free from misapprehension, he has realized within himself the state of perfect peace. Having understood as they really are the origin and the passing away of feelings, their satisfaction, their unsatisfactoriness, and the escape from them, the Tathāgata, bhikkhus, is emancipated through non-clinging.

73. "These are those dhammas, bhikkhus, that are deep, difficult to see, difficult to understand, peaceful and sublime, beyond the sphere of reasoning, subtle, comprehensible only to the wise, which the Tathāgata, having realized for himself with direct knowledge, propounds to others; and it is concerning these that those who would rightly praise the Tathāgata in accordance with reality would speak.

IV. Speculations about the Future (*Aparantakappika*)

74. "There are, bhikkhus, some recluses and brahmins who are speculators about the future, who hold settled views about the future, and who on forty-four grounds assert various conceptual theorems referring to the future. And owing to what, with reference to what, do these honorable recluses and brahmins frame their speculations?

A. Doctrines of Percipient Immortality (*Saññīvāda*): Views 19–34

75. "There are, bhikkhus, some recluses and brahmins who maintain a doctrine of percipient immortality[15] and who on sixteen grounds proclaim the self to survive percipient after death. And owing to what, with reference to what, do these honorable recluses and brahmins proclaim their views?

76. "They proclaim: 'The self is immutable after death, percipient, and:

A. 1. material
   2. immaterial

---

15. This might have been translated "doctrines of conscious survival" to accord with common idiom, but I have used a more literal rendering to maintain consistency with the commentarial explanation.

3. both material and immaterial
4. neither material nor immaterial

B. 1. finite
2. infinite
3. both finite and infinite
4. neither finite nor infinite

C. 1. of uniform perception
2. of diversified perception
3. of limited perception
4. of boundless perception

D. 1. exclusively happy
2. exclusively miserable
3. both happy and miserable
4. neither happy nor miserable.'

77. "It is on these sixteen grounds, bhikkhus, that those recluses and brahmins who maintain a doctrine of percipient immortality proclaim the self to survive percipient after death. Whatever recluses or brahmins maintain a doctrine of percipient immortality, all of them do so on these sixteen grounds, or on a certain one of them. Outside of these there is none.

"This, bhikkhus, the Tathāgata understands ... and it is concerning these that those who would rightly praise the Tathāgata in accordance with reality would speak.

B. Doctrines of Non-percipient Immortality (*Asaññīvāda*): Views 35–42

78. "There are, bhikkhus, some recluses and brahmins who maintain a doctrine of non-percipient immortality, and who on eight grounds proclaim the self to survive non-percipient after death. And owing to what, with reference to what, do these honorable recluses and brahmins proclaim their views?

79. "They proclaim: 'The self is immutable after death, non-percipient, and:

A. 1. material
2. immaterial
3. both material and immaterial
4. neither material nor immaterial

B. 1. finite
2. infinite
3. both finite and infinite
4. neither finite nor infinite.'

80. "It is on these eight grounds, bhikkhus, that those recluses and brahmins who maintain a doctrine of non-percipient immortality proclaim the self to survive non-percipient after death. Whatever recluses or brahmins maintain a doctrine of non-percipient immortality, all of them do so on these eight grounds, or on a certain one of them. Outside of these there is none.

"This, bhikkhus, the Tathāgata understands … and it is concerning these that those who would rightly praise the Tathāgata in accordance with reality would speak.

C. Doctrines of Neither Percipient Nor Non-Percipient Immortality (*N'evasaññī-nāsaññīvāda*): Views 43–50

81. "There are, bhikkhus, some recluses and brahmins who maintain a doctrine of neither percipient nor non-percipient immortality and who on eight grounds proclaim the self to survive neither percipient nor non-percipient after death. And owing to what, with reference to what, do these honorable recluses and brahmins proclaim their views?

82. "They proclaim: 'The self is immutable after death, neither percipient nor non-percipient, and:

A. 1. material
2. immaterial
3. both material and immaterial
4. neither material nor immaterial

B. 1. finite
2. infinite
3. both finite and infinite
4. neither finite nor infinite.'

83. "It is on these eight grounds, bhikkhus, that those recluses and brahmins who maintain a doctrine of neither percipient nor non-percipient immortality proclaim the self to survive neither percipient nor non-percipient after death. Whatever recluses or brahmins maintain a doctrine of neither percipient nor non-percipient

immortality, all of them do so on these eight grounds, or on a certain one of them. Outside of these there is none.

"This, bhikkhus, the Tathāgata understands ... and it is concerning these that those who would rightly praise the Tathāgata in accordance with reality would speak.

D. Annihilationism (*Ucchedavāda*): Views 51–57

84. "There are, bhikkhus, some recluses and brahmins who are annihilationists and who on seven grounds proclaim the annihilation, destruction, and extermination of an existent being. And owing to what, with reference to what, do these honorable recluses and brahmins proclaim their views?

85. "Herein, bhikkhus, a certain recluse or a brahmin asserts the following doctrine and view: 'The self, good sir, has material form; it is composed of the four primary elements and originates from father and mother. Since this self, good sir, is annihilated and destroyed with the breakup of the body and does not exist after death, at this point the self is completely annihilated.' In this way some proclaim the annihilation, destruction, and extermination of an existent being.

86. "To him another says: 'There is, good sir, such a self as you assert. That I do not deny. But it is not at that point that the self is completely annihilated. For there is, good sir, another self—divine, having material form, pertaining to the sense sphere, feeding on edible nutriment. That you neither know nor see, but I know it and see it. Since *this* self, good sir, is annihilated and destroyed with the breakup of the body and does not exist after death, at this point the self is completely annihilated.' In this way others proclaim the annihilation, destruction, and extermination of an existent being.

87. "To him another says: 'There is, good sir, such a self as you assert. That I do not deny. But it is not at that point that the self is completely annihilated. For there is, good sir, another self—divine, having material form, mind-made, complete in all its limbs and organs, not destitute of any faculties. That you neither know nor see, but I know it and see it. Since *this* self, good sir, is annihilated and destroyed with the breakup of the body and does not exist after death, at this point the self is completely annihilated.' In this way others proclaim the annihilation, destruction, and extermination of an existent being.

88. "To him another says: 'There is, good sir, such a self as you assert. That I do not deny. But it is not at that point that the self is completely annihilated. For there is, good sir, another self belonging to the base of infinite space, (reached by) the complete surmounting of perceptions of material form, by the disappearance of perceptions of resistance, by non-attention to perceptions of diversity, (by contemplating) "Space is infinite." That you neither know nor see, but I know it and see it. Since *this* self, good sir, is annihilated and destroyed with the breakup of the body and does not exist after death, at this point the self is completely annihilated.' In this way others proclaim the annihilation, destruction, and extermination of an existent being.

89. "To him another says: 'There is, good sir, such a self as you assert. That I do not deny. But it is not at that point that the self is completely annihilated. For there is, good sir, another self belonging to the base of infinite consciousness, (reached by) completely surmounting the base of infinite space (by contemplating): "Consciousness is infinite." That you neither know nor see. But I know it and see it. Since *this* self, good sir, is annihilated and destroyed with the breakup of the body and does not exist after death, at this point the self is completely annihilated.' In this way some proclaim the annihilation, destruction, and extermination of an existent being.

90. "To him another says: 'There is, good sir, such a self as you assert. That I do not deny. But it is not at that point that the self is completely annihilated. For there is, good sir, another self belonging to the base of nothingness, (reached by) completely surmounting the base of infinite consciousness (by contemplating): "There is nothing." That you neither know nor see. But I know it and see it. Since *this* self, good sir, is annihilated and destroyed with the breakup of the body and does not exist after death, at this point the self is completely annihilated.' In this way some proclaim the annihilation, destruction, and extermination of an existent being.

91. "To him another says: 'There is, good sir, such a self as you assert. That I do not deny. But it is not at that point that the self is completely annihilated. For there is, good sir, another self belonging to the base of neither perception nor non-perception, (reached by) completely surmounting the base of nothingness (by contemplating): "This is the peaceful, this is the sublime." That you neither know nor

see. But I know it and see it. Since *this* self, good sir, is annihilated and destroyed with the breakup of the body and does not exist after death, at this point the self is completely annihilated.' In this way some proclaim the annihilation, destruction, and extermination of an existent being.

92. "It is on these seven grounds, bhikkhus, that those recluses and brahmins who are annihilationists proclaim the annihilation, destruction, and extermination of an existent being. Whatever recluses or brahmins proclaim the annihilation, destruction, and extermination of an existent being, all of them do so on these seven grounds, or on a certain one of them. Outside of these there is none.

"This, bhikkhus, the Tathāgata understands ... and it is concerning these that those who would rightly praise the Tathāgata in accordance with reality would speak.

E. Doctrines of Nibbāna Here and Now (*Diṭṭhadhammanibbānavāda*): Views 58–62

93. "There are, bhikkhus, some recluses and brahmins who maintain a doctrine of Nibbāna here and now and who, on five grounds, proclaim nibbāna here and now for an existent being. And owing to what, with reference to what, do these honorable recluses and brahmins proclaim their views?

94. "Herein, bhikkhus, a certain recluse or a brahmin asserts the following doctrine or view: 'When this self, good sir, furnished and supplied with the five strands of sense pleasures, revels in them—at this point the self attains supreme nibbāna here and now.' In this way some proclaim supreme nibbāna here and now for an existent being.

95. "To him another says: 'There is, good sir, such a self as you assert. That I do not deny. But it is not at that point that the self attains supreme nibbāna here and now. What is the reason? Because, good sir, sense pleasures are impermanent, suffering, subject to change, and through their change and transformation there arise sorrow, lamentation, pain, grief, and despair. But when the self, quite secluded from sense pleasures, secluded from unwholesome states, enters and abides in the first jhāna, which is accompanied by initial and sustained thought and contains the rapture and happiness born of seclusion—at this point, good sir, the self attains supreme nibbāna here and now.' In this way others proclaim supreme nibbāna here and now for an existent being.

96. "To him another says: 'There is, good sir, such a self as you assert. That I do not deny. But it is not at that point that the self attains supreme nibbāna here and now. What is the reason? Because that jhāna contains initial and sustained thought; therefore it is declared to be gross. But when, with the subsiding of initial and sustained thought, the self enters and abides in the second jhāna, which is accompanied by internal confidence and unification of mind, is free from initial and sustained thought, and contains the rapture and happiness born of concentration—at this point, good sir, the self attains supreme nibbāna here and now.' In this way others proclaim supreme nibbāna here and now for an existent being.

97. "To him another says: 'There is, good sir, such a self as you assert. That I do not deny. But it is not at that point that the self attains supreme nibbāna here and now. What is the reason? It is declared to be gross because of the mental exhilaration connected with rapture that exists there. But when, with the fading away of rapture, one abides in equanimity, mindful and clearly comprehending, and still experiencing happiness with the body, enters and abides in the third jhāna, so that the ariyans announce: "He abides happily, in equanimity and mindfulness"—at this point, good sir, the self attains supreme nibbāna here and now.' In this way some proclaim supreme nibbāna here and now for an existent being.

98. "To him another says: 'There is, good sir, such a self as you assert. That I do not deny. But it is not at that point that the self attains supreme nibbāna here and now. What is the reason? It is declared to be gross because of the mental concern with pleasure that is there. But when, with the abandoning of pleasure and pain, and with the disappearance of previous joy and grief, one enters and abides in the fourth jhāna, which is without pleasure and pain and contains purification of mindfulness through equanimity—at this point, good sir, the self attains supreme nibbāna here and now.' In this way some proclaim supreme nibbāna here and now for an existent being.

"This, bhikkhus, the Tathāgata understands … and it is concerning these that those who would rightly praise the Tathāgata in accordance with reality would speak.

99. "It is on these five grounds, bhikkhus, that these recluses and brahmins who maintain a doctrine of nibbāna here and now proclaim supreme nibbāna here and now for an existent being. Whatever recluses or brahmins proclaim supreme nibbāna here and now for an

existent being, all of them do so on these five grounds, or on a certain one of them. Outside of these there is none.

"This, bhikkhus, the Tathāgata understands ... and it is concerning these that those who would rightly praise the Tathāgata in accordance with reality would speak.

100. "It is on these forty-four grounds, bhikkhus, that those recluses and brahmins who are speculators about the future and hold settled views about the future, assert various conceptual theorems referring to the future. Whatever recluses or brahmins, bhikkhus, are speculators about the future, hold settled views about the future, and assert various conceptual theorems referring to the future, all of them do so on these forty-four grounds, or on a certain one of them. Outside of these there is none.

"This, bhikkhus, the Tathāgata understands ... and it is concerning these that those who would rightly praise the Tathāgata in accordance with reality would speak.

101. "It is on these sixty-two grounds, bhikkhus, that those recluses and brahmins who are speculators about the past, speculators about the future, and speculators about the past and the future together, who hold settled views about the past and the future, assert various conceptual theorems referring to the past and the future.

102. "Whatever recluses or brahmins, bhikkhus, are speculators about the past or speculators about the future or speculators about the past and the future together, hold settled views about the past and the future, and assert various conceptual theorems referring to the past and the future, all of them do so on these sixty-two grounds, or on a certain one of them. Outside of these there is none.

103. "This, bhikkhus, the Tathāgata understands. And he understands: 'These standpoints, thus assumed and thus misapprehended, lead to such a future destination, to such a state in the world beyond.' He understands as well what transcends this, yet even that understanding he does not misapprehend. And because he is free from misapprehension, he has realized within himself the state of perfect peace. Having understood as they really are the origin and the passing away of feelings, their satisfaction, unsatisfactoriness and the escape from them, the Tathāgata, bhikkhus, is emancipated through non-clinging.

104. "These are those dhammas, bhikkhus, that are deep, difficult to see, difficult to understand, peaceful and sublime, beyond the

sphere of reasoning, subtle, comprehensible only to the wise, which the Tathāgata, having realized for himself with direct knowledge, propounds to others; and it is concerning these that those who would rightly praise the Tathāgata in accordance with reality would speak.

V. The Round of Conditions and Emancipation from the Round

A. Agitation and Vacillation (*Paritassitavipphandita*)

105. Therein, bhikkhus, when those recluses and brahmins who are eternalists proclaim on four grounds the self and the world to be eternal—that is only the feeling of those who do not know and do not see; that is only the agitation and vacillation of those who are immersed in craving.

106. "When those recluses and brahmins who are eternalists in regard to some things and non-eternalists in regard to other things proclaim on four grounds the self and the world to be partly eternal and partly non-eternal—that too is only the feeling of those who do not know and do not see; that is only the agitation and vacillation of those who are immersed in craving.

107. "When those recluses and brahmins who are extensionists proclaim on four grounds the world to be finite or infinite—

108. "When those recluses and brahmins who are endless equivocators on four grounds resort to evasive statements and endless equivocation when questioned on this or that point—

109. "When those recluses and brahmins who are fortuitous originationists proclaim on two grounds the self and the world to originate fortuitously—

110. "When those recluses and brahmins who are speculators about the past and hold settled views about the past assert on eighteen grounds various conceptual theorems referring to the past—

111. "When those recluses and brahmins who maintain a doctrine of percipient immortality proclaim on sixteen grounds the self to survive percipient after death—

112. "When those recluses and brahmins who maintain a doctrine of non-percipient immortality proclaim on eight grounds the self to survive non-percipient after death—

113. "When those recluses and brahmins who maintain a doctrine of neither percipient nor non-percipient immortality proclaim on eight grounds the self to survive neither percipient nor non-percipient after death—

114. "When those recluses and brahmins who are annihilationists proclaim on seven grounds the annihilation, destruction, and extermination of an existent being—

115. "When those recluses and brahmins who maintain a doctrine of nibbāna here and now proclaim on five grounds supreme nibbāna here and now for an existent being—

116. "When those recluses and brahmins who are speculators about the future and hold settled views about the future assert on forty-four grounds various conceptual theorems referring to the future—

117. "When those recluses and brahmins who are speculators about the past, speculators about the future, speculators about the past and the future together, who hold settled views about the past and the future, assert on sixty-two grounds various conceptual theorems referring to the past and the future—that too is only the feeling of those who do not know and do not see; that is only the agitation and vacillation of those who are immersed in craving.

B. Conditioned by Contact (*Phassapaccayavāra*)

118 (131). "Therein, bhikkhus, when those recluses who are eternalists proclaim on four grounds the self and the world to be eternal—that is conditioned by contact. That they can experience that feeling without contact—such a case is impossible.[16]

119 (132). "When those recluses and brahmins who are eternalists in regard to some things and non-eternalists in regard to other things proclaim on four grounds the self and the world to be partly eternal

16. In order to avoid excessive repetition, the following section of the sutta has been combined with the present section by deleting its repetition of each view and adding its novel feature, the declaration that the experience of feeling without contact is impossible, to the end of each statement in the present section.

and partly non-eternal—that too is conditioned by contact. That they can experience that feeling without contact—such a case is impossible.

120 (133)—129 (142). "When those recluses and brahmins who are extensionists proclaim their views; when those who are fortuitous originationists proclaim their views; when those who are speculators about the past and hold settled views about the past assert on eighteen grounds various conceptual theorems referring to the past; when those who maintain a doctrine of percipient immortality, non-percipient immortality, or neither percipient nor non-percipient immortality proclaim their views; when those who are annihilationists proclaim their views; when those who maintain a doctrine of nibbāna here and now proclaim their views; when those who are speculators about the future and hold settled views about the future assert on forty-four grounds various conceptual theorems referring to the future—that too is conditioned by contact. That they can experience that feeling without contact—such a case is impossible.

130 (143). "When those recluses and brahmins who are speculators about the past, speculators about the future, speculators about the past and the future together, who hold settled views about the past and the future, assert on sixty-two grounds various conceptual theorems referring to the past and the future—that too is conditioned by contact. That they can experience that feeling without contact—such a case is impossible.

C. Exposition of the Round
(*Diṭṭhigatikādhiṭṭhānavaṭṭakathā*)

144. "Therein, bhikkhus, those recluses and brahmins who are eternalists and proclaim on four grounds the self and the world to be eternal; and those who are eternalists in regard to some things and non-eternalists in regard to others; and those who are extensionists; and those who are endless equivocators; and those who are fortuitous originationists; and those who are speculators about the past; and those who maintain a doctrine of percipient immortality; and those who maintain a doctrine of non-percipient immortality; and those who maintain a doctrine of neither percipient nor non-percipient immortality; and those who are annihilationists; and those who maintain a doctrine of nibbāna here and now; and those who are speculators about the future; and those who are speculators about the past, speculators about the future, speculators about the past and the

future together, hold settled views about the past and the future, and assert on sixty-two grounds various conceptual theorems referring to the past and the future—all these recluses and brahmins experience these feelings only by repeated contacts through the six bases of contact. With feeling as condition, there arises in them craving; with craving as condition, clinging arises; with clinging as condition, existence; with existence as condition, birth; and with birth as condition, aging and death, sorrow, lamentation, pain, grief, and despair arise.

D. The Ending of the Round
(*Vivaṭṭakathādi*)

145. "When, bhikkhus, a bhikkhu understands as they really are the origin and passing away of the six bases of contact, their satisfaction, unsatisfactoriness, and the escape from them, then he understands what transcends all these views.

146. "Whatever recluses or brahmins, bhikkhus, are speculators about the past, speculators about the future, speculators about the past and the future together, hold settled views about the past and the future, and assert various conceptual theorems referring to the past and the future—all are trapped in this net with its sixty-two divisions. Whenever they emerge, they emerge caught within this net, trapped and contained within this very net.

"Just as, bhikkhus, a skillful fisherman or a fisherman's apprentice, after spreading a fine-meshed net over a small pool of water, might think: 'Whatever sizeable creatures there are in this pool, all are trapped within this net, trapped and contained in this very net'—in the same way, all those recluses and brahmins are trapped in this net with its sixty-two divisions. Whenever they emerge, they emerge caught within this net, trapped and contained within this very net.

147. "The body of the Tathāgata, bhikkhus, stands with the leash that bound it to existence cut. As long as his body stands, gods and men shall see him. But with the breakup of the body and the exhaustion of the life-faculty, gods and men shall see him no more.

"Just as, bhikkhus, when the stalk of a bunch of mangoes has been cut, all the mangoes connected to the stalk follow along with it, in the same way, the body of the Tathāgata stands with the leash that bound it to existence cut. As long as his body stands, gods and men shall see him. But with the breakup of the body and the exhaustion of the life-faculty, gods and men shall see him no more."

148. When this was said, the Venerable Ānanda said to the Exalted One: "It is wonderful, venerable sir, it is marvelous! What is the title, venerable sir, of this exposition of the Dhamma?"

"Ānanda, you may remember this exposition of the Dhamma as the Net of the Good, as the Net of the Dhamma, as the Supreme Net, as the Net of Views. You may remember it also as the Incomparable Victory in Battle."

149. Thus spoke the Exalted One. Elated in mind, the bhikkhus delighted in the word of the Exalted One. And while this exposition was being spoken, the ten-thousandfold world system shook.

Here ends the Brahmajāla Sutta.

Part Two

THE COMMENTARIAL EXEGESIS OF THE BRAHMAJĀLA SUTTA

[**Note:** The chapter, section, and passage numbers of the commentarial exegesis correspond with the chapter, section, and passage numbers of the sutta text. Hence the explanation of any particular sutta passage, if commented upon, can be located by consulting the corresponding number below. The sutta passage, either in its entirety or by way of its key words, is given first in New Century Schoolbook font, sometimes followed by the Pāḷi. The explanation from the commentary (*aṭṭhakathā*) is prefixed by **CY.**, from the subcommentary (*ṭīkā*) by **Sub.Cy.**, and from the new subcommentary (*abhinavaṭīkā*) by **N.Sub.Cy.** Since normally N.Sub.Cy. simply reproduces the old subcommentary, expanding and elaborating on it for the sake of greater clarity, phrases from the N.Sub.Cy. have sometimes merely been inserted into the selections from the Sub.Cy., marked off by square brackets. English portions in parenthesis are my own additions.]

I. Talk on Wanderers
(*Paribbājakakathā*)

1. Thus have I heard.

CY. This is the introduction or beginning to the Brahmajāla Sutta, spoken by the Venerable Ānanda on the occasion of the First Great Council. For at the First Council, after the compilation of the Vinaya Piṭaka was completed, the Venerable Mahākassapa questioned the Venerable Ānanda about the Brahmajāla, the first sutta in the first collection (*nikāya*) of the Sutta Piṭaka, asking: "Friend Ānanda, where was the Brahmajāla Sutta spoken?" and so on. When the questionnaire was finished, the Venerable Ānanda explained everything, where it was spoken, the reason, etc., beginning with the words: "Thus have I heard." By this he meant: "Thus have I heard" concerning the Brahmajāla."

On one occasion the Exalted One

CY. By this phrase, implying the non-existence of the Exalted One (at the time it was recited), the Venerable Ānanda shows the parinibbāna of the form-body (*rūpakāya*) of the Buddha. Thus he inspires a sense of spiritual urgency (*saṃvega*) in people intoxicated with the vanity of life and arouses in them a desire to hear the true Dhamma, as though telling them: "Even the Exalted One, the Teacher of the ariyan Dhamma, the Bearer of the Ten Powers,[17] whose body was like a mass of diamonds, has passed away. Who then can hope to live forever?"

Reciting the word "thus," he shows that the sutta possesses a teaching; by the words "have I heard," that it possesses a listener; by the words "on one occasion," that it possesses a specific time; and by the words "the Exalted One," that it possesses a teacher.

with a great company of bhikkhus

CY. That company was "great" on account of the greatness of its noble qualities and on account of the greatness of its number. Because its members were endowed with such noble qualities as fewness of wishes, etc., the company of bhikkhus was great in noble qualities; and because it was composed of five hundred bhikkhus, it was great in number.

the wanderer Suppiya

CY. A pupil of Sañjaya.[18] He was a clothed wanderer (i.e., not a naked ascetic).

---

17. The ten powers of knowledge pertaining to a Buddha. See MN 12,9–21.
18. The wanderer Sañjaya was the teacher of Sāriputta and Moggallāna before they encountered the Buddha.

He spoke in many ways

CY. (In the phrase *anekapariyāyena*), the word "way" (*pariyāya*) occurs in the senses of turn, teaching, and reason. Here it is employed in the sense of reason (*kāraṇa*). Therefore the meaning is: "for many a reason," "with many reasons."

in dispraise of the Buddha

CY. Although the Exalted Buddha was altogether flawless and possessed countless praiseworthy qualities, he spoke in dispraise, criticism, and blame of the Buddha, groundlessly charging him with one of the following faults: "The recluse Gotama does not perform the proper duties such as salutation, etc., towards those advanced in years. These duties are called, in common idiom, 'the taste of concord'; therefore the recluse Gotama is lacking in taste. He is worthless. He teaches a doctrine denying the moral efficacy of action. He is an annihilationist, a detester, a nihilist, a tormentor, incapable of higher rebirth. The recluse Gotama has attained no state transcending the merely human level, no distinguished knowledge and vision worthy of the ariyans. He teaches a doctrine hammered out by reason, deduced from his investigations, following his own flight of thought.[19] The recluse Gotama is not omniscient, not a knower of the worlds, not supreme, not the foremost individual."

N.Sub.Cy. This is the meaning of these accusations:—The "taste of concord" acknowledged by worldly convention consists in paying homage to elders, rising up for them, saluting them reverentially,[20] doing the proper duties for them, and offering them a seat. Because he does not practice this "taste of concord," the Buddha is said to be "lacking in taste." Because he does not possess the "worth" of the taste of concord, he is called "worthless." Because he does not teach this practice, he is said to hold to the inefficacy of action. Similarly, he is an "annihilationist" because he teaches that such conduct should be annihilated, a "detester" because he treats beauty and birth as though

---

19. See AN 8:11, Svibh Pārājikā 1, and MN 12.2 for the scriptural sources for these charges.

20. *Añjali,* the traditional East Asian gesture of respectful greeting, made by extending the joined hands held at head or breast level towards the recipient of the greeting.

they were filth, a "nihilist" because he destroys this convention and because he himself should be destroyed, a "tormentor" because he torments those advanced in years by not observing this custom or because he is despicable for neglecting such conduct, and "incapable of higher rebirth" because by not observing this custom he has fallen away from rebirth in the world of gods and is bound for an inferior rebirth. Thus the Buddha's non-practice of homage, etc., is the reason for the charges that he is lacking in taste, etc.

"He has attained no distinguished knowledge and vision": because he did not (seem to) know about the death of the female wanderer Sundarī (see Ud 4.8); because he claims that a first point of saṃsāra cannot be discovered; because he dismisses certain questions as unanswerable, etc.—these may be adduced as the grounds for this charge.

"He teaches a doctrine hammered out by reason," etc.: because here and there, in this way and that, his teaching of the Dhamma proceeds through his own penetration, acquired by himself without a teacher. Sometimes, when answering the questions of others, he uses logical procedures, etc.—such are the reasons for this accusation.

"He is not omniscient ... not the foremost individual": because he can only comprehend all dhammas in succession (not simultaneously), because he does not know the end of the world, does not recognize the utility of austerities, etc.

(in dispraise of) the Dhamma, and the Saṅgha

CY. Just as he spoke in dispraise of the Buddha, he also spoke in dispraise of the Dhamma, groundlessly declaring: "The Dhamma of the recluse Gotama is wrongly expounded, wrongly penetrated, not liberating, not conducive to peace." And as he spoke in dispraise of the Dhamma, he also spoke in dispraise of the Saṅgha: "The recluse Gotama's community of disciples is practicing wrongly and perversely. It has entered upon a warped, distorted, unrighteous course of practice."

But his pupil the youth Brahmadatta, spoke in many ways in praise of the Buddha, the Dhamma, and the Saṅgha

CY. His pupil Brahmadatta thought: "Our teacher misapprehends something that should not be misapprehended and attacks something that should not be attacked. For if he speaks in dispraise of the praiseworthy Triple Gem he will come to ruin and destruction as surely as if he were to swallow fire, seize a sword with his hand, try to shatter Mount Sineru with his fist, play with the teeth of a saw, or try to stop a ferocious rutting elephant with his hand. If the teacher were to tread upon dung, fire, thorns, or a black viper, or to mount a stake, eat deadly poison, step into a violent stream, or throw himself down a cliff, there is no reason for the pupil to follow suit. For beings are the owners of their kamma and they each go their own way according to their own kamma. The father does not inherit the son's kamma, nor the son the father's; the mother does not inherit the son's kamma, nor the son the mother's; the brother does not inherit the sister's kamma, nor the sister the brother's; the teacher does not inherit the pupil's kamma, nor the pupil the teacher's. My teacher speaks in dispraise of the Triple Gem; this is a terrible blameworthy deed—the reviling of the ariyans." Emerging from such wise reflections, since he was a naturally intelligent young man he began to speak in many ways in praise of the Triple Gem, confuting his teacher's views and supporting himself with cogent reasons.

Thus these two ... followed closely behind the Exalted One and the company of bhikkhus

CY. Why was the Exalted One travelling along that highway? And why did Suppiya follow behind him? And why did he speak in dispraise of the Triple Gem?

At that time the Exalted One had been residing in one of the eighteen large monasteries in the vicinity of Rājagaha. In the morning, after attending to his bodily needs, the Exalted One walked for alms in Rājagaha at the time for the almsround, surrounded by the company of bhikkhus, by his presence making it easy for the bhikkhus to obtain alms. Following the meal, after returning from the almsround, he made the bhikkhus bring his bowl and outer robe and announced: "Now I will set out for Nālandā." He then left Rājagaha and set out on the highway. At the same time Suppiya too was residing in the vicinity of Rājagaha, in one of the monasteries reserved for the wanderers. Surrounded by his company of wanderers, he walked for alms in Rājagaha that morning, by his presence making it easy for the wanderers to obtain alms. When he had finished his morning meal, he made his wanderers bring his set of requisites and announced: "Now I will set out for Nālandā." Thus he set forth on his journey following closely behind the Exalted One, without realizing that the Exalted One was travelling along the same highway. For if he had known he would not have followed behind. While going along unknowingly, he lifted his neck, looked around, and saw the Exalted One ahead of him, radiant with the glory of a Buddha like the shimmering crest of a golden mountain enveloped in a crimson mantle.

At that time, it is told, the six-colored rays of the Bearer of the Ten Powers issued forth from his body, filling and pervading an area eighty feet on all sides. The forest clearing through which they were walking appeared then as though it were bestrewn with garlands and wreathes made of gems or with the dust of pulverized gems, as though it were a beautiful golden cloth embroidered with gems, as though it were sprinkled over with the essence of red gold or filled with a hundred meteors or bestrewn with clustered (golden) *kanikāra* flowers, as though it were bestrewn with red China lead reduced to powder and scattered about by gusts of wind or as though it were irradiated and illuminated throughout by the splendor of rainbows, streaks of lightning, and the multitudinous host of stars.

The Exalted One's body, adorned with the eighty minor marks of physical beauty, was like a lake filled with blooming lotus flowers and water lilies, like a pāricchattaka tree in full blossom, like the canopy of the sky sparkling with the light of the stars, smiling down with glory from above. And with his thirty-two characteristics of physical beauty woven, as it were, into a garland shining with splendor for a fathom all around, he surpassed in glory the glory of a garland composed of thirty-two moons or thirty-two suns, the glory even of thirty-two world-ruling monarchs, of thirty-two celestial kings, or of thirty-two Mahābrahmās.

Surrounding the Exalted One stood bhikkhus all of few wishes, content, fond of solitude, aloof, exhorters, censors of evil, teachers, tolerant of correction, endowed with virtue, concentration, wisdom, emancipation, and the knowledge and vision of emancipation. Standing in their midst, the Exalted One was like a golden pillar surrounded by a red woolen rampart, like a golden boat amidst a cluster of red lotus flowers, like a tower of flame encircled by a coral railing or like the full moon surrounded by the host of stars. The sight filled the eyes even of the birds and beasts with joy, much more, then, did it bring joy to the eyes of gods and humans.

On that day most of the eighty great disciples accompanied the Exalted One. With their cloud-colored rag-robes arranged over one shoulder, carrying their walking sticks, they appeared like perfumed elephants clad in solid armor—all free from corruptions, their corruptions ejected, their defilements shattered, their tangles disentangled and their bonds cut. The Exalted One, free from lust, hatred, and delusion himself, stood surrounded by those free from lust, hatred, and delusion; free from craving himself, he stood surrounded by those free from craving; devoid of defilements himself, he stood surrounded by those devoid of defilements; enlightened himself, he stood surrounded by those enlightened after him. Travelling along that road like the moon across the sky with the inconceivable, incomparable grace of a Buddha, produced through the power of merit accumulated over an immeasurable period of time, the Exalted One appeared like the filament (of a lotus flower) surrounded by petals, like a pericarp surrounded by filaments, like a six-tusked elephant king surrounded by eight thousand bull elephants, like a royal swan surrounded by ninety thousand swans, like a world-ruling monarch surrounded by his complete army, like Sakka the king of the gods surrounded by the multitude of gods, like the Mahābrahmā Hārita surrounded by the multitude of Brahmā gods.

Having seen the Exalted One moving with the incomparable grace of a Buddha and those bhikkhus with downcast gaze, tranquil faculties and tranquil minds honoring the Exalted One like the full moon in the vault of heaven, the wanderer Suppiya then surveyed his own assembly. He saw his followers leaning on the poles they were carrying, heaped up with a big load of requisites—dilapidated stools, tridents, peacock-fans, earthen bowls, sacks, water-pots, etc. They were loose-tongued, noisy, vociferous, unsightly, and uninspiring. Seeing them, he was filled with remorse. Now, just then it would have been proper for him to have praised the Exalted One. But since his gain and honor as well as his following had diminished (on account of the Buddha), he was constantly jealous of the Buddha. For so long as a Buddha does not appear in the world, the monks of other sects acquire abundant gain and honor. But when a Buddha appears, then their gain and honor diminish, just as the light of the glow-worm becomes indiscernible with the rising of the sun. Moreover, when Upatissa and

Kolita (i.e., Sāriputta and Moggallāna) went forth into homelessness under Sañjaya, their assembly swelled with numbers.[21] But when these two left him (to follow the Buddha) the assembly of wanderers was split. Thus for these two reasons, the diminishing of his gains and the loss of his followers, the wanderer Suppiya was constantly jealous of the Buddha. Vomiting up the poison of his jealousy, he spoke in dispraise of the Triple Gem.

2. There, too, (in the royal resthouse) the wanderer Suppiya spoke in many ways in dispraise of the Buddha, the Dhamma, and the Saṅgha

CY. When night had fallen, the wanderer Suppiya, having arrived at the resthouse, looked across at the Exalted One. At the time, lamps were burning all around like scattered stars. The Exalted One was sitting in their midst, surrounded by the company of bhikkhus. Not even one bhikkhu fidgeted with his hands or feet or made any sound of coughing or sneezing. The entire assembly, through its masterly self-discipline and out of reverence for the Teacher, sat together as still and motionless as the flame of a lamp in a windless place. Having seen this wonder, the wanderer then surveyed his own assembly. There, some were playing with their hands, some with their feet, some were chitchatting, while others slept, their tongues hanging out of their mouths, dribbling, gnashing their teeth, snoring and snorting in their sleep. Then too he should have praised the noble qualities of the Triple Gem; but because of his jealousy he spoke in dispraise. Brahmadatta, however, again spoke in their praise.

3. It is wonderful and marvellous, friends, how the Exalted One, he who knows and sees ... has so thoroughly penetrated the diversity in the dispositions of beings

CY. The Exalted One, after fulfilling the complete thirty pāramīs and destroying all defilements, awakened to the supreme perfect enlightenment. He is one "who knows," because he knows the propensities and latent tendencies (*āsayānusaya*) of the various kinds of sentient beings. He is one "who sees," because he sees all knowable

21. As a pupil of Sañjaya, Suppiya would have shared his teacher's indignation over the loss of these two disciples.

dhammas (*sabbañeyyadhamma*) as clearly as a fruit held in the palm of the hand. He *knows* through the knowledge of past lives, etc.; and he *sees* through the divine eye. He knows through the three kinds of clear knowledge (*vijjā*) and the six kinds of direct knowledge (*abhiññā*); and he sees through the universal eye (*samantacakkhu*) of unimpeded penetration.[22] He knows through the wisdom that is capable of knowing all dhammas; and with the fully purified fleshly eye he sees things outside the visual range of other beings, such as forms hidden behind walls, etc. He knows through the wisdom of penetration which secures his own welfare and has concentration as its proximate cause; and he sees through the wisdom of teaching which secures the welfare of other beings and has compassion as its proximate cause. By this statement it is meant that the Exalted One has perfectly penetrated the truth: "Beings, bhikkhus, come together and encounter one another because of some common element. Those of low disposition meet and encounter those of low disposition, those of noble disposition meet and encounter those of noble disposition. So it was in the past, so it will be in the future, and so it is at present" (SN 14:14). Thus, as though measuring them with a ruler or weighing them on a pair of scales, the Buddha has realized through his knowledge of omniscience and his comprehension of the dispositions of beings, that beings have diverse dispositions, inclinations, views, acquiescences, and preferences. It is hard to find even two beings of identical inclinations in the world. If one person wants to go, the other wants to stay; if one wants to drink, the other wants to eat.

4. The Exalted One, realizing the turn their discussion had taken

CY. He heard it through his knowledge of omniscience. But what was he doing that he heard it? He was engaged in the activity of the last watch of the night. There are two kinds of activities (*kicca*), the beneficial and the useless. Of these, all tendencies to useless activity

---

22. The three kinds of *clear knowledge* are the knowledge of recollecting past lives, the knowledge of the passing away and re-arising of beings, and the knowledge of the destruction of the cankers. The six kinds of direct knowledge include these three, preceded by the knowledge of the modes of psychic power, the divine ear-element, and the penetration of others' minds. The *universal eye* is the knowledge of omniscience.

were abolished by the Exalted One with his attainment of the path of arahatship at the foot of the Bodhi Tree. But from then on he remained engaged in beneficial activity.

(The Buddha's Daily Routine)

The Exalted One's activities were divided into five groups: the activities of the morning, of the afternoon, of the first watch of the night, of the middle watch, and of the last watch.

(1) These were his *morning activities:* The Exalted One would rise early in the morning and attend to his morning ablutions, out of compassion for his attendant (by giving him the opportunity to acquire merit) and for the sake of his physical well-being. Then he would remain seated in seclusion until the time for the almsround. When the time for the almsround arrived, he would change his lower robe, fasten the waistband, put on the upper robe, and taking his bowl, enter the village or town for alms. Sometimes he would go alone, sometimes with a retinue of bhikkhus; sometimes he would enter in a natural manner, sometimes giving a display of wonders. Thus when the Lord would walk for alms, gentle winds would precede him at each step, clearing the ground. Clouds would sprinkle drops of water to still the dust along the path, and then remain as a canopy overhead. Other winds would gather flowers and strew them along the road. The elevated areas of the ground would lower themselves and the depressed areas raise themselves, so that the ground was always level beneath the tread of his feet. Sometimes delicate lotus flowers would spring up to receive his feet. As soon as he placed his right foot within the town-gate, the six-colored rays issuing from his body would radiate in all directions, adorning the mansions, gabled houses, and other buildings, so that they appeared as though enveloped in the sheen of rarefied gold or in a cloak of many hues. Elephants, horses, and birds, standing in their own places, would break out into melodious sounds, while musical instruments such as drums and lutes, as also the ornaments of the people, would spontaneously give forth music.

By these signs the people would know: "The Exalted One has come for alms." Then, well dressed and well groomed, bringing scents, flowers, and other offerings, they would issue forth from their houses into the street, respectfully present their offerings to the Exalted One, do homage to him, and say; "Lord, give us ten bhikkhus for alms, give us twenty, give us fifty, give us a hundred." Taking the Exalted One's bowl, they would lead him to a seat and respectfully serve him with almsfood. When he had finished his meal, the Exalted One would survey the mental dispositions of the people present. Then he would teach the Dhamma to them in such a way that some would become established in the refuges, some in the five precepts, some in the fruits of sanctity—the fruits of stream-entry, once-returner or non-returner. Others, having gone forth into homelessness, would attain to the supreme fruit of arahatship. After benefitting the multitude in this way, he would rise from his seat and return to the monastery. Upon his return he would sit down in the pavilion, in the special seat prepared just for him, and wait until the bhikkhus finished their meal. When the bhikkhus had finished eating, the attendant would inform the Exalted One. The Exalted One would then enter the Fragrant Cottage.

(2) These were his *afternoon activities:* With the morning activities completed, the Exalted One would sit down in the antechamber of the Fragrant Cottage and wash his feet. Then, getting up on a footstool, he would exhort the Bhikkhu Saṅgha: "Bhikkhus, strive for your deliverance with diligence. Rare is the appearance of a Buddha in the world, rare the acquisition of the human state, rare the gain of optimal supporting conditions, rare the going forth into homelessness, rare the opportunity of hearing the true Dhamma." Some bhikkhus would then request a subject of meditation and the Exalted One would assign them subjects appropriate for their particular temperaments. Thereupon all the bhikkhus would do homage to the Master and retire to their individual day and night quarters—some to the forest, some to the foot of a tree, some to a place in the mountains, and some to the various sense-sphere heavens.

Following this the Exalted One would enter the Fragrant Cottage. If he wished, he would lie down for a few moments on his right side, in the lion posture, mindful and clearly comprehending. When his body was refreshed, he would rise and pass the second part of the afternoon surveying the world. In the third part of the afternoon, the people of the village or town near which he was dwelling, who had given alms in the morning, would assemble in the monastery, well-dressed and well-groomed, bringing scents, flowers, and other offerings. The Exalted One would approach, displaying whatever wonders were appropriate for the assembly present. Then, sitting down in his special seat in the assembly hall, he would teach the Dhamma in a way fitting the time and occasion. When the discourse was finished, he would dismiss the assembly, and the people, having done homage to him, would depart.

(3) These were his activities during *the first watch of the night:* When he had finished his afternoon activities, if he wanted to bathe, he would rise up from his seat, enter the bathroom, and refresh his body with water brought by his attendant. The attendant would also take the seat and prepare it in a cell in the Fragrant Cottage. The Exalted One, having put on a fresh well-dyed lower robe, fastened the waistband and arranged his upper robe over one shoulder, would return to his cell and sit alone for a few moments in solitary meditation. Thereafter the bhikkhus would arrive from various directions to attend upon the Master. Some would ask questions, some would request meditation subjects, some would ask about points of Dhamma. The Exalted One would pass the first watch of the night complying with their requests.

(4) These were his activities during *the middle watch of the night:* When the first watch activities were completed and the bhikkhus had paid homage to the Master and departed, the deities of the entire ten-thousandfold world system would gain the opportunity to see the Exalted One. Having approached him, they would ask whatever questions might occur to them, even one only four syllables in length,[23] and the Exalted One would pass the middle watch of the night replying to their questions.

(5) These were his activities during *the last watch of the night:* he divided the last watch of the night into three parts. Because his body ached from sitting continuously since early morning, he would spend one part pacing up and down to dispel the discomfort. In the second part, he would enter the Fragrant Cottage and lie down on his right side, in the lion posture, mindful and clearly comprehending. In the third part, he would rise, take a seat, and survey the world with the Buddha-eye in order to discover individuals who had observed their course of duties, such as giving alms and observing precepts, in the presence of the Buddhas of the past.

On that day the Exalted One, after concluding his morning activities in Rājagaha, set out on his journey in the afternoon. In the first watch of the night he explained meditation subjects to the

---

23. The Pāḷi has *"antamaso caturakkharampi." Akkhara* according to DP can mean either "letter", "character", or "syllable", but not a "full line".

bhikkhus, and in the middle watch answered the questions of the deities. In the last watch, while pacing up and down on the walkway, he learned of the discussion taking place among the bhikkhus concerning his knowledge of omniscience, having heard it with his knowledge of omniscience itself. Hence it was said above: "He heard it through his knowledge of omniscience."

Realizing this, he thought: "These bhikkhus are holding a discussion concerning my knowledge of omniscience. The working of the knowledge of omniscience is not clear to them; it is clear only to me. But when I have gone there, they will immediately tell me all about their discussion. Then, making their discussion the occasion for a discourse, as though lifting up Mount Sineru or pounding the sky with a golden mallet, I will teach the Brahmajāla Sutta. Within it I will analyze the three classes of virtue, roar my irreversible lion's roar over the sixty-two cases of views, subsume the views under the law of conditionality, and having elucidated the Buddha-qualities, I will bring the teaching to a climax with the attainment of arahatship, causing the ten-thousandfold world system to quake. This teaching of mine will help beings to attain the deathless, the supreme state of nibbāna, even five thousand years following my parinibbāna."

Sub.Cy. The "lion's roar" will be sounded in the portions of the teaching beginning "These viewpoints", etc. The views will be subsumed under the law of conditionality in the passage beginning "With feeling as condition there arises in them craving," etc. The pair of similes about Mount Sineru and the golden mallet has the purpose of showing the extreme difficulty of teaching the Brahmajāla Sutta, for that lies beyond the capacity of anybody other than (a perfectly enlightened Buddha).

sat down on the prepared seat

CY. In the time of the Buddha, it is told, wherever even a single bhikkhu dwelt, a seat was always prepared for the Master. Why? When a bhikkhu had received a meditation subject from the Master and went to dwell at a place convenient to himself, the Exalted One would direct his attention to him, thinking: "such and such a bhikkhu has received a meditation subject from me and gone away. Will he be able to attain a state of spiritual distinction or not?" Then he would see that bhikkhu, having dropped his meditation subject, reflecting upon an unwholesome thought. The Exalted One would think: "How is this? After this clansman has received a subject of meditation from a Master such as myself, should unwholesome thoughts overwhelm him and drive him on through the suffering of the beginningless round of existence?" In order to help him, the Exalted One would show himself to the bhikkhu, admonish him, and rising into the air, return to his own dwelling place. Then those bhikkhus who had been admonished would reflect: "The Master, knowing our minds, came here and showed himself, standing in our presence. If, at that moment, we have to go about searching for a seat where the Master could be invited to sit, that would be troublesome." Therefore they kept a seat prepared. He who had a chair prepared his chair. He who had none prepared a bed, a bench, a log, a rock, or a heap of sand. If that was not available, they gathered old leaves and spread a rag over them. But here (in the royal resthouse) there was a royal seat. The bhikkhus dusted it by beating, prepared it, and sat around it, praising the excellence of the Exalted One's knowledge of the dispositions of others.

At this point (i.e., through §4 of the sutta) the introductory narrative (*nidāna*) spoken by the Venerable Ānanda is completed. The introduction, by mentioning the time, place, teacher, background story, assembly, and region, helps facilitate comprehension of this sutta, perfect in meaning and phrasing, illustrating the greatness of the spiritual power of the Buddha-qualities.

(The Purpose of the Introduction)

Sub.Cy. *Query:* What was the purpose in including the introductory narrative in the compilation of the Dhamma and Vinaya? Shouldn't the collection only have included the actual words spoken by the Buddha?

Reply: The introductory narrative serves to promote the durability, non-obscuration, and credibility of the discourse. For a discourse provided with an indication of the time, place, teacher, background story, and assembly endures long, remains free from obscuration, and is credible, like a business contract provided with notations of the place, date, merchandise, and conditions. Therefore, at the First Great Council, the Venerable Mahākassapa asked about the place where the Brahmajāla Sutta was spoken, etc., and the Venerable Ānanda, the treasurer of the Dhamma, recited the introduction in reply.

Furthermore, the introduction reveals the excellence of the Master. By showing that the Exalted One has no need for prior preparation, inference or reasoning based on scripture, it points to his attainment of perfect Buddhahood. For, as a perfectly enlightened Buddha, he requires no previous preparation, [no inferential judgments of probability and no reliance on reasoning from outside scriptures]; for him there is only one authoritative source of knowledge—the movement of his unimpeded knowledge (of omniscience) in all knowable dhammas. Again, by showing that the Master has no "closed fist" of a teacher,[24] no stinginess in sharing the Dhamma, and no favoritism towards disciples, it points to his freedom from cankers (*āsavas*). For through the destruction of cankers he has eliminated all "closed-fistedness" and rendered his activity of benefitting others fully pure. Thus the Master's perfect Buddhahood and complete inner purity, respectively, indicate his accomplishment in knowledge and in the abandonment (of defilements), and point to his freedom from ignorance and craving, those corruptions which corrode a teacher's attainments in wisdom and virtue. They further prove that he is endowed with the first two of the Tathāgata's grounds of self-confidence.[25] The Master's lack of any confusion in regard to states obstructive to spiritual progress and in regard to the liberating potency of his doctrine prove that he is endowed with the third and fourth grounds of self-confidence.[26] Thus the introduction, by describing the Exalted One as "he who knows and sees," and by exhibiting his ingenuity in creating an opportunity to deliver a discourse appropriate to the inclinations of the assembly present, reveals his endowment with the four grounds of self-confidence and his conduct for the welfare of himself and others. Therefore it is said: "The introduction reveals the excellence of the Master."

Furthermore, the introduction also reveals the excellence of the Dispensation (*sāsana*).[27] For the Exalted One, whose every deed is

24. See DN 16.2.25.
25. Namely, his assurance that he is perfectly enlightened about all dhammas, and that he has destroyed all the cankers. See MN 12.23.
26. The third and fourth grounds, referred to just below, are his assurance that the things he declares to be obstacles are truly obstructive, and that his teaching leads one who practices it to complete liberation from suffering.
27. For this paragraph the clearer and more complete version of the N.Sub.Cy. has been used.

accompanied by knowledge and compassion, does not engage in any useless activity, nor in any activity directed to his own welfare alone. Every deed of the perfectly enlightened Buddha is directed to the welfare of others. Since this is so, all the actions of the Buddha, bodily, verbal, and mental, described (in the text) as they actually occurred, constitute his Dispensation, in the sense that they instruct (*anusāsanaṭṭhena*) other beings in their own good—in the good pertaining to the present life, to the life to come, and to ultimate deliverance. It is not mere poetry. For along with the indication of the time, place, teacher, story, and assembly, the introduction here and there shows, as far as possible, the conduct of the Master. Or else, the introduction reveals the authoritativeness of the Dispensation by revealing the authoritativeness of the Master. The Master's authoritativeness is indicated by the title "the Exalted One" (*bhagavā*), signifying his supremacy among all beings by reason of his distinguished qualities, and by the epithet "he who knows and sees," signifying his attainment of the knowledge of the propensities and latent tendencies of others, etc.

The above is a mere outline of the purposes served by the introductory narrative. For who can exhaustively explain all the purposes of the introduction spoken by the treasurer of the Dhamma (Venerable Ānanda), who was enlightened after the Buddha himself?

5. **CY.** Now, with the words "If, bhikkhus, others speak in dispraise of me," the time has come to comment on the sutta delivered by the Exalted One. And since this commentary will be clearer if we first examine the grounds on which the Exalted One delivers a sutta, we will deal with this latter point first.

(THE FOUR GROUNDS FOR THE DELIVERY OF A SUTTA)
(*suttanikkhepa*)

There are four grounds for the delivery of a sutta: (1) personal inclination (*attajjhāsaya*), (2) the inclinations of others (*parajjhāsaya*), (3) the proposal of a question (*pucchāvasika*) and (4) the occurrence of a special incident (*aṭṭhuppattika*).

Among these, (1) those suttas that the Exalted One declares entirely through his own inclination, without being requested by others, have personal inclination as the ground for their delivery. Some examples of this class are the Ākaṅkheyya Sutta (MN 6), the Vattha Sutta (MN 7), the Mahāsatipaṭṭhāna Sutta (DN 22), the

Mahāsaḷāyatana Sutta (MN 137), the Ariyavaṃsa Sutta (A 4:28), and many suttas on the right endeavors, the bases of spiritual success, the faculties, powers, factors of enlightenment, and factors of the path.

(2) Those suttas that he declares by reason of the inclinations of others, after discerning their inclination, acquiescence, state of mind, aspiration, and capacity for understanding, have the inclinations of others as the ground for their delivery. An instance is the case of Rāhula: when the Exalted One perceived that the factors maturing in emancipation had reached maturity in Rāhula, he thought: "Let me now lead Rāhula to the destruction of the cankers." Some suttas of this class are: the Cūḷarāhula Sutta (MN 147), the Mahārāhula Sutta (MN 62), the Dhammacakkappavattana Sutta (SN 56:11), and the Dhātuvibhaṅga Sutta (MN 140).

(3) When the four assemblies, the four classes, nāgas, supaṇṇas, gandhabbas, asuras, yakkhas,[28] the gods of the sense-sphere heavens, and Mahābrahmas approach the Exalted One and ask questions—about the factors of enlightenment, hindrances, clinging aggregates, the "best treasure of man," and so on—and the Exalted One speaks a sutta in reply, those suttas have the proposal of a question as the ground for their delivery. To this class belong numerous suttas of the Saṃyutta Nikāya and the Sakkapañha (DN 21), Cūḷavedalla (MN 44), Mahāvedalla (MN 43), Sāmaññaphala (DN 2), and other suttas.

(4) And those suttas declared because a special incident had occurred—these have the occurrence of a special incident as the ground for their pronouncement. Examples are the suttas Dhammadāyāda (MN 3), Cūḷasīhanāda (MN 11), the Candūpama, Puttamaṃsūpama, Dārukkhandhūpama, Aggikkhandūpama, Phenapiṇḍūpama, and Pāricchattakūpama.

Of the four, this Brahmajāla Sutta has the occurrence of a special incident as the ground for its delivery, since it was delivered by the Exalted One on account of the occurrence of a special incident. And what was that incident? Praise and dispraise. The teacher Suppiya spoke in dispraise of the Triple Gem, while his pupil Brahmadatta spoke in their praise. Thus, making praise and dispraise the occasion, the Exalted One, skilled in teaching, began the discourse with the

---

28. Various types of non-human beings. The nāgas are dragons, the supaṇṇas large birds, the gandhabbas celestial musicians, the asuras titans, and the yakkhas ogres.

words "If, bhikkhus, others speak in dispraise of me." Although there was no resentment in those bhikkhus, the Buddha set up a guideline in order to prohibit clansmen in the future from arousing unwholesome states of mind under similar circumstances.

In the passage (§5 of text), by the first statement ("you should not give way to resentment") the Master prohibits ill will. By the second, "if you were to become angry or upset … you would only be creating an obstacle for yourselves," he shows the danger involved in ill will: that anger or displeasure would present an obstacle to attaining the first jhāna, etc. Having thus shown the danger, by the third statement in the form of the question "would you be able to recognize whether their statements are rightly or wrongly spoken?," he shows that an angry person cannot even recognize the meaning of a statement. As it is said:

The angry person does not know the meaning,
The angry person does not see the Dhamma.
Only a mass of blinding gloom remains
When anger overpowers a person.

Anger is an agent of harm,
Anger is a disturbance of mind,
The danger produced on account of this—
That the people do not understand (AN 7:60)

You should unravel what is false and point it out as false

CY. Having thus prohibited ill will, now the Master shows the proper course of conduct. This is the interpretation: "If you should hear others say: 'Your teacher is not omniscient, the Dhamma is badly expounded, the Saṅgha is practicing wrongly,' etc., you should not remain silent. You should reply: 'What you say is false. For this reason it is false; for this reason it is untrue. There is no such thing in us; this is not found among us. Our teacher is omniscient, the Dhamma is well expounded, the Saṅgha is practicing the good path. Such and such is the reason.' This unraveling should be undertaken only in the case of dispraise, not in other cases. For if someone were to say: 'You are depraved and your teacher did this and that,' you should remain silent and bear it patiently. You should be cautious. Putting away ill will, you may unravel the dispraise. But if anyone should abuse you with any of the ten forms of abuse—calling you a buffalo, an ox, etc.—you should look upon him with equanimity and practice forbearance and patience."

6. **CY.** In the previous section he showed equipoise in the case of dispraise; now he shows the same quality in the case of praise. By the first statement ("you should not give way to jubilation") he prohibits exhilaration. By the second, "if you were to become jubilant," etc., he shows the danger therein: that exhilaration would present an obstacle to the first jhāna, etc.

Query: Why is this said? Hasn't the Buddha, in many suttas, spoken in praise of the rapture and joy that arise over the Triple Gem?

Reply: This is true; he has praised it. But that is the rapture and joy connected with renunciation. Here the intention is the rapture and joy that arise connected with worldliness, the kind that arise by thinking: "Our Buddha, our Dhamma, our Saṅgha." For that is what creates an obstacle to attaining the first jhāna, etc. This rapture is associated with greed, and greed is similar to anger. As it is said:

The greedy person does not know the meaning;
The greedy person does not see the Dhamma.
Only a mass of blinding gloom remains
When greed overpowers a person.

Greed is an agent of harm,
Greed is a disturbance of mind,
The danger produced on account of this—
That the people do not understand. (It 3:39)

A third statement has not come down here, but it should be understood as implicit. For the greedy man, like the angry man, does not understand the meaning of what is spoken.

This is the interpretation of the section showing the proper course of practice: "If you should hear others say: 'Your teacher is omniscient, a Worthy One, a perfectly enlightened Buddha; the Dhamma is well expounded; the Saṅgha is practicing the good path,' you should not remain silent. You should acknowledge it: 'What you say is a fact. For this reason it is a fact; for this reason it is true. The Exalted One, for such and such a reason, is a Worthy One, a perfectly enlightened Buddha; the Dhamma, for such and such a reason, is well expounded, visible here and now; the Saṅgha, for such and such a reason, is practicing the good path, practicing the straight path.' If asked: 'Are you virtuous?', you may claim: 'I am virtuous.' If asked: 'Have you gained the first jhāna?,' etc., or 'Are you an arahat?' then you may admit the fact (if it is true), but only to fellow bhikkhus." In this way domination by evil desires is avoided and the fruitfulness of the Dispensation of the Buddha is made plain.

II. The Analysis of Virtue

7. **CY.** What is the sequential structure (*anusandhi*) of this sutta? This sutta is bound together by two terms: praise and dispraise. Dispraise is refuted by pointing out: "For such and such a reason this is false, this is untrue," etc., just as fire is extinguished by submerging it in water. And praise is confirmed by acknowledging fact as fact thus: "For such and such a reason this is a fact." Praise is of two kinds: that spoken by Brahmadatta and that spoken by the company of bhikkhus. The Master will show the sequel (*anusandhi*) to the praise spoken by the company of bhikkhus later in the sutta, in the section on the elucidation of emptiness (§§ 36–37, etc.). Here he begins the teaching by showing the sequel to the praise spoken by Brahmadatta.

> It is, bhikkhus, only to trifling and insignificant matters, to the minor details of mere moral virtue

CY. *Query:* (In regard to the description of virtue as "trifling and insignificant")—Isn't it true that virtue is the supreme ornamentation of a yogi? As it is said by the ancients:

> Virtue is the adornment of a yogi,
> Virtue is a yogi's ornament.
> A yogi adorned with virtuous conduct
> Has gained the very foremost ornament.

And the Exalted One himself has extolled virtue in many hundreds of suttas, e.g.: "If, bhikkhus, a bhikkhu should wish: 'May I be dear and agreeable to my companions in the holy life, revered and esteemed,' he should be perfect in fulfilling the rules of conduct" (MN 6.3), etc. And so too in many other suttas virtue is extolled. Then why is virtue here said to be trifling?

Reply: Virtue is trifling in comparison with higher qualities. For virtue does not reach the level of the excellence of concentration and concentration does not reach the level of the excellence of wisdom. Therefore, in comparison with the higher qualities, the inferior ones are called "insignificant."

How is it that virtue does not reach the level of the excellence of concentration? In the seventh year following the enlightenment, the Exalted One, while sitting beneath a celestial white parasol three yojanas wide, on a divan a yojana wide, in a jewelled pavilion twelve yojanas wide at the foot of Kaṇḍa's mango tree by the city-gate of Sāvatthī, performed the twin miracle (*yamakapāṭihāriya*) before an assembly of people extending for twelve yojanas in all directions.[29] Thereby he showed his acceptance of the challenge posed by the sectarians and quelled their forces. "From the upper part of his body a mass of fire issued forth, from the lower part a stream of water issued forth ... from each single hair-pore a mass of fire issued forth and from each single hair-pore came a stream of water of six colors" (Patis 1.593–95). The golden-colored rays, issuing from his golden-colored body, continued on to the summit of existence, adorning the entire ten-thousandfold world sphere. The remaining colored rays, issuing from his body in turn according to color, came forth (in such rapid succession) that they appeared to come forth simultaneously, at a single moment.

(To explain why the word "appeared" is used:) There is no occurrence of two acts of consciousness at a single moment. But in the case of the Buddhas, by reason of the brevity of their stay in the *bhavaṅga*[30] and through their fivefold mastery (over the meditative attainments),[31] the differently colored rays (in the display of the twin miracle) *appeared* to come forth at a single moment. But in reality the adverting, preparation, and resolution for each colored ray is done separately. The Exalted One attains the blue kasiṇa absorption in order to produce the blue rays, the yellow kasiṇa in order to produce the yellow rays, the red and white kasiṇas in order to produce the red and

29. A *yojana* is equal to about seven miles, according to one system of reckoning.

30. The "life-continuum" or subconscious flow of mind, which occurs between moments of active thought-processes.

31. The "five masteries" over a meditative attainment are mastery in adverting to the attainment, in entering it, in resolving on its duration, in emerging from it at the specified time, and in reviewing its occurrence.

white rays, the fire kasiṇa in order to produce the mass of fire, and the water kasiṇa in order to produce the stream of water.[32] The Master paces up and down, while projected images (*nimmita*) of himself stand or sit or lie down and so on; all may be explained at length (by reversing the places of the original and the projected images in succession). In all this, there is not even one thing that was accomplished by virtue. All was accomplished by concentration. Therefore virtue does not reach to the excellence of concentration.

(To explain why concentration does not reach to the excellence of wisdom, it is said:) After fulfilling the pāramīs for four incalculables and a hundred thousand great aeons, the Exalted One, in his twenty-ninth year, renounced his palace, which was like the glorious abode of a world-ruling monarch, went forth into homelessness on the bank of the Anomā River, and devoted himself to striving and exertion for six years. On the full moon day of the month of Visākha, he ate a meal of honeyed milk-rice infused with celestial nectar, offered by Sujātā in Uruvelā. That evening he entered the "terrace of enlightenment" via the path running from north to south, circumambulated the royal assattha tree three times, and standing on the northeastern side, spread a seat of straw fourteen feet across. Taking his seat on that excellent divan, with the Bodhi tree fifteen feet behind him—its trunk standing like a silver column upon a golden pedestal, its branches towering above like a jewelled parasol and its tendrils drooping like veins of coral on a golden cloth—he folded his legs crosswise in the triple-jointed posture, developed the preliminary meditation of loving kindness complete in four factors, and made a firm determination not to relax his energy until he attained enlightenment.

N.Sub.Cy. "Loving kindness complete in four factors": occurring equally in regard to four persons—oneself, a friend, a neutral person and a hostile person. The four-factored completeness may also be interpreted as a qualification of the determination of energy, thus: "(1) Willingly, let the flesh and blood of my body dry up, (2) until only skin, sinews, and bones remain, but (3) so long as I have not attained what can be attained by manly fortitude, energy, and courage, (4) I will not relax my energy."[33]

32. The kasiṇas are circular devices presenting a color or element used as the object of meditation. Initially a physical device is used, but this is dropped once a clear mental image of the object is obtained.

CY. As the sun set, he defeated the army of Māra. In the first watch of the night he recollected his past lives, in the middle watch he purified the divine eye, and in the early hours of dawn he immersed his faculty of knowledge in the law of conditionality. Then, as is the custom of all Buddhas, he entered the fourth jhāna by mindfulness of breathing, and making that the basis, developed insight. Thereby he attained in succession each of the four supramundane paths, until with the attainment of the path of arahatship he expelled all defilements and penetrated all the Buddha-qualities. This was all accomplished by wisdom. Thus concentration does not reach to the excellence of wisdom.

Thus when each lower quality is compared to each higher quality, virtue is found to be "trifling" and "insignificant."

a worldling would refer (to) when speaking in praise of the Tathāgata

CY. Here—

The Enlightened One, the kinsman of the sun,
Speaks of the worldling in a twofold way:[34]
One is the worldling blinded by darkness,
The other the worldling noble and good.

The blind worldling (*andhaputhujjana*) is the worldling who has not studied, interrogated, learned, memorized, and reviewed the teachings on the aggregates, elements, sense bases, etc. The worldling who has done so is the good worldling (*kalyāṇaputhujjana*). The derivation is twofold:

He is called a worldling for such reasons
As that he generates a multitude of things,

---

33. See MN 70.27, SN 12:22; see too MN 32.17.

34. *Puthujjana.* The Pāḷi word *puthu* actually represents two different Sanskrit words: *pṛthu,* many or numerous, and *pṛthak,* separate or distinct. Prefixed to the noun *jana*, "person," it gives the resultant compound, *puthujjana,* a double meaning: a common person, and a person who is distinct. The former is the correct derivation, but the commentator also tries to draw out the implications of the latter.

Because he is immersed in the herd,
And because he is a person who is distinct.

The worldling is so-called because he generates a multitude of diverse defilements, etc.[35] As it is said: "They generate a multitude of defilements, hence they are worldlings. They have not destroyed the multiple forms of personality view, they look up to a multitude of teachers, they have not emerged from the multitude of destinations, they form multiple kamma-formations, they are swept away by a multitude of floods, afflicted by a multitude of afflictions, consumed by a multitude of fevers—hence they are worldlings. They are lustful and greedy for the five multiple strands of sense pleasure; therein they are bound, infatuated, addicted, attached, fastened, and confined—hence they are worldlings. They are obstructed, hindered, and enveloped by the five multiple hindrances; there they are enclosed, concealed, and incarcerated—hence they are worldlings" (Nidd I 191). Again, one who is included among the incalculable multitude of people who live according to an inferior doctrine and are averse to the doctrine of the ariyans is called a worldling. And a person distinct or remote from the ariyans endowed with such noble qualities as virtue, learning, etc., is called a worldling.[36]

8. Having abandoned the destruction of life, the recluse Gotama abstains from the destruction of life

CY. The word "life" (*pāṇa*) signifies, in conventional discourse, a living being (*satta*); in the ultimate sense, it is the life-faculty (*jīvitindriya*). The "destruction of life" (*pāṇātipāta*) is the volition of killing in one who perceives a living being as such, [which volition] occurs through the door of either the body or of speech and occasions an act of cutting off the life-faculty of that living being. In the case of beings devoid of moral qualities such as animals, the act of killing is less blameworthy when the being is small in size, more blameworthy when the being is big. Why? Because of the magnitude of the effort

35. "Multitude" is *puthu* and "generates" is *janana*, a pun that does not occur in English.
36. At this point the Cy. presents its lengthy disquisition on the word "Tathāgata," incorporated here separately as Part Five. **Sub.Cy.** in turn takes this as a cue for introducing its treatise on the pāramīs, included here as Part Four.

involved in killing a being with a big body. But even when the effort is the same, the act of killing a big-bodied being is still more blameworthy because of the magnitude of its physical substance. In the case of beings endowed with moral qualities such as humans, the act of killing is less blameworthy when the being has low moral qualities and more blameworthy when the being has high moral qualities. But when the physical body and moral qualities of the victims are equal, the act of killing is less blameworthy when the defilements and force of the effort are mild, more blameworthy when they are powerful.

The act of killing has five components (*sambhāra*): a living being, the perception of the living being as such, the thought of killing, the act, and the death of the being by means of the act. There are six means (*payoga*) of killing: one's own person (i.e., by oneself), commanding (another to kill), mobile weapons (such as spears or arrows), stationary devices (traps), magical formulas, and psychic power.

(THE ACT OF KILLING IN TERMS OF THE DOCTRINE OF NON-SELF) [37]

Sub.Cy. *Query:* When formations are subject to constant cessation from moment to moment, who kills and who is killed? If it is said that the continuum of consciousness and its concomitants kills and is killed, this answer has to be rejected. For such a continuum is immaterial, and because it is immaterial it is incapable of inflicting any harm by cutting, breaking, etc., nor can it be harmed itself. If it is said that "killing" and "being killed" apply to the material continuum, this alternative too must be rejected. For the material continuum is devoid of consciousness, like a block of wood, and so the destruction of life by cutting, etc., can no more apply to the body than to a lifeless corpse.

Again, the means of destroying life, such as striking a blow, etc., must apply to formations either in the past, the future, or the present. But it is impossible that the means could apply to past or future formations, since those do not exist (at the time the blow is struck). In the case of present formations, any application of the means would be useless. For the present formations, due to their momentary nature, are subject to complete cessation anyway, and hence are already heading towards their own destruction by themselves. Since, therefore, their

37. For the Pāḷi text of the following passage, see Appendix 2, No.1.

destruction occurs without any extraneous cause (but follows from their nature), death would not be caused by the striking of blows or by other means. Because the formations are devoid of personal initiative (*nirīhaka*), to whom do the means of killing belong? And who should be bound by the kamma of destroying life if, due to momentariness, the intention of killing breaks up at the very same time it arises, and does not last up to the time of the act's completion?

Reply: The "killer" is the assemblage of formations conventionally called a "being," containing the aforementioned volition of killing. That which "is killed" by him is the aggregation of material and immaterial dhammas that would have been capable of arising (in continued succession) if the aforementioned means of killing had not been applied, but which now continues as a bare procession (of material dhammas) conventionally termed "dead," deprived of vital warmth, consciousness, and the life-faculty due to the application of the means of killing by the killer. Or else (that which "is killed" may be defined as) the continuum of consciousness and its concomitants alone. Although the mental continuum does not itself form the actual object of the means of killing (since the victim's body is the object), still the notion of life-destruction remains valid (even with this definition). For, in the five-constituent existence,[38] the mental continuum occurs in dependence upon the material continuum; so when an enemy applies the means of cutting off the life-faculty to the material continuum in such a way that the successive arising of the vital material states linked up with and supporting the correlative mental continuum is impaired, then the disruption (of the mental continuum) takes place (and the being is said to be killed). Again, the destruction of life is not without a specific cause, nor is the application of the means of killing useless. Death is not without a specific cause:

38. "Five-constituent existence" (*pañcavokārabhava*) refers to those planes of existence where all five aggregates—material form, feeling, perception, mental formations, and consciousness—are found. It is contrasted with one-constituent existence (*ekavokārabhava*), the plane of impercipient beings, and with four-constituent existence (*catuvokārabhava*), the immaterial planes, where the aggregate of materiality is absent. In the five-constituent existence the mental aggregates occur in dependence on the body, so when the physical life-force is extinguished, the flow of mental states is disrupted and the being is said to be dead.

(1) because if the means of killing are applied to the present formations, the aggregation of formations due to arise in immediate succession to them will not arise; (2) because in the present context it is not the "momentary death" of the momentary formations that is intended by the designation "death"; and (3) because the death of the life-continuity (which is meant here) does occur through specific causes, as explained above.[39] Therefore, death is not causeless. Nor are the means of destroying life void of agency (*katturahita*). Though formations lack personal initiative, nevertheless, the conventional designation of agency is applicable to causes that are effective through their contiguity and are fixed in their capacity to give results adequate to themselves, just as in the statements "the lamp illuminates" and "the moon brings in the night" (agency is ascribed to the lamp and to the moon).

The act of destroying life must be recognized to pertain not only to the aggregation of consciousness and mental concomitants existing simultaneously with the intention of killing, but must also be admitted to apply to the (entire sequence of states) that endures by way of (the unity and individuality of) the continuum. Just as the accomplishment of activity is seen in the case of lamps, etc., which likewise exist by way of continuity, so too there certainly does exist one who is bound by the kamma of destroying life.

The same method of investigation may, with due alterations, be applied in the case of taking what is not given, etc., as well.

It is in this way, bhikkhus, that a worldling would speak.

CY. This is a synopsis: The worldling, speaking in praise of the Tathāgata, would speak thus: "The recluse Gotama does not kill living beings or order others to do so, nor does he approve of such action. He abstains from this depravity. Oh, how great are the Buddha's qualities!" Having aroused great zeal, desiring to speak praise, he mentions only something trifling and insignificant, mere virtue and

---

39. The Pāḷi commentarial tradition recognizes two kinds of death, *upacchedamaraṇa,* the cutting off of the life-faculty of the living being, and *khaṇikamaraṇa,* the "momentary death," the dissolution of the formations taking place each moment. The disputant's objection draws its force by blurring the distinction between these two. The reply clears this objection by bringing the distinction to light.

good conduct. The worldling is unable to speak praise referring to those qualities of the Tathāgata that he does not share in common with others. But not only the worldling. Stream-enterers, once-returners, non-returners, arahats, and even *paccekabuddhas* cannot speak of that. The Tathāgata alone can do so.

Having abandoned taking what is not given, the recluse Gotama abstains from taking what is not given

CY. "Taking what is not given" is stealing the belongings of others, theft or robbery. When another person exercises free control over a particular article, and is unimpeachable and irreproachable for so doing, that article is his or her property. "Taking what is not given" is the volition of theft in one who perceives another's property as such, which volition occasions the act of taking away that property from the owner. The act is less blameworthy when the article stolen is low in value, more blameworthy when it is high in value. Why? Because of the superior value of the article. When the articles stolen are equal in value, the stealing of an article belonging to one of superior moral qualities is more blameworthy, the stealing of an article belonging to one of inferior moral qualities is less blameworthy. The act of stealing has five components: property belonging to another, the perception of the property belonging to another as such, the thought of stealing, the act, and the removal of the article.

Having abandoned unchaste living, the recluse Gotama lives the life of chastity

Sub.Cy. By the phrase "lives the life of chastity," abstinence from sexual intercourse is meant; by the phrase "he dwells remote" abstinence from the seven bonds of sexuality is shown.[40] Here "unchastity" denotes the volition of indulgence in impure conduct, reaching expression through the bodily door and occasioning sexual union. But in the offence of sexual misconduct (in the third precept for

---

40. The "seven bonds of sexuality" are (1) while abstaining from actual sexual intercourse with women, one agrees to being massaged, rubbed, and bathed by them; (2) one jokes and plays with them; (3) one stares at them; (4) one relishes the sound of their voices; (5) one recalls past pleasures with them; (6) one watches a householder enjoying sense pleasures; and (7) one leads the holy life for the sake of a heavenly rebirth (see AN 7:47).

lay people), the volition of having sexual intercourse with an inviolable person, such as a girl under the care of her parents, etc., should be substituted. Transgression against persons of inferior moral qualities is less blameworthy. But forceful compulsion is highly blameworthy, even in the case of persons of inferior qualities. If the persons transgressed against are of equal qualities and give their consent, then the act is less blameworthy when the defilements and force of the effort are mild, more blameworthy when they are strong.

For unchastity there are two components: the lustful thought of indulgence and the union of sexual organs. For sexual misconduct there are four components: the inviolable person, the thought of indulgence, the effort to indulge and the tolerance of sexual union.[41] Some, however, say that in the case of a forceful transgression, there is no offence of sexual misconduct for the violated individual even though he or she tolerates the union, since he or she made no effort for union prior to the act of intercourse. But others reply that so long as the lustful thought or desire for indulgence arises, the lack of effort is no criterion, since women generally do not make effort for indulgence (even when they consent beforehand to the relationship). (So on the first position) one would be led to the untenable conclusion that a woman incurs no offence of sexual misconduct even when she has already aroused the lustful thought of indulgence beforehand. Therefore it should be understood that four factors are mentioned as the maximum in the case of a man.

Otherwise there would be no offence of sexual misconduct even for a man at a time when a woman is playing the active role, since the effort for indulgence would be lacking on his part.

This, then, is the ruling: For one who engages through one's own desire, there are three components [the inviolable person, the effort to indulge and the tolerance of union, the lustful thought of indulgence being already implied by the effort to indulge]. For one who engages because one is forced to, there are three components. [Because of the absence of any effort for union prior to the act, there are only the inviolable person, the lustful thought of indulgence, and the tolerance

41. Here there seems to be an erroneous reading in Sub.Cy. I follow the reading in N.Sub.Cy., which is confirmed by the commentary to the Majjhima Nikāya, as well as by the ensuing discussion in the Sub.Cy. itself.

of union]. But when all are mentioned without omission, there are four. There is only one means: one's own person.

9. Having abandoned false speech, the recluse Gotama abstains from false speech

CY. Here falsity (*musā*) is the bodily or vocal effort destroying the welfare of others of one who is bent on deceiving. "False speech" is the volition with intention to deceive occasioning the bodily or vocal effort to deceive others. Another method of explanation is as follows. "False" is a situation that is not fact, untrue. "False speech" is the intimation that such a case is fact or truth. According to characteristic, "false speech" denotes the volition occasioning such an act of intimation in one who wishes to make another believe that an untrue situation is true. When the welfare that it destroys is slight, it is less blameworthy; when the welfare is great, it is more blameworthy. Further, when a householder, reluctant to part with a certain possession, denies that he owns it, it is of little blame; but when he is called to witness and lies for the sake of destroying another's welfare, then the blame is heavy. For monks, the blame is light when they exaggerate in jest, e.g., if after getting a little oil or ghee they say, "Oil flows like a river in the village today." But the blame is heavy when they claim to have seen something they did not see (i.e., when they bear false witness in monastic disciplinary proceedings). There are four components: an untrue situation, the thought of deceiving, the corresponding effort, and the communication of the meaning to another.

Sub.Cy. Even though an effort is made with the intention to deceive, if the meaning is not understood by another the act of deceiving is incomplete; thus the communication of the meaning to another is one factor.

CY. There is one means, one's own person, and it operates by the action of deceiving another with the body or with an object connected with the body or with speech. If another understands the meaning conveyed, one is bound by the kamma of false speech at the very moment the volition occurred occasioning the act (of false intimation).

Having abandoned slander

CY. "Slander" is the volition occasioning bodily or vocal effort in one who, with a defiled mind, aims at dividing others or winning the affection of others for oneself. The act is less blameworthy when the person one divides is of inferior moral qualities, more blameworthy when he or she is of superior moral qualities. There are four components: a person to be divided, the disposition to create a division or to win affection and trust for oneself, the effort, and the communication of the meaning.

Sub.Cy. Whether one at whom the slander is directed suffers division or not, as long as the meaning is communicated it is sufficient (for an act of slander to take place). But the act reaches the level of a course of kamma (*kammapatha*) only when division occurs.

Having abandoned harsh speech

CY. "Harsh speech" is the definitely harsh volition occasioning bodily or vocal effort that cuts into the quick of another's heart. Though there is such effort cutting into the quick of another's heart, it does not count as harsh speech when it is backed by tenderness of mind. For parents sometimes tell their children: "May robbers cut you into bits!" But in truth they do not want even a lotus leaf to fall on them. And preceptors and teachers sometimes say to their pupils: "What is the use with you shameless rascals. Get out!" Yet they wish their success in study and spiritual achievement. Harsh speech is less blameworthy when the person at whom it is directed is of inferior moral qualities, more blameworthy when the person is of superior moral qualities. There are three components: a person to be abused, an angry mind, and the act of abusing.

Having abandoned idle chatter

CY. "Idle chatter" is the unwholesome volition occasioning the bodily or vocal effort to communicate something useless. It is less blameworthy when indulgence is mild, more blameworthy when indulgence is great. There are two components: the disposition to engage in useless talk, such as talk on the great war of India or the abduction of Sīta,[42] and the act of engaging in such talk.

III. Speculations about the Past
(*Pubbantakappika*)

28. **CY.** Having explained in detail the three classes of moral virtue as the sequel to the praise spoken by Brahmadatta, with the words: "There are, bhikkhus, other dhammas," the Exalted One begins the elucidation of emptiness (*suññatāpakāsana*) as the sequel to the praise spoken by the company of bhikkhus.

Sub.Cy. The praise spoken by the company of bhikkhus was that beginning "It is wonderful and marvelous, friends." This is the connection: "Those qualities that are clear to you, bhikkhus, are not the only qualities of the Buddha. But there are, bhikkhus, other dhammas that are not clear." These he will now explain in detail.

"The elucidation of emptiness": this teaching has the explication of emptiness as its principal theme for the following reasons. (1) With its refrain, "These standpoints thus assumed," etc., it reveals the emptiness of the mode in which these standpoints such as eternalism, etc., are assumed. (2) With its refrain, "yet even that understanding he does not misapprehend," signifying that the non-misapprehension of virtue (and the other spiritually beneficial qualities) is essential to liberation, it reveals the absence of any permanent substance (to be clung to in those qualities). (3) In the passage, "Having understood as they really are the origin and passing away of feelings," it is indicated that these vacillations of views arise in outside recluses and brahmins because they have not gotten rid of lust for feelings. Now, by showing the absence of any specific-natured experiencer (*vedaka*) behind the feelings (on account of which these views arise) and the absence of any specific-natured agent (*kāraka*) behind the delusion (and other mental states) functioning as conditions for those feelings, the teaching reveals the absence of a self and of any property of a self in all dhammas.[43] And (4) with its refrain, "the Tathāgata is emancipated through non-clinging," it points to the state of parinibbāna without clinging (which is ultimate emptiness).

---

42. An allusion to the Mahābhārata and the Rāmāyaṇa, the two classical epics of Brahmanic India.

There are, bhikkhus, other dhammas

CY. The word "dhamma" is used in various senses: noble quality (*guṇa*), the teaching (*desanā*), the scriptures (*pariyatti*), impersonal states (*nissatta*), etc. In the following verse, "dhamma" means noble quality:

> Dhamma and non-dhamma are two different things,
> Which lead to two dissimilar results:
> Non-dhamma will lead to hell in the end,
> While dhamma finally leads to heaven. (Th 304).

In the passage, "I will teach you the Dhamma, bhikkhus, good in the beginning," etc., it means the teaching. In the passage, "Herein, a bhikkhu masters the Dhamma—the suttas, songs," etc. (MN 22.10), it means the scriptures. And in the passage: "On that occasion there are dhammas, there are aggregates," etc. (Dhs §121, etc.), it means impersonal states.

Sub.Cy. Some other meanings of the word "dhamma" are: the truths (*sacca*), things endowed with a specific nature (*sabhāva*), concentration (*samādhi*), wisdom (*paññā*), nature (*pakati*), merit (*puñña*), a disciplinary offence (*āpatti*), the knowable (*ñeyya*), etc. In the passage, "It is through not understanding four dhammas, bhikkhus" (DN 16.4.2), it means the (four noble) truths; in the passage, "wholesome dhammas, unwholesome dhammas" (Dhs *Mātikā*), things endowed with a specific nature; in the passage, "Those Exalted Ones were of such dhammas" (DN 28.1), concentration; in the passage, "truth, dhamma, fortitude, and renunciation, with these one does not sorrow in leaving this world" (Sn 190), it means wisdom; in the passage, "to beings of a dhamma to be born, such a wish arises," etc. (DN 22.18), it means nature; in the passage "Dhamma well-practiced issues in happiness" (Sn 184), it means merit; in the passage "four dhammas entailing defeat" (Svibh Pārājika 4.9.7), it means a disciplinary offence; and in the passage "All dhammas in all their

---

43. A specific-natured experiencer or agent would be an experiencer or agent who possesses a specific nature (*sabhāva*) and hence exists as a reality in the ultimate sense. In terms of the dhamma theory, what exists as conditioned realities are only dhammas arising and passing away in accordance with conditions. Feelings arise and active mental states occur but without anything substantial subsisting behind them as a separate self.

modes enter the threshold of the Exalted One's portal of knowledge" (Nidd I 277), it means the knowable.

CY. Here the meaning "noble quality" (*guṇa*) applies. Thus the sentence means: "There are other noble qualities of the Tathāgata."

deep, difficult to see, difficult to understand, peaceful, and sublime, beyond the sphere of reasoning, subtle, comprehensible only to the wise.

CY. "Deep": just as a mosquito cannot get a footing on the great ocean, so the knowledge of anyone other than the Tathāgata cannot get a footing in these dhammas. They are "difficult to see" because of their depth, and "difficult to understand" because they are difficult to see. They are "peaceful" because all the fevers of passion become pacified (in those dhammas) or because they occur in regard to peaceful objects. They are "sublime" because one cannot be satiated with them, as with delicious food. They are "beyond the sphere of reasoning" because the objective domain of the uttermost knowledge cannot be encompassed by reasoning. They are "subtle" because they are abstruse and recondite in nature. And they are "comprehensible only to the wise," that is, they must be understood by the wise for they are not the objective domain of fools.

What are these dhammas extolled by the Tathāgata? The knowledge of omniscience (*sabbaññutañāṇa*). If so, why is it described in the plural (with the word "dhammas")? Because it is associated with multiple classes of consciousness and because it takes a multiplicity of objects. For the knowledge of omniscience is found in the four great functional classes of consciousness associated with knowledge (*catūsu ñāṇasampayuttamahākiriyacittesu*), (thus it is associated with multiple classes of consciousness).[44] And the knowledge of omniscience does not take only a single dhamma as its object, (thus it takes a multiplicity of objects). As it is said: "It knows the entire past, thus it is the knowledge of omniscience. It knows

44. These are the four sense-sphere classes of consciousness accompanied by knowledge which occur in the active *javana* phase of the cognitive process of a Buddha or an arahat. They are functional (*kriyā*) rather than wholesome (*kusala*) because they no longer bring about the accumulation of kamma. The four are obtained according to whether they are associated with joyful or equanimous feeling and whether they are prompted or spontaneous.

everything therein without obstruction, thus it is the unobstructed knowledge (*anāvaraṇañāṇa*)," etc. (Paṭis 1.599). Therefore, because it is associated with multiple classes of consciousness and because it takes a multiplicity of objects on the successive occasions of its arising, it is described in the plural.

Sub.Cy. "It takes a multiplicity of objects": by this he shows that it accomplishes the functions of the numerous types of knowledge. For the knowledge of omniscience, according to circumstances, accomplishes the functions of the numerous types of knowledge divisible into many hundreds of thousands of kinds: the unimpeded knowledge of the three times, the knowledge encompassing the four modes of origin (*yoni*) and the five destinations (*gati*), the remainder among the six types of knowledge not held in common with others, the knowledge illuminating the seven types of ariyan individuals, the unwavering knowledge of the eight assemblies, the knowledge fully understanding the nine abodes of beings, the ten powers of knowledge, etc. [It does this by taking as its own object the many dhammas that serve as object for these kinds of knowledge].

N.Sub.Cy. "On the successive occasions of its arising": rejecting the view that the knowledge of omniscience takes a multitude of objects on a single occasion, the commentator says this to show that (it comprehends a multiplicity of objects) by occurring in succession on a number of occasions. For the knowledge of omniscience occurs in its objective domain only in succession and not, as outsiders assert, simultaneously: "He who is omniscient knows everything simultaneously, not in succession." [45]

Sub.Cy. *Query:* If this is so, how is it possible for a single, limited type of knowledge to penetrate without omission the entire range of the knowable with its inconceivable, immeasurable subdivisions?

Reply: Who says the Buddha-knowledge is limited? Like the knowable itself the Buddha-knowledge is infinite. For it is said: "As far as that knowledge extends, so far does the knowable extend; as far as the knowable extends, so far does that knowledge extend" (Paṭis 1.599). It may be objected that if the knowable, with its numerous subdivisions by way of class, plane, specific nature, etc., and by way of direction, place, time, etc., is apprehended in

45. According to the Buddhist suttas, this was the claim made by Nigaṇṭha Nāṭaputta, leader of the Jains.

succession, it is impossible to penetrate it in its totality, without remainder. But that is not so. Why? Because whatever it is that the Exalted One wishes to know, whether in its entirety or in part, that he knows by direct experience through the unimpeded movement (of his knowledge) in that object. And on the basis of the statement, "The knowledge of the Exalted Buddha is subject to his wish,"[46] it cannot be denied that the Exalted Buddha, who is always concentrated with an undistracted mind, is able to know by direct experience whatever he wishes to know. For the Buddha's knowledge, at the time he is comprehending numerous dhammas, does not occur in an undifferentiated mode like the cognition of those seeing a painting from a distance or the insight of those contemplating all dhammas as non-self. This should be accepted. For the spiritual power (*ānubhāva*) of the Buddha-knowledge is inconceivable. Hence it is said: "The objective domain of the Buddha is inconceivable" (AN 4:77). This is the ruling: With the abandoning of the entire obstruction of the knowable, the Exalted One gained the unobstructed knowledge that occurs subject to his wish and is capable of comprehending all dhammas in all their modes. By means of this knowledge the Exalted One was capable of penetrating all dhammas in continuous succession (*santānena*); therefore he was omniscient or all-knowing in the way fire is called "all-consuming" through its ability to burn all its fuel in continuous succession. He was not, however, omniscient in the sense that he could comprehend all dhammas simultaneously.[47]

29. There are, bhikkhus, some recluses and brahmins

CY. Why is this teaching undertaken in this way? Because on four occasions the thundering of the Buddhas becomes truly great, their knowledge enters its proper field, the greatness of the Buddha-knowledge becomes manifest and their teaching becomes deep, stamped with the three characteristics, connected with emptiness. What are these four occasions? (1) The promulgation of the Discipline (*vinayapaññatti*), (2) the classification of the diversity of planes (*bhūmantara*), (3) the exposition of conditionality (*paccayākāra*), and (4) the classification of the diversity of creeds (*samayantara*).

46. Nidd I 278; slightly different in text.

47. A fuller version of this discussion is given in the *ṭīkā* to the *Visuddhimagga* translation at Vism 7, n.7.

(1) The "promulgation of the Discipline" is the promulgation of a training rule in a particular case which has arisen thus: "This is a light offence, this a heavy offence. This is curable, this incurable. This is an offence, this not an offence. This leads to expulsion, this to rehabilitation, this to confession. This is a fault according to the world, this according to the rules of the Order. In such a case, such should be promulgated." In this matter others have neither the capacity nor the power, for this is not the domain of others. It is the domain only of the Tathāgata. Thus, in the promulgation of the Discipline, the thundering of the Buddhas becomes truly great, their knowledge enters its proper field, and so on.

(2) The "classification of the diversity of planes" is the analysis of the Abhidhamma Piṭaka with its twenty-fourfold universal pattern and its infinite methods proceeding thus: "These are the four foundations of mindfulness ... this the Noble Eightfold Path. There are five aggregates, twelve sense bases, eighteen elements, four truths, twenty-two faculties, nine root causes, four nutriments, seven contacts, seven feelings, seven perceptions, seven volitions, and seven types of consciousness. Among these, so many dhammas pertain to the sense sphere, so many to the fine-material and immaterial spheres. So many dhammas are mundane, so many are supramundane." Others have neither the capacity nor the power to explain this matter, for this is not the domain of others. It is the domain only of the Tathāgata. Thus in the classification of the diversity of planes the thundering of the Buddhas becomes truly great, their knowledge enters its proper field, and so on.[48]

(3) The "exposition of conditionality" is the analysis of dependent origination; that is, the occurrence of a particular dhamma as a condition in such and such ways for some other dhamma. This has three rounds, three periods of time, three links, four sections, and twenty modes[49] and is expounded as follows: Ignorance is a condition for kamma-formations in nine modes: it is a condition as arising,

---

48. **Sub.Cy.** "The 'diversity of planes' is the distinction of the modalities and positions of dhammas (*dhammānaṃ avatthāvisesañ ca ṭhānavisesañ ca*). The 'distinction of modality' is the division of dhammas such as mindfulness, etc., into such categories as the foundations of mindfulness, faculties, powers, enlightenment factors, path factors, etc. The distinction of position is their division into the sense sphere, etc."

49. These terms are explained at Vism 17.284–98.

occurrence, sign, accumulation, conjunction, impediment, origination, cause, and condition. As it is said: "What is wisdom in the discernment of conditions, the knowledge of the structure of dhammas? Ignorance is the basis for kamma-formations, as the arising, occurrence, sign, accumulation, conjunction, impediment, origination, cause, and condition for kamma-formations. Ignorance is a condition in these nine modes, the kamma-formations are conditionally arisen, both these dhammas are conditionally arisen—this is wisdom in the discernment of conditions, the knowledge of the structure of dhammas. In the past it was so, in the future it will be so. And so on as far as: Birth is the basis for aging and death, as the arising ... and condition for aging and death. Birth is a condition in these nine modes, aging and death are conditionally arisen, both these dhammas are conditionally arisen—this is wisdom in the discernment of conditions, the knowledge of the structure of dhammas (Paṭis 1.271).

Others have neither the capacity nor the power to explain this matter, for this is not the domain of others. It is the domain only of the Tathāgata. Thus in the exposition of conditionality the thundering of the Buddhas becomes truly great, their knowledge enters its proper field, and so on.

(4) The "classification of the diversity of creeds" is the analysis, disentangling, and unraveling of the sixty-two speculative views, proceeding thus: "There are four eternalists, four partial-eternalists, four extensionists, four endless equivocators, and two fortuitous originationists; there are sixteen who hold doctrines of percipient immortality, eight who hold doctrines of non-percipient immortality, and eight who hold doctrines of neither percipient nor non-percipient immortality; there are seven annihilationists and five who hold doctrines of nibbāna here and now. Depending upon this, they assume this."

Others have neither the capacity nor the power to explain this matter, for this is not the domain of others. It is the domain only of the Tathāgata. Thus, in the classification of the diversity of creeds the thundering of the Buddhas becomes truly great, their knowledge enters its proper field, and so on.

Sub.Cy. "Depending upon this, they assume this" (*idaṃ nissāya idaṃ gaṇhanti*): depending upon ignorance of specific conditionalilty. So also, depending upon the apprehension of the aspect of unity (*ekattagahaṇa*) found in the succession [of dhammas] actually existing in the ultimate sense, without applying to it the method of diversity (*nānattanaya*), due to a failure to analyze the compact continuity (of successive dhammas composing the individual) into its component factors connected together by the relation of cause and effect. "They assume this": adhering to the assumption of eternalism, they express their views. Partial-eternalism and the other views can also be explained by the same method, making changes where appropriate.[50]

CY. In this place, (from these four occasions) the classification of the diversity of creeds is found. Therefore, in order to show the greatness of his knowledge of omniscience and in order to give, through the discourse, an explication and elucidation of emptiness, the King of the Dhamma enters into the diversity of creeds and begins his answer to the question (he posed) with the words:

29. There are, bhikkhus, some recluses and brahmins who are speculators about the past

CY. "Speculators about the past (*pubbantakappikā*)": they apprehend (their views) after thinking and speculating about the past (*pubbantaṃ kappetvā vikappetvā gaṇhanti*).

Sub.Cy. This is said because they first think about the past with the initially formed thought-constructions of craving and views (*purimasiddhehi taṅhādiṭṭhikappehi kappetvā*), then speculate (*vikappetvā*) about it when their thoughts gain force through repetition and diversified considerations and finally apprehend (*gaṇhanti*) their views through the subsequently formed assumptions (*gāha*) of craving and views; through these, as modes of adherence, they adhere to these views and tenaciously cling to them. Or the thinking and apprehending can be understood by way of craving and clinging respectively, since craving is the condition for clinging (as thinking is for apprehending).

CY. The word *anta* (in *pubbanta*, lit. "the past end") here has the meaning of "portion" (*koṭṭhāsa*). *Kappa* (the base of *kappika*) here signifies craving and views. As it is said: "There are two thought constructions: the thought construction governed by craving (*taṇhākappa*) and the thought construction governed by views (*diṭṭhikappa*: Nidd I 74).[51] Therefore the meaning of "speculators

50. In the analysis of each view below it will be shown at greater length how each of the major views originates through a failure to apply, in a correct and balanced way, the complementary methods of unity and diversity.

about the past" should be understood as follows: they persistently think and speculate about the past portion of the aggregates by way of craving and views.

Sub.Cy. "By way of craving and views": by way of the craving which is (a) the decisive support (*upanissaya*) for a wrong view (arising at a subsequent time) and (b) the co-nascent (*sahajāta*) delight (accompanying a wrong view simultaneous with itself); and by way of the false assumption (*micchāgāha*) of one adhering to eternalism, etc.

"The past portion of the aggregates": since it is speculation having as its domain the dhammas that occurred in the past that is intended here, the word *pubba* signifying past time is used; and since there is no base for speculation apart from the aggregates of material form (feeling, perception, mental formations, and consciousness), the word *anta* signifying a portion is used.

who hold settled views about the past

CY. As they thus persistently speculate about the past, their views, by arising repeatedly, become settled on the past (*pubbantam eva anugatā diṭṭhi*); thus they "hold settled views about the past (*pubbantānudiṭṭhino*)."

and who on eighteen grounds assert various conceptual theorems referring to the past.

CY. Holding such views, they try to convert other people to their views by asserting on eighteen grounds various conceptual theorems referring to the past. (1) The word "conceptual theorems" (*adhivuttipadāni*)[52] means "designational terms (*adhivacanapadāni*)."

Sub.Cy. (a) "Designational terms": this signifies conceptual terms (*paññatipadāni*). A designation is a concept (or appellation, *paññatti*) as, for example, in calling servants one uses as an aid (*adhikāra*) a mere word (*vacanamatta*) like Sirivaḍḍhaka. (b) Or else the prefix *adhi* signifies "existing above" (*uparibhāva*). A designation is a word

51. The word *kappa* comes from the root *kapp,* meaning both to think and to construct, hence the rendering "thought construction." *Taṇhākappa* may be explained as wishful thinking or the emotional bias in thought, *diṭṭhikappa* as theorizing or the intellectual bias in thought.

52. Here I prefer the Roman and Sinhalese texts to the Burmese, which reads *adhimuttipadāni.* The commentary supports the former, as shown.

for what exists above; that is, it is a derivative concept (*upādāpaññatti*), conceived in reference to something (assumed to exist) above (the actually existing things) such as primary and derived matter, etc. Therefore "conceptual theorems" should be considered as terms signifying conceptual entities (*paññattidīpakapadāni*). For things such as "self" and "world" (the themes of the views to follow) are mere conceptual entities (*paññattimatta*), not ultimate realities (*paramattha*) like material form, feeling, etc.

CY. (2) Views are called *adhivutti* because they do violence to the real meaning (*bhūtaṃ atthaṃ*) and do not apprehend things according to their true nature (*yathāsabhāvato*). *Adhivuttipadāni,* therefore, are terms signifying views.

N.Sub.Cy. "They do violence to the real meaning": because they exceed the real true nature of things; or they overshoot the mark and bypass (the real nature).

Sub.Cy. Views are called *adhivutti* because of their excessive character (*adhikavuttitā*). For views superimpose (*ajjhāropetvā*) upon the specific-natured dhammas a superfluous, unreal meaning such as eternity, nature, substantiality, soul and body, etc.[53]

A. Eternalism (*Sassatavāda*): Views 1–4

30. There are, bhikkhus, some recluses and brahmins who are eternalists and who on four grounds proclaim the self and the world to be eternal.

CY. Apprehending one of the aggregates, such as material form, etc., to be the self and the world, they proclaim it to be eternal, immortal, permanent, and stable. As it is said: "They proclaim the self and the world thus: 'Material form is the self and the world; it is eternal.' Again, they proclaim the self and the world thus: 'Feeling …

53. The notion of superimposition (Skt. *adhyāropaṇa, adhyāsa)* plays a central role in the philosophy of Advaita Vedānta, according to which the phenomenal world and individual soul are false superimpositions upon the undifferentiated substratum of ultimate reality, Ātman or Brahman. According to the position taken here, the reverse is the case. The impermanent mental and material events arising through conditions are the ultimate realities, and the notions of a self, substance, and substratum the illusory superimpositions.

perception … mental formations … consciousness is the self and the world; it is eternal'" (see Paṭis 2.323).

Sub.Cy. This refers to five kinds of personality view (*sakkāya-diṭṭhi*): that is, he regards material form, feeling, perception, mental formations, or consciousness as the self. The remaining fifteen kinds of personality view, beginning with the view of the self as possessing material form, etc., are obtained as follows: In each case he apprehends four aggregates to be the self and proclaims the fifth to be the world. Again, apprehending one aggregate to be the self, he proclaims the remaining four to be the world, i.e., the field for the self's enjoyment. Or he apprehends the aggregates included in his own continuum to be the self and proclaims anything other than that to be the world.[54]

(THE STATIONARY AND UNPRODUCTIVE VIEW OF THE WORLD)

31. He speaks thus: 'The self and the world are eternal, barren, steadfast as a mountain peak, standing firm like a pillar …'

CY. "Barren" (*vañjo*): like barren cattle or barren land, the self and the world do not bear fruit and do not produce anything. By this statement, he denies that the jhānas, etc.—apprehended as the self and the world—produce anything such as material form, etc.

Sub.Cy. The jhānas are mentioned here because the dhammas constituting the jhānas enter the jhāna-attainer's threshold of awareness with particular distinctness. The remaining dhammas are comprised under that heading. He denies that they produce anything, for if they had a productive capacity they would exist in dependence on conditions, like material form, etc., and like happiness, etc., and therefore would have an origin. But if they had an origin they would inevitably also have a cessation, and there would be no room for their permanence.

---

54. Personality view (*sakkāyadiṭṭhi*) is the viewing of the aggregates constituting the personality (*sakkāya*) as either a self or the adjuncts of a self. The suttas list twenty kinds of personality view. Five are obtained by identifying each aggregate with the self, the remaining fifteen by regarding the self as alternatively possessing, containing, or contained within each of the five aggregates.

CY. By the two expressions, "steadfast as a mountain peak" (*kūṭaṭṭho*) and "standing firm like a pillar" (*esikaṭṭhāyiṭṭhito*), he illustrates the indestructibility of the world.[55]

Sub.Cy. By the expression "steadfast as a mountain peak" the absence of impermanence is maintained; by the expression "firm as a pillar" the absence of mutation.

(The eternalist doctrine of emergent manifestation)

CY. But some read the text as *īsikaṭṭhāyiṭṭhito* (instead of *esikaṭṭhāyiṭṭhito*), explaining the term thus: "The world stands like a reed (*īsika*) in (a sheath of) *muñja* grass." This is the purport: that which is said to be born emerges as something already existing (*vijjamānam eva nikkhamati*), like a reed that comes out from a sheath of *muñja* grass. Because (the self and the world) exist immanently like a reed, it is said: "these beings roam on in saṃsāra," i.e., from here they go elsewhere.

Sub.Cy. "Something already existing" (*vijjamānam eva*): by showing the existence of the effect in the cause, he indicates the doctrine of emergent manifestation (*abhibyattivāda*)[56]. "It emerges": it comes to full manifestation (*abhibyattiṃ gacchati*).

N.Sub.Cy. "That which is said to be born" is the kind of thing called "self," which is held to be "already existing" in the past in the mode of potentiality (*sattirūpa*)[57] and to "emerge" (at a subsequent time) in the mode of manifestation (*byattirūpa*), meaning that it comes to full manifestation. By the phrase "already existing," signifying the existence of the effect in the cause, he points to the doctrine of emergent manifestation by way of the mode of manifestation. The

55. The word *kūṭastha* occurs in the Bhagavadgītā at 15.16–17. The passage runs thus: *Dvāv imau puruṣau loke kṣaras cākṣara evaḥ sarvāni bhūtāni kūṭastho' kṣara ucyate/Uttamaḥ puruṣas tvan yaḥ paramātmetya udāhataḥ.*

"Two kinds of spirit are found in the world,
the perishable and the imperishable.
All beings are the perishable.
That which is imperishable, steadfast as a
mountain peak, is the ultimate spirit,
which they call the supreme self."

56. For the identification of the *abhibyattivāda* as a tenet of the Sāṅkhya school, see Dasgupta, op. cit., pp. 254ff.

57. *Satti.* Skt. *śakti*, energy, force, potentiality.

mode of potentiality is like the ear of rice existing still encased in the sheath of the rice-plant; the mode of manifestation is like the ear of rice that has emerged from the sheath.

Sub.Cy. How can something already existing [in the mode of potentiality], previously unmanifest, afterwards come to full manifestation [in the mode of manifestation]?[58] (It is said:) As a jar concealed by darkness becomes manifest by means of light.

This must be examined. What does the light actually do to reveal the jar? If it is said that it [reveals the jar] by producing a cognition (*buddhi*) that has the jar as its object, the doctrine of emergent manifestation would be invalidated, for this assertion implies the arising of a previously unarisen cognition.[59] If, next, it is held that it reveals the jar by dispelling the darkness that obstructs the cognition of the jar (existing in the mode of potentiality), the doctrine of emergent manifestation is again invalidated. For if the cognition of the jar exists, how can the darkness obstruct it? Just as it is not correct to hold to the manifestation of the jar, so too [it is not correct to hold to the manifestation] of the self [postulated by our theorist]. Then too, if the arising of a hitherto unarisen cognition occurs through the concurrence of the sense-faculty, sense-object, etc., the doctrine of emergent manifestation is invalidated by the very term "arising"; [for that term exceeds the bounds of the mere manifestation (of something previously existent but unmanifest) and signifies the actual arising of an unarisen cognition]. So once again the doctrine of eternalism is invalidated, [for the very same reason].

(For the following, the more elaborate version of **N.Sub.Cy.** has been used): Suppose next, it is held that the cognition arises by the dispelling of the delusion which, in place of the darkness, here obstructs the occurrence of the cognition.[60] If this is so, i.e., if the cognition having the thing as its object exists, how can delusion obstruct it? The doctrine of emergent manifestation is thus invalidated.

---

58. For the Pāḷi text of the following argument, see Appendix 2, No. 2.

59. The origination of cognition contradicts the notion of the manifestation of something already existent, and hence invalidates the doctrine.

60. The position set forth here assumes the cognition to be present in the mode of potentiality, but only obstructed in its actual occurrence due to delusion. The dispersing of delusion does not, on this view, originate the cognition, but only allows it to become manifest as a function.

And what is more, the doctrine of emergent manifestation is also invalidated in view of the existing diversity (of cognition and its object). For the diversity of things to be made manifest, such as the jar, etc., does not obtain through the diversity of the manifestors (*abhibyañjanaka*), such as the moon, sun, gems, lamps, etc.; and the diversity in cognition does obtain through the diversity in the objects, since the cognition arises in accordance with its object. Thus, to a still greater extent, the doctrine of emergent manifestation is invalidated.[61]

And here too, (the postulation of) the exercise of a function by way of the manifesting of (unmanifest) existence is not correct, since the identity of the function, i.e., the activity of manifesting (unmanifest) existence, and the agent exercising the function is admitted. For the activity, i.e., the aforesaid function, is not different from the base possessing it, just as the state of contacting, etc., (*phusanādibhāva*) is not different from contact (*phassādi*), etc.[62] Therefore, since there is no difference between the function, i.e., the activity of manifesting (unmanifest) existence, and the agent exercising this function, the doctrine of emergent manifestation that some thinkers postulate is not correct.

---

61. If all cognitions exist *a priori* in a state of potentiality, then a sufficient reason must be given why, on a particular occasion, a cognition of one kind rather than of another, e.g., of a jar rather than of a pencil, occurs. If it is said that the cognition is existent but obstructed by darkness, or by delusion in place of darkness, then the cause for the manifestation of the particular cognition should be the manifestor, i.e., the source of illumination. In such a case one would expect the cognition to reflect the differences in the sources of illumination. But contrary to expectation, the same cognition occurs despite differences in manifestors, implying the dependence of cognition on something external to the cognizing mind and hence its actual production, not merely its passage from a state of potentiality to a state of manifestation. And the cognition does invariably conform to the object, which proves its *a posteriori* origination in dependence on the object.

62. The activity of contacting is in essence not different from contact, the thing exercising that activity.

(The eternalist's view of change)

> and though these beings roam and wander (through the round of existence), pass away and re-arise...

CY. "(They) wander": they transmigrate from one state of existence to another. "Pass away": they are reckoned thus (*evaṃ sankhaṃ gacchanti*).

N.Sub.Cy. Having marked out the words "pass away" (i.e., putting them, as it were, in quotation marks), the commentator reveals the (merely conventional) significance (of those words for the eternalist) by glossing them, "they are reckoned thus."

Sub.Cy. "They are reckoned thus": because of its permanence (*niccasabhāvattā*) there can be, according to the eternalist, no real passing away or re-arising of the self (considered eternal); and because of its omnipresence (*sabbabyāpitāya*), it cannot really roam and wander. They are "reckoned thus" (i.e., as passing away and re-arising) by a distinction in the modes of occurrence of mere attributes. The purport is that they are conventionally designated (*voharīyati*) thus. The commentator thereby shows the doctrine of change (*vipariṇāmavāda*), according to which the mere attributes of the attribute-bearer, i.e., of an enduring self, arise and perish.[63] This view will be examined below.

CY. Our theorist here undermines his own doctrine, for having first said "the self and the world are eternal," he now says "these beings roam and wander." The theorist's view is inconsistent. It is fickle, like a stake implanted in a heap of chaff. The good and the bad alike are mixed in it like pieces of cake, feces, and cowdung in the basket of a madman.

Sub.Cy. By the use of the word "roaming," which implies the fact of impermanence, he undermines the eternalist doctrine he himself previously proposed.

---

63. *Avaṭṭhitasabhāvassa attano dhammino ca dhammamattaṃ uppajjati c'eva vinassati ca. Pariṇāmavāda* (or, in Sub.Cy., *vipariṇāmavāda*) is a technical name for the Sāṅkhya theory of causation, the view that the cause is transformed into its effect through mere change of form without change of fundamental substance. The examination is given below, in Sub.Cy. §36.

> yet the self and the world remain the same just like eternity itself.

CY. He conceives them to be like the great earth, Mount Sineru, the sun, or the moon, on account of their permanent existence. Conceiving the self to be like these, he asserts "they remain the same just like eternity itself."

(Recollection of past lives as proof of an eternal self)

> What is the reason? Because I ... recollect my numerous past lives ... for this reason I know this: the self and the world are eternal.

CY. Now in order to prove his assertion that the self and the world are eternal, the theorist gives his reason. With the words, "for this reason I know this," he shows: "through this distinguished achievement (i.e., the recollection of past lives) I know this through direct experience (*paccakkhato*). I do not speak from mere faith alone."

Sub.Cy. "Gives his reason": the theorist gives the reason for his assertion to those before whom he proclaims the self and the world to be eternal. He has not proven the reality of his own view even to himself through direct experience. But by means of a fact directly experienced by himself (i.e., the recollection of past lives), he tries to prove a fact that he has not directly experienced (i.e., the eternity of the self and the world); and he communicates it to others as if it were ascertained by himself, not as unascertained.

This is his argument: "Throughout the course of these many hundreds of thousands of births, this my self and the world have remained one and the same, as proven by the fact of recollection. For the one who recollects an experience is the same as the one who originally experienced it, not someone else. It is not possible for one person to recollect something experienced by a different person; e.g., Dhammarakkhita cannot recollect what was experienced by Buddharakkhita. And as it is with these existences (recollected by me), so it is with earlier ones too. Therefore my self and the world are eternal. And as it is with me, so it is with other beings; for them too, the self and the world are eternal." Thus, leaping into the jungle of views by way of eternalism, the theorist establishes others in his view as well. According to the statements in the text, "they assert various conceptual theorems" and "he speaks thus," the argument is intended for the purpose of converting others.

This, bhikkhus, is the first case.

CY. This is the first among the four cases referred to by the word "ground" (*vatthu*) in the phrase "on four grounds." The meaning is: the first cause (*kāraṇa*) consisting in the recollection of several hundred thousand past lives.

Sub.Cy. Causes (*kāraṇa*) are of three kinds:

(1) Cause of obtainment (*sampāpakakāraṇa*): e.g., the noble path is the cause for the obtainment of nibbāna.

(2) Cause of generation (*nibbattakakāraṇa*): e.g., the seed is the cause for the generation of the sprout.

(3) Cause of communication (*ñāpakakāraṇa*): e.g., the conditioned arising of things, etc., is the cause for communicating the truth of impermanence, etc.

Here, (in the sutta), the cause of communication alone is intended. For that which communicates is the cause for the knowledge which has the meaning to be communicated for its domain.

(The second and third cases of eternalism)

32–33. **CY.** The same method of explanation applies to the following two sections only; where the first section speaks in terms of the recollection of many hundred thousands of past births, the following two speak in terms of the recollection of ten and forty aeons of world contraction and expansion, respectively. For a sectarian with dull intelligence can recollect several hundred thousand past births; one with medium intelligence can recollect ten aeons of world contraction and expansion; and one with keen intelligence can recollect forty aeons, but not more than that.

N.Sub.Cy. *Query:* If the only distinction between the first three sections is the difference of time recollected, why is eternalism analyzed into four positions? Shouldn't it be analyzed instead into two positions, like the doctrine of fortuitous origination?

Reply: The threefold division of time is made in order to show that the sectarians who gain the knowledge of recollecting past lives fall into three groups, according to whether their intelligence is dull, medium, or keen. Together with the view based on mere reasoning, eternalism is analyzed into four positions.

Query: It is possible to divide those who gain states of distinction (i.e., recollection of past lives) with dull intelligence, etc., still further by way of the inferior (medium and superior) members of each class, just as the rationalists can be divided into those who depend on hearsay, etc. And so their classification should become still more complex. Why are all the gainers of distinction classified into only three categories?

Reply: Because the Exalted One wishes to show them by delimiting (the recollective capacity) of the superior. For among these three categories of sectarians, those who possess inferior and medium intelligence can recollect only a number of past births below the maximum stated for sectarians. And those who possess superior intelligence cannot recollect more than the maximum. Thus, because the Exalted One wishes to show them by delimiting (the recollective capacity) of the superior, they are classified into only three categories—those who can recollect several hundred thousand past births, those who can recollect ten aeons of world contraction and expansion, and these who can recollect forty such aeons.

"But not more than that": the sectarians cannot recollect more than forty aeons of world contraction and expansion. Why? Because of the weakness of their wisdom. For it is said in the commentaries that their wisdom is weak, since they lack the knowledge delimiting mentality and materiality.[64]

34. Some recluse or brahmin is a rationalist, an investigator

CY. "Rationalist" (*takkī*) is a designation for a theorist who assumes his views via reasoning (*takka*) and initial thought (*vitakka*). "Investigation" (*vīmaṃsā*) is pondering, preferring, acquiescing (*tulanā ruccanā khamanā*). Just as a man descends into water after investigating its depth with a stick, the investigator ponders, forms a preference, acquiesces, and assumes his view.

Sub.Cy. "Reasoning" is discursive thought, characterized by striking or discrimination, serving as a basis for views. "Investigation"

---

64. *Nāmarūpaparicchedа,* the ability to analyze experience in terms of bare mentality and materiality. Because such a mode of analysis is not found outside the Buddha's dispensation, sectarian yogis are limited in their capacity for recalling past lives. See Vism 13.13–71

is examination. According to its denotation, it is an act of consciousness accompanied by greed, functioning as a counterfeit of wisdom (*paññāpaṭirūpaka*); or it is unwise reflection (*ayoniso manasikāra*), that is, a wrong adherence (*micchābhinivesa*); or it is the antecedent phase of the vacillation of views.

N.Sub.Cy. Investigation is twofold, wisdom and counterfeit wisdom. Here it is counterfeit wisdom.

CY. There are four kinds of rationalists:

(1) One who reasons from hearsay (*anussutika*). He hears about King Vessantara and reasons: "If the Exalted One was Vessantara (in a past birth) there must be an eternal self." Then he assumes this view.

(2) One who reasons from memory (of a small number) of past births (*jātissara takkika*). He remembers two or three past births and reasons: "I myself was so and so in the past, therefore there must be an eternal self."

(3) One who reasons from fortune (*lābhītakkika*). He reasons on the basis of his fortune: "As my self is happy now, so it was in the past, and so it will be in the future," and then assumes his view.

(4) One who follows pure reason (*suddhatakkika*). The pure rationalist is one who assumes his view as a result of mere reasoning alone, thus: "If this exists, that exists."

Sub.Cy. Here the commentator shows the way the rationalist searches for a proof (*yutti*) for his eternalist view. He reasons: "If things were impermanent, it would follow that one individual acts and another experiences the results. Such being the case, there would be the destruction of kamma performed and the encounter with results of kamma that was not performed. But if things are permanent, then the one who acts and the one who experiences the results are the same, and one does not commit any errors."

"As a result of mere reasoning alone": by pure reason without the aid of scripture or spiritual achievement, and apart from hearsay, etc.

Query: The eternalists who gain spiritual distinction (i.e., the recollection of past lives) identify the self and the world with their own mental continua and what has transpired therein through the experience of several hundred thousand past births, ten aeons, or forty aeons, which they can recollect by means of this achievement. Now isn't it true that they become adherents of eternalism by drawing inferences (*anuvitakkanamukhena*)? That is, they infer that the continuum which had evolved thus far back existed in retrogressively earlier births, and also that the same state of affairs holds with regard to all beings.[65] If so, shouldn't all the eternalists be classified as rationalists since like those who reason from hearsay, etc., these form their views by reasoning based upon a ground experienced by themselves? And surely the aforementioned kinds of reasoning must be admitted as valid. Otherwise the eternalist who gains spiritual distinction would have to be classified with partial-eternalist or with the fortuitous originationist.[66]

Reply: The matter should not be seen in this way. For the recollection of the aggregate-continuum (*khandhasantāna*) over a long period of time—whether minimum, medium, or maximum—in the case of those who gain spiritual distinction is a special cause for the assumption of eternalism not held in common with the others. Thus, when it was said: "I recollect my numerous past lives ... For this reason I know this," his recollection itself is shown as the principal cause. The reasoning that occurs (consequent to the recollection) is not the principal cause here, for it is subordinate to and dependent upon the recollection of past lives.

Query: If so, doesn't it follow that the hearsay, etc., is the principal cause (in the case of the rationalists)?

Reply: No. For these latter, their reasoning is the principal cause, since they lack realization. And both in the Buddha's Dispensation and in worldly discourse, a descriptive term is phrased with reference to the principal cause, as in the terms "eye-consciousness" and "corn sprout."

Or else: the achievement of spiritual distinction is stated as a separate cause for the assumption of eternalism in order to show reasoning that is not grounded in spiritual achievement as a distinct cause for the eternalist view.

---

65. Having recollected as a maximum forty aeons, he infers that the self and the world have existed eternally back into the beginningless past. And he infers that as his own self is eternal, so too are the selves of other beings.

66. Since if the validity of these kinds of reasoning is not admitted, he would have no legitimate ground to justify his inference from the past lives he can recall to the eternity preceding them, or from his own situation to that of other beings, and would therefore have to conclude that the stream of experience he recollects and identifies as "self" was either created by God or arose spontaneously without a cause.

35. **Outside of these there is none.**

CY. The Buddha roars his irreversible lion's roar: "Outside of these grounds, there is not even one cause for the proclaiming of eternalism."

Sub.Cy. *Query:* Are these four grounds the theorist's reason for his own adherence to eternalism or for establishing others in his view? If they are the reasons for his own adherence, why are only recollection of past lives and reasoning mentioned, and not the inversion of perception (*saññāvipallāsa*), etc.? For an inverted perception, unwise reflection, the company of bad people, and listening to false doctrine are also grounds for the origination of wrong views. And if they are the means for establishing others in his view, scripture (*āgama*) should be mentioned along with spiritual achievement and rational proof, for like them it also is a means for establishing others. In either case it is going too far to say "outside of these there is none."

Reply: That is not so. Why? Firstly, in regard to his own adherence to eternalism, the theorist adheres to the aggregates as an eternal self and world through the aforementioned recollection and reasoning only after he has kept company with bad people, listened to false doctrine, emerged from unwise reflection, acquired thereby a perverted perception, overshot the bounds of rational proof by not comprehending the momentary dissolution of the aggregates, and wrongly applied the method of unity.[67] Recollection of past lives and reasoning are alone mentioned here because they are the proximate and principal causes for eternalism, and because when they are mentioned, the other conditions are implicitly included along with them. Then, in regard to the establishment of others, scripture is grouped under rational proof, which is alone shown in order to take a particular case of the use of reason [i.e., by outsiders who have no

67. *Ekattanayaṃ micchā gahetvā.* Misapplying the method of unity, the theorist takes the continuity and coherence of his experience as evidence for the existence of a permanent underlying self. Because he lacks the right understanding of the Buddha's teaching, he does not see that this coherence obtains between occasions of experience that are subject to momentary dissolution and hence do not provide the core of substantiality required of a permanent self.

recognized scriptures]. Thus recollection and reasoning are alone mentioned as the grounds for these views.

Moreover, there are two kinds of characteristics pertaining to ultimately real dhammas (*paramatthadhamma*): (1) the characteristic of the specific nature (*sabhāvalakkhaṇa*); and (2) the general characteristic (*sāmaññalakkhaṇa*).[68] The comprehension of the characteristic of the specific nature is direct experiential knowledge (*paccakkhañāṇa*); the comprehension of the general characteristic is inferential knowledge (*anumānañāṇa*). Scripture, as the means for acquiring wisdom born of learning (*sutamayī paññā*), issues only in inferential knowledge. But by considering the things learned, one becomes established in reflective acquiescence, gives rise to the wisdom born of reflection (*cintāmayī paññā*), and by meditative development (*bhāvanā*) gradually achieves direct experiential knowledge.[69] Thus scripture does not transcend the sphere of reasoning, and so is implied by the reference to reasoning through hearsay in the commentary. Therefore it is correct to say: "Outside of these there is none." On the basis of the statements "they assert various conceptual theorems" and "they proclaim the self and the world to be eternal," the intention here is that these are grounds for establishing others in his view.

36. This, bhikkhus, the Tathāgata understands and he understands: 'these standpoints, thus assumed and thus misapprehended, lead to such a future destination, to such a state in the world beyond...'

CY. The first sentence may be paraphrased: "Bhikkhus, the Tathāgata understands this fourfold speculative view (*diṭṭhigata*) in its diverse aspects." Showing what he understands in addition to this, he says: "These standpoints,"[70] etc. Here the views themselves are called

68. The "ultimately real dhammas" are the concrete actualities of developed Theravāda ontology. Their specific characteristics are the features particularizing each type of dhamma. Their general characteristics are the marks of impermanence, suffering, and non-self.
69. The allusion is to the threefold classification of wisdom according to its mode of acquisition: learning, reflection, and meditation. See Vism 14.14.
70. *Diṭṭhiṭṭhāna,* lit. "stands for views."

"standpoints." And further, a reason, ground, or cause (*kāraṇa*) for views is also a standpoint. As it is said:

> What are the eight standpoints (i.e., grounds for views)? The aggregates, ignorance, contact, perception, initial thought, unwise reflection, evil friends, and the voice of another. The aggregates are a cause and condition, in the sense of an origin for a standpoint; thus the aggregates are also a standpoint. Ignorance ... the voice of another is a cause and condition, in the sense of an origin for a standpoint; thus the voice of another is also a standpoint. (Paṭis 2.3-4).

"Thus assumed" (*evaṃgahitā*). Firstly, the standpoints consisting in the views that hold the self and the world to be eternal are "assumed," i.e., taken up and made to occur. [**N.Sub.Cy**: "Taken up" in one's own mental continuity and "made to occur" in the continuities of others, i.e., propagated.] They are "thus misapprehended" (*evaṃparāmaṭṭhā*), i.e., apprehended again and again with an unquestioning mind and consummated with the conclusion: "This alone is truth, any other view is false."

Secondly, since the standpoints consisting in the grounds for views give rise to views when they are assumed, they are assumed by way of object (*ārammaṇa*) [**N.Sub.Cy.**: that is, the aggregates among the eight grounds]; by way of occurrence (*pavatti*) [that is, ignorance, contact, perception, initial thought, and unwise reflection]; and by way of association (*āsevana*) [that is, evil friends and the voice of another]. They are misapprehended by assuming them again and again as long as the danger inherent in them is not perceived.

They "lead to such a future destination" (*evaṃgatikā*), that is, they lead to the hells, the animal kingdom, or the realm of ghosts. The following phrase is a synonym for the former.

Sub.Cy. "Lead to such a future destination": this may also be interpreted, "they go thus," i.e., they are concluded thus. [They are broken up, destroyed, and consummated by the following cross-examination.] This is meant: these standpoints called views are assumed and misapprehended by the superimposition of eternal existence upon a self which is non-existent in the ultimate sense.[71]

71. *Paramatthato asantaṃ attānaṃ sassatabhāvañ c'assa ajjhāropetvā.* It should be noted that a dual error is involved here: first a self is assumed to exist, and then eternal existence is ascribed to this self.

They are the mere prattle of fools, which continue only so long as the wise do not cross-examine them. But when they are cross-examined by the wise, lacking any durable ground and unable to stand up under pressure, they break up, perish, and disappear, like drops of dew or the light of a glow-worm with the rising of the sun.

(AN EXAMINATION OF ETERNALISM)

Sub.Cy. Now follows a brief examination of eternalism.[72] If the self or the world postulated by the opponent were eternal, it would be impossible to take them as the basis for attaining any state of spiritual distinction. For on account of their immutability, they would always retain their original form (*purimarūpa*), and then any instruction the eternalist may give for the purpose of turning away from evil and practicing virtue would be useless. For if they cannot undergo alteration, how could such instruction be effective? And for such a self, meritorious actions such as giving, etc., and harmful actions such as injuring, etc., would no more be possible than for empty space. So too, it is not tenable for the eternalist to hold that the self is determined to experience pleasure and pain, for such a self cannot be bound by kamma. And because it is impossible for an eternal self to undergo birth, etc., what need does it have for liberation?

If the opponent asserts: "Expressions such as action, etc., do pertain to the self insofar as its mere attributes (*dhammamatta*) arise and perish," we reply that it is impossible to ascribe "mere attributes" to an enduring self that always retains its original form. Those attributes of the self that constitute its modes (*avatthā*) must be either different from the self or identical with it. If they are different (*aññe*), it must be admitted that those attributes through which the self acts, experiences (the results of action), passes away, and re-arises, make no difference to the self (i.e., they are without any effect on the self). Therefore this alternative leads to the same position as that discussed above. It is saddled with the same error and, moreover, makes even the postulation of attributes purposeless. On the other hand, if the self and its attributes are identical (*anaññe*), then, when the modes are subject to arising and destruction, the self, which is identical with them, must likewise be subject to arising and destruction. And in such a case, how could one maintain that it is permanent? If one holds that the attributes

72. For the Pāḷi text of this passage, see Appendix 2, No. 3.

as well as the self are permanent, bondage and emancipation would be impossible. Thus eternalism is not tenable. There is no eternalist capable of giving a perfectly sound proof (*yutti*) of the eternal existence of things. And a doctrine that cannot be proven is not satisfying to the minds of the wise. Thus it was said above: "They continue only so long as the wise do not cross-examine them."

He understands as well what transcends this....

CY. The Tathāgata does not understand only this fourfold speculative view together with its grounds and destinations, but he understands all that, and he understands what transcends it; that is, virtue, concentration, and the knowledge of omniscience.

Sub.Cy. The knowledge of omniscience is mentioned because that is the subject under analysis here. But when the omniscient knowledge is mentioned, its foundation—the knowledge of the destruction of the cankers (*āsavakkhayaṭāṇa*)—and all the Buddha's ten powers of knowledge, etc., which are inseparable from it, are also implied.

yet even that understanding he does not misapprehend.

CY. Although he understands such incomparable states of distinction, he does not think: "I understand this," etc., misapprehending it by way of craving, views, and conceit.

Sub.Cy. This is meant: The Tathāgata does not even adhere to those essential states of distinction, the qualities such as virtue, etc., which transcend speculative views, much less to the bait of the round (*vaṭṭāmisa*). "I understand this": here "I" indicates misapprehension by way of views [and conceit], while "etc." implies misapprehension by way of craving as "mine." A "misapprehension" is an apprehension of dhammas in a mode contrary to actuality, overshooting their true nature.[73] For there is nothing in the aggregates which can be held to as "I" or "mine."

And because he is free from misapprehension, he has realized within himself the state of perfect peace.

CY. With non-misapprehension as condition, he has realized within himself the state of perfect peace (*paccattaṃ yeva nibbuti viditā*), the

73. *Dhammasabhāvaṃ atikkamitvā parato āmasanaṃ parāmāso.*

pacification of the defilements of misapprehension. He shows: "Bhikkhus, nibbāna is evident to the Tathāgata."

> Having understood as they really are the origin and passing away of feelings, their satisfaction, their unsatisfactoriness, and the escape from them, the Tathāgata, bhikkhus, is emancipated through nonclinging.

CY. In order to show the practice (*paṭipatti*) by means of which he achieved the state of perfect peace, the Tathāgata now explains the meditation subject (*kammaṭṭhāna*) in terms of those very feelings enamored with which the sectarians enter the jungle of views, thinking: "Here we shall be happy! We shall be happy here!"

Sub.Cy. "Those very feelings": Among the numerous discourses of the Buddha dealing with the Four Noble Truths in terms of the aggregates, sense bases, etc., this (discourse is given in terms of feelings) in order to show that the theorists leap into the jungle of views on account of their wrong practice [in regard to feelings]; thus feeling alone is brought forth in order to show the ground for full understanding (*pariññāya bhūmi*). The meditation subject referred to is the meditation subject of the four truths.

CY. "Having understood as they really are" (*yathābhūtaṃ viditvā*): He understood as it really is the origin (*samudaya*) of feelings by way of the following five characteristics:

> He sees the rise (*udaya*) of the aggregate of feelings, in the sense of its conditioned origination (*paccayasamudaya*), thus: through the origination of ignorance, feelings originate; through the origination of craving ... of kamma ... of contact, feelings originate. Seeing as well the characteristic of production (*nibbattilakkhaṇa*), he sees the rise of the aggregate of feelings. (Paṭis 1.288)

He understood as it really is the passing away (*atthaṇgama*) of feelings by way of the following five characteristics:

> He sees the fall (*vaya*) of the aggregate of feelings, in the sense of its conditioned cessation (*paccayanirodha*), thus: with the cessation of ignorance, feelings cease; with the cessation of craving ... of kamma ... of contact, feelings cease. Seeing as well the

> characteristic of change (*vipariṇāmalakkhaṇa*), he sees the fall of the aggregate of feelings. (Paṭis 1.288)

He understood as it really is the satisfaction (*assāda*) in feelings thus: "The pleasure and joy that arise in dependence on feelings, this is the satisfaction in feelings" (SN 22:26). He understood as it really is the unsatisfactoriness (*ādīnava*) in feelings thus: "That feelings are impermanent, suffering, subject to change, this is the unsatisfactoriness in feelings" (*ibid.*). He understood as it really is the escape (*nissaraṇa*) from feelings thus: "The removal and abandoning of desire-and-lust for feelings, this is the escape from feelings" (*ibid*). And having understood all this: "The Tathāgata, bhikkhus, devoid of clinging through the disappearance of desire-and-lust, is emancipated through non-clinging." Since one might cling to something so long as clinging is present, through the absence of clinging and of any aggregates that might exist as a result of past clinging, the Tathāgata is emancipated without clinging to anything whatsoever.

Sub.Cy. "Having understood as they really are": having known, i.e., having penetrated, the origin of feelings, etc., with insight-wisdom (*vipassanāpaññā*) by way of the penetration of the object (*ārammaṇapaṭivedha*), and with path-wisdom (*maggapaññā*) by way of the penetration of non-delusion (*asammohapaṭivedha*).[74]

"In the sense of their conditioned origination": their origination because they have not been extirpated by the noble path, and through the arising of their conditions such as ignorance, etc., as described in the standard formula: "This being, that exists; through the arising of this, that arises." The characteristic of production is the characteristic of arising (*uppādalakkhaṇa*); that is, their genesis (*jāti*).

"In the sense of their conditioned cessation": the meaning should be understood as the reverse of the method stated for origination. [That is, their cessation because they have been extirpated by the noble path, and through the cessation of their conditions as described in the standard formula: "When this has ceased, that has ceased; with the

---

74. Insight-wisdom is the knowledge which penetrates the five aggregates as impermanent, suffering, and non-self, through repeated contemplation of the aggregates in the light of these characteristics in the course of insight-meditation. The wisdom of the four noble paths penetrates nibbāna as object. Whereas insight penetrates the aggregates as direct object, path-wisdom penetrates them by dispelling delusion about them through the realization of nibbāna.

cessation of this, that ceases."[75] The characteristic of change is the characteristic of cessation (*nirodhalakkhaṇa*); that is, their dissolution (*bhaṅga*).]

"The satisfaction": a [previous] feeling's capacity to serve as an object-condition for [subsequent] pleasure and joy, or the pleasure and joy themselves. This is the meaning in brief: when joy has arisen taking as object a previously arisen feeling, the previous feeling's quality of giving satisfaction [by serving as a condition], and joy's quality of finding satisfaction—this is the satisfaction [in the previously arisen feeling].

"The unsatisfactoriness": by the term "impermanent," he states the unsatisfactoriness in equanimous feeling (*upekkhā vedanā*), or in all feelings, by way of the suffering inherent in formations. By the other two terms (i.e., "suffering" and "subject to change") he shows the unsatisfactoriness in painful and pleasant feeling, respectively, by way of the other two types of suffering. Or all three terms can be applied to all feelings without distinction.[76] This is the unsatisfactoriness in feelings: their impermanence in the sense of their non-existence after having been; their subjection to suffering in the sense of their oppression by rise and fall; and their twofold changeableness through aging and death.

---

75. The first part of the formula for cessation that has come down in the suttas actually reads: "This not being, that does not exist" (*imasmiṃ asati idaṃ na hoti*).

76. The general notion of suffering (*dukkha*) comprises three subsidiary types: affective suffering (*dukkhadukkhatā*), which is physical and mental painful feeling; suffering in change (*vipariṇāmadukkhatā*), which is the suffering due to the termination of pleasant experience; and suffering inherent in formations (*saṅkhāradukkhatā*), which is the inadequacy inherent in conditioned existence. According to the first method of interpretation given in the Sub.Cy., the term "impermanent" applies to equanimous feeling, or all feeling, and signifies the suffering inherent in formations; the term "suffering" applies to painful feeling, and signifies affective suffering; and the term "subject to change" applies to pleasant feeling, and signifies the suffering in change. The second method extends all three terms to all three types of feeling. This interpretation gives a clear example of the intricate interconnection of the diverse categorical schemes underlying the Buddha's teaching, and the precision in the Master's selection of words in formulating his discourse.

"The escape from feeling": as long as one does not abandon the desire and lust bound up with feeling, one is attached to feeling; but when one abandons desire and lust, then one is released and detached from feeling. And here, when feeling is mentioned, the material and immaterial dhammas that are co-nascent, support, and object conditions for feeling are also included. Thus all the five aggregates of clinging are included. The five clinging-aggregates included by the mentioning of feelings make up the truth of suffering (*dukkhasacca*). The ignorance, etc., included by mentioning the origin of feelings make up the truth of the origin (*samudayasacca*). The terms "passing away" and "escape" imply the truth of cessation (*nirodhasacca*). And the understanding of feelings "as they really are" implies the truth of the path (*maggasacca*). Thus the Four Noble Truths can be found in this passage.[77]

"Devoid of clinging through the disappearance of desire-and-lust": this is said because clinging to sense pleasures (*kāmupādāna*) is the root of the other types of clinging, and because when clinging to sense pleasures is abandoned, the other types of clinging come to an end.

"(The Tathāgata) is emancipated through non-clinging": the Exalted One shows his own attainment of the paths and fruits.

By this entire passage on feelings, the King of the Dhamma shows the ground for the origination of his knowledge of omniscience together with its preliminary practice; for that is the element of Dhamma (*dhammadhātu*) the full penetration of which enabled him to analyze in detail these speculative views together with their grounds and destinations.

37. These are those dhammas, bhikkhus, ...

CY. This is a paraphrase: "I asked: 'What, bhikkhus, are those dhammas that are deep, etc.?' It is these dhammas pertaining to the knowledge of omniscience, expounded in the above passage, that are deep, difficult to see ... comprehensible only to the wise. Concerning these, neither the worldling, the stream-enterer, nor anyone else can speak in praise of the Tathāgata in accordance with reality. The Tathāgata alone can do so." Asking thus, he asked only in reference to

77. This refers back to the earlier statement that the passage gives the meditation subject of the four truths.

the knowledge of omniscience, and answering, he answered by reference to the same. But other views remain to be analyzed.

B. Partial-Eternalism (*Ekaccasassatavāda*): Views 5–8

38. There are, bhikkhus, some recluses and brahmins who are eternalists in regard to some things, and non-eternalists in regard to other things ...

CY. Partial-eternalists are of two kinds: partial-eternalists in regard to beings (*sattekaccasassatikā*) and partial-eternalists in regard to formations (*saṅkhārekaccasassatikā*). Both kinds are included here.

Sub.Cy. Partial-eternalism is the doctrine that something among beings and formations is eternal. The first three doctrines (in the sutta) are analyzed in terms of beings, the fourth in terms of formations. When the expression "partial-eternalists in regard to formations" is used, this is intended to show the dhammas assumed to be eternal in accordance with their true nature, not to show them in the way they are conceived by the partial-eternalist himself. For in his theory, the things conceived to be eternal are regarded as unconditioned (*asaṅkhata*).[78] Hence he says: "That which is called 'mind' ... is a permanent, stable self..." For it is impossible for anyone in his right mind to maintain that some entity he admits to be produced by conditions is permanent and stable.

(The Jain doctrine of the sevenfold predicable (*sattabhaṅga*) and of relativism (*anekavāda*)

Sub.Cy. Hence the doctrine of the "sevenfold predicable,"[79] which maintains that entities possessing rise, fall, and stability may be permanent (*siyā niccā*), may be impermanent (*siyā aniccā*), or may be unclassifiable (*siyā na vattabbā*) can be demonstrated to be untenable. The demonstration follows.

If one should say: "That nature (*sabhāva*) in terms of which a thing is said to be (*atthi*) is the very same nature in terms of which it is said not to be (*natthi*)," etc.—this may be the doctrine of relativism,

78. And hence he does not himself regard them as formations. The meaning of formations that is relevant here is *saṅkhatasaṅkhārā,* "formations consisting of the conditioned."

79. For a discussion of these Jain tenets, see Introduction, p. 19.

and again it may not be the doctrine of relativism. It is not fitting to mention here the relation to a different place, etc., for everyone acknowledges this and hence there is no dispute concerning it.[80]

Some, however, say: "When an ornament is made out of a golden jar, the state of a jar is destroyed and the state of an ornament arises, but the state of gold remains. So for all entities: one attribute (*dhamma*) is destroyed, another attribute arises, but the intrinsic nature (*sabhāva*) remains."[81] They should be refuted thus: "What is the gold that remains the same in both the jar and the ornament?" If it is said to be materiality, etc., then it is impermanent like sound. If it is said to be an aggregation of materiality, etc., an aggregation (*samūha*) is a mere conventional term to which neither existence nor non-existence nor permanence apply. Thus no doctrine of relativism can obtain here. The error in affirming either the difference or identity of the attributes and attribute-bearer has already been dealt with in the examination of eternalism; therefore it should be understood by the method explained above.[82] Furthermore, it cannot be maintained that the self and the world are existent in the ultimate sense but possess a nature that may be permanent, impermanent, or unclassifiable, depending on the point of view, as in the example of lamps, etc. For lamps, etc., are subject by their nature to rise and fall, and hence no intrinsic nature that may be permanent, impermanent, or unclassifiable can be discerned in them.[83] And so too, no such nature can be discerned for a soul (*jīva*). Thus the sevenfold scheme of predication, as well as any other divisioned scheme of predication, is impossible. In this way the doctrine of the sevenfold predicable is shown to be untenable.

---

80. If it is the same nature in terms of which a thing is said both to be and not to be, one is already at the outset violating the law of contradiction and is therefore on such insecure ground that one cannot even be said to be maintaining a single doctrine. On the other hand, if one is using the words "to be" and "not to be" in the context of the predication of place, time, material, or state, e.g., "My pen is in my hand but is not on the table," the issue is so trivial as to be beyond disagreement, and it is mere sophistry to try to inject ontological implications into this matter of verbal usage.

81. This argument is intended to prove the co-existence of arising, ceasing, and stability, the initial thesis which provoked this discussion.

82. See p. 143.

83. The lamps, possessing rise and fall, are decidedly impermanent.

Partial-eternalists in regard to beings are, for example, the theists (*issaravāda*), who maintain that God (*issara*) is permanent and other beings impermanent. Partial-eternalists in regard to formations are, for example, the followers of Kaṇāda,[84] who maintain that the atoms (*paramāṇu*) are permanent and stable, the molecules, etc., (*aṇukādayo*) impermanent. [That is, the combinations of atoms (*dviaṇukādayo*) are impermanent. Those who maintain that the eye and other physical sense-organs are impermanent, and consciousness permanent, are also partial-eternalists in regard to formations.]

(Is partial-eternalism in part a correct view?)

Sub.Cy. *Query:* Isn't it true that in the doctrine that some dhammas are eternal, some non-eternal, the conviction that the eye, etc., are non-eternal is a comprehension of things according to their true nature (*yathāsabhāvāvabodha*)? If so, then why is it a wrong view?

Reply: Who says the conviction that the eye, etc., are non-eternal is a wrong view? The wrong view (in this doctrine) is the adherence to some of the non-eternal things as eternal. And since they maintain a wrong view in one section of their doctrine, their comprehension that the eye, etc., are non-eternal is vitiated by the admixture with wrong view just as cream of ghee is vitiated by the admixture with poison. It cannot be classified under right view because it is incapable of performing the proper function of right view. Moreover, it is impossible to deny that their comprehension is a wrong view, for though the eye, etc., are recognized to be non-eternal, the theorists still attribute to them the nature of a soul (*samāropitajīvasabhāva*) when they say: "The eye ... the body, that self is impermanent...," etc.

When this point is made clear, there is no room for the criticism that the doctrine of analysis,[85] in maintaining a distinction between the unconditioned and conditioned elements, becomes a form of partial-eternalism which holds: "Some dhammas are eternal, some non-eternal." For the doctrine of analysis accords with the unperverted true nature of dhammas (*aviparītasabhāva-sampaṭipattibhāvato*).

---

84. The founder of the Vaiśesika system, one of the six orthodox systems of Indian philosophy.

85. *Vibhajjavāda*: an ancient name that the Theravāda school uses for itself. The unconditioned element is nibbāna, all others are conditoned.

N.Sub.Cy. It accords with the unperverted true nature of dhammas because it is free from any admixture with wrong views and because (unlike partial-eternalism) it does not attribute to dhammas the nature of a soul.

(For the following the more elaborate version of **N.Sub.Cy.** has been used): Objection: Admittedly, in the former doctrine (of eternalism), the apprehension of non-eternal dhammas as eternal is a decidedly wrong view; and the conception of eternal things as eternal (in the doctrine of analysis) is not a wrong view, since it apprehends things in accordance with their true nature. But such being the case, no doctrinal difference should be drawn between the present doctrine of partial-eternalism (and the doctrine of analysis), for both involve the conception of eternity only in regard to some dhammas.

Reply: A difference should be drawn, for the present doctrine, discriminating between the dhammas to be apprehended, postulates "some dhammas are eternal, some non-eternal" when they are all exclusively non-eternal.

Query: Since the part is included within the whole, shouldn't this limited conception of eternalism be incorporated in the former, unlimited conception of eternalism?

Reply: This, too, cannot be maintained, for the two doctrines are differentiated on account of the distinction between their respective domains. For some theorists adhere to the view that all things are eternal, others to the view that some things are eternal and some non-eternal. (When the two doctrines are distinguished), the fact that one doctrine treats all formations exhaustively without omission, while the other embraces only a part, is made perfectly clear.

And what is more—(it cannot be maintained that partial-eternalism should be incorporated in eternalism) for one adherence (i.e., eternalism) is based on the succession of aggregates extending over a number of existences, the other (i.e., partial-eternalism) on the succession contained only in one existence.[86] Thus all four kinds of

86. That is, the eternalist recollects (or supposes) a number of lives, and on this basis postulates an eternal self transmigrating from life to life through beginningless time, while the partial-eternalist recollects one past life and postulates an eternal self—either as a creator God or a multitude of deities—existing eternally through a single life, without going through death and rebirth.

eternalists become adherents of eternalism in regard to the assemblage of immaterial dhammas occurring in dependence upon diverse physical bodies through the course of different births, either through direct-knowledge (in the case of those who recollect past births), or (in the case of the rationalists) who follow hearsay, etc., by assuming a diversity of physical bodies. Thus they say: "Passing away thence, I re-arose there," "they pass away and re-arise," etc. But the partial-eternalist who gains spiritual distinction forms his adherence by assuming eternal existence in regard to the succession of dhammas (in a single existence) without taking into account a number of different existences; for his adherence has as its objective domain only the aggregate-continuum included in a single existence. Thus for three forms of the doctrine, only this much is said: "He recollects his immediately preceding life, but none previous to that." The distinction between the two types of rationalists—the eternalist and the partial-eternalist—is also clear by way of the distinction in their objective domains of material and immaterial dhammas.

(THE ORIGIN OF BELIEF IN A CREATOR GOD)

39. beings for the most part are reborn in the Ābhassara Brahma-world.

CY. "For the most part": that is, except those who are reborn in the higher Brahma-worlds or in the immaterial realms or (elsewhere).

Sub.Cy. "In the higher Brahma-worlds": in the fine-material Brahma-worlds such as the Parittasubha plane. The destruction of the aeon by fire is intended here, since this occurs most frequently.

The word "or" (at the end of the commentary's remark) signifies the alternative, "or in world systems other than those that are contracting." For it is inconceivable that all beings in the planes of misery will then re-arise in the fine-material or immaterial spheres, since it is impossible for those with the longest life spans in the planes of misery to be reborn in the human world.

N.Sub.Cy. And they cannot be reborn from the plane of misery into the higher worlds without being first reborn in the human world. One with wrong views of fixed consequences[87] will not be released from hell when the world system contracts. It is said in the commentaries that he is then reborn on the other side of the world sphere.

There they dwell, mind-made

CY. "Mind-made" (*manomaya*): because they have been reborn through the jhāna-mind.

Sub.Cy. Although for all beings rebirth occurs through the kammically formative states of consciousness, the beings of the fine-material sphere are called "mind-made" because they are reborn through mind alone without external conditions. Such being the case, one might ask, shouldn't the state of being "mind-made" also apply to beings of spontaneous origin in the sense-sphere existence? No, it should not. For the expression "mind-made" applies only to beings reborn through the distinguished type of mind pertaining to the higher consciousness.[88] Showing this, the commentator says: "because they have been reborn through the jhāna-mind."

Does the state of being "mind-made" also apply to beings in the immaterial sphere? No, for it is unnecessary to emphasize that they have been reborn through mind alone, since there is not even a suspicion that they could be reborn there through external conditions. And in common usage the expression "mind-made" is applied to beings of the fine-material sphere. Thus the teachers of the Vedas speak about a fivefold self: "a self made of food, made of breath, made of mind, made of bliss, made of consciousness."[89]

40. an empty palace of Brahmā appears.

CY. The plane of Brahmā's company (*brahmakāyikabhūmi*) is produced.[90] It was originally empty, since no beings were as yet reborn there. It has no maker or creator, but is a gem-studded plane produced through kamma as condition and temperature as mode of origin, in the way described in the *Visuddhimagga*. Gardens, celestial

---

87. *Niyatamicchādiṭṭhika:* one who holds a wrong view that undermines the principles of ethics, such as moral nihilism (*natthikavāda*), non-action (*akiriyavāda*), or non-causality (*ahetukavāda*); see e.g. MN 60.5, 13, 21; MN 76.7, 10, 13.

88. *Adhicitta:* a technical term for the higher states of consciousness produced through meditative development, in particular, the four jhānas.

89. *Annamaya, pāṇamaya, manomaya, ānandamaya, viññāṇamaya.* A key tenet of classical Vedānta, the origin of which goes back to the Upanishads. However, according to the Vedānta these are not a "fivefold self" but five sheaths (*kośa*) surrounding the self (*ātman*), which transcends them all.

wishing trees, etc., are produced here in the natural places for their production.

> Then a certain being, due to the exhaustion of his life span or the exhaustion of his merit, passes away from the Ābhassara plane and re-arises in the empty palace of Brahmā.

Sub.Cy. How is it that beings living in the superior plane of the second jhāna (i.e., the Ābhassara world) re-arise in the inferior plane of the first jhāna (i.e., the plane of Brahmā's company)? In order to explain how the commentator says:

CY. Then an attachment (*nikanti*) to their dwelling place spontaneously arises in those beings. Having developed the first jhāna, they descend from there (i.e., take rebirth in the lower plane).

"Due to the exhaustion of his life span": those beings who have done lofty deeds of merit and are reborn in a celestial world with a short life span cannot remain there solely by the power of their merit, but pass away because of the (limited) length of the life span in that world. These beings are said to pass away due to the exhaustion of their life span. "Or the exhaustion of his merit": those beings who have done inferior deeds of merit and are reborn in a celestial world with a long life span cannot remain for the full life span of that world, but pass away in the middle of their life. These are said to pass away due to the exhaustion of their merit.

Sub.Cy. "Due to the (limited) length of the life span of that world": due to the limited length of the maximum life span.

Query: But what is this "maximum life span" (*paramāyu*)? And how is it of a limited length?

---

90. This plane, the lowest in the sphere of fine-material existence, includes three subsidiary realms: Brahmā's assembly (*brahmapārisajja*), Brahmā's ministers (*brahmapurohita*), and Mahābrahmās. It is produced as the objective counterpart of the first jhāna, just as the Ābhassara world is produced as the objective counterpart of the second jhāna. According to Buddhism, all the so-called objective realms of existence are in actuality "ontological crystallizations" of the kammic energy generated in the volitionally active states of consciousness, so that it is mind which, through its volitional faculty, is the ultimate creator of the entire world of sentient existence.

Reply: The life span is the specific duration of the succession of resultant aggregates (i.e., of the *bhavaṅga* or life-continuum) of the various beings in each particular realm of existence. Like their distinctive bodies, organs, colors, shapes, sizes, etc., it is generally of fixed limits (*niyatapariccheda*) for the different destinations, orders of beings, etc.; it is determined by the decisive support of a previously formed longing for existence, and is fortified by present conditions, such as semen, blood, temperature, and food, etc., in the case of mammals, temperature and food, etc., in the case of sense sphere deities, and temperature, etc., in the case of beings of the fine-material sphere. The material and immaterial life-faculties, which support the momentarily enduring material and immaterial dhammas respectively co-nascent with themselves, maintain them not only by causing their momentary duration, but also by causing the non-disruption of the continuous succession (of life-phenomena) until the bhavaṅga is cut off (i.e., until physical death takes place). Therefore, because the specific duration of life is rooted in the life-force (*āyu*), by a metaphorical use of the cause's name for its fruit, it is itself called the "life span" (*paramāyu*). For gods and denizens of hell, the life span is generally of fixed limits; for human beings living in Uttarakuru, it is exclusively of fixed limits.[91] For animals, ghosts, and the remainder of humankind, the life span is without fixed limits, since at a time when kamma conducive to longevity is prevalent, it may be longer or shorter, depending upon such conditions as the continuum connected with the kamma, the semen and blood (from which the foetus) is produced, and upon certain conditions rooted in the kamma, such as the evenness or unevenness of the revolutions of the sun and moon, etc., and the evenness or unevenness of the temperature and nutriment from which it is produced, etc. Just as the distinctive color, shape, etc., of the beings in the different destinations, orders of beings, etc., is determined by way of a previously formed longing for existence, as well as by the completion of their apprehension from the beginning as a result of seeing, hearsay, etc., so too the limitation of the life span—the specific duration of which is generally the same for the beings reborn in the same plane of rebirth—is determined from the beginning by way of the effected longing for existence, which is formed as a

91. According to ancient Indian belief, the inhabitants of this semi-mythological country in Central Asia all lived to the age of 120.

result of seeing, hearsay, etc., and adheres (to that state of existence) as supreme.

Although kamma is capable of producing, in the various planes of rebirth, the specific colors, etc., that are fixed for the beings in each plane, as well as deviations from the norm, it cannot produce resultants exceeding the limits of the life span in planes of rebirth where the life span is of fixed limits. Therefore it is said: "they pass away because of the limited length of the life span."

41. There arises in him discontent and agitation

CY. "Discontent" (*anabhirati*): the longing for the arrival of another being. But dissatisfaction (*ukkaṇṭhitā*) associated with aversion (*paṭigha*) does not exist in the Brahma-world.

Sub.Cy. "Dissatisfaction" is the mental distress over the lack or loss of a loved object. It denotes an act of consciousness accompanied by grief (*domanassacittuppāda*).

CY. "Agitation" (*paritassanā*):[92] anxiety (*ubbijjanā*), trembling (*phandanā*). This is fourfold:

(1) Agitation through fear (*tāsatassanā*): this is "the fear, fright, consternation, horripilation, and mental disquietude, that arise on account of birth, aging, disease, and death."

(2) Agitation through craving (*tāṇhātassanā*): this occurs in the wish, "Oh, that other beings might come to this place!"

(3) Agitation through views (*diṭṭhitassanā*): this is agitation and vacillation (see below §§105–17).

(4) Agitation through knowledge (*ñāṇatassanā*): this is found in the passage, "Those gods, on hearing the Tathāgata's discourse on Dhamma, generally feel fear, a sense of urgency, and terror" (SN 22:78).

In the above passage, both agitation through craving and agitation through views apply.

Sub.Cy. "Agitation" here signifies the craving and views based on his discontent which arise in him as he enjoys the delight of the

92. The Pāḷi word *paritassanā* may be derived from two different Sanskrit verb roots: (1) *tṛṣ, tṛṣyati,* to be thirsty, to crave, yields Skt. *tṛṣnā* and Pāḷi *taṇhā*, craving; and (2) *tras, trasati,* to fear, yields Pāḷi *utrāsa,* disquietude, *tāsa* fear, and *santāsa,* terror. Hence the primary explanations are in terms of craving and fear, with views and knowledge added in a secondary sense.

jhānas over a long period of time and become the causes for the assumptions of "mine" and "I." When, in drawing out the meanings, the passage "Oh, that other beings might come to this place!" was cited to illustrate the agitation through craving, this was done to elicit from the statement the agitation of craving alone, since a separate citation was given for the agitation of views. It should not be taken to mean that the agitation of views is absent on such an occasion (for it is present as well).

(In the passage on the agitation through knowledge), "fear" (*bhaya*) is the knowledge of fearfulness (*bhayañāṇa*) arisen as the fear of all formations in one practicing contemplation of dissolution (*bhaṅgānupassanā*). A "sense of spiritual urgency" (*saṃvega*) is knowledge together with moral dread, or just moral dread (*ottappa*). "Terror" (*santāsa*) is knowledge terrified of all formations, resulting from the contemplation of danger and the contemplation of disenchantment (*ādīnavanibbidānupassanā*).[93]

42. "I am … the lord, the maker and creator…"

CY: (Paraphrase:) "I am the Lord (*issara*) of the world, I am the Maker and Creator of the world; the earth, the Himalayas, Mount Sineru, the world-spheres, the great ocean, the moon and the sun have been created by me."

"… the ordainer …"

CY. "I am the one who appoints beings to their place: 'You be a khattiya, you a brahmin, you a merchant, you a serf. You be a householder, you a monk. You be a camel, you a cow."

"What is the reason?"

CY. Now, after claiming "These beings have been created by me," he sets out to substantiate this with a reason.

Sub.Cy. Although this Brahmā had acquired the knowledge of the ownership of kamma in previous births, due to the instability of a worldling's views he discarded it. Induced by his (supposed) creation of beings through a mere act of consciousness exercising the psychic power of transformation, he deceived himself, and leaping upon the

93. See Vism 21.29–44.

doctrine of the creative play of God (*issarakuttadassana*), thinking "I am the Lord, the Maker and Creator," he became established in it as his conviction. But this statement does not yet serve to establish others (in this view), since it is said: "(He) thinks to himself." In order to show that this conviction was formulated also as a means of establishing others in his view, it is said "after claiming" and "desiring to substantiate this with a reason."

"We have been created by him."

CY. Although they passed away and re-arose by reason of their own kamma, through sheer imagination alone they imagined that they had been created by him, and bowing before him like crooked pegs being inserted into crooked holes, they flocked to his feet (i.e., they became his devotees).

Sub.Cy. *Query:* Isn't it true that immediately after they are reborn, gods possess the reviewing knowledge: "Having passed away from such a destination, we have re-arisen here as a result of such and such kamma"?

Reply: This is true in the case of those whose dispositions in previous births were perfectly grounded in the knowledge of the ownership of kamma. But these beings adhered to the view of the creative play of God in previous births as well. Therefore they thought: "We have been created by him."

"He is permanent, stable, eternal, not subject to change..."

CY. Not having seen him re-arise, they say he is "permanent" (*nicca*). Not seeing him die, they say he is "stable" (*dhuva*). "Eternal" means ever-existing. He is not subject to change (*avipariṇāma-dhamma*) due to the absence of change by way of aging.

(The second and third cases of partial-eternalism)

45. There are, bhikkhus, certain gods called "corrupted by play."

CY. "Corrupted by play" (*khiḍḍāpadosika*). They are corrupted (*padussanti*), i.e., destroyed (*vinassanti*), by play.

> These gods spend an excessive time indulging in the delights of laughter and play. As a consequence they become forgetful, and when they become forgetful they pass away from that plane.

CY. They become forgetful about their food. These gods, it is said, celebrate a festival in honor of their own great beauty and splendor, attained through their distinguished merit. They then become so absorbed in their great enjoyment that they do not even know whether or not they have eaten. But when they have passed up the time even for a single meal, though they eat and drink immediately afterwards, they pass away and cannot remain. Why? Because of the strength of their kamma-born heat element[94] and the delicacy of their material bodies (*karajakāya*). In the case of humans, the kamma-born heat element is delicate and the material body strong. Because of the delicacy of their heat and the strength of their bodies they can subsist for even seven days on warm water, clear gruel, etc. But in the case of gods, the heat element is strong and the body delicate. If they pass up the time even for a single meal, they cannot endure. Just as a red or blue lotus placed on a heated rock at mid-day in the hot season would not be able to resume its original condition in the evening even if one were to pour a hundred jars of water over it, but would only perish, in the same way, though they eat and drink immediately after (missing their meal) these gods pass away and cannot remain.

But who are these gods? This matter is not investigated in the Commentary.[95] But since it is said, "In the case of gods, the heat element is strong and the body delicate," without making any distinctions, we can understand that all gods living on material food who act thus pass away. Some, however, say that only the Nimmānarati and the Paranimmitavasavattī gods are meant.[96]

> 47. There are, bhikkhus, certain gods called "corrupted by mind."

CY. "Corrupted by mind" (*manopadosika*): they are corrupted, i.e., destroyed, by mind.

---

94. *Kammajatejo:* the primary force in the process of digestion.
95. That is, the old commentary on which Buddhaghosa based his work.
96. The gods of the two highest sense-sphere heavenly worlds.

Sub.Cy. By a mind corrupted through an envious nature. Or the meaning can be understood as mental corruption; i.e., the corruption of the mind by jealousy is the cause of their destruction, thus they are "corrupted by mind."

CY. These are the Cātumahārājika gods.[97] One young god among these, it is told, wishing to celebrate a festival, set out by chariot on the roadway along with his retinue. Another of those gods, going out for a walk, saw the first one riding ahead of him. He became angry and exclaimed: "That miserable wretch! There he is going along puffed up with rapture to the bursting point, as if he had never seen a festival before." The first, turning around and realizing that the other was angry—angry people being easy to recognize—became angry in turn and retorted: "What have you got to do with me, you hot-headed fellow? My prosperity was gained entirely by my own meritorious works. It has nothing to do with you!"

Now if one of these gods gets angry, but the other remains unangered, the latter protects the former (from passing away). But if both get angry, the anger of one will become the condition for the anger of the other, and both will pass away with their harems weeping. This is the natural law (*dhammatā*).

Sub.Cy. If one remains unangered, the anger of the other, not getting any fuel, will arise for only one turn and then subside. It will become extinguished like fire immersed in water, and cannot cause his death. But if both get angry, the anger of each will grow stronger and stronger, intensifying the anger of the other, and become fierce in its attacks, capable of consuming the support (of the vital processes). Then their anger will burn up the heart-base (*hadayavatthu*) and destroy their extremely delicate material body. Subsequently, the entire individual form will disappear.

"The natural law": the purport is that their passing away from that plane is due to the delicacy of their material bodies and the strength of their arisen anger, as well as to the specific nature of their material and immaterial dhammas.

(The Rationalist Dualism of a Transient Body and an Eternal Mind)

49. **CY.** The rationalist sees the breakup of the eye, etc.; but because every preceding act of consciousness (*citta*), in ceasing, conditions the

97. The gods of the lowest sense-sphere heavenly world.

arising of its successor, he does not see the breakup of consciousness, even though the latter is more prominent than the breakup of the eye, etc. Since he does not see the breakup of consciousness, he assumes that when the bodily frame breaks up (at death) the consciousness goes elsewhere, in the same way a bird leaves one tree and settles on another. This he declares as his view.

Sub.Cy. "He sees the breakup of the eye, etc.": due to the grossness of the breakup of material dhammas, he sees their destruction when he sees them undergo alteration in the encounter with contrary conditions and finally disappear from sight (with death).

"Conditions the arising": becomes a condition by proximity condition, etc.[98]

"(The breakup of consciousness) is more pronounced": this is said because the breakup of consciousness is quicker. For in the time a single material dhamma endures, sixteen acts of consciousness break up.

"He does not see the breakup of consciousness": although consciousness is breaking up moment after moment, each act of consciousness, in breaking up, becomes the proximity condition for the following act of consciousness. Because each succeeding act of consciousness arises concealing, as it were, the absence of its predecessor, the aspect of presence (*bhāvapakkha*) alone is strong and clear, not the aspect of absence (*abhāvapakkha*). Thus he does not see the destruction of consciousness. This matter becomes very clear by the example of the fire-disc (i.e., the unbroken disc of flame formed by swinging a firebrand in rapid circular motion). Because the rationalistic partial-eternalist is still more remote from understanding and applying the method of diversity, and wrongly applies the method of unity, he arrives at the conviction: "This very consciousness which always occurs with a single nature is a permanent self."[99]

---

98. The proximity condition (*anantarapaccaya*) is the relation each act of consciousness and its concomitants bear to each immediately succeeding act of consciousness and its concomitants.

99. He does not apply the method of diversity, which reveals the discreteness of the acts of consciousness making up the mental continuum, and wrongly applies the method of unity by taking similarity of form and function to indicate identity of substance.

C. Doctrines of the Finitude and Infinity of the World (*Antānantavāda*): Views 9–12

53–57. **CY.** "Extensionists" (*antānantika*) are those who profess the doctrines of finitude or infinity, i.e., doctrines occurring with reference to finitude, infinity, finitude and infinity, or neither finitude nor infinity.

Sub.Cy. The finitude or infinity of what? Of the self (*attā*), which is here called "the world" (*loka*) because it is "looked upon" (*lokīyati*) by theorists desiring to escape from saṃsāra, or because merit, demerit, and their results are "looked for" (*lokīyanti*) there (i.e., as applying to such a self) by those theorists. Thus the Exalted One has said: "They proclaim the world to be finite or infinite." But what is that self? It is the sign of the kasiṇa functioning as the objective domain of jhāna. For it is this that the theorist perceives as the world. Thus it is said below: "Having apprehended that as the world." But some say that the jhāna itself together with its concomitant dhammas is apprehended as the self or the world.

Query: It is proper to describe the first three doctrines as forms of extensionism, since these refer to the finitude, infinity, and (conjunctive) finitude and infinity (of the world), respectively. But how can the last doctrine be described as a form of extensionism, when it repudiates both terms (i.e., finitude and infinity)?

Reply: (It can be so described) precisely because it repudiates both terms. For the doctrine that repudiates the finitude and infinity of the world, since it refers to that matter, has the world's finitude and infinity as its objective domain. Referring to this, it is said in the commentary: "occurring with reference to..."

Or else: just as, in the case of the third doctrine, both the finitude and infinity of one and the same world are included by way of a distinction in spatial direction (*desabheda*), in the same way the rationalist doctrine includes both by way of a distinction in time (*kālabheda*), speaking of them in terms of their mutual incompatibility. Infinity is implied by the repudiation of finitude, and finitude by the repudiation of infinity. The inclusion of finitude and infinity here, however, is not identical with that of the third doctrine, for in the present case a distinction in time is intended (whereas the third involves a distinction in spatial direction). This is meant: Since, through hearsay, he has heard that the great seers who achieved spiritual distinction sometimes witnessed the self—here labelled "the world"—to be infinite, the rationalist concludes that it is not finite.

And since he has heard that those same seers sometimes witnessed the self to be finite, he concludes that it is not infinite. What is said here concerning the rationalists who reason from hearsay can also be applied, with due alterations, to those who reason from memory of past births and the other types of rationalist.

After extending the previously unextended counterpart sign,[100] the rationalist does not (in either case) directly experience (the self posited to be experienceable), either before or during the extension of the sign. Therefore, referring to the time when the sign is extended, he takes his stand upon mere hearsay, etc., and rejects (the finitude of the self), objecting: "it is not finite." And referring to the time when the sign is unextended, he rejects (the infinity of the self), objecting: "it is not infinite." This position does not assert the complete absence of finitude and infinity, but should be taken, rather, like the term "neither perception nor non-perception," (as an elliptical expression.)[101] His own rejection of the first three doctrines is based on the discrepancy of characteristics pertaining to each case. Surely this must be understood in such a way. Otherwise the fourth doctrine would have to be classified under the category of equivocation.[102] For there is no conception of the self altogether divorced from finitude, infinity, or the conjunction of both; and the rationalist is one who searches for a rational proof; and there is nothing untenable in attributing both terms to one and the same world by way of a distinction in time.

But some explain the fourth doctrine to originate through the following process of reasoning: "If the self were finite, its rebirth in distant places could not be recollected. And if it were infinite, one living in this world would be able to experience the happiness of the heavenly worlds and the suffering in the hells, etc. If one holds it to be both finite and infinite, one would incur the errors of both the previous

---

100. *Paṭibhāganimitta,* the purified internalized image of the meditation subject which appears when concentration has reached a high level of intensity. Once developed, the sign can be extended to cover successively larger areas of the inward visual sphere. See Vism 4.31.126–128.

101. This term signifies neither the complete absence of perception nor its non-absence, but rather that the perception has become so subtle as to evade characterization. See Vism 10.49.

102. See following set of views.

positions. Therefore the self cannot be declared to be either finite of infinite."

Query: It is proper to describe the doctrines of the last two theorists as forms of extensionism, for these doctrines have both the finitude and infinity of the world as their objective domain. But how can the first two views be separately described as forms of extensionism (lit. "finite-infinitism") (when those views have only one of the two alternatives as their objective domain?)

Reply: By a figurative application (*upacāravutti*). For the word "extensionist," which occurs in reference to the last two theorists by way of the total (objective domain) of their views (i.e., the finitude and the infinity of the world) also applies by linguistic convention to the first two theorists individually (because their doctrines take part of that total as their domain), just as the term "method of the eight liberations" applies individually to each immaterial jhāna, or as the term "abode of beings" applies to the world. Or else the expression ("finite-infinitizer") was given to them by way of its applicability to the times prior to their adherence. For these theorists, at a time prior to their achievement of such mental concentration, were "finite-infinitizers" insofar as their reasoning was suspended in between both positions, (as they pondered): "Is the world finite, or is it infinite?" But even after they make a definite assumption through their gain of distinction, the older expression is still applied to them.

(THE ORIGIN OF THE FOUR VIEWS)

CY. Without having extended the counterpart sign to the boundaries of the world-sphere, apprehending it as the world, he abides perceiving the world as finite. But he who has extended the kasiṇa-image to the boundaries of the world-sphere perceives the world to be infinite. Not extending the sign in the upward and downward directions, but extending it across, he perceives the world as finite in the upward and downward directions, and infinite across. The rationalist doctrine should be understood by the method stated. These four theorists are included among the speculators about the past because they apprehend their view as a consequence of what was previously seen by themselves.

Sub.Cy. "As a consequence of what was previously seen": that is, by recollecting the finite (sign), etc., which was previously experienced by consciousness, here called "seeing." Having made this clear, the rationalists who reason from hearsay and the pure rationalists are included by implication. Or else, by mentioning the seen, the heard, (sensed, and cognized) should be understood as implied. Since these four doctrines occur as the misapprehension (of the view asserting) an ever-existent self claimed to be finite, etc., they are included in eternalism.

D. The Doctrines of Endless Equivocation (*Amarāvikkhepavāda*): Views 13–16

61. **CY.** "Endless equivocation" (*amarāvikkhepa*): it does not die, thus it is endless (*amarā,* lit. "immortal"). What is this? The view and speech of this theorist, which go on hedging without limits. "Equivocation" (*vikkhepa*): tossing back and forth in diverse ways (*vividha khepa*). "Endless equivocation": equivocation through endless views and speech.

Another method of derivation: *amarā* is the name of a kind of fish (perhaps eel). Because they roam about in the water diving in and out, it is impossible to catch hold of them. Analogously, this doctrine roams about here and there and is impossible to catch hold of; therefore it is called "eel-wriggling."

62. (He) does not understand as it really is what is wholesome and what is unwholesome.

CY. He does not understand as they really are the ten courses of wholesome and unwholesome kamma. "That would distress me": it might distress me by producing remorse over having spoken falsely. The meaning is that it would be painful. "That distress would be an obstacle for me": i.e., an obstacle to attaining heaven or the path. "Out of fear and loathing of making a false statement": due to moral dread and shame.

"I do not take it thus" (*evam ti me no*): this is indeterminate equivocation.

"I do not take it in that way" (*tathā ti pi me no*): he rejects the eternalist doctrine that the self and the world are eternal.

"Nor do I take it in some other way" (*aññathā ti pi me no*): i.e., in some way other than eternalism; by this he rejects partial-eternalism.

"I do not say that it is not" (*no ti pi me no*): he rejects the annihilationist doctrine that "the Tathāgata does not exist after death."

"Nor do I say that it is neither this nor that" (*no no ti pi me no*): he rejects the rationalist doctrine that "the Tathāgata neither exists nor does not exist after death."

(Another method:) When asked, he does not himself declare anything as wholesome or unwholesome. When asked: "Is this wholesome?", he says: "I do not take it thus." Asked: "What, is it then unwholesome?", he says: "I do not take it that way." Asked: "Is it then something other than these two?", he says: "Nor do I take it in some other way." Asked: "If it is neither of these three, what is your opinion?", he says: "I do not say that it is not." Asked: "In your opinion is it neither this nor that?", he says: "Nor do I say that it is neither this nor that." Thus he resorts to equivocation and does not take a stand on any single side.

Sub.Cy. The equivocators do not have sufficient intelligence even to know the difference between the natures of unwholesome states and states superior to the human level. They do not understand the terms "wholesome" and "unwholesome" by way of the wholesome and unwholesome courses of kamma. (In the explanation of the five types of evasion) the first method serves to illustrate endless equivocation as indefinite equivocating, the second to illustrate the similarity of the equivocation to the wriggling of an eel.

63. desire and lust ... might arise in me

CY. Without understanding, he suddenly declares the wholesome to be wholesome and the unwholesome to be unwholesome. Then afterwards he asks other wise men: "I explained thus to so and so. Was my explanation right?" If they should say: "You explained rightly, gold-mouth, you declared the wholesome to be wholesome and the unwholesome to be unwholesome," he might think: "There is no wise man equal to me,"—thus "desire and lust (*chando vā rāgo vā*) might arise in me." Here "desire" is weak attachment, "lust" strong attachment.

or hatred and aversion might arise in me.

CY. If he declares the wholesome to be unwholesome and the unwholesome to be wholesome, and asks wise men about his reply, they will say: "You explained wrongly." Then he will think: "I do not even know this much"—thus "hatred and aversion (*dosa vā paṭigho* *vā*) might arise in me." Here "hatred" is weak anger, "aversion" strong anger.

That would be clinging on my part. Such clinging would distress me...

CY. "The pair, desire and lust, would be clinging (*upādāna*) on my part; the pair, hatred and aversion, would distress (*vighāta*) me." Or both pairs are clinging because they are forms of holding firmly, and both are distress because they cause distress. For lust takes hold of the object like a leech, not desiring to let go of it. And hatred takes hold of it like a poisonous snake, desiring to destroy it. And both pairs cause distress, in the sense that they are afflicting. Thus they are called both "clinging" and "distress."

Sub.Cy. The pair, desire and lust, are alone said to be clinging according to the Abhidhamma method. For in the Abhidhamma only craving (*taṇhā*) and views (*diṭṭhi*) are set down as clinging. But in the suttas, hatred is also sometimes called clinging.

64. They might cross-examine me

CY. "They might ask me my opinion: 'What is wholesome? What is unwholesome? State your opinion.'"

They might press me for reason

CY. "If I say: 'This is my opinion,' they might ask for my reasons: 'For what reason do you hold this?'"

They might refute my statements

CY. "If I say: 'For this reason,' they would point out the errors in my reasons and would examine me thus: 'You do not understand this. Accept this. Answer this.'"

These four endless equivocators are included among the speculators about the past because they apprehend their view as a consequence of some dhamma occurring in the past.

Sub.Cy. Although the first three equivocators are dull insofar as they do not comprehend the nature of wholesome and unwholesome dhammas, they at least distinctly comprehend the fact that they do not comprehend these dhammas. But the fourth lacks even this much intelligence and is thus said to be dull and stupid.[103]

Query: But isn't it true, on the basis of his equivocal statement, that he does comprehend his own non-comprehension of these dhammas?

Reply: Although he does, unlike the first three, he does not have fear and loathing of making false statements, etc., in declaring things he has not fully understood. Therefore he is extremely deluded. Or else the fact that he does not comprehend his own non-comprehension of those dhammas is shown by the way he sets up the question, "If you should ask me whether there is another world," etc., in order to equivocate over the reply: "But I do not take it thus," etc. Thus he alone is distinguished as "dull and stupid." Hence Sañjaya Belaṭṭhaputta was called "the dullest and stupidest of all these recluses and brahmins."[104]

Among the questions, the question "Is there a world beyond?" is asked from the standpoint of eternalism, or from the standpoint of right view; the question, "Is it there no world beyond?" from the nihilist standpoint (*natthikadassana*) or from the standpoint of right view; the question, "Is it that there both is and is not a world beyond?" from the standpoint of annihilationism (*ucchedadassana*) or of right view; since no alternative mode is possible when the first three modes have been rejected, the question, "Is it that there neither is nor is not a world beyond?" is asked from the standpoint of right view, when it means that the world beyond is indescribable in terms of existence or non-existence, or out of a preference for equivocation. The remaining three tetrads should be understood in conformity with the method stated. For just as the triad of kamma-formations concerned with merit is included by the triad of kamma-formations through body, speech, and mind, so the meaning of the latter three tetrads is included by the first. These three have the same significance by way of the misapprehension of a self and a criticism of the fruitfulness of merit, etc.

---

103. See Dhp 63: "A fool who knows his foolishness is wise at least to that extent; but a fool who thinks himself wise is called a fool indeed."

104. A skeptical philosopher in the time of the Buddha. Precisely this view is ascribed to him in the Sāmaññaphala Sutta (DN 2.32).

Since the endless equivocator does not approve of the eternalist view of the self (or of any other view), he practices equivocation by saying: "I do not take it thus," etc. These statements of his equivocate by repudiating each point on which he is questioned.

Query: Isn't it true that insofar as he takes a stand on the side of equivocation, he makes a positive affirmation of the equivocal position?

Reply: No, because he is utterly deluded about that as well, and because the doctrine of equivocation occurs only by way of rejection. For example, when Sañjaya Belaṭṭhaputta was asked by King Ajātasattu about an immediately visible fruit of recluseship, he equivocated by repudiating the triad of views on the world beyond, etc.

Query: All the endless equivocators resort to mere equivocation when questioned on this or that point because they do not comprehend as they really are the wholesome dhammas, etc., and the triad on the world beyond, etc. If so, how can they be characterized as theorists? Like someone who does not desire to speak, he cannot be properly called a theorist merely because he resorts to equivocation when he does not understand the matter he is questioned about.

Reply: He is not called a theorist merely because he resorts to equivocation when asked a question, but because he holds a wrong conviction. For this person actually holds the wrong conviction of eternalism, but due to his dull intelligence he cannot comprehend wholesome dhammas as they really are, etc., or the triad of views on the world beyond, etc. So because he is afraid of making a false statement, and because he cannot convince others of a matter he has not understood himself, he resorts to equivocation. Thus the commentator will afterwards classify him with the eternalists.

Another explanation is possible. The doctrine of endless equivocation can be considered as a single distinct view, like the Jain doctrine of the sevenfold predicable. It arises when one who does not comprehend or believe in merit and evil and their respective results resorts to equivocation in response to a question having these matters as its domain. Acquiescing in and approving of such equivocation as good, he adheres to it. Hence the commentator says: "The view and speech of this theorist are without limits."

But how does his view come to be included under eternalism? Because he does not hold the conviction of annihilationism. Besides, there is to be found in his view a fragment of eternalism (indicated by the assumptions in his statements): "Considering the multitude of (*philosophical*) disputations in the world, there is no one who has understood things as they really are. Yet, since beginningless time, there has been reflection upon teachings leading to such exclamations as 'This is the way it is.'"[105]

E. Doctrines of Fortuitous Origination (*Adhiccasamuppannavāda*): Views 17–18

67. (They) proclaim the self and the world to originate fortuitously

CY. "To originate fortuitously" (*adhiccasamuppannaṃ*): to originate without a cause (*akāraṇa*).

68. There are, bhikkhus, certain gods called "non-percipient beings"

CY. "Non-percipient beings" (*asaññasattā*): this is the heading of the teaching. Because they arise without mind, their individual forms consist of mere materiality (*rūpamattattabhāvā*). Their origin is explained as follows.

Someone who has gone forth into a sectarian order practices the preliminary work of meditation on the wind kasiṇa and develops the fourth jhāna. After emerging from the jhāna he sees the fault in mind (*citta*) thus: "When there is mind, one is exposed to the suffering of having one's hands mutilated, etc., and to all kinds of perils. Enough with mind! The unconscious state alone is peaceful." Having thus seen the fault in mind, if he passes away without having fallen away from the jhāna, he is reborn among the non-percipient beings. With the cessation of his final death-consciousness, his mental process desists here in the human world, and the mere aggregate of material form becomes manifest in the non-percipient realm.

---

105. The passage is obscure and the translation, therefore, tentative. The eternalist assumptions seem to be conveyed by such words as *koci*, "anyone" and *vedī*, "one who understands," which suggest belief in a substantial subject. The word *anādikālika*, "since beginningless time," likewise implies the eternal existence of those subjects.

Just as an arrow driven by the propulsive force of the bow-string travels through space to a distance exactly proportional to the propulsive force of the string, in the same way this being, taking rebirth (among the non-percipient beings) through the propulsive force of the jhāna, remains in that realm for a time exactly proportional to the propulsive force of the jhāna. When the force of the jhāna is exhausted, the aggregate of material form disappears there (in the realm of the non-percipient beings) and a rebirth-linking perception (*paṭisandhisaññā*) arises here (in the human world). Because their passing away from the non-percipient realm is discerned through the arising of perception here, it is said: "When perception arises in them, those gods pass away from that plane." The rest is evident.

Sub.Cy. "The heading of the teaching": perception is mentioned as the principal factor in the teaching. For the Exalted One delivered this teaching making perception alone the burden,[106] but he did not intend to suggest that the other immaterial dhammas exist there. Hence he says: "Because they arise without mind." For when the Exalted One teaches supramundane (*lokuttara*) dhammas, he makes concentration or wisdom the burden; and when he teaches mundane (*lokiya*) dhammas, he makes mind or perception the burden. This is illustrated by the following citations. On the supramundane: "On the occasion when one develops the supramundane jhāna" (Dhs 277), "right concentration endowed with five factors" (DN 34), "right concentration endowed with five kinds of knowledge" (DN 34), and "having seen with wisdom, his cankers are eliminated" (MN 30), etc. On the mundane: "On the occasion when a wholesome state of consciousness pertaining to the sense sphere has arisen" (Dhs 1), "What were you conscious of, bhikkhu?" (Svibh Pārājika 1.2), "mind is the forerunner of dhammas" (Dhp 1) "there are, bhikkhus, beings diverse in body and diverse in perception" (AN 9:24) and "the base of neither perception nor non-perception."

"A sectarian order": in a creed of the sectarians outside the Buddha's Dispensation. For the sectarians, perceiving emancipation (to be attained through) a distinguished form of rebirth, or seeing the danger in perception and the benefits in its fading away, develop the non-percipient meditative attainment and take rebirth in an

106. *Dhura,* a technical expression indicating the main theme or vehicle for conveying the teaching.

inopportune plane of existence.[107] But not those belonging to the Buddha's Dispensation.

"He practices the preliminary work of meditation on the wind kasiṇa": having attained the first three jhānas on the wind kasiṇa, having achieved mastery over the third jhāna, he emerges from it and practices the preliminary work for the attainment of the fourth jhāna.

Query: Why is the preliminary work on the wind kasiṇa alone mentioned?

Reply: Just as the particular immaterial meditative attainment called "the development of the fading away of the material" (*rūpavirāgabhāvanā*) is realized by the elimination of materiality in the particular kasiṇas which serve as the counterparts of materiality, in the same way the particular material attainment called "the development of the fading away of the immaterial" (*arūpavirāgabhāvanā*) is attained by the elimination of the immaterial factors in the particular kasiṇa (i.e., the wind kasiṇa) which, because it lacks a distinct shape, serves as the counterpart of the immaterial. Herein, the determination upon the material attainment is formed by seeing the danger in the occurrence of the immaterial through the contemplation: "Perception is a sickness, perception is a boil," etc., or: "Away with consciousness, consciousness is despicable," etc., and by holding the conviction that the peaceful and sublime state is to be found in the absence of the immaterial. The "development of the fading away of the material" is the immaterial attainments together with their access; in particular, the first immaterial jhāna.

Query: If so, shouldn't the limited space kasiṇa also be mentioned? For this, too, is a counterpart of the immaterial.

Reply: This is actually accepted by some, but because it was not included by the ancient teachers it is not stated here. However, there is nothing wrong if it is said that the fading away of the immaterial can be accomplished in virtue of the fact that certain dhammas (i.e., the immaterial dhammas) can be made to fade away, and that it becomes

---

107. *Akkhaṇabhūmi.* The non-percipient realm is regarded as an inopportune plane of existence because it is neither itself a true deliverance from saṃsāra, nor, due to the absence of perception and mind, a plane favorable to the attainment of true deliverance. Particularly at a time when a Buddha appears in the world, the non-percipient plane is inopportune because its inhabitants have no opportunity to see him or listen to his teachings.

manifest in any particular domain serving as the counterpart of those dhammas. But because this is the practice the sectarians themselves must undertake for this attainment, and because they practice this jhāna (i.e., the fourth jhāna on the wind kasiṇa) which is closely connected with the objective domain (of the immaterial attainment), the keen-visioned teachers of old have mentioned only the preliminary work on the wind kasiṇa as the practice for the development of the fading away of the immaterial. Moreover, it is common knowledge that the jhāna on the first three element kasiṇas (i.e., the kasiṇas of earth, water, and fire), like that on the color kasiṇas, takes as its conceptual object the after-image of a color; therefore the *Visuddhimagga* (IV, 31) describes the earth-kasiṇa by the similes of the mirror and the disc of the moon. But the kasiṇa of the fourth element enters the range of the jhāna only as the after-image of the element. Thus it is proper to call it the counterpart of the immaterial and to mention the preliminary work on the wind kasiṇa alone.

Query: If, as the commentary says, the mere aggregate of material form becomes manifest in the non-percipient realm, how can materiality occur there without dependence on the immaterial factors? [Isn't it true that the aggregate of material form must originate in dependence on the immaterial factors, for it is never seen to originate independently here, in five-constituent existence?]

Reply: [This is no objection, and it is not applicable to other cases]. (For one might just as well ask in return) how the immaterial factors in the immaterial realm can occur without dependence on materiality. This state of affairs belongs to the same category. Why? Because it is never seen here. Along the same lines, no materiality should occur in the fine-material realm without edible nutriment. For what reason? Because it is never seen here. Furthermore, the mental continuum that has for its generative cause the non-disappearance of craving for materiality, because it originates together with materiality, occurs in dependence on the latter. The mental continuum that has for its generative cause the disappearance of craving for materiality, because of its indifference to materiality, occurs without the latter. Similarly, the succession of material dhammas that has for its generative cause the disappearance of craving for the immaterial occurs without the immaterial dhammas.[108]

N.Sub.Cy. In the five-constituent existence, due to the absence of the power of meditative development, the material and immaterial dhammas originate together; in the four-constituent existence, through the power of meditative development, the immaterial alone originate; and in the non-percipient existence, again due to the power of meditative development, the material alone originate.

Sub.Cy. *Query:* How can it be believed that the bare succession of material dhammas continues there (in the non-percipient realm) for such a long time without contemporaneous conditions for its support? And for how long a time does it occur?

Reply: Anticipating such a question, the commentary says: "Just as an arrow, by the propulsive force of the bow-string," etc. By this he shows that not only scripture, but this analogy as well demonstrates the point. The non-percipient beings remain in that realm for at most five hundred great aeons. The "propulsive force of the jhāna" is the force of the kamma accumulated in the non-percipient meditative attainment.

Query: How, after the lapse of many hundreds of aeons, can consciousness again originate from a consciousness series that has ceased so long ago? No visual consciousness is ever seen to originate when the eye has ceased.

Reply: This should not be considered one-sidedly. For if no consciousness of the same class has arisen in the interval, even the consciousness that has ceased long ago can act as a proximity condition (*anantarapaccaya*) for the rebirth-consciousness. It is not the seed; kamma alone is the seed. But on account of that kamma functioning as the seed, when beings pass away from the non-percipient realm a rebirth-consciousness with its conditions such as object condition, etc., arises in the sense sphere. Thus the commentary says: "A rebirth-linking perception arises here."

When a scion is removed from a tree which, in accordance with the order of the seasons, blossoms at a fixed time, by the force of the scission the blossoming of the scion does not necessarily occur at the same time as that of the parent tree. In the same way, when, by the development of the fading away of the material, or of the immaterial, a scission is made in the material and immaterial dhammas occurring

---

108. The disappearance of craving for the material and the immaterial referred to here is the temporary suppression of craving through these meditative developments and not its complete eradication, which can only come about through the wisdom of the supramundane paths.

inseparably in five-constituent existence, by reason of the incisive force of the attainment the aggregates in the immaterial realm and in the non-percipient realm occur devoid of their material and immaterial counterparts, respectively.

Query: Isn't it possible to divide the fortuitous originationists after the manner of the eternalists, according to whether their existence in the non-percipient realm endures for a hundred thousand births, for ten aeons of world contraction, etc., or for some period within these intervals?

Reply: True, it is possible. But because existence in the non-percipient plane occurs without intermission, the fortuitous originationist is shown as singlefold merely to point out the method. Or else, because the doctrine of fortuitous origination is included in eternalism, the entire method of teaching that has come down in the discussion of eternalism can be applied to the doctrine of fortuitous origination, wherever appropriate. For the sake of showing this distinction the Exalted One has explained the doctrine of fortuitous origination without subdividing its adherents who gain jhāna.

And surely it must be admitted that the doctrine of fortuitous origination is included in eternalism, for the defiled inclinations of beings are two [towards eternalism and towards annihilationism, and the present case is not one of annihilationism].

Query: But isn't it incorrect to include the doctrine of fortuitous origination in eternalism? For the former maintains: "Previously I did not exist, but now I am. Not having been, I sprang into being." In maintaining this thesis, it assumes the manifestation of a previously non-existent being, while eternalism, in contrast, assumes the all-time existence of the self and the world, maintaining that "they exist just like eternity itself."

Reply: No, it is not incorrect, because the doctrine of fortuitous origination does not recognize any end point in the future. For although this doctrine, in maintaining its thesis that "previously I did not exist," etc., wrongly assumes a first beginning for the self and the world, it still does not recognize any end for them from the present onwards into the future. And because it does not recognize any end for them in the present or in the future it is distinctly a doctrine of eternalism. As the eternalist says: "They will remain the same just like eternity itself."

Query: If so, then isn't it incorrect to include this doctrine, as well as eternalism, etc., among the "speculations about the past," since they involve a misconception about the future?

Reply: No, because they begin with considerations about the past. For they originate through the knowledge of previous lives, which belongs to the past, and through reasoning grounded in hearsay, etc., conformable to such knowledge. And thus it is explained. And besides, these views were propounded by the Lord of the Dhamma, the most excellent speaker, endowed with unimpeded knowledge, after he had realized for himself with direct knowledge everything that comes within their scope and all that is excluded from their scope. Therefore whatever views the Exalted One has explained, and the way they have been explained, should be accepted with conviction precisely in that way. No demonstration or examination is pertinent here, for this is the domain of the Buddha's knowledge, and the domain of the Buddha's knowledge is inconceivable.

IV. Speculations about the Future (*Aparantakappika*)

A. Doctrines of Percipient Immortality (*Saññīvāda*): Views 19–34

(The first tetrad)

76. **CY.** "The self is material" (*rūpī attā*): apprehending the material form of the kasiṇa object as the self, and the perception (of the kasiṇa) as the self's perception, or by mere reasoning as in the case of the Ājīvakas,[109] etc., they proclaim: "The self is immutable after death, percipient, and material."

Sub.Cy. *Query:* Shouldn't the self here be distinct from material form, since the latter, like perception, is held to be the property of the self (*attaniya*)? When it is said that the self is percipient (*saññī attā*), perception itself is not the self (but the self's property); hence it is said above "apprehending ... the perception (of the kasiṇa) as the self's perception." Such being the case, why is the material form of the kasiṇa apprehended as the self?[110]

109. A sect of ascetic philosophers contemporary with the Buddha.

Reply: It shouldn't be thought that the self is material in the sense that material form belongs to it, but rather in the sense that it is characterized by deformation (*ruppanasīla*). And the deformation of the material form of the kasiṇa, which makes it resemble (ordinary) material form, is the differentiation it undergoes when at one time it is extended and at another unextended. And it is impossible to deny that this is so, since kasiṇas do undergo such differentiation as limited and expanded.

Query: If so, isn't it wrong to include this doctrine in eternalism?[111]

Reply: No, it is not wrong. For it is the immutability of the self following the breakup of the body that is intended. Thus it is said: "the self is immutable after death."

"Or by mere reasoning as in the case of the Ājīvakas": none of the Ājīvakas gain the jhānas, for they are fatalists and reject kamma and its fruits. [The Ājīvakas are only rationalists]. Some Ājīvakas maintain that there is a self among the six classes of man, the dark class, etc.

"Immutable" (*aroga*, lit. "healthy"): it undergoes no sickness, i.e., no dissolution. The word *aroga* is a synonym for permanent (*nicca*). By means of this term, the theorist claims the permanence of the self due to its immutability.

CY. (On the remaining three views of the first tetrad:) Apprehending the signs of the immaterial attainments as the self, and the perception occurring (in these attainments) as the self's perception, or by mere reasoning as in the case of the Nigaṇṭhas (Jains), etc., they proclaim: "The self is immutable after death, percipient, and immaterial." The third view arises by combining the views, the fourth through reasoning.

Sub.Cy. "The signs of the immaterial attainments": the space left by the removal of the kasiṇa, the consciousness of the first immaterial attainment, the non-existence (of that consciousness), and the base of

---

110. He asks why, when *rūpī attā* and *saññī attā* are of the same grammatical form, the self is identified with material form while perception is held only to be an accessory of the self.

111. That is, if change or "deformation" is attributed to the kasiṇa form identified as self, how can the self be eternal? The reply points out that eternalism does not preclude all change, but only dissolution.

nothingness, [these are the respective signs (or objects) of the four immaterial attainments].

"As in the case of the Nigaṇṭhas": the Nigaṇṭhas hold that the immaterial self abides in the body, extending over it like the bitter taste in a nimba leaf.

"By combining the views": by apprehending the signs of the material and immaterial attainments together as a single self, and the perceptions occurring in these attainments as the self's perceptions. For this theorist, when he gains the material and immaterial attainments, apprehends their signs as a self with a material aspect and an immaterial aspect, and therefore formulates his conviction that "the self is both material and immaterial," like the Ajjhattavādins.[112] Or else, by apprehending the combinations of material and immaterial dhammas through mere reasoning, he holds "the self is both material and immaterial."

"The fourth through reasoning": through the reasoning that occurs thus: "The self is not material like a conglomerate of posts, wattle, and daub, or of hands, feet, etc., for like the subtle residual formations (of the base of neither perception nor non-perception), it is incapable of performing the specific function (of materiality) on account of its extremely subtle nature; yet it is not immaterial, for it does not transcend the specific nature of materiality." Or else the meaning can be understood by way of the mutual contradiction (of the first two positions) as in the tetrad of extensionist doctrines. Only there is this distinction: in the earlier case, the third and fourth doctrines were shown to originate through a difference in spatial direction and time respectively, while here they originate through a difference in time and base (*kālavatthuvasena*). For the third doctrine originates through a difference in time, since the signs of the material and immaterial attainments cannot be present simultaneously. And the fourth doctrine originates through a difference in base, since it maintains, by way of reasoning, that the aggregation of material and immaterial dhammas is a single self.[113]

---

112. This may refer to the *adhyātmavidyā*, "the knowledge of the supreme self," a tenet of the Vedānta. Cf. Bhagavadgītā, 8.3; "The imperishable is the supreme brahman, its true nature is the supreme self" (*adhyātmā*). The lines following speak of the *adhibhūta*, "what belongs to the elements," which may be the material aspect of the supposed self posited by the theorist.

CY. The second tetrad should be understood by the method stated in the discussion of extensionism. In the third tetrad: (1) the doctrine that the self is of uniform perception (*ekattasaññī*) pertains to one who gains the meditative attainments; (2) the doctrine that the self is of diversified perception (*nānattasaññī*) pertains to the non-attainer; (3) the doctrine that the self is of limited perception (*parittasaññī*) pertains to one who employs a limited kasiṇa; and (4) the doctrine that the self is of boundless perception (*appamāṇasaññī*) pertains to one who employs an expanded kasiṇa.

Sub.Cy. Since each attainment has a different perception, the doctrine that the self has diversified perception may also be held by the theorist who possesses the eight attainments. Nevertheless, because the perception in the attainment presents itself as uniform, the commentary ascribes to the attainer the doctrine that the self is of uniform perception. Or else this doctrine may pertain to one who possesses only a single attainment. And though there is a difference in perceptions corresponding to the differences in attainments, the doctrine that the self is of diversified perception is ascribed to the non-attainer in order to show the perceptual diversity by way of the gross diversity of perception arising through a multiplicity of external objects.

The statement of the third doctrine indicates that this doctrine identifies perception itself with the self, since the kasiṇa is here a dhamma separate from the perception. The kasiṇa is mentioned in order to show the object of the perception. [The perception is limited because of its object.] The same method should also be applied to the case of the expanded kasiṇa (the fourth doctrine). When this is done, a valid distinction is made between these two doctrines on the one hand, and the first and second extensionist doctrines (among the speculations about the past) and the finite and infinite doctrines of the present section (B1 and B2) on the other.[114] Otherwise these two doctrines would be distinguishable from one pair (i.e., from the first and second extensionist doctrines) merely in terms of the difference between the

---

113. And since it is a single self, the self cannot be identified exclusively with either set, and so is "neither material nor immaterial."

114. The difference is that the present doctrines identify perception with the self, and regard the kasiṇa as only the object of the self, while the other doctrines identify the kasiṇa sign with the self.

periods of time with which their speculations are concerned (the past and the future), and would be indistinguishable from the other (i.e., from the finite and infinite doctrines of the present section).

Or else "of limited perception" may mean that the self is percipient and limited, as in the views of those who say "the self is the size of a thumb, or the size of corn, or is a mere atom," like Kapila, Kaṇāda, etc.[115] And "of boundless perception" may mean that the self is percipient and boundless, as is held by those who claim that the self is all-pervasive.[116]

CY. With the fourth tetrad, having seen with the divine eye a being taking rebirth on the plane of the first three, or four, jhānas,[117] he holds that the self is "exclusively happy." Having seen a being reborn in hell, he holds that the self is "exclusively miserable." Having seen a being reborn in the human world, he holds that the self is "both happy and miserable." Having seen a being reborn among the Vehapphala gods,[118] he holds that the self is "neither happy nor miserable." Generally, those who gain the recollection of past lives speculate about the past, those who gain the divine eye speculate about the future.

---

115. The founders of the Sāṅkhya and Vaiśeṣika systems of orthodox Indian philosophy. N.Sub.Cy. reads "the followers of Kapila and Kaṇāda."

116. *Sabbagatabhāva:* most likely the Vedāntins are meant.

117. The first three according to the Suttanta method, the first four according to the Abhidhamma method. The suttas divide the jhānas according to a fourfold scheme, the transition from the first to the second being effected by the simultaneous elimination of initial thought (*vitakka*) and sustained thought (*vicāra*). The Abhidhamma distinguishes a stage in the development of concentration intermediate to the first and second jhānas of the Suttanta scheme, where initial thought has dropped away but sustained thought remains. When this stage is taken into account, the original fourfold scheme becomes fivefold. Rebirth into the various planes in the fine-material world is achieved through the jhāna whose level of consciousness corresponds, in purity and intensity, to that prevailing in each particular plane.

118. A class of gods in the realm of fine-materiality. Rebirth among them is gained through the fourth jhāna, and their predominant affective experience is equanimity or "neither pleasant nor painful feeling."

B. Doctrines of Non-percipient Immortality (*Asaññīvāda*): Views 35–42

C. Doctrines of Neither Percipient Nor Non-percipient Immortality (*N'evasaññīnāsaññīvāda*): *Views* 43–50

79, 82. **CY.** The doctrines of non-percipient immortality and also those of neither percipient nor non-percipient immortality should be understood in terms of the first two tetrads of the doctrine of percipient immortality. Only those theorists held the view that the self is percipient, while these respectively hold that it is non-percipient and neither percipient nor non-percipient. No special reason need be sought for this, for the theorists' assumptions are like the basket of a madman.[119]

Sub.Cy. In the doctrine of non-percipient immortality, the first doctrine (i.e., that the self is material) arises through the experience of beings reborn in the non-percipient realm. The second takes perception to be the self, and maintains a non-percipient immortality on the ground that no other perception exists belonging to this self as its property.[120] The third doctrine arises when the material dhammas together with perception, or all the material and immaterial dhammas together, are apprehended as the self. And the fourth is maintained by way of reasoning. In the second tetrad, taking "non-percipient" to signify that the materiality of the kasiṇa lacks the specific nature of perceiving, the four doctrines should be understood according to the method stated in the discussion of the extensionist doctrines.

In the doctrines of neither percipient nor non-percipient immortality, the first doctrine recognizes, in the case of a being reborn in the realm of neither perception nor non-perception, the existence of a subtle perception incapable of performing the decisive function of perception at death and rebirth-linking, or on any occasion.[121] The second (and remaining) doctrines are maintained by acknowledging

---

119. See p. 134.

120. Since according to this view the self is identified with perception, though the self continues to perceive after death, it is called "non-percipient" because it does not "own" another perception subordinate to itself.

121. Because perception continues to exist in that realm, it is called "not non-percipient"; but because the perception is too subtle to perform the decisive function of perception, it is called "not percipient".

the specific nature of perceiving and the subtlety of the perception, according to the method stated for the doctrine of non-percipient immortality. In order to show the unreasonableness of the theorists' doctrines, even when reasons are offered, he says: "No special reason need be sought for this." Because these doctrines of percipient, non-percipient, and neither percipient nor non-percipient immortality all state that the self is immutable after death, it is clear that they are included in eternalism.

D. Annihilationism (*Ucchedavāda*): Views 51–57

84. (They) proclaim the annihilation, destruction, and extermination of an existent being.

CY. There are two types of people who hold the annihilationist view, the possessor (of the divine eye) and the non-possessor. The possessor adopts the annihilationist view when, with the divine eye, he perceives the passing away of an arahat without seeing any rebirth, or when he perceives the mere passing away (of others) without seeing their rebirth.[122] The non-possessor adopts the annihilationist view because he does not know of any world beyond, or because he is greedy for sense pleasures, or by way of reasoning, e.g., as follows: "Beings are just like leaves which fall from a tree and never grow again."

Sub.Cy. Since the destruction of the non-existent (*asato*) is impossible, the words "(*annihilation*) of an existent being" (*sato sattassa ucchedaṃ*) are used, signifying annihilation based on existence (*atthibhāvanibandhano upacchedo*). The word "being" is used in order to show the following.

The specific-natured dhammas occurring as causes and effects included in a single (multi-life) continuum exhibit a certain distinction insofar as they may belong to different (individual life) continuities (within that single multi-life continuum).[123] Misapplying the method of diversity (*nānattanaya*), these theorists misapprehend the real differentiation between the causes and the effects, and arrive at the conclusion that the differentiation is absolute, as though (the causal

122. He does not see the rebirth of an arahat because the arahat is not reborn; he does not see the rebirth of others because his divine eye is not sufficiently developed.

and resultant continuities) belonged to completely different continua (*bhinnasantāna*). Hence the reason for the adherence to annihilationism is the misapplication of the method of diversity. A second reason is the misapplication of the method of unity (*ekattanaya*). Here, despite the existing differentiation in their specific natures, the dhammas occurring as causes and effects in a single continuity are apprehended as an absolutely undifferentiated whole on account of their inclusion in a single continuity (*ekasantati*). In order to show this [i.e., that it is a being possessed of existence which serves as the objective domain of the theorist's doctrine], the word "being" is used in the text. For the assumption of a being arises when the compact of aggregates occurring in the form of a continuum is not dissected (into its components).[124] And since it is held that "the self exists so long as it is not annihilated," the assumption of annihilationism is based on the assumption of the existence of a being.[125]

---

123. It should be noted that in this passage the word *santāna,* here translated "continuum," is consistently used to signify the single beginningless series of life-processes extending into the indefinite future and containing within itself a countless number of individual life-terms. The word *santati* (from the same root *tan,* with prefix *san,* to stretch out, to continue), here translated "continuity," is used in contradistinction to signify the individual life-terms themselves. Thus a single, beginningless multi-life continuum will contain innumerable individual continuities, each with a distinct beginning ("birth") and a distinct end ("death"). The continuities in turn, as their name implies, are constituted of a succession of "*dhammas*," momentary mental and material factors following each other in a rapidly changing process of rising and passing away, held together by laws of causal relationship. How the misapplication of the methods of diversity and unity gives rise to the wrong view of annihilation is explained in the Introduction (p. 28.)

124. The "dissection of the compact" (*ghanavinibbhoga*) is a technical expression for a phase in the development of insight wherein the mass of human personality, which appears to untutored perception as a uniform whole, is broken down into its components. It is seen "temporally" as a succession of momentary factors following one another without the transmission of any enduring subject, and "spatially" as an assemblage of aggregates functioning together without any unitary entity binding them together. This dissection leaves no room for the assumption of a substantial being.

125. For the Pāḷi text of this passage, see Appendix 2, No. 4.

The non-possessor adopts the annihilationist position because he does not understand that there is a world beyond this, due either to his nihilistic scepticism[126] or to his stupidity. Or he holds that "the domain of the world extends only as far as the range of the senses" due to his greed for sense pleasures, like the king who took hold of his own daughter's hand [because of his infatuation with sense pleasures]. Or he holds the opinion that "just as a withered leaf separated from its branch cannot be rejoined to it, in the same way all beings undergo death with no further rebirth-linkage; [they do not take rebirth, they are consummated by death, they do not undergo any renewed existence]. For beings are like water bubbles [because they never re-arise]."

CY. The seven annihilationist views arise on account of craving and views, in one way or another or by proceeding eclectically.

N.Sub.Cy. "In one way": in the way stated by the example of the possessor (of the divine eye) who does not see the re-arising of an arahat, etc. "Or another": in some other way, since they originate through numerous modes of reasoning. "Or by proceeding eclectically": these views also arise in the case of the possessor through reasoning when he does not see any being re-arise following its passing away.

85. **CY.** "Originates from mother and father": What is that? Semen and blood. Thus the first theorist asserts the human form (*manussattabhāva*), under the heading of the material body, to be the self.

N.Sub.Cy. "Under the heading of the material body": this is said in order to show that they may also take the immaterial factors to be the self.

86. **CY.** The second, rejecting this doctrine, asserts the divine form (*dibbattabhāva*) to be the self. "Divine" means originating in the world of the gods. "Pertaining to the sense sphere" means included among the six classes of sense-sphere gods. "Not destitute of any faculties": complete in its faculties. This is said by way of the faculties existing in the Brahma-world and the figures of the others.[127]

---

126. The nihilist view (*natthikavāda*) denies the existence of any afterlife and of the moral efficacy of actions.

127. In the Brahma-world the nose, tongue, and body remain only as material forms but no longer function as bases of sense experience.

87–91. **CY.** In the third, "mind-made" means produced through the jhāna mind. The meaning of the fourth, etc., is explained in the *Visuddhimagga* (Vism X).

(THE METHOD OF THE TEACHING)

Sub.Cy. *Query:* Unlike the doctrines of endless equivocation, which are shown exclusively in terms of the non-possessor (of meditative attainments), and unlike the tetrad of doctrines on percipient immortality, which are shown exclusively in terms of the possessor, the present doctrine (of annihilationism) is held by both possessors and non-possessors, like eternalism, partial-eternalism, etc. For it is said: "There are two types of people who hold the annihilationist view." If so, why is the method of teaching employed here different from that used in the exposition of eternalism, etc.?

Reply: For the sake of displaying elegance of teaching (*desanāvilāsa*). For the Exalted Buddhas display elegance of teaching when they teach the Dhamma in diversified modes to conform to the inclinations of the beings to be trained. Thus here, as well as elsewhere, the Exalted One could have given the teaching by distinguishing between the possessor of spiritual distinction and the rationalist as follows: "Herein, bhikkhus, some recluse or brahmin, by means of ardor … with his mind thus concentrated he directs his mind to the knowledge of the passing away and re-arising of beings. With the divine eye, purified and surpassing the human, he sees the death-consciousness (*cuticitta*) of an arahat, or of ordinary beings, but does not see any re-arising following it. He declares," etc. Therefore, in order to conform to the inclinations of the beings to be trained through elegance of teaching, the method of teaching employed here is different from that used in the exposition of eternalism, etc.

Or else the Exalted One has taught the annihilationist doctrine in a way distinct from the previous doctrines in order to reveal this difference: in the case of annihilationism the doctrine held by the meditative attainer does not involve a mode of formulation different from the doctrine held by the rationalist (as does partial-eternalism, etc.). But rather, since their classification is identical, their modes of formulation are also identical.[128] For the doctrine is formulated by the rationalist in the same way it is by the one possessing the attainments.

Or else the Exalted One does not teach these views either as future occurrences or as mere probable postulations (*parikappanavasena*).[129] But in whatever way the theorists proclaim their views, saying: "This alone is truth, any other view is false," in exactly that way the Exalted One has delimited them with his knowledge of omniscience and revealed them as they really are. It is through this that the deep, transcending Buddha-qualities are disclosed, and it is by praising it that the Tathāgatas are rightly extolled. And since the annihilationists who perceive successively higher states of existence establish their respective doctrines by repudiating the doctrines of those who perceive lower states, the teaching occurs thus (in conformity with the way the doctrines are established). Therefore, the employment of a teaching method different from those used earlier should not be criticized. Further, it should be recognized that the annihilationist position could have been further broken down by way of the subdivisions in the sense sphere and fine-material sphere (views 1–3), as was done in the case of the immaterial sphere (views 4–7). Or alternatively, it could have been stated without having broken down the immaterial sphere, by a concise method as in the case of the treatment of the sense sphere and fine-material sphere. Such being the case, there is no room for the criticism that the annihilationist doctrine contains either more or fewer divisions than the seven stated by the Exalted One.

Query: In the first three doctrines it is right to say "with the breakup of the body" (*kāyassa bhedā*), for these refer to an individual form included in five-constituent existence.[130] But why is this expression used in the last four views, when those refer to an individual form in four-constituent existence? Isn't it true that the immaterial beings do not own a body?

---

128. That is, each of the seven versions of annihilationism may be presented either by the attainer or by the rationalist.

129. N.Sub.Cy. "Postulating: these views might occur thus."

130. *Pañcavokārabhava*: that is, realms of existence which include five aggregates, with the aggregate of material form as the foundation for the four mental aggregates. Four-constituent existence, which excludes the material aggregate, is the immaterial sphere of existence.

Reply: That is true. But the theorist himself uses this expression, attributing the word "body," which is usually used in reference to the material form, to the immaterial individual form. And the Exalted One shows their views in exactly the way the theorists proclaim them. Or else the descriptive term "body" can be considered to apply to the immaterial form—that is, to the aggregation (*samūha*) of dhammas such as contact, etc.—since this has the character of an immaterial body.

Query: The characterization of the second and following doctrines as speculations about the future is correct, for these doctrines—proclaiming the extermination without remainder of the individual form of sense-sphere gods, etc.—take the future period as their domain. But isn't that characterization out of place in the case of the first doctrine; for the latter, which proclaims the annihilation of the human form directly experienced by the theorist, takes the present as its domain? The second and following doctrines, because they teach the annihilation of a self arisen in some state of existence successively higher than the self mentioned in each immediately preceding doctrine, are correctly classed as speculations about the future. Thus they say: "But it is not at that point that the self is completely annihilated." And when they say: "For there is, good sir, another self," this is said in reference to the distinction [between (that self and) the lower individual forms beginning with the human form]. But there is no such contrast in every case. [Since the first doctrine does not teach the annihilation of a self re-arising in the future in some state of existence higher than the human, and does not mention any other self by way of contrast, isn't it incorrect to class it as a speculation about the future?]

Reply: No, it is not incorrect. For though the self spoken of by the first doctrine is included in the present world, it is the future time that is intended as the domain of the doctrine. [For what is intended by the first doctrine is the annihilation after death, hence in the future, of the self included in the present world]. Thus there is no contradiction in the characterization of the first doctrine as a speculation about the future.

E. Doctrines of Nibbāna Here and Now (*Diṭṭhadhammanibbānavāda*): Views 58–62

93. **CY.** "Here and now" (*diṭṭhadhamma*, lit. "a visible state"): a directly experienceable dhamma (*paccakkhadhamma*). This is a designation for the individuality obtained in this or that state of existence. "Nibbāna here and now" means the subsiding of suffering (*dukkhavūpasama*) in this very individuality.

N.Sub.Cy. Here, "nibbāna" means only the subsiding of suffering. It is not the supreme fruit and not the unconditioned element, for these are beyond the domain of these theorists.[131]

94. When this self, good sir, furnished and supplied with the five strands of sense pleasure, revels in them ...

CY. "Revels": he allows his sense faculties to roam and wander among the strands of sense pleasure according to his wish and indulges in them in this way and that. Or else: he sports, delights, and plays with them. The strands of sense pleasure are twofold, the human and the divine. The human are like those enjoyed by King Mandhātu, the divine are like those enjoyed by the king of the Paranimmitavasavattī gods.[132] The theorists proclaim the achievement of nibbāna here and now only for those who have acquired such sense pleasures.

N.Sub.Cy. By this he shows that they proclaim nibbāna here and now only for those who enjoy the ultimate in the strands of sense pleasure. For the sense pleasures of King Mandhātu and the king of the Vasavattī gods illustrate the ultimate.

Sub.Cy. (The reasoning of the first theorist is as follows:) "Just as the longing for delicious food, etc., increases in one overcome by hunger and thirst, so the longing for objects of clinging distinctly increases in one who deprives himself of sense pleasures. But just as one who has eaten his fill of deliciously flavored food no longer has any appetite, so one who has satisfied himself with as much as he wants of excellently flavored sense pleasures no longer has any thirst

---

131. The supreme fruit (*aggaphala*) is the fruit of arahatship, metaphorically called *nibbāna* after the object of its realization. The unconditioned element is *nibbāna* itself, the supramundane goal, which is beyond the experience of the theorists.

132. On King Mandhātu, see Ja II 310–11. The Paranimmitavasavattī devā are the highest class of sense-sphere gods.

for them. And when one has lost one's longing for the object, like a leech one will automatically let go even of tantalizing objects." Emerging from such unwise reflections, the first theorist declares the suffering of saṃsāra to subside by the satiation of (desire for) sense pleasures. The second and following theorists, seeing the unsatisfactoriness in sense pleasures, and the peacefulness of the happiness of the first jhāna, etc., declare that the suffering of saṃsāra ends by satisfying (the desire for) the happiness of the first jhāna, etc.

The examination (of the method of teaching) given in the section on annihilationism may be brought in here too, with due alterations. There is, however, the following distinction: these five doctrines (of nibbāna here and now) are found in a single individuality.[133] [According to the first doctrine, if the self is furnished with the strands of sense pleasure, then it has attained nibbāna here and now. And if, in the second and following doctrines, this same self is endowed with the first jhāna, etc., in that case it has attained nibbāna here and now. Thus in the text, no separate mention is made of "another self," as is made in the section on annihilationism.]

Query: But why, when it proclaims the absolute extension[134] of the self, is the doctrine of the nibbāna here and now of the self included in the eternalist rather than in the annihilationist view?

Reply: Because they teach the persistence of the purified self in its own form (*sakarūpena*) when it is liberated from bondage by obtaining this or that particular endowment of happiness.

N.Sub.Cy. For in their opinion, the self which has become purified through liberation from the bondage of kamma and has attained nibbāna here and now still persists in its own form.

100.–101. **CY.** At this point, all the sixty-two views have been explained. Seven of these views belong to annihilationism, the remainder (fifty-five) to eternalism. Now, collecting into one all the speculators about the future in the section beginning "it is on these

---

133. That is, all these five types of *nibbāna* are obtainable in a human existence, whereas only the first of the seven types of annihilation discussed in the earlier doctrine applies to a human existence, the other six being obtainable only as a deity or a brahma.

134. *Accantanibbāna.* The word "*nibbāna*" here seems to be taken in its literal meaning of extinction. The reply indicates that these theorists still hold to the persistence of the self on a trans-phenomenal plane.

forty-four grounds" (§100), the Exalted One reveals his knowledge of omniscience. And collecting into one all the speculators about the past, the future, (and their combination) in the section beginning "it is on these sixty-two grounds" (§101), he again reveals this same knowledge of omniscience. Thus, when in the beginning he asked: "And what, bhikkhus, are those dhammas that are deep, etc?", he asked only in reference to the knowledge of omniscience. And answering this question, the Exalted One answers by means of the same knowledge of omniscience, bringing forth the sixty-two speculative views just as if he were weighing the inclinations of beings with a pair of scales or removing the sand from the foot of Mount Sineru.

Sub.Cy. *Query:* What is the reason why only the past and the future (separately) are shown as the objective domains of the adherence to views, and not the two in conjunction?

Reply: Because it is impossible to do so. For whereas theoretical speculations are possible in regard to the past and the future, due to its evanescence no such speculations are possible in regard to the exact mid-point between the two apart from the two themselves, [since it is the mere interval between the past and the future]. On the other hand, if the middle term is taken as the present individuality, insofar as its nature relating to past and future is amenable to theoretical speculation, it is already comprised under the speculations about the past and the future.

Or alternatively, because it possesses a past and a future, the exact mid-point is called "the past and the future together." That can be considered to be referred to by the Exalted One separately from the past and the future when he says, "Recluses and brahmins who are speculators about the past and the future together, hold settled views about the past and the future (together)." In the commentary also it can be considered to be included under the common description "all the speculators about the past, the future, (and their combination)," or under a single division of that description. Otherwise it would be meaningless to combine the speculators together with a single expression. And who are these speculators about the past and the future together? [Those who adhere to a combination of speculations about the past and the future, such as] those who are extensionists (with regard to the past) and hold the doctrine of nibbāna here and now (with regard to the future), etc.

102. all of them do so on these sixty-two grounds, or on a certain one of them. Outside of these there is none.

Sub.Cy. According to this statement of the sutta, there are no theorists outside of these three groups: those who speculate about the past, the future, and both together. Therefore, those doctrines found in the Sāmaññaphala Sutta (DN 2) and in various other suttas, such as the doctrines of the inefficacy of action (*akiriyavāda*), of moral acausality (*ahetukavāda*), of nihilism (*natthikavāda*), etc., as well as the speculative views about God (*issara*), the Lord of Creation (*pajāpati*), the Primordial Spirit (*purisa*), time (*kāla*), nature (*sabhāva*), fate (*niyati*), chance (*yadicchā*), etc., found outside the suttas, should all be included and comprised in these three groups.

How? The doctrine of the inefficacy of action, because it denies the reality of morally efficacious action and holds that deeds are "barren and steadfast like a mountain peak,"[135] is comprised within eternalism. So too is the doctrine of Pakudha Kaccāyana, which maintains: "These seven groups (are barren and steadfast like a mountain peak)," etc. The doctrine of moral acausality, because it asserts "there is no cause or condition for the defilement (and purification) of beings,"[136] is comprised in the doctrine of fortuitous origination. Nihilism, because it asserts "there is no world beyond,"[137] is comprised in annihilationism. Thus in the same passage it is said: "With the breakup of the body, fools and the wise alike are annihilated."

By the first "etc." (after nihilism above), the doctrines of the Nigaṇṭhas (the Jains) and others are included. Although the doctrine of Nāṭaputta (Mahāvīra) has come down in the texts by way of the "fourfold restraint" (*cātuyāmasaṃvara*), nevertheless, because of the evasiveness involved in its method of the sevenfold predicable (see pp. 151–52), it is included in the doctrine of endless equivocation, just as Sañjaya's doctrine is. The doctrines that maintain "the soul and the

---

135. The *akiriyavāda* is ascribed to Pūraṇa Kassapa in the Sāmaññaphala Sutta, but the phrase "steadfast as a mountain peak" does not occur there. The classification of this and the following view under eternalism seems questionable; as formulated in the suttas they are much closer to annihilationism.

136. The doctrine of Makkhali Gosāla.

137. The doctrine of Ajita Kesakambala.

body are the same" and "the soul and the body are different" are included in the doctrines that the self is immutable after death and material/immaterial. The doctrines that "the Tathāgata exists after death" and "there are beings spontaneously reborn" are included in eternalism; the doctrines "the Tathāgata does not exist after death" and "there are no beings spontaneously reborn," in annihilationism; the doctrines "the Tathāgata both exists and does not exist after death" and "there both are and are not beings spontaneously reborn," in partial-eternalism; the doctrines "the Tathāgata neither exists nor does not exist after death" and "there neither are nor are not beings spontaneously reborn," in endless equivocation. The doctrines of God, the Lord of Creation, the Primordial Spirit, and time are comprised in partial-eternalism; so also is the doctrine of Kaṇāda (see note 115). The doctrines of nature, fate, and chance are included in the doctrine of fortuitous origination.

In this way, the speculative views found in various suttas, and those outside them [in the creeds of the sectarians], are comprised within these sixty-two views.

"Just as if he were weighing the inclinations of beings with a pair of scales": "inclination" here is the inclination towards views. For the inclination of beings subject to defilement is twofold: towards eternalism and towards annihilationism. And though this twofold inclination is divided into numerous classes insofar as it arises in the immeasurable domain of knowledge of innumerable beings in innumerable world systems, the Exalted One has delimited it with his knowledge of omniscience and summarized it into sixty-two categories beginning with the four types of eternalists, just as if he had placed it on a measuring scale.

"As if removing the sand from the foot of Mount Sineru": by this he shows that it is impossible for any other kind of knowledge than the knowledge of omniscience to originate this teaching, due to its extreme profundity.

(The sequence of meaning)

CY. This teaching has come down by way of a sequence of meaning dictated by the natural structure of the teaching. For suttas have three kinds of sequence of meaning: (1) a sequence of meaning based on a question (*pucchānusandhi*); (2) a sequence of meaning dictated by inclination (*ajjhāsayānusandhi*); and (3) a sequence of meaning dictated by the natural structure of the teaching (*yathānusandhi*). Herein, the "sequence of meaning based on a question" is found in those suttas the Exalted One pronounced in response to those who questioned him, as the following passage illustrates: "When this was said, a certain bhikkhu said to the Exalted One: 'What, Lord, is the lower shore? What is the further shore? What is sinking in the middle? What is being thrown up on dry land? What is seizure by humans, by non-humans and by a whirlpool? What is inner putridity?" (SN 35:241).

(2) The "sequence of meaning dictated by inclination" can be understood through those suttas the Exalted One pronounced after he had understood the inclinations of others, as the following passage illustrates: "Then the following line of thought arose in the mind of a certain bhikkhu: 'It is said, sir, that material form is not-self, feeling is not-self, perception is not-self, mental formations are not-self, consciousness is non-self. What self, then, do kammas done without a self affect'? Then the Exalted One, discerning with his mind this bhikkhu's thought, addressed the bhikkhus: 'It is possible, bhikkhus, that a certain foolish man here, confused, immersed in ignorance and dominated by craving, may imagine in his mind that he can overshoot the dispensation of the Master, thus: "'It is said, sir, that material form is non-self,' etc. What do you think, bhikkhus, is material form permanent or impermanent?" etc. (MN 109.14–15).

Sub.Cy. "It is said," etc., this bhikkhu reveals his own disapproval of the emptiness of selfhood (*attasuññatā*) as it is taught by the Exalted One. "Kammas done without a self": kammas not done by any self, or kammas done by the aggregates that are non-self. He asks: "If there is no self, and the aggregates are momentary, what self do kammas affect when they produce their fruits?" The meaning is: "Who experiences the fruit of kamma?" He is "confused" because he is unskilled in the ariyan dhamma due to lack of learning, etc.; he is "immersed in ignorance" because he has not abandoned ignorance due to lack of discipline in the ariyan dhamma; and he is "dominated by craving" because he has come under the domination of craving, thinking: "If there is no one called 'I,' who experiences the fruit of the kamma done by me? But if there is an 'I,' there may well be the enjoyment of the fruit." "In his mind": in a mind accompanied by clinging to a doctrine of self. "That he can overshoot the dispensation of the Master": though formations are momentary, the kamma and the fruit in the assemblage of dhammas (constituting an individual) are connected together by the fact that the fruit arises in the same continuum in which the kamma was originally done. But because he wrongly applies the method of unity to this connection, he concludes that there must be a single self-identical agent (*kāraka*) and experiencer (*vedaka*) (in order to establish a connection between kamma and its fruit). Thus he conceives that he can pass beyond the dispensation of the Master, which elucidates the emptiness of a self and of any property of a self.

CY. (3) The "sequence of meaning dictated by the natural structure of the teaching" can be understood through those suttas in which the teaching progresses from its initial subject to its culmination by way of counterparts or by way of the opposites of the initial subject. For example, in the Ākaṅkheyya Sutta (MN 6) the teaching is set up at the beginning by way of virtue and culminates in the six kinds of direct knowledge. In the Vattha Sutta (MN 7), the teaching is set up by way of the defilements and culminates in the sublime abodes (*brahmavihāra*). In the Kosambiya Sutta (MN 48), the teaching is set up by way of schism and culminates in the principles of fraternal harmony. In the Simile of the Saw (MN 21), the teaching is set up by way of impatience and culminates in the simile. And in this Brahmajāla Sutta, the teaching is set up at the beginning by way of views and culminates in the elucidation of emptiness. Thus it is said: "This teaching has come down by way of a sequence of meaning dictated by the natural structure of the teaching."

Sub.Cy. The first example (the Ākaṅkheyya Sutta) shows the sequence of meaning by way of counterparts, the others the sequence of meaning by way of opposites. In the Brahmajāla Sutta the teaching is set up by way of the speculative views proclaiming a permanent substance, etc., and concludes with the elucidation of the emptiness of any permanent substance, etc.

V. The Round of Conditions and Emancipation from the Round

A. Agitation and Vacillation (*Paritassitavipphandita*)

105. **CY.** Now, in order to mark the boundaries, the following teaching is undertaken.

N.Sub.Cy. "In order to mark the boundaries": that is, in order to reveal the absolute discrepancy between the Tathāgatas' knowledge and vision and the theorists' misapprehension through craving and views, and between right view and the wrong views such as eternalism, etc. Through the following teaching he marks the boundaries thus: "Those views are only their misapprehensions resulting from craving and views; they are not at all similar to the Tathāgatas' knowledge and vision of things as they really are. And this 'feeling of wrong views' is only vacillation due to craving and views; it is not unshakable like the stream-enterer's 'feeling' of right vision."

> That is only the feeling of those who do not know and do not see; that is only the agitation and vacillation of those who are immersed in craving.

CY. (This is the paraphrase:) "The satisfaction of views (*diṭṭhi-assāda*), the pleasure of views (*diṭṭhisukha*), the feeling of views (*diṭṭhivedayita*), on account of which those recluses and brahmins on four grounds joyously proclaim the self and the world to be eternal—that is only the feeling of those who do not know and do not see the true nature of dhammas as it really is (*yathābhūtaṃ dhammānaṃ sabhāvaṃ ajānantānaṃ apassantānaṃ vedayitaṃ*); it is only the feeling of those who are entirely immersed in craving." And "it is only the agitation and vacillation" (*paritassitavipphanditameva*): it is only vacillation, shaking, and wavering, caused by the agitation of craving and views. Like a stake planted in a heap of chaff, it is not unshakable like the vision of a stream-enterer. The same method applies to all the views.

N.Sub.Cy. "The satisfaction of views": the satisfaction which serves as a condition for the view. "Pleasure of views" and "feeling of views" are synonyms for the same.

Sub.Cy. Though it is said in the commentary, "who do not know and do not see the true nature of dhammas as it really is," the theorists do not form a wrong adherence simply because they do not know the true nature of conditioned dhammas. This general explanation conceals a distinction. When this distinction is brought to light the following interpretation is made: "Who do not know and do not see": who do not know and do not see as it really is: "This standpoint—that the self and the world are eternal—thus assumed and thus misapprehended, leads to such a future destination, to such a state in the world beyond." So too, (the phrase "who do not know and do not see" may be taken to mean): who do now know and do not see as they really are the origin [and passing away, etc.] of that feeling on account of which, in their craving for feeling, they cling to such a speculative view. In this way he shows that whereas the Tathāgatas, through the unobstructed knowledge of their universal eye, know and see this matter as it really is, the theorists only misapprehend through craving and views. Thus this teaching was given in order to mark the boundaries between the two (i.e., between the Buddha and the theorists).

"Feeling" (*vedayita*): the affective tone of experiencing (*anubhavana*) which accompanies the proclamation of the view "the self and the world are eternal" and is experienced (along with) that view. This feeling, the bait of the round (*vaṭṭāmisa*), is fickle, for it arises as the exhilaration of one who is pierced by the thorns of craving and views; it does not persist with a steady tone like the pleasurable feeling of the noble paths and fruits.

Or, as an alternative explanation (for the present section): having analyzed the sixty-two speculative views according to their specific causes (*visesakāraṇa*), the present teaching is now undertaken to show their common cause (*avisesakāraṇa*); for feeling, ignorance, and craving are causes common to all the views. Therein, "that" (*tadapi*), i.e., that proclamation that the self and the world are eternal, is made by those who do not know and do not see as they really are the three types of feeling—pleasant, painful, and neither-pleasant-nor-painful feeling—as suffering, a thorn, and impermanent, respectively, and who do not know and see all feeling without exception in terms of its origin, passing away, satisfaction, unsatisfactoriness, and escape.[138]

138. See SN 36:5–6.

And then, because it originates through the longing for pleasure, etc., in those who, through their involvement in craving, are "immersed in craving," this proclamation is only the vacillation and shaking of views caused by the agitation of craving. Or it is the mere active expression (*copanappattimatta*) of the view through the doors of body and speech, as when it is said: "If there is no self, who experiences feeling?" The point is that there is no eternal dhamma to be proclaimed as such (as eternal) through that view. This same method should be applied to the doctrine of partial-eternalism, etc.

B. Conditioned by Contact
(*Phassapaccayavāra*)

118. that is conditioned by contact.

CY. This teaching is undertaken in order to show the succession of conditions (*paramparapaccaya*). By this the Master shows that the satisfaction, pleasure, or feeling of views on account of which these recluses and brahmins joyously proclaim the self and the world to be eternal, is a palpitation (*pariphandita*) of craving and views, a feeling conditioned by contact (*vedayitaṃ phassapaccayā ti dasseti*).

Sub.Cy. "The succession of conditions" (*paramparapaccaya*): this teaching is undertaken in order to elicit the succession of conditions thus: "These speculative views occur due to the agitation of craving. Craving is conditioned by feeling, and feeling is conditioned by contact."

[If so, what is the purpose of showing the succession of conditions? The purpose is to communicate a difference in meaning, thus:] Just as the dhamma of proclamation, i.e., the view itself, and the dhammas which condition the view, arise only through their respective conditions and do not arise without them, so too the dhammas about which the proclamation is made—i.e., material form, feeling, etc.—(arise only through conditions and do not arise without them). There is no eternal self or world at all to be found here. [The point is that the "palpitation of craving and views," i.e., the feeling that functions as the condition for craving, which in turn functions as the cause for the view, is conditioned by contact.]

That they can experience that feeling without contact—such a case is impossible.

CY. This statement is made in order to show the strength of the condition (i.e., of contact) for the feeling of views. Just as a prop is a strong condition for bolstering up a dilapidated house, which would not be able to stand if it were not bolstered up by the prop, in the same way contact is a strong condition for feeling, and without contact there would be no "feeling of views."

Sub.Cy. The "feeling of views" is the feeling that functions as condition for the view. This feeling is produced through its own conditions, among which contact is the chief.

"The strength of the condition": feeling sometimes arises without the eye-base, etc., and without some of its concomitant dhammas, but it can never arise without contact; thus contact is a strong cause for feeling. For if a sense object is within range, but the act of consciousness does not contact the object, the latter will not become an object condition (*ārammaṇapaccaya*) for consciousness. Thus contact is a special condition for all the concomitant dhammas (in an act of consciousness). Hence when the Exalted One analyzed an act of consciousness (in the Dhammasaṅgaṇī), he brought forth contact first. But it is the foundation especially for feeling.

C. Exposition of the Round
(*Diṭṭhigatikādhiṭṭhānavaṭṭakathā*)

144. All these recluses and brahmins experience these feelings only by repeated contacts through the six bases of contact.

CY. In the present passage the Exalted One lumps together all the "feelings of views." Why? In order to relate them once more to contact. How? By the statement: "All these recluses and brahmins experience these feelings only by repeated contacts through the six bases of contact." The six bases of contact are the eye as a base of contact; the ear, nose, tongue, body, and mind as bases of contact.

The word "base" (*āyatana*) occurs in the texts with four meanings: (1) place of origin (*sañjāti*); (2) place of convergence (*samosaraṇa*); (3) cause (*kāraṇa*); and (4) as a mere designation of place (*paṇṇattimatta*).

(1) In the statement: "Kamboja is the base for horses, the southern region the base for cows," it signifies place of origin.

(2) "The birds resort to that delightful base"—here it signifies place of convergence.

(3) "When there is a basis (for a meditative attainment)"—here it signifies cause.

(4) "They lived in leaf-huts in a forest base"—here it is a mere designation of place.

In the present case, the first three meanings apply. For the pentad of contact[139] originates in and converges upon the sense faculties, and these latter are its cause; thus they are called "bases." Here, the bases of contact, etc., are mentioned in order to show the succession of conditions, making contact the starting point and arranging the teaching under the heading of contact, in accordance with the method of the following passage: "Dependent on the eye and visible forms, eye-consciousness arises. The meeting of the three is contact," etc. (SN 12:43)[140]

Sub.Cy. "Relating feeling to contact" means showing the conditioning role of contact thus: "The experiencing of the six objects through the six internal bases invariably occurs by reason of the six types of contact."

"The meeting (*saṅgati*) of the three": contact is to be apprehended as the meeting of the three factors—object (*visaya*), faculty (*indriya*), and consciousness (*viññāṇa*). Thus it has concurrence (*sannipāta*) as its manifestation.

"In accordance with the method of the following passage": although other concomitant dhammas [such as perception] are also found, in the sutta cited the teaching is set up under the heading of contact in order to show contact as the principal cause for feeling. In the same way, here in the Brahmajāla Sutta, when it is said "by repeated contacts through the six bases of contact," contact is made the starting point of the sequence beginning "with contact as condition, feeling,"

---

139. *Phassapañcamakā dhammā*: consciousness, feeling, perception, volition, and contact. The name derives from the last member.

140. In this sutta the contact resulting from the meeting of object, faculty, and consciousness is made the starting point for the rest of the usual formula of dependent origination.

etc., in order to show the succession of conditions by teaching dependent origination as extending into the future (*aparanta-paṭiccasamuppāda*).

CY. Although the statement "by repeated contacts through the six bases of contact" gives the impression that the six bases themselves exercise the function of contacting, this would be a wrong interpretation. For it is not the bases that contact the object; rather, it is contact itself that contacts the various objects. The bases are shown as incorporated within contact. Therefore the meaning of the present passage should be understood thus: "All these recluses and brahmins experience the feeling of views by contacting objects such as visible forms, etc., by means of contact originating through the six bases of contact."

Sub.Cy. "It is contact itself that contacts the various objects": contact, though an immaterial dhamma, occurs as though contacting (or touching, *phusanto viya hoti*), i.e., it occurs in the mode of contacting without adhering to the object on any one side. Hence it is said: "Contact has contacting as its characteristic, the act of impingement as its function."[141] The bases themselves do not exercise the function of contacting, but they are shown as possessing this function by an attributive expression, as when it is said: "The beds made a sound." They are "incorporated in contact," included within contact, set up metaphorically in the role of contact. For a metaphor (*upacāra*) is a mere expression, and not the basis for a derivation of meaning.

With feeling as condition, there arises in them craving

CY. "Feeling" is here the feeling originating through the six bases of contact. It is a condition for craving—divided into craving for visible forms, etc.—under the crest of decisive-support condition.[142] Thus it is said: "With feeling as condition there arises in them craving." Craving in turn is a condition for the four types of clinging (*upādāna*) under the crests of decisive-support (*upanissaya*) and co-nascence (*sahājāta*). Clinging is a condition for existence (*bhava*) in the same way. Existence is a condition for birth under the crest of decisive-support. "Birth" here is the five aggregates together with their alterations (*savikārā pañcakkandhā*). Birth is a condition for aging and death, and

141. Vism 14.134.

for sorrow, etc., under the crest of decisive-support. This is a brief explanation. The detailed explanation can be found in the discussion of dependent origination in the *Visuddhimagga* (ch. XVII). But what is given here is sufficient.

Sub.Cy. Feeling is, in brief, sixfold, by way of the six types of contact that function as its respective conditions: i.e., feeling born of eye-contact, down to feeling born of mind-contact. In detail, it is divided into a hundred and eight kinds in accordance with the hundred-and-eightfold method.

N.Sub.Cy. The hundred and eight kinds obtain thus: feeling becomes sixfold according to contact. These each divide into three types according to object of inspection (*upavicāra,* whether desirable, undesirable, or neutral), and again these eighteen are divided into two depending on the support (whether an internal or external object). And finally each of these thirty-six divide into three according to time—past, present or future. The dwellers of the Mahāvihāra[143] say that like consciousness, mentality-materiality, and the six-fold base, the contact and feeling included in a single continuity, whether as condition or conditionally arisen, should (in the context of the dependent origination formula) be recognized only as resultant. Others, however, say that whenever contact and feeling function as a condition, in one way or another, they cannot be excluded, and therefore that all contact and feeling should be recognized (as included by the terms "contact" and "feeling" in the dependent origination formula).

Sub.Cy. Craving is, in brief, of six classes: craving for visible forms, etc., down to craving for mental objects. In detail it is of a hundred and eight types.[144]

---

142. *Upanissayakoṭiyā paccayo.* The word *koṭi,* here translated "crest," is used technically in Pāḷi commentarial literature to signify that the term it follows is the principal member of a group of factors all implied by the key term. Thus "decisive-support," though the primary condition, is only one of a group of conditions relating feeling to craving, as the Sub. Cy. will show. The conditions are selected from the twenty-fourfold scheme of the Paṭṭhāna. Their full application to dependent origination is given in Vism XVII. Much of the following discussion will be unintelligible to one not familiar with that chapter.

143. The "Great Monastery," the ancient seat of Theravāda orthodoxy in Anurādhapura. It was here that Buddhaghosa edited the commentaries.

144. See Vism 17.234–235.

"Under the crest of decisive-support condition (relating feeling to craving)." *Query:* Why is only the decisive-support condition brought forth here? Aren't pleasant feeling and neither-pleasant-nor-painful feeling conditions for craving in a fourfold way: by way of simple-object (*ārammaṇa-matta*), object-predominance (*ārammaṇādhipati*), object-decisive-support (*ārammaṇūpanissaya*), and natural decisive-support (*pakatūpanissaya*)? And is not painful feeling a condition in a twofold way: by way of simple-object and natural decisive-support?

Reply: This is true. But all of those are already comprised in the decisive-support condition.

Query: It is correct to include the object-decisive-support within decisive-support, for both have the common nature of decisive-support. But how can the simple-object and object-predominance conditions be included therein?

Reply: Because they are included within object-decisive-support, since they all have the common nature of the object. But they are not included within natural-decisive-support. In order to express the aforementioned fact, the commentary does not say simply that feeling is a decisive-support condition, but that it is a condition under the crest of decisive-support condition.

"Craving is a condition for the four types of clinging": that is, for clinging to sense pleasures, clinging to views, clinging to rules and observances, and clinging to a doctrine of self.

Query: Is not craving itself the same as clinging to sense pleasures? [If so, how can one thing be a condition for itself?][145]

Reply: This is true. But one may understand the distinction between them as follows. In the present context, weak craving is stated as craving itself, and powerful craving as clinging to sense pleasures. Or else, craving is the longing for an object that has not yet been acquired, like a thief stretching out his hand in the dark; clinging is the grasping of an object that one has obtained, like the thief grasping the treasure reached with his hand. Craving is opposed to fewness of wishes, clinging to contentment. Craving is the root of the suffering involved in searching for what one needs, clinging is the root of the suffering involved in protecting one's acquisitions.

---

145. Both craving and clinging to sense pleasures ultimately reduce to the same mental factor, namely, greed (*lobha*); hence the question arises how a single mental factor can condition itself.

N.Sub.Cy. These are the distinctions the teacher Dhammapāla shows by drawing upon the explanations of various teachers. But the orthodox explanation, as given in the *Visuddhimagga*, is that previous craving (=craving) is a condition for subsequent craving (=clinging to sense pleasures), since the latter becomes firm by the influence of previous craving, which acts as its decisive-support condition.

Sub.Cy. Craving is a condition for non-co-nascent clinging under the crest of decisive-support; for the other (i.e., co-nascent) clinging under the crest of co-nascence.[146] Herein, craving is a condition for the proximate clinging[147] as a proximity, contiguity, proximate-decisive-support, absence, disappearance, and repetition condition; for the non-proximate clinging as a decisive-support condition; and when it becomes the object of clinging, as either an object-predominance and object-decisive-support condition, or as a simple-object condition. When it is said "under the crest of decisive-support condition," all of this is included within decisive-support. Since one who, through craving, finds satisfaction in visible forms, etc., acquires a thirst for sense pleasures, craving is the decisive-support for clinging to sense pleasures. And since one who is confused about visible forms, etc., takes hold of the wrong view that "there is no (fruit of) giving," etc., while one desiring liberation from saṃsāra takes what is not the path to purity to be the path or adopts a personality view (*sakkāyadiṭṭhi*) which recognizes a self and self's property in the five aggregates, craving is also the decisive support for the other three types of clinging.[148] And finally, craving is a condition for co-nascent clinging by way of co-nascence, mutuality, support, association, presence,

---

146. Since craving is the same mental factor as clinging to sense pleasures, the former can never condition the latter contemporaneously as a co-nascence condition, but only across an interval of time, as a decisive-support condition. But since the other three types of clinging reduce to the mental factor of views (*diṭṭhi*), which can co-exist with craving, craving may be either a decisive-support or a co-nascence condition for these three types. The decisive-support relation is found when earlier craving results in the clinging to a certain view at a subsequent time; the co-nascence relation when craving and wrong view are simultaneously present in the same act of consciousness.

147. *Anantarassa,* i.e., for the clinging contained in the immediately following act of consciousness.

148. These phrases are allusions to the clinging to views, to rules and observances, and to a doctrine of self, respectively.

non-disappearance, and root cause conditions. All this is implied when it is said "under the crest of co-nascence."

"Clinging is a condition for existence in the same way": that is, under the crest of decisive-support and under the crest of co-nascence. "Existence" is kamma-existence (*kammabhava*) and rebirth-existence (*upapattibhava*). Herein, "kamma-existence" is all kamma that leads to existence, i.e., volition and its concomitants. "Rebirth-existence" consists in the nine states of existence.[149] The fourfold clinging is a condition for rebirth-existence as a natural-decisive-support, since it is the cause and concomitant of kamma-existence, which is in turn the cause of rebirth-existence. But at a time when kamma is taken as object, the clinging to sense pleasures co-nascent with the kamma becomes an object condition for rebirth-existence.[150] The co-nascent clinging is a condition for co-nascent kamma-existence in numerous ways: as co-nascence, mutuality, support, association, presence, and non-disappearance condition, and also as a root cause and path condition. For the non-co-nascent [and proximate] kamma-existence, clinging is a proximity, contiguity, proximate-decisive-support, absence, disappearance, and repetition condition; for the other [i.e., the non-proximate] it is a natural-decisive-support condition. At times of insight comprehension, etc., it is an object condition. Having incorporated the proximity condition, etc., in the decisive-support condition, and the co-nascence condition, etc., in the co-nascence condition, it is said "under the crest of decisive-support and under the crest of co-nascence."

"Existence is a condition for birth": here, it is kamma-existence alone, and not rebirth-existence, that is intended by "existence," for kamma-existence alone is a condition for birth. Rebirth-existence is birth itself, since the latter consists in the aggregates that are first produced at the initial moment of rebirth. Thus it is said: "'Birth' here

149. The nine states of existence are obtained by dividing the realms of existence into three divisions according to three alternative methods: (1) sense-sphere, fine-material, and immaterial existence; (2) five-constituent, one-constituent, and four-constituent existence; and (3) percipient, non-percipient, and neither percipient nor non-percipient existence.

150. This refers to the transition from one life to the next, when a previous kamma becomes the object of the last thought-process before death, and then the object of the rebirth-consciousness in the next life.

is the five aggregates together with their alterations." The phrase "with their alterations" means: with their alterations due to the alteration of production. Those aggregates are the rebirth-existence itself, which cannot be its own cause. Kamma-existence is a condition for rebirth-existence [that is, for birth] as a kamma condition and decisive-support condition. Thus he says: "existence is a condition for birth under the crest of decisive-support." And since aging and death arise only when there is birth, not in its absence, and since sorrow, etc., arise in a fool afflicted by aging and death, etc., birth is the condition for aging and death, etc.

CY. When he gives an exposition of the round, the Exalted One sometimes discusses it under the heading of ignorance, as when he says: "No first point of ignorance can be discerned, bhikkhus, before which there was no ignorance and after which it arose. And though this is said, bhikkhus, nevertheless it can be discerned that ignorance has a specific condition" (AN 10:61). Sometimes he discusses it under the heading of craving: "No first point of craving for existence can be discerned, bhikkhus, etc., … nevertheless craving for existence has a specific condition" (AN 10:62). And sometimes he discusses it under the heading of the view of existence (*bhavadiṭṭhi*): "No first point of the view of existence can be discerned, bhikkhus, etc…. nevertheless the view of existence has a specific condition."[151] Here he discusses it under the heading of views. Having first explained the views that arise through lust for feeling, he discusses dependent origination as rooted in feeling.[152] In this way he shows: "These theorists, holding these views, roam and wander here and there, back and forth, through the three realms of existence, the four modes of origin, the five destinations, the seven stations of consciousness, and the nine abodes of beings. Like an ox yoked to a mill-wheel, like a dog chained to a post, or like a ship tossed about in a storm, they revolve in the round of suffering and are not even able to lift their heads up out of the round."

N.Sub.Cy. In this passage, the commentator shows the reason, together with citations, why the Exalted One discusses dependent origination in the text only by the single section showing how feeling becomes the cause for views. Thereby he shows the purport to be as follows: "The Exalted One, giving an exposition of the round,

151. No such sutta has been traced in the Sutta Piṭaka.
152. *Vedanāmūlakaṃ paṭiccasamuppādaṃ kathesi.*

discusses it under one of the three headings—ignorance, craving, or views. Here, discussing it under the heading of views, he explains dependent origination by a single section rooted in feeling in order to show that feeling is a powerful cause for views."

"No first point of ignorance can be discerned": that is, "because no initial boundary exists, not even my unimpeded knowledge of omniscience can discern a first boundary of ignorance of which it can be said: 'Ignorance first arose in the time of such and such a perfectly enlightened Buddha or of such and such a world-ruling monarch. It did not exist before that." Admittedly, ignorance is said to lack an initial boundary. "Nevertheless," though it is said to lack an initial boundary in terms of temporal determination (*kālaniyāmena*), "ignorance has a specific condition," that is, ignorance arises with the five hindrances as its condition. And therefore, a first point of ignorance can be discerned in terms of the order of dhammas (*dhammaniyāmena*). For it is said in the same sutta: "And what is the nutriment for ignorance? The reply is: the five hindrances."

"Craving for existence" (*bhavataṇhā*): craving that functions as the fetter of existence (*bhavasaṃyojana*). Its specific condition is ignorance. For it is said in the sutta: "And what is the nutriment for craving for existence? The reply is: ignorance."

"The view of existence": the eternalist view. Its specific condition is feeling.

Query: Isn't it true that the views have already been discussed? What purpose, then, does this exposition of dependent origination serve?

Reply: This exposition of dependent origination in direct order is the exposition of the round. By means of this discussion the Exalted One shows that so long as these theorists do not relinquish their wrong view, for so long they are driven through the succession of conditions and remain submerged in the round.

D. The Ending of the Round
(*Vivaṭṭakathādi*)

145. When, bhikkhus, a bhikkhu understands as they really are the origin and passing away of the six bases of contact, their satisfaction, unsatisfactoriness, and the escape from them, then he understands what transcends all these views.

CY. Having discussed the round in terms of the theorists, the Exalted One now shows the ending of the round, expressing it in terms of a bhikkhu devoted to meditation.

"The six bases of contact": the same six bases of contact as those on account of which the theorists, experiencing feelings by means of contact, revolve in the round. The origin, etc., of the six bases of contact should be understood in accordance with the method stated in the meditation subject of feeling, thus: "Through the origination of ignorance, the eye originates," etc.[153] But while it was said above that feeling originates and ceases through the origination and cessation of contact, here it should be noted that the eye and the other physical sense bases originate and cease through the origination and cessation of nutriment (*āhāra*). But the mind-base originates and ceases through the origination and cessation of mentality-materiality (*nāmarūpa*).[154]

Sub.Cy. "Nutriment" is edible nutriment. Since edible nutriment is a condition, as nutriment condition, for this body, it follows that edible nutriment is a condition fortifying [the physical sense bases such as the eye] that originate through kamma.[155]

CY. "He understands what transcends all these views": the theorist knows only his view, but this bhikkhu understands these views and also what transcends these views, namely, virtue, concentration, wisdom, and emancipation, culminating in arahatship. Who understands this? The canker-free arahat understands, the non-returner, the once-returner, the stream-enterer, the bhikkhu who is a

---

153. See above, pp. 145ff.

154. The mind-base (*manāyatana*) is the same as consciousness, which is conditioned by both mentality and materiality together.

155. The sensitive material of the sense organs, called *pasādarūpa*, is originated by past kamma, but once arisen is maintained and strengthened by physical food.

learned master of the scriptures, and the bhikkhu who has aroused insight. But the teaching is concluded with its culmination in arahatship.

Sub.Cy. Although the stream-enterer, etc., understand these as they really are, the teaching is concluded with its culmination in arahatship in order to show the supremacy of the arahat's understanding. And by the above passage of the sutta, the Exalted One shows the liberating character of the Dhamma together with the Saṅgha's practice of the good path. For when the commentary, after asking: "Who understands?," replies "The canker-free arahat," etc. the Bhikkhu Saṅgha is shown.

146. All (those recluses and brahmins) are trapped in this net with its sixty-two cases. Whenever they emerge, they emerge caught within this net, they emerge trapped and contained within this very net.

CY. Having discussed the ending of the round, the Exalted One now expounds the above statement in order to show that there are no theorists free from the net of this teaching.

"Whenever they emerge" (*ummujjamānā*), etc. This is meant: "Whether they sink downwards or rise upwards, they sink and rise caught within the net of my teaching, contained within the net of my teaching. There are no theorists not included herein."

Sub.Cy. "Sink downwards" by way of rebirth in the plane of misery, "rise upwards" by way of a favorable realm of rebirth. So too, the two terms may be interpreted by way of a limited plane and an exalted plane of existence, by way of sticking fast and going too far, and by way of settled views about the past and settled views about the future, respectively.

CY. The application of the simile of the fisherman is as follows. The Exalted One is like the fisherman; the teaching is like the net; the ten-thousandfold world system is like the small pool of water; the theorists are like the sizable creatures. Just as the fisherman, standing on the shore surveying the net, sees all the sizable creatures trapped within his net, so the Exalted One sees all the theorists caught within the net of this teaching.

147. The body of the Tathāgata, bhikkhus, stands with the leash that bound it to existence cut. As long as his body stands, gods and men shall see him. But with the breakup of the body and the exhaustion of the life-faculty, gods and men shall see him no more.

CY. Having shown that because their views are all included in these sixty-two views all the theorists are included in the net of this teaching, the Exalted One makes the above statement in order to show that he himself is not contained anywhere.

"The leash that bound it to existence" (*bhavanetti*): they lead by this (*etena nayanti*), thus it is called a leash (*netti*). This is the name for a rope with which they drag an animal along after tying it around his neck. Here it is craving for existence (*bhavataṇhā*) that is intended by the word "leash," since such craving is similar to a leash. For craving for existence, tied around the neck of the multitude, leads and drags the multitude to one realm of existence or another. But for the Tathāgata, the "leash of existence" has been cut off with the sword of the path of arahatship; thus his body stands "with the leash that bound it to existence cut."

"The exhaustion of the life-faculty": when he has reached the state where there is no further rebirth-linkage (*puna appaṭisandhikabhāva*). "Gods and men shall see him no more:" he will go to the indescribable state (*apaṇṇattikabhāvaṃ gamissati*).

N.Sub.Cy. "He himself is not contained anywhere": through his skillfulness in teaching, he shows that he himself is not confined anywhere in the realms of existence, the places where the theorists emerge and sink.

"The indescribable state": the state wherein he is indescribable by any description referring to something presently existing. But with reference to the past, the designation "Tathāgata" continues up to the disappearance of the Dispensation, and even beyond that, to the times when other Buddhas arise in the world, as now it is used in reference to the Buddha Vipassī, etc. Thus he will say: "It will be a mere expression." "Body" (*kāya*): individuality (*attabhāva*), i.e., the aggregation of material and immaterial dhammas.

CY. The application of the mango simile is as follows. The body of the Tathāgata is like the mango tree. The craving that occurred in the past supported by that body is like the great stalk growing on the tree. Like the bunch of mangoes connected to the stalk, numbering five, twelve, or eighteen fruits, are the five aggregates, twelve bases, and eighteen elements connected with craving, which would have been produced in the future if craving were to continue to exist. But just as, when the stalk is cut, all those mangoes follow along with and accompany the stalk, and with the cutting off of the stalk are also cut off, in the same way all those dhammas—the five aggregates, twelve bases, and eighteen elements—that would have arisen in the future if the stalk of the "leash of existence" (i.e., craving for existence) were not cut off, all follow along with and accompany the leash of existence; when the leash is cut, they also are cut.

When the tree is gradually withered and killed by contact with a poisonous *maṇḍuka* thorn, no one sees the tree anymore, but people say: "In this place such and such a tree stood," using the word "tree" as a mere expression (*vohāramatta*). In the same way, when the body of the Tathāgata, brought into contact with the noble paths, is gradually withered and broken up through the exhaustion of the moisture of craving, with the breakup of the body and the exhaustion of the life-faculty, gods and men shall see the Tathāgata no more. When people say: "This is the Dispensation of such and such a Master," (the word "Tathāgata") will be a mere expression. Thus the Exalted One concludes the teaching by bringing it to a climax with the nibbāna-element without residue (*anupādisesanibbānadhātu*).

148. **CY.** When the Exalted One had finished speaking this sutta, the Elder Ānanda, who had been attending to the entire sutta from the beginning thought: "The Exalted One, elucidating the power of the Buddha, has not given a title to the sutta he has just expounded. Let me, then, ask him to give it a title." Thus he said to the Exalted One: "What, venerable sir, is the title of this exposition of the Dhamma?" The Master replied:

> Ānanda, you may remember this exposition of the dhamma as the Net of the Good, as the Net of the Dhamma, as the Supreme Net, as the Net of Views. You may remember it also as the Incomparable Victory in Battle.

CY. This is the interpretation of the meaning: "Ānanda, because the good pertaining to the present world (*idh'attha*) and the good pertaining to the world beyond (*par'attha*) have been analyzed in this exposition of the Dhamma, you should remember it as the 'Net of the Good' (*atthajāla*). And because many threads of Dhamma have been discussed here, you should remember it as the 'Net of the Dhamma' (*dhammajāla*). And because the knowledge of omniscience, called 'Brahma' in the sense of supreme (*seṭṭha*), has been analyzed here, you should remember it as the 'Supreme Net' (*brahmajāla*). And because the sixty-two views have been analyzed here, you should remember it as the 'Net of Views' (*diṭṭhijāla*). And because, after hearing this exposition, one is able to crush Māra—i.e., the deity Māra, the Māra of the aggregates, the Māra of death, and the Māra of the defilements—therefore you should remember it as the 'Incomparable Victory in Battle' (*anuttara saṅgāmavijaya*)."

Sub.Cy. Another method of interpretation is as follows. *Atthajāla* is the "Net of Meaning" because it is perfect in meaning.[156] *Dhammajāla* is the "Net of the Dhamma" because it is perfect in phrasing (*byañjana*) and because it expounds blameless dhammas such as virtue, etc. *Brahmajāla* is the "Supreme Net" because it analyzes the paths, fruits, and nibbāna, which are called "Brahma" in the sense of supreme. *Diṭṭhijāla* is the "Net of Views" because it demonstrates right view by elucidating emptiness through the refutation of wrong views. And it is the "Incomparable Victory in Battle" because it provides the means for crushing the doctrines of the sectarians.

149. Thus spoke the Exalted One

CY. By speaking this entire sutta from the end of the introduction up to the concluding words "the Incomparable Victory in Battle," the Exalted One revealed his supremely deep knowledge of omniscience wherein the wisdom of others cannot find a footing, and he dispelled the great darkness of speculative views just as the sun dispels the darkness of the night.

---

156. The word *attha* can mean "meaning" as well as "good" or "goal." The Dhamma, or doctrine as expounded, is said to be perfect (*paripuṇṇa*) insofar as it is "perfect in meaning," the meaning being also the good or goal towards which the doctrine points, and "perfect in phrasing," that is, in the formulated expression of that meaning.

And while this exposition was being spoken, the ten-thousandfold world system shook.

CY. "Ten-thousandfold world system": a world system numbering ten thousand world-spheres (*cakkavāḷa*). It should not be thought that the world system shook only at the conclusion of the sutta. For it is said "while it was being spoken" (a present participle). Therefore, it should be understood that while these sixty-two speculative views were being taught and unravelled, it shook on sixty-two occasions, namely, at the conclusion of the exposition of each of the sixty-two views.

Herein, there are eight causes for an earthquake: a disturbance of the elements; the exercise of psychic power; the conception of the bodhisattva; the birth of the bodhisattva; the attainment of enlightenment; the setting in motion of the Wheel of the Dhamma; the relinquishing of the remainder of the life span; and the parinibbāna. But the great earth also shook on eight other occasions: when the bodhisattva made his great renunciation; when he approached the terrace of enlightenment; when he took up dust-heap rags; when he washed them; and on the occasions of teaching the Kālakārāma Sutta (AN 3:65), the Gotamaka Sutta (AN 3:123), the Vessantara Jātaka, and the Brahmajāla Sutta. Herein, on the occasions of the great renunciation and the approaching of the terrace of enlightenment, the earth shook through the power of energy (*viriyabala*). On the occasion of taking up dust-heap rags, the earth shook through being struck by the impact of wonder, as if thinking: "The Exalted One has indeed done something extremely difficult—abandoning dominion over the four great continents and their retinue of two thousand islands, going forth into homelessness, going to the charnel ground, and taking up dust-heap rags!" On the occasions of washing the rags and the teaching of the Vessantara Jātaka, it shook through the shock of surprise. At the teaching of the Kālakārāma Sutta and of the Gotamaka Sutta it shook as a way of bearing witness, as if saying: "I am a witness, Lord."

But in the case of the Brahmajāla Sutta, when the sixty-two speculative views were taught, disentangled, and unravelled, it shook as a sign of applause.

Sub.Cy. It shook at the great renunciation through the power of energy the bodhisattva displayed in relinquishing the glory of a world-ruling monarch. At the approaching of the terrace of enlightenment it shook through the power of his energy endowed with four factors.[157] In the case of washing the dust-rags, some say it shook through the splendor of merit, but the impact of wonder appears to apply here also. In the case of the Vessantara Jātaka, it shook numerous times through the splendor of the merit acquired in the fulfillment of the pāramīs. In the teaching of the Brahmajāla, it shook as a sign of applause, as it did with the setting in motion of the Wheel of the Dhamma and at the time of the councils, etc.

CY. It was not only on these occasions that the earth shook, but also at the time of the three councils,[158] and on the day when the Elder Mahinda the Great, after coming to this island of Sri Lanka, taught the Dhamma while sitting in the Grove of Light. Further, a Piṇḍapātika Elder at the Kalyāṇa Vihāra, after sweeping the terrace around the shrine, sat down there and, filled with rapture by meditating on the Buddha, started to recite this sutta; at the conclusion of the recital, the earth shook to its boundaries of water. Again, east of the Brazen Palace (at Anurādhapura) there is the "Place of the Mango Shoot" (Ambalaṭṭhakaṭṭhāna). There the elders who were reciters of the Dīgha Nikāya sat down and started to recite the Brahmajāla Sutta. At the conclusion of their recitation, the earth shook to its boundaries of water.

Therefore the wise should thoroughly master
The meaning and text of this supreme sutta,
The net of Brahmā proclaimed by the Self-Awakened,
Which caused the earth to tremble many times.
And when they have fully grasped the meaning,
Let them practice it with mind set straight.

The commentary to the Brahmajāla Sutta is concluded.

---

157. See note 15.

158. The three councils convened to rehearse the Dhamma and Discipline at Rājagaha, Vesālī, and Pāṭaliputta.

PART THREE

THE METHOD OF THE EXEGETICAL TREATISES

[**Note:** The basic text here is from the Sub.Cy. Additions from the N.Sub.Cy. are in brackets.]

So far we have explained the meaning of obscure passages in the commentary. Now follows the explanation of the meaning of the text according to the method of the exegetical treatises (*pakaraṇanayena*).[159]

The sutta's meaning will be easily explained and readily intelligible once its origin (*samuṭṭhāna*), purpose (*payojana*), receptacle (*bhājana*), and condensed meanings (*piṇḍattha*) have been elicited. Therefore these points will be treated here first.[160]

[The origin is the source of the teaching (*desanānidāna*).] It is twofold: general and particular. The general origin is likewise twofold: the internal and the external. Herein, the internal general origin is the great compassion (*mahākaruṇā*) of the Exalted One. For, inspired by his great compassion, the Lord of the World decided to teach the Dhamma to the beings to be trained. In reference to this, it is said: "Out of compassion for beings, he surveyed the world with the eye of a Buddha" (MN 26). The great compassion in its three stages can be included here, since the teaching originates from the great compassion for the purpose of conveying beings across the great flood of saṃsāra

159. The treatises referred to are the *Nettippakaraṇa* and the *Peṭakopadesa*. See Introduction, p. 36.

160. The following bracketed passage taken from the N.Sub.Cy. to the present sutta is also found, with minor variations in readings, in the subcommentary to the Majjhima Nikāya.

with the helping hand of the true Dhamma. And like the great compassion, the knowledge of omniscience, the ten powers of knowledge, and the other Buddha-qualities also make up the internal general origin of the teaching. For the Exalted One, knowing as they really are all that is knowable, the propensities and latent tendencies of beings, and the mode in which they should be taught, through his skill in distinguishing causal occasion from non-causal occasion, employs a teaching with variegated methods appropriate for the inclinations of the beings to be trained. The external general origin of the teaching was the request of Brahmā Sahampati together with his retinue of ten thousand great Brahmās (MN 26). For in response to that request, the Lord of the Dhamma silenced the inclination to inaction that had arisen in him when he reviewed the profundity of the Dhamma and became filled with zeal to teach.

The particular origin is also twofold: internal and external. Herein, the internal is the great compassion and knowledge of teaching through which this sutta originated. For though compassion and knowledge, in their common mode, are the general origin of this sutta, in their specific mode they are its particular origin. The external particular origin is the speaking of praise and dispraise referred to in the commentary.] The following facts also contribute to the external particular origin of the sutta: the need to teach the beings to be trained not to give way to jubilation and resentment towards others on account of praise and blame, and to show the dangers these involve; the ignorance of beings about the proper way to behave in the face of praise and blame; their ignorance about the various kinds of virtue that form the object of praise; their ignorance of the unobstructed movement of the omniscient knowledge in the sixty-two standpoints of views and in that which transcends them; and their ignorance of the fact that the Tathāgata cannot be contained anywhere [in any of the realms of existence].

The purpose is likewise twofold: general and particular. Herein, the general purpose of the entire teaching of the Exalted One is the attainment of parinibbāna without clinging, since the entire teaching is permeated by the taste of emancipation. The particular purpose should be understood by the inversion of the external particular origin. Thus the Exalted One undertakes this teaching to instruct the beings to be trained how to maintain equipoise; to abolish the diverse kinds of wrong livelihood such as scheming and talking; to unravel the net of the sixty-two views; to elucidate the law of conditionality under the heading of views; to expound the meditation subject of the four truths by way of the six bases of contact; to exhaust all speculative views without omission; and to reveal his own parinibbāna without clinging.

The receptacle of this teaching is the people to be trained, whose minds are possessed by favoring and opposing because of praise and dispraise, who engage in the diverse kinds of wrong livelihood such as scheming, etc., who are immersed in the mire of the sixty-two views, and who, because they have not fulfilled the aggregate of virtue (and the other stages of training), do not understand the distinguished qualities of a Buddha.

The condensed meaning [is the summarized meaning of the entire sutta or of single passages]. These are some examples:

(1) By the words "you should not give way to resentment," etc., the bhikkhus are enjoined to display the conduct of recluses in accordance with their vows; to maintain patience and meekness; to apply themselves to the development of the sublime abodes (*brahmavihāra*); to harmonize faith and wisdom; to apply mindfulness and clear comprehension; to perfect their powers of reflection and meditative development; to abandon the obsessions and latent tendencies; to practice for the welfare of themselves and for the welfare of others; and to remain untainted by the vacillations of the world.

(2) By the words "abstains from the destruction of life," etc., the purification of virtue is shown; together with this are also shown endowment with shame and moral dread; the possession of loving kindness and compassion; the abandoning of transgressions; the abandoning by factor-substitution;[161] the abandoning of defilement by wrong conduct; the perfecting of the three abstinences;[162] becoming dear, agreeable, and worthy of reverence; the obtaining of gains, honor, and fame; the foundation of serenity and insight; the diminution of the unwholesome roots; the planting of the wholesome roots;

---

161. *Tadaṅgappahāna*: by observing a precept, one factor of moral conduct is accepted which eclipses the particular evil deed the precept prohibits.

162. *Viratittaya*: the three abstinences of right speech, right action, and right livelihood. These are the three morality factors of the Noble Eightfold Path, which in the Abhidhamma method of mental analysis become three distinct mental factors.

remoteness from both kinds of harm (to oneself and to others); self-confidence in assemblies; abiding in diligence; being unassailable by others; and freedom from remorse.

(3) By the words "deep, (difficult to see)," etc., the following is indicated: the depth of the Dhamma, which does not allow any foothold (to those outside the Dispensation) and only becomes manifest at rare intervals over immeasurable aeons; the near impossibility of penetrating it through direct experience even by subtle intellects; its being unachievable by inferential knowledge, i.e., by drawing reasonable conclusions; its tranquilizing of all distress; its peaceful nature; the beauty of its consummation; its abolishing of worldly complacency; its leading to the attainment of the supreme state; its being the range of knowledge of things as they really are; the subtlety of its specific nature; and the demonstration of great wisdom.

(4) By the passages dealing with the various views, in brief, the views of eternalism and annihilationism are shown. The following are also shown: sticking fast and going too far,[163] engagement and bondage, wrong adherence, the practice of a wrong path, inverted assumptions, misapprehension and misappropriation, views concerning the past and views concerning the future, views of existence and views of non-existence, the occurrence of craving and ignorance, views of the finitude and infinity of the world, the entering upon the two extremes, and the classification (of views) into the categories of canker, deadly flood, bond, defilement, knot, fetter, and clinging.

(5) By the words "the origin of feeling," etc., the following is shown: the understanding and penetration of the Four Noble Truths, the abandoning through suppression and eradication, the disappearance of craving and ignorance, the discernment of the basis and structure of real dhammas, the acquisition of scriptural learning and spiritual achievement, practice for the welfare of oneself and others, the attainment of the threefold knowledge, the establishing of mindfulness and clear comprehension, the harmonization of faith and wisdom, the proper balancing of energy and serenity, and accomplishment in serenity and insight.

---

163. Eternalist views "stick fast" (*olīyanti*) because they adhere to impermanent substanceless dhammas as a permanent self; annihilationist views "go too far" (*atidhāvanti*) because they declare the annihilation of a non-existent self. See It 2:22.

(6) By the words "who do not know and do not see" ignorance is shown; by the words "the agitation and vacillation of those immersed in craving" craving is shown; and by both expressions the hindrances and fetters, the non-termination of the beginningless round of saṃsāra, the set of conditions inherited from the past and the set extending into the future,[164] the analysis of the causes by way of the past and the present,[165] the mutual support of ignorance and craving through their mutually intertwined occurrence, and their obstruction to emancipation by wisdom and emancipation by mind are respectively shown.

(7) By the words "that too is conditioned by contact," signifying that the proclamation of eternalism, etc., occurs in dependence on conditions, the notion of permanence in dhammas is rejected and the truth of impermanence established. This phrase further refutes the notion of an agent existing as an ultimate reality, discloses the actual nature of dhammas, reveals the truth of emptiness, and indicates conditions and characteristics capable of functioning without an initiating agent.

(8) By the words "Tathāgata's body stands with the leash that bound it to existence cut" he shows the Exalted One's achievement of abandoning (all defilements), his mastery over knowledge and emancipation, his completion of the threefold training (in virtue, concentration, and wisdom), the distinction between the two elements of nibbāna,[166] the fulfillment of the four foundations,[167] and his transcendence over all the realms of existence, modes of origin, etc.

And from the entire sutta, the following ideas may be elicited: the Exalted One's equipoise under desirable and undesirable circumstances; his establishing others in this quality; the exposition of the pair of qualities that form the foundation of wholesome dhammas;

---

164. In the twelve-factored formula of dependent origination, the factors from ignorance through feeling are the inheritance from the past, and the factors from craving on are the extension into the future.

165. In the same formula, ignorance is the principal factor among the past conditions, craving the principal factor among the present conditions.

166. The nibbāna-element with residue (*sa-upādisesanibbānadhātu*), i.e., the nibbāna experienced by the arahat while alive, and the nibbāna-element without residue (*anupādisesanibbānadhātu*), the nibbāna attained with the arahat's final passing away.

167. Of truth, relinquishment, peace, and wisdom. See MN 140.11.

instruction in the threefold training; the four types of individuals, i.e., the one who torments himself, etc. (MN 51.8); the four kinds of kamma, dark and bright, with their results (MN 57); the exposition of the domain of the four boundless states;[168] the comprehension of the five facts—origin, (passing away, satisfaction, unsatisfactoriness, and escape)—as they really are; the six principles of fraternal behavior;[169] the ten qualities that provide one with a refuge;[170] etc.

I. The Sixteen Modes of Conveyance

1. The Mode of Conveying a Teaching (*desanāhāra*)

The five aggregates of clinging that function as the foundation for views about the self and the world: indicated by the reference to feelings and bases of contact: these five aggregates of clinging, except for craving, are the truth of suffering (*dukkhasacca*).

Craving is the truth of the origin of suffering (*samudayasacca*). This is indicated in the text by the term "agitation" (*paritassanā*), is referred to in its own nature by the phrases "immersed in craving" and "with feeling as condition, craving arises," and is again implied by the expressions "the origin (of feelings)" and "the leash of existence." This is the treatment according to the sutta method.

According to the Abhidhamma method, the truth of the origin is kamma and defilements, indicated in brief by any words signifying mundane wholesome or unwholesome dhammas; e.g., by the words "resentment" and "exultation," by the phrases "by means of ardor" and "corrupted by mind," by all terms signifying views, by the mentioning of wholesome and unwholesome, realms of existence, sorrow, etc., and by the term "origin" in its different contexts.[171]

The non-occurrence of both (kamma and defilements) is the truth of cessation (*nirodhasacca*). It is indicated in the text by the

168. Identical with the four *brahmavihāras*.

169. Loving acts of body, speech, and thought, common views and virtues, and the sharing of material possessions. See MN 48.6.

170. *Nāthakaraṇadhammā*. See AN 10:17.

171. According to Vbh 4.2, the origin of suffering, in its widest application, includes all wholesome and unwholesome kamma as well as the totality of unabandoned defilements which maintain the continuity of saṃsāra.

expositions of the passing away of feelings and the escape from them, by the phrase "he has realized within himself the state of perfect peace," and by the expression "emancipated through non-clinging."

The way leading to the understanding of cessation is the truth of the path (*maggasacca*). It is referred to in the several passages about understanding as they really are the origin, etc., of feelings, in the passage about understanding as they really are the origin etc., of the six bases of contact, and in the passage about the cutting off of the leash of existence.

"Satisfaction" should be understood as the truth of the origin, "unsatisfactoriness" as the truth of suffering, and "escape" as the truths of cessation and the path. This is the interpretation by way of the four truths, but satisfaction, unsatisfactoriness, and escape have come down in the text in their own nature. The "fruit" (*phala*) is the purpose; this, as stated above, is to instruct the beings to be trained how to maintain equipoise, etc. The "means" (*upāya*) is the method by which the various purposes are to be achieved; that is, not giving way to resentment, etc., remembering that the fruits of resentment, etc., do not affect any other mental continuum (than one's own), acknowledging and unravelling the true nature of praise and blame, etc. The "injunction" (*āṇatti*) of the Lord of the Dhamma is the prohibition against giving way to resentment, etc.

2. The Mode of Conveying an Investigation (*vicayahāra*)

(Here omitted, as concerned only with investigating the choice of words.)

3. The Mode of Conveying a Construing (*yuttihāra*)

"Not giving way to resentment under any circumstances leads to equipoise"—this is the construing, because in this way the mind proceeds evenly under both desirable and undesirable circumstances.

"When resentment, etc., arise in a certain mental continuum, the obstacles that they create lead to the destruction of the achievements (developed in the continuum)"—this is the construing, because there is no transference of the kammas (sown in one's own continuum) to the mental continua of others.

"When the mind is overwhelmed by the arising of resentment, etc., it will be incapable even of distinguishing what is rightly and wrongly spoken"—this is the construing, because of the mental blindness and darkness of those overcome by anger and greed.

"Abstinence from the destruction of life, etc., leads to receiving the joy and praise of all beings"—this is the construing, because a highly favorable report circulates concerning one who is endowed with virtue.

"Though the praising of the Tathāgata on account of his qualities such as profound knowledge, etc., refers to only one part (of what is praiseworthy in him), yet it leads to understanding all the qualities of the Omniscient One"—this is the construing, because (it refers to those qualities) he does not hold in common with others.

"Meditative achievements and reasoning based on unwise reflection lead to the adherence to eternalism, etc."—this is the construing, because the net of speculative thought-constructions has not yet been extirpated.

"When there is no comprehension of the unsatisfactoriness in feeling, craving for feeling will increase"—this is the construing, because one only contemplates the satisfaction in feelings.

"When there is lust for feeling, the assumption of a self and a self's property, and the assumption of eternalism, etc., will agitate (the mind)"—this is the construing, because of the proximity of the cause. For craving is the condition for clinging (to views and to a doctrine of self).

"Contact is the cause for the proclamation of such views as eternalism, etc., and for the experiencing of feelings corresponding to such views"—this is the construing, because these latter cannot occur without the meeting of object, faculty, and consciousness (constituting contact).

"With the six bases of contact as the foundation, there is an unbroken continuation of the round of existence"—this is the construing, because ignorance and craving have not yet been abandoned.

"Understanding the origin, etc., of the six bases of contact transcends the ideas of all the theorists"—this is the construing, because (such understanding leads to) the penetration of the Four Noble Truths.

"All the theorists are trapped in these sixty-two views"—this is the construing, because those who deny the moral efficacy of action, etc., as well as the theists, etc., are also included in this net; this has been explained above (pp. 134ff.).

"The body of the Tathāgata stands with the leash that bound it to existence cut"—this is the construing, since the Exalted One, by developing the seven factors of enlightenment as they really are with a mind established in the four foundations of mindfulness, has achieved his original aspiration.

"With the breakup of the body he will attain to parinibbāna, and (gods and men) shall see him no more"—this is the construing, since with the attainment of the nibbāna-element without residue none (of the aggregates) such as material form, etc., will remain.

4. The Mode of Conveying the Proximate Cause (*padaṭṭhāna-hāra*)

Unacceptable, abusive, critical speech referring to those deserving praise is a proximate cause for the various kinds of loss (*vipatti*). Acceptable, laudatory, appreciative speech referring to those deserving praise is a proximate cause for the various kinds of achievement (*sampatti*).

Giving way to resentment, etc., is a proximate cause for suffering in the hells, etc. Not giving way to resentment, etc., is a proximate cause for all achievements, such as a heavenly rebirth, etc.

Abstinence from the destruction of life, etc., is a proximate cause for the aggregate of noble virtue, the aggregate of noble virtue for the aggregate of noble concentration, and the aggregate of noble concentration for the aggregate of noble wisdom.

The Exalted One's knowledge of penetration, possessing profundity of objective domain, is the proximate cause for his knowledge of teaching. His knowledge of teaching is the proximate cause for enabling the beings to be trained to escape from all the suffering of the round.

All views, as the clinging to views, are the proximate cause for the ninefold existence; existence is the proximate cause for birth, and birth for aging and death, as well as for sorrow, etc.

The penetration of the origin and passing away of feelings as they really are is also the understanding and penetration of the Four Noble Truths. Therein, the understanding of the truths is the proximate cause for their penetration, and their penetration is the proximate cause for the four fruits of recluseship.

"Who do not know and do not see"—this is a reference to ignorance. Ignorance is the proximate cause for kamma-formations, and so on through the chain of dependent origination down to feeling as the proximate cause for craving. "The agitation and vacillation of those immersed in craving"—here, craving is the proximate cause for clinging.

"That too is conditioned by contact"—here, the proclamation of eternalism, etc., is the proximate cause for establishing others in a wrong adherence. The wrong adherence is the proximate cause for aversion to hearing the true Dhamma, to associating with good people, to reflecting wisely, and to practicing in accordance with the Dhamma; and for their hearing false Dhamma, etc."

"Without contact"—contact is the proximate cause for feeling. The six bases of contact are the proximate cause for contact itself and for all the suffering of the round. Understanding the origin, etc., of the six bases as they really are is the proximate cause for disenchantment (*nibbidā*), dispassion (*virāga*), etc., down to parinibbāna through non-clinging.

The Exalted One's cutting off of the leash of existence is the proximate cause for his knowledge of omniscience, as well as for his parinibbāna through non-clinging.

5. The Mode of Conveying the Characteristic (*lakkhaṇahāra*)

By mentioning resentment, etc., anger, malice, denigration, domineering, envy, stinginess, presumption, and the belittling of others may also be included, for these all have a single characteristic insofar as they are all contained in the classes of consciousness associated with aversion (*paṭighacittuppāda*).

By mentioning jubilation, etc., covetousness, unrighteous greed, conceit, arrogance, vanity, and negligence may also be included, for these all have the same characteristic insofar as they are all contained in the classes of consciousness associated with greed (*lobhacittuppāda*).

Again, by mentioning resentment, the remaining bodily knots and hindrances may be included, since they all share the common characteristic of being knots and hindrances.[172] And by mentioning jubilation, contact and the remaining factors of the aggregate of mental

172. Resentment (*āghāta*), as an equivalent of ill will (*byāpāda*), implies the other three knots (*gantha*) and four hindrances (*nīvaraṇa*).

formations may be included, since they all share the characteristic of belonging to the formations aggregate.[173]

By mentioning virtue, the training in the higher consciousness and in the higher wisdom may also be included, since they all share the characteristic of being forms of higher training. The restraint of the senses should be considered as part of virtue.

By mentioning views, the remaining types of clinging may be included, since they all share the characteristic of being forms of clinging.

By mentioning feelings, the remaining aggregates of clinging may be included, since they all share the characteristic of being aggregates of clinging. So too, since feeling is included in the base of mental objects (*dhammāyatana*) and in the element of mental objects (*dhammadhātu*), all the other sense bases and elements that come within the range of insight-comprehension (*sammasana*) may be included, since they all share the characteristic of being sense bases and elements.

By referring to ignorance with the words "who do not know and do not see," the other roots, cankers, floods, bonds, hindrances, etc., may be included, since they all share with ignorance the characteristic of belonging to the same group, such as roots, etc. The same applies to the reference to craving, i.e., "the agitation and vacillation of those immersed in craving."

By mentioning contact—"that too is conditioned by contact"—perception, mental formations, and consciousness may be included, since they share the characteristic of being aggregates and causes for the inversions (*vipallāsa*).

By mentioning the six bases of contact, the aggregates, faculties, elements, etc., may be included, since they all share the characteristic of being causal bases for the arising of contact and come within range of insight-comprehension.

And by mentioning the leash of existence, the defilements such as ignorance, etc., may also be included, since they share the characteristic of being roots of the round.

---

173. Jubilation (*ānanda*), a synonym for rapture (*pīti*), is a member of the formations aggregate and so implies the remaining members of the aggregate.

6. The Mode of Conveying the Fourfold Array (*catubyūhahāra*)

(i) The Source (*nidāna*). The source of this teaching consists in those beings who are capable of training yet whose minds are shaken by praise and blame, who do not refrain from wrong livelihood, who adhere to such false views as eternalism, etc., and who cannot appreciate the flavor of the perfectly enlightened Buddha's noble qualities because they are not established in the training-aggregate of virtue, etc.

(ii) The Purport (*adhippāya*). The Exalted One's purport is this: "How can these beings be freed from the aforementioned faults and devote themselves to their own welfare and the welfare of others by following the right path of practice?"

(iii) Linguistics (*nirutti*). This deals with the derivation of words. It can be easily understood by consulting the derivation of words given in the commentary, but we do not deal with it at length for fear of getting caught up in excessive details.

(iv) The Sequence (*sandhi*). The sequence is sixfold: (a) the sequence of words (*padasandhi*); (b) of the meanings of words (*padatthasandhi*); (c) of exposition (*niddesasandhi*); (d) of delivery (*nikkhepasandhi*); (e) of the sutta (*suttasandhi*); and (f) of the teaching (*desanāsandhi*).

(a) The "sequence of words" is the connection between one word and another, [e.g., between "of me" and "dispraise" (in §5 of sutta)].

(b) The "sequence of word-meanings" is the connection between the meaning of one word and the meaning of another, [between the Exalted One, signified by "of me," and the lack of noble qualities attributed to him by others, signified by the word "dispraise"].

(c) The "sequence of exposition" is the connection between the consecutive sections of a sutta with several sections, and between the earlier and later portions of a sutta with a single section. This may be illustrated by the connection between the Master's teaching that begins: "If, bhikkhus, others should speak in dispraise of me," etc., and the dispraise spoken by the wanderer Suppiya; between his teaching that begins: "If, bhikkhus, others should speak in praise of me," etc., and the praise spoken by the youth Brahmadatta; and between his teaching that begins: "There are, bhikkhus, other dhammas, deep, difficult to see," etc., and the praise spoken by the bhikkhus.

(d) The "sequence of delivery" has been explained above by way of the four grounds for the delivery of a sutta (pp. 104–5).

(e) The "sequence of the sutta" has already been examined in the commentary. It is analyzed into the three sequences of meaning: the sequence based on a question, the sequence dictated by inclination, and the sequence dictated by the natural structure of the teaching (pp. 193–96).

(f) The "sequence of teaching" is the coherence between the teaching (in this sutta) and the teaching (in other suttas). It may be illustrated by the following examples.

The teaching, "If others speak in dispraise of me ... you should not give way to animosity in your heart," this links up with the simile of the saw: "If, bhikkhus, robbers should cut you up limb for limb with a double-handled saw, he who feels anger in his heart would not be a follower of my teaching" (MN 21.20).

"You would only be creating an obstacle for yourselves"—this links up with the teaching that "beings are owners of their kamma, heirs to their kamma" (MN 135.4).

"Would you be able to recognize whether their statements are rightly or wrongly spoken?" —this links up with the teaching: "The angry man does not know the meaning" (AN 7:60).

"If others speak in praise of me ... you should not give way to exultation in your heart"—this links up with the simile of the raft: "Even (wholesome) dhammas must be abandoned, bhikkhus, much more, then, what is contrary to (wholesome) dhammas" (MN 22.13).

"You would only be creating an obstacle for yourselves"—this links up with the teaching: "The greedy person does not know the meaning" (It 3:38).

"Trifling and insignificant matters, the minor details of mere moral virtue"—this links up with passages showing the inferiority of virtue to jhānas, since even the first jhāna is of greater fruit and greater benefit than moral virtue, e.g.: "When he abides having entered the first jhāna—this, brahmin, is a sacrifice less difficult and less troublesome than the previous one, but of greater fruit and greater benefit" (DN 5.75).

"Having abandoned the destruction of life"—this links up with such teachings as: "The recluse Gotama is virtuous, he is endowed with wholesome ways of conduct" (DN 4.6).

"There are other dhammas, deep," etc.—this links up with other texts illustrating the profundity of the Buddha's knowledge through its penetration of dhammas possessing profundity of objective domain, e.g.: This Dhamma discovered by me is deep," etc. (MN 26.19).

"There are, bhikkhus, some recluses and brahmins who are speculators about the past ... speculators about the future"—these link up with the teaching in the Pañcattaya Sutta (MN 102).[174] And the passage: "Having understood the origin of feelings ... the Tathāgata is emancipated through non-clinging"—this links up with the teaching (in the same sutta): "This is conditioned and gross. But there is cessation of formations. Having understood that there is, perceiving the escape from this, the Tathāgata has transcended this."

"That is only the feeling of those who do not know and do not see, the agitation and vacillation of those who are immersed in craving"—this links up with the teaching (again in the same sutta): "That these honorable ones, apart from faith, apart from preference, apart from hearsay, apart from ratiocination, apart from reflective acquiescence in a view, will have pure and lucid personal knowledge (of their doctrines)—this is impossible. And since they have no pure and lucid personal knowledge (of their doctrines), whatever section of knowledge these honorable recluses and brahmins (claim to) clarify, this can be declared to be mere clinging on their part."

"That too is conditioned by contact"—this links up with the following teachings: "Dependent on the eye and visible forms, eye-consciousness arises. The meeting of the three is contact. With contact as condition, feeling arises; with feeling as condition, craving arises; and with craving as condition, clinging arises" (SN 12:44–45); and: "These dhammas, friend, are rooted in desire, originated by attention, subsumed under contact, and they converge upon feeling" (AN 8:83).

"When a bhikkhu understands the six bases of contact"—this links up with the teaching: "When, Ānanda, a bhikkhu does not regard feeling as the self, or perception, or mental formations or consciousness—not regarding them thus he does not cling to anything in the world. Not clinging he is not agitated, and free from agitation, he inwardly attains to nibbāna" (untraced; cf. SN 22:45).

---

174. Here the subcommentator brings in the summary passages from the sutta, which list in condensed form the same set of views as those given in the Brahmajāla Sutta.

"All these are trapped in this net with its sixty-two divisions" — this links up with the teaching: "Whoever declares (these views), all declare views belonging to these five groups or to a certain one of them" (MN 102.13).

"With the breakup of the body ... gods and men shall see him no more"—this links up with the following teaching:

> "Just as a flame flung into the wind,
> Upasiva"—said the Lord,
> "Flies to its end, no more to enter concept's range,
> The sage set free, released from the mental-group,
> Attains the end, no more to enter concept's range."
>
> (Sn 1074)

7. The Mode of Conveying Conversion (*āvattahāra*)

By the phrase "you should not give way to resentment," etc., acting in conformity with patience and meekness (is indicated). Therein, along with patience, faith and wisdom enabling one to endure the pain caused by the wrongs of others may be included; and along with meekness, virtue may be included. By mentioning faith (and wisdom), the faculties of faith (and wisdom) and all the other constituents of enlightenment[175] turn up (*āvattati*). By mentioning virtue, freedom from remorse and all the other benefits of virtue turn up (AN 10:1).

By the statement "he abstains from the destruction of life," etc., abiding in diligence (is indicated). With this, the entire holy life of the Dispensation turns up. By mentioning dhammas possessing profundity of objective domain, the supreme enlightenment is extolled. For the supreme enlightenment is both the knowledge of the destruction of the cankers, having the unobstructed knowledge as its proximate cause, and the unobstructed knowledge, having the knowledge of the destruction of the cankers as its proximate cause. With this, all the Buddha-qualities such as the ten powers, etc., turn up.

By mentioning the views of eternalism, etc., ignorance and craving are implied. With these, the beginningless round of saṃsāra turns up. The penetration of the origin, etc., of feelings as they really

---

175. *Bodhipakkhiyadhammā.* The faculties of faith and wisdom belong to the five faculties, which constitute one set among the thirty-seven constituents of enlightenment.

are implies the Exalted One's purification of the three kinds of full understanding.[176] With these, all his pāramīs headed by the perfection of wisdom (*paññāpāramī*) turn up. By referring to ignorance with the words "who do not know and do not see," unwise reflection is included. With this, the dhammas rooted in unwise reflection turn up. By referring to craving with the words "the agitation and vacillation of those immersed in craving," the nine dhammas rooted in craving turn up.[177] With the words, "that too is conditioned by contact," he shows that the proclamation of eternalism, etc., occurs in dependence on conditions. With this, the three characteristics of impermanence, suffering, and non-self turn up. The understanding of the six bases of contact as they really are points to the achievement of emancipation. With this, the seven purifications turn up.[178] The words "the body of the Tathāgata stands with the leash that bound it to existence cut" imply the abandoning of craving. With this, the Exalted One's abandoning of all defilements turns up.

8. The Mode of Conveying Classification (*vibhattihāra*)

Resentment and jubilation, etc., are unwholesome dhammas; their proximate cause is unwise reflection, etc. Those dhammas by means of which one does not give way to resentment and jubilation, etc., by which one desists from them—those are wholesome dhammas, such as benevolence, etc.; their proximate cause is wise reflection. Among these, resentment, etc., pertain to the sense sphere; benevolence, etc., to all four planes. So too, abstinence from the destruction of life, etc., may be wholesome or indeterminate; their proximate cause is shame and moral dread. Therein, the wholesome may pertain to the sense sphere, or they may be supramundane; the indeterminate is exclusively supramundane. The dhammas referred to in the phrase: "There are, bhikkhus, other dhammas deep," etc., may be wholesome, or they may be indeterminate. The proximate cause for the wholesome dhammas is insight leading to emergence;[179] the proximate cause for the indeterminate is the dhammas of the path, insight, or advertance.

176. The full understanding of the known (*ñātapariññā*), full understanding through scrutinization (*tīraṇapariññā*), and full understanding through abandoning (*pahānapariññā*). See Vism 20:3–5.

177. See DN 15.9, AN 9:23.

178. See MN 24.9–15.

Among these, the wholesome are exclusively supramundane; the indeterminate may pertain to the sense sphere or they may be supramundane. All views are unwholesome dhammas pertaining to the sense sphere. Their proximate cause, without distinction, is unwise reflection over a wrong adherence. But taken separately, the proximate cause for eternalism is the misapplication of the method of unity due to the failure to dissect the compact of the continuity (of successive dhammas into its discrete components); this may be conjoined with reasoning or the recollection of past lives. The proximate cause for annihilationism is the misapplication of the method of diversity due to the failure to apprehend the interconnection (between the dhammas functioning) as causes and effects (in the successive life-continuities within the same general continuum); this is conjoined with the corresponding act of attention. The proximate causes for the remaining views may be stated as is appropriate for each case.

"Of feelings"—here, feelings may be wholesome, unwholesome, or indeterminate; they may pertain to the sense sphere, to the fine-material sphere, or to the immaterial sphere. Their proximate cause is contact. The penetration of the origin of feelings, etc., as they really are, is the knowledge of the path; emancipation through non-clinging is the fruit. The classification of these dhammas should be made by way of the method given in the section on "deep dhammas." Ignorance and craving are unwholesome dhammas pertaining to the sense sphere. Of these, the proximate cause for ignorance is the cankers, or unwise reflection; the proximate cause for craving is perceiving satisfaction in dhammas subject to the fetters. "That too is conditioned by contact"—here, the classification of dhammas, etc., in the case of contact should be understood in the same way as in the case of feeling. By this method, the classification of dhammas, etc., in the case of the bases of contact, etc., should also be brought in, as is fitting in each case.

9. The Mode of Conveying Reversal (*parivattahāra*)

Not giving way to resentment, etc., having fortified patience and meekness, by perfecting the powers of reflection and meditative development results in practice for the welfare of both oneself and others. But if resentment, etc., are allowed to continue, they will result in

179. *Vuṭṭhānagāmaṇīvipassanā*: The stage of insight immediately preceding the attainment of the supramundane path. See Vism 21.83.

ugliness, uneasiness, the loss of wealth, disrepute, and inaccessibility to others; they will finally lead to great suffering in the hells.

Abstinence from the destruction of life, etc., results in the entire sequence of noble states beginning with freedom from remorse (AN 10:1). But the destruction of life, etc., results in the entire sequence of ignoble states beginning with remorse.

The knowledge possessing profundity of objective domain, by comprehending the true nature of all that is knowable, helps the beings to be trained attain to such distinguished qualities as the (threefold) knowledge, the (six) direct knowledges, etc., according to their fitness. But knowledge lacking such profundity of objective domain, because it is obstructed by the knowable, cannot lead to the aforesaid distinguished qualities.

All views veering to the two extremes of eternalism and annihilationism cannot transcend the "shore of personality" (*sakkāyatīra*), for they are incapable of leading to liberation (*aniyyānikasabhāvattā*). But the right view pertaining to the Middle Way, together with its requisites,[180] crosses beyond the "shore of personality" and arrives at the further shore (i.e., nibbāna), for it tends to liberation by its very nature.

The penetration of the origin, etc., of feelings as they really are results in emancipation through non-clinging, for it belongs to the path. But non-penetration of the origin, etc., of feelings leads to confinement in the prison of saṃsāra, for it functions as the condition for kamma-formations.[181]

The delusion concealing the true nature of feelings results in delight in feelings. But the comprehension (of feelings) as they really are results in disenchantment and dispassion towards feelings. Craving conjoined with unwise reflection upon wrong adherences spreads out the complex net of views. The eradication of this craving by the first path (i.e., the path of stream-entry) shrivels up this net of views.

Contact is the condition for the proclamation of eternalism, etc., for there is no (such proclamation) in the absence of contact.

---

180. The requisites (*parikkhārā*) of right view are the other seven factors of the Noble Eightfold Path.

181. Non-penetration is here synonymous with ignorance, the condition for kamma-formations, according to dependent origination.

When there is no cessation of the bases of contact, etc., in those bound by the bondage of views, there is no cessation of contact, etc., and thus no ceasing of the suffering of saṃsāra. Through the full understanding of the bases of contact, etc., in accordance with their nature, one transcends all speculative views. But when the bases of contact, etc., are not fully understood, one does not transcend the holding to views.

The cutting off of the leash of existence conduces to the non-production of another individual form (*attabhāva*). But so long as the leash of existence is not cut off, the succession of existences revolves onwards into the future.

10. The Mode of Conveying Synonyms (*vevacanahāra*)

(Since this mode merely gives synonyms for the words occurring in the text, it is here omitted).

11. The Mode of Conveying a Description (*paññatti*)

Resentment may be described by way of its base as of ten or nineteen types. Displeasure may be described by way of the objects of inspection (*upavicāra*) as of six types. Jubilation may be described by way of rapture, etc., as of nine types; rapture, its synonym, may be described as of five types—as minor, (momentary, showering, uplifting, and pervading). Joy may be described by way of the object of inspection as of six types. Virtue may be described as of many types—as avoidance and performance, etc. The knowledge possessing profundity of objective domain is of four or twelve types by way of classes of consciousness; but by way of objective domain it is of many types. Views are described in terms of sixty-two divisions, as eternalism, etc., but by analyzing their contents further, they become even more multitudinous. Feeling is described as of six, a hundred and eight, and many types. Its origin and passing away are each described as of five types. The satisfaction (in feelings) is described as of two types; its unsatisfactoriness as of three types; and the escape (from feeling) as of one and of four types. Emancipation through non-clinging is described as of two types.

Ignorance, indicated by the phrase "who do not know and do not see," is described by way of its objective domain as of four and of eight types. Craving, indicated by the phrase "immersed in craving," is described as of six, a hundred and eight, and many types. Contact is described as of six types by way of its support. Clinging is described as of four types; existence, of two or many types; birth, by way of its synonyms, as sixfold, aging as sevenfold, and death as eightfold or ninefold. Sorrow is described as fivefold, lamentation as sixfold, pain and grief as fourfold, and despair also as fourfold.

"Such is the origin" is a description of the source. "He understands as they really are" is a description of the full understanding of suffering, a description of the abandoning of its origin, a description of the realization of its cessation, and a description of the development of the path (leading to its cessation). "They are all trapped (in this net)," etc., is a description of the inclusion of all views. "Stands with the leash that bound it to existence cut" is a description of the two kinds of parinibbāna.

So too, the wholesome and unwholesome dhammas beginning with resentment may be analyzed as a description of the source, etc.; and again, resentment may be analyzed as a description of a synonym for ill will, displeasure as a description of a synonym for grief, and so on.

12. The Mode of Conveying Ways of Entry (*otaraṇahāra*)

By mentioning resentment and animosity, the aggregate of mental formations is included; by mentioning displeasure, the aggregate of feeling is included. This is the entry by way of the aggregates. Again, by mentioning resentment, etc., the mental-object base, the mental-object element, the truth of suffering, and truth of the origin are implied. This is the entry by way of the sense bases, elements, and truths.

The ignorance co-nascent with resentment, etc., is their condition as root cause, co-nascence, mutuality, support, association, presence, and non-disappearance conditions. The non-co-nascent ignorance is their condition as proximity, contiguity, proximate-decisive-support, absence, and disappearance conditions. The non-proximate is a condition only by way of decisive-support.

The way in which craving, clinging, etc., and contact, etc., function as conditions may be explained as is appropriate for each case, according to whether (the conditioned states) are co-nascent with them or not. Some factors are a condition as predominance condition, some as kamma condition, some as nutriment condition, some as faculty condition, some as jhāna condition, and some as path condition—this distinction should be recognized. This is the entry by way of dependent origination.

Through the same method the entry by way of the aggregates, etc., may be explicated in the case of jubilation, etc.

Again, virtue is the abstinence from the destruction of life, a volition, and the mental concomitants such as benevolence, etc. The destruction of life, etc., consist only in volition. These, and the dhammas that assist them such as conscientiousness, kindness, etc., are included in the aggregate of mental formations, the mental-object base, etc. This is the entrance by way of the aggregates, etc., according to the method given above. This method also applies to knowledge, views, feeling, ignorance, craving, etc. The references to escape and to emancipation through non-clinging imply the unconditioned element; the entry here may be made by way of elements.

The passage: "Having understood as they really are … the Tathāgata is emancipated through non-clinging" implies the Exalted One's five aggregates (virtue, concentration, wisdom, emancipation, and knowledge and vision of emancipation) and his thirty-seven constituents of enlightenment, beginning with the four foundations of mindfulness. These give entry under the corresponding headings. The phrase: "That too is conditioned by contact," signifying the conditional dependence of the proclamation of views, gives entry by way of the fact of impermanence. As the actual nature of dhammas, this gives entry by way of dependent origination. The suffering and absence of selfhood inherent in the impermanent give entry by way of the wishless and by way of emptiness, respectively. The same method may be applied to the remaining terms.

13. The Mode of Conveying a Clearing Up (*sodhanahāra*)

"If others speak in dispraise of me"—this is a starting point (*ārambha*). "Or in dispraise of the Dhamma, or of the Saṅgha"— this is a clearance of terms (*padasuddhi*), not a clearance of the starting point. "You should not give way to resentment," etc.— this is a clearance of terms and a clearance of the starting point. The same method applies to the passage giving the opposite case.

"It is only to trifling matters," etc.—this is a starting point. "And what are those?" etc.—this is a question. "Having abandoned the destruction of life," etc.—this is a clearance of terms, not a clearance of the starting point, not a clearance of the question. "These are those trifling matters," etc.—this is a clearance of the question, a clearance of terms, and a clearance of the starting point.

"There are, bhikkhus, other dhammas," etc.—this is a starting point. "And what are those dhammas?," etc.—this is a question. "There are some recluses and brahmins," etc.—this is a starting point. "And owing to what?", etc.—this is a question. "That with his mind thus concentrated," etc.—this is a clearance of terms, not a clearance of the starting point, not a clearance of the question. "These are those recluses and brahmins," etc.—this is a clearance of terms, a clearance of the question, and a clearance of the starting point.

In the same way, the starting point, etc., may be understood in each case.

14. The Mode of Conveying Terms of Expression (*adhiṭṭhānahāra*)

"Dispraise" is a general term of expression (*sāmaññato adhiṭṭhānaṃ*). Without differentiating this, the particular terms (*visesavacana*) "of me, or of the Dhamma, or of the Saṅgha" (are extracted). The same method with the bright side (i.e., in the case of praise).

"Virtue" is a general term of expression. Without differentiating this, the particular terms "abstains from the destruction of life," etc. (are extracted).

"Other dhammas," etc., is a general term of expression. Without differentiating this, the particular terms "this the Tathāgata understands," etc. (are extracted).

"Speculators with regard to the past," etc., is a general term of expression. Without differentiating this, the particular terms "eternalists," etc. (are extracted).

Along the same lines, the general and particular terms should be elicited in each case.

15. The Mode of Conveying Requisites (*parikkhārahāra*)

The nineteen bases of resentment, such as the thought: "He did me harm," etc., are the cause (*hetu*) for resentment, etc. Excessive affection for the object is the cause for jubilation, etc. Shame and moral dread, together with such qualities as fewness of wishes, etc., are the cause for virtue. The cause for the dhammas described as "deep," etc., are the pāramīs, particularly the perfection of wisdom. The causes for views are, in general, association with bad men, listening to false doctrine, and unwise reflection upon wrong adherences; in particular, the recollection of past lives is a cause for eternalism, etc. Ignorance, craving, kamma, and contact are the causes for feeling. The noble path is the cause for emancipation through non-clinging. Unwise reflection is the cause for the proclamation (of views). The contemplation of satisfaction in dhammas subject to the fetters is the cause for craving. The six bases are the cause for contact, and mentality-materiality is the cause for the six bases. And the development of purity is the cause for cutting off the leash of existence.

16. The Mode of Conveying Coordination (*samāropanahāra*)

By the phrase "you should not give way to resentment," etc., accomplishment in patience is shown; by the phrase "it is only to trifling matters," etc., accomplishment in meekness; by the phrase "there are other dhammas," etc., accomplishment in knowledge. The two phrases "because he is free from misapprehension he has realized within himself the state of perfect peace," and "having understood as they really are the origin, etc., of feelings, the Tathāgata is emancipated through non-clinging," indicate the Buddha's accomplishment in mastery over knowledge and emancipation together with his accomplishment in concentration.

Therein, the accomplishment in patience, perfected by the power of reflection, is the proximate cause for the accomplishment in meekness. The accomplishment in meekness is, in denotation, virtue itself. So too, the phrase "abstinence from the destruction of life" shows the analytical synonyms for virtue. Virtue is the proximate cause for concentration, and concentration the proximate cause for wisdom. By virtue the abandoning of transgressions and the abandoning of defilement by wrong conduct are perfected. By concentration the abandoning of obsessions, the abandoning by suppression, and the abandoning of defilement by craving are perfected. And by wisdom the abandoning of latent tendencies, the abandoning by eradication, and the abandoning of defilement by views are perfected. Thus by the three aggregates—virtue, concentration, and wisdom—the development of serenity and insight is fulfilled and the three kinds of abandonment are perfected.

II. The Five Methods
(*Pañcavidhanaya*)

1. The Method of the Conversion of Delight (*nandiyāvattanaya*)

By the phrase "you should not give way to resentment," etc., the reduction of craving and ignorance is shown. For when there is affection and confusion regarding objects that can be taken as a self or as the property of a self, resentment arises, expressed in the thought: "He did me harm," etc.

Again, by the phrases "he abstains from the destruction of life," etc., "he has realized within himself the state of perfect peace," "he is emancipated through non-clinging," "he understands as they really are the origin, etc., of the six bases of contact," etc., the ultimate abandoning of craving and ignorance is shown. Material and immaterial dhammas are the foundation (*adhiṭṭhāna*) for ignorance and craving, which are shown in their own nature in such passages as "speculators about the past," etc., and "who do not know and do not see," etc. Serenity (*samatha*) and insight (*vipassanā*) are their opposites (i.e., of craving and of ignorance, respectively). Emancipation by mind (*cetovimutti*) and emancipation by wisdom (*paññāvimutti*) are their respective fruits.[182]

Therein, craving, or craving and ignorance together, is the truth of the origin. The material and immaterial dhammas that serve as their foundation are the truth of suffering. Their non-occurrence is the truth of cessation. The serenity and insight that understand cessation are the truth of the path. This is the interpretation in terms of the four truths.

By mentioning craving, the entire faction of unwholesome states may be brought in by way of hypocrisy, craftiness, conceit, arrogance, vanity, negligence, evil desires, evil friendship, lack of shame and moral dread, etc. And by mentioning ignorance, the faction of unwholesome states may be brought in by way of inverted reflection, anger, malice, denigration, domineering, envy, stinginess, presumption, recalcitrance, views of existence, views of non-existence, etc. By reversing what has been said, the wholesome faction

---

182. See AN 2:3.10, which explains serenity as the means for abandoning lust and achieving emancipation by mind, and insight as the means for abandoning ignorance and achieving emancipation by wisdom.

may be brought in by way of absence of hypocrisy and craftiness, etc., and by way of uninverted reflection, etc. And again, the wholesome faction may be introduced by way of the factors on the side of serenity, such as the faculty of faith, etc.; and by way of the factors on the side of insight, such as the perception of impermanence, etc.

2. The Method of the Trefoil (*tipukkhalanaya*)

By the phrase "you should not give way to resentment," etc., as well as by the references to abstaining from the destruction of life and from harsh speech, non-hatred is shown. By the phrase "you should not give way to jubilation," etc., as well as by the reference to abstaining from unchastity, non-greed is shown. By mentioning the abstinence from taking what is not given, etc., both are shown. "This the Tathāgata understands"—by this non-delusion is shown. Thus the three wholesome roots are shown as the opposites of the three unwholesome roots and by the injunctions not to give way to resentment, etc. From the three unwholesome roots the entire faction of unwholesome states may be elaborated by way of the three kinds of wrong conduct, defilements, stains, unrighteous ways, unwholesome perceptions and thoughts, evil dhammas, etc. And from the three wholesome roots the entire faction of wholesome states may be derived by way of the three kinds of right conduct, kinds of cleansing, righteous ways, wholesome perceptions and thoughts, kinds of wisdom, good dhammas, concentrations, doors to deliverance, deliverances, etc.

Here too an interpretation in terms of the four truths may be established. How? Greed, or all wholesome and unwholesome roots, are the truth of the origin. The clinging-aggregates produced through these, serving as their foundation and objective range, are the truth of suffering. [Their non-occurrence is the truth of cessation. And the deliverances, etc., understanding cessation are the truth of the path].

3. The Method of the Lion's Play (*sīhavikkīḷitanaya*)

By the injunction not to give way to resentment and jubilation, etc., mindfulness is shown. For through mindfulness one recognizes blameworthy and blameless states, discerns the dangers in the former and the benefits in the latter, abandons the blameworthy, and undertakes the blameless.

Again, by mentioning abstinence from wrong livelihood, energy is shown. For through energy one dispels thoughts of sensual desire, ill will, and aggression. And the perfecting of energy is the (means for) virtue through purification of livelihood.

By mentioning abstinence from the destruction of life, etc., mindfulness is shown. For through mindfulness one recognizes blameworthy and blameless states, discerns the dangers in the former and the benefits in the latter, abandons the blameworthy, and undertakes the blameless. Thus mindfulness is said to have as its manifestation confrontation with the objective domain.

"This the Tathāgata understands"—by this concentration and wisdom are shown. For through wisdom one comprehends things as they really are; and one who is concentrated understands things as they really are.

By the words "permanent, stable," etc., the inversion of holding the impermanent to be permanent (*anicce niccan ti vipallāso*) is shown; by the words "(the self is) immutable after death and exclusively happy," and "attains supreme nibbāna here and now," etc., the inversion of holding that which is unpleasurable to be pleasurable (*asukhe sukhan ti vipallāso*) is shown; by the words "furnished and supplied with the five strands of sense pleasure," the inversion of holding the impure to be beautiful (*asubhe subhan ti vipallāso*) is shown; and by all these passages setting forth the various views, the inversion of holding that which is non-self to be self is shown (*anattani attā ti vipallāso*). Thus the four inversions are shown. The four foundations of mindfulness are implied as their opposites.[183]

Therein, four types of individuals may be explained through the four faculties. How? The individual with a craving temperament (*taṇhācarita*) is of two types: one with dull faculties and one with keen faculties. So too is the individual with a theorizing temperament (*diṭṭhicarita*). The first of these (the craving type with dull faculties), having conceived the inverted view of the impure as beautiful, comes to recognize the true nature of the body as it really is by the power of

183. Mindfulness of the impurity of the body corrects the inversion of holding the impure to be beautiful. Mindfulness of the unsatisfactoriness and inadequacy in all feeling corrects the inversion of holding the unpleasurable to be pleasurable. Mindfulness of the fleeting nature of consciousness or mind corrects the inversion of holding the impermanent to be permanent. And mindfulness that all dhammas are non-self corrects the inversion of holding what is non-self to be self.

mindfulness and thereby enters the order of rightness.[184] The second (the craving type with keen faculties), having conceived the inverted view of the unpleasurable as pleasurable, dispels this inversion by the power or energy, called "restraint by energy," as it is said: "He does not tolerate an arisen thought of sensual desire" (MN 2.20) The third (the theorizing type with dull faculties), holding the impermanent to be permanent contrary to its actual nature, penetrates the momentariness of formations as it really is with a mind well concentrated through the power of serenity. The fourth (the theorizing type with keen faculties), deceived by its apparent compactness of continuity, aggregation, function, and object, wrongly adheres to the idea of a self in what is not a self but a mere assemblage of dhammas such as contact, etc. He dispels this wrong adherence by reflection upon four-cornered emptiness.[185]

And here, through the four inversions, the entire faction of unwholesome states can be brought in by way of the four cankers, floods, bonds, bodily knots, evil courses, arisings of craving, and types of clinging, the seven stations of consciousness, the absence of full understanding, etc. So too, through the four foundations of mindfulness, the entire faction of wholesome states can be brought in by way of the four jhānas, abidings, foundations, dhammas partaking of happiness, immeasurables, right endeavors, bases of spiritual success, etc.

The perception of beauty and the perception of pleasure (in the impure and unpleasurable, respectively), or all four inversions, indicate the truth of the origin. The five aggregates of clinging that serve as their foundation and object are the truth of suffering. [Their non-occurrence is the truth of cessation. And the foundations of mindfulness, etc., that understand cessation are the truth of the path]. This is the interpretation in terms of the four truths.

4. The Method of Plotting the Directions (*disālocananaya*)
5. The Method of the Hook (*ankusanaya*)

By showing the three methods dealing with meaning, the two methods dealing with their expression (*vohāranaya*) are shown. For the plotting (*samālocana*) of the dhammas according to the directions of the three

184. *Sammattaniyāma:* the supramundane path.

185. *Catukoṭisuññatā.* The four "corners" are the emptiness of both a self and the property of a self (*atta-attaniya*) in both internal and external aggregates.

methods dealing with meaning is the method of "plotting the directions." The guiding together of these dhammas is the "method of the hook." Thus the five methods are laid down.

III. The Pattern of the Dispensation (*Sāsanapaṭṭhāna*)

In the sixteenfold pattern of the Dispensation, this sutta is classified as a sutta dealing with defilement, morality,[186] and the adept,[187] [since it analyzes the defilements of craving and views, etc., the making of merit by virtue, etc., and the adept's aggregates of virtue, etc.]. Or it is classified as a sutta dealing with defilement, morality, penetration, and the adept, [since it analyzes the aforesaid items, and also the learner's aggregate of virtue, etc.].

In the twenty-eight-fold pattern of the Dispensation, it should be understood as mundane and supramundane in scope, as expressed in terms of both beings and dhammas, as dealing with knowledge and the knowable, vision and meditative development, the Buddha's doctrine and the doctrine of outsiders, the answerable and the unanswerable, the wholesome and the unwholesome, the allowable and the refused, and eulogy.

---

186. *Vāsanā*, elsewhere translated as mental impressions. Here the term indicates those aspects of the teaching which induce wholesome "mental impressions" conducive to spiritual progress but do not pertain directly to the supramundane path.

187. *Asekha*, lit. "one beyond study," an arahat. The "learner" (*sekha*) is a noble disciple below the level of arahat training for the goal.

Part Four

A TREATISE ON THE PĀRAMĪS

We now undertake a detailed explanation of the pāramīs for clansmen following the suttas who are zealously engaged in the practice of the vehicle to great enlightenment (*mahābodhiyāna*), in order to improve their skillfulness in accumulating the requisites for enlightenment.[188]

This is the schedule of the questions: (i) What are the pāramīs? (ii) In what sense are they called pāramīs? (iii) How many are there? (iv) What is their sequence? (v) What are their characteristics, functions, manifestations, and proximate causes? (vi) What is their condition? (vii) What is their defilement? (viii) What is their cleansing? (ix) What are their opposites? (x) How are they to be practiced? (xi) How are they analyzed? (xii) How are they synthesized? (xiii) By what means are they accomplished? (xiv) How much time is required to accomplish them? (xv) What benefits do they bring? (xvi) What is their fruit?

The answers follow:

(i) What are the pāramīs?

The pāramīs are the noble qualities such as giving, etc., accompanied by compassion and skillful means, and untainted by craving, conceit, and views.[189]

---

188. For the translation of this treatise, the full-length version of the *Cariyāpiṭaka Aṭṭhakathā* has been used rather than the abridged version of Sub.Cy. Likewise, N.Sub.Cy. gives the full version, with minor variations in readings.

(ii) In what sense are they called "pāramīs"?

The bodhisattvas, the great beings, are supreme (*parama*), since they are the highest of beings by reason of their distinguished qualities such as giving, virtue, etc. The pāramīs—the activities of giving, etc.—are their character or their conduct. Or else: he excels, thus he is supreme (*paratī ti paramo*). the bodhisattva is the fulfiller and guardian of the noble qualities such as giving, etc.; that which belongs to the supreme—the character or conduct of the one who is supreme (i.e., of the bodhisattva)—is a pāramī, i.e., the activities of giving, etc.[190]

(iii) How many are there?

In brief there are ten. These have come down in the texts in their specific character. As it is said:

Reflecting then I saw: the first pāramī is giving,
The great way followed by the sages of the past. (Bv II v.117)

And again it is said:

"How many dhammas are there, venerable sir, culminating in Buddhahood?"

"There are, Sāriputta, ten dhammas culminating in Buddhahood. What are the ten? Giving, Sāriputta, is a dhamma culminating in Buddhahood. Virtue, renunciation, wisdom, energy, patience, truthfulness, determination, loving kindness, and equanimity are dhammas culminating in Buddhahood."[191] Thus spoke the Exalted One. Having spoken thus, the Well-Farer, the Teacher, further said:

Giving, virtue, then renunciation,
Wisdom and energy come to five;
Patience, truth, resolution, love,
With equanimity, these are ten.[192]

---

189. *Taṇhāmānadiṭṭhī anupahatā karuṇūpāyakosallapariggahitā dānādayo guṇā pāramiyo.*

190. Some further derivations, intelligible only in Pāḷi, are here omitted.

191. *Dāna, sīla, nekkhamma, paññā, viriya, khanti, sacca, adhiṭṭhāna, mettā, upekkhā.*

192. Bv II v.76, somewhat different in text.

But some say there are six. This is said by way of their synthesis, which we will explain below (see section xii).

(iv) What is their sequence?

Here "sequence" means sequence of teaching. This sequence is rooted in the order in which the pāramīs are initially undertaken, which in turn is rooted in the order in which they are investigated.[193] The quality that is investigated and undertaken at the beginning is taught first. Therein, giving is stated first, for giving assists (the development of) virtue and is easy to practice. Giving accompanied by virtue is abundantly fruitful and beneficial, so virtue is stated immediately after giving. Virtue accompanied by renunciation ... renunciation by wisdom ... wisdom by energy ... energy by patience ... patience by truthfulness ... truthfulness by determination ... determination by loving kindness ... and loving kindness accompanied by equanimity is abundantly fruitful and beneficial; thus equanimity is stated immediately after loving kindness. Equanimity is accompanied by compassion and compassion by equanimity. (Someone may ask:) "How can the bodhisattvas, the great compassionate ones, look upon living beings with equanimity?" Some teachers say: "Sometimes they show equanimity towards living beings when it is necessary to do so." But others say: "They do not show equanimity towards living beings but towards the offensive actions performed by beings."

Another method (of explaining the sequence) may be given:

(1) *Giving* is stated at the beginning: (a) because it is common to all beings, since even ordinary people practice giving; (b) because it is the least fruitful; and (c) because it is the easiest to practice.

(2) *Virtue* is stated immediately after giving: (a) because virtue purifies both the donor and the recipient; (b) to show that, while giving benefits others, virtue prevents the affliction of others; (c) in order to state a factor of abstinence immediately after a factor of positive activity; and (d) in order to show the cause for the achievement of a

---

193. An allusion to the first stage in the active career of a bodhisattva. After the bodhisattva makes his original aspiration at the feet of a living Buddha and receives from the him prediction of his future attainment of Buddhahood, he goes into solitude and investigates each of the pāramīs in terms of its specific character. Following the investigation, he then undertakes their practice. See Bv II, vv.116–66

favorable state of future existence right after the cause for the achievement of wealth.[194]

(3) *Renunciation* is mentioned immediately after virtue: (a) because renunciation perfects the achievement of virtue; (b) in order to list good conduct of mind immediately after good conduct of body and speech; (c) because meditation (*jhāna*) succeeds easily for one who has purified virtue; (d) in order to show that the purification of one's end (*āsaya*) through the abandoning of the offensive mental defilements follows the purification of one's means (*payoga*) by the abandoning of offensive actions; and (e) to state the abandoning of mental obsessions immediately after the abandoning of bodily and verbal transgressions.[195]

(4) *Wisdom* is mentioned immediately after renunciation: (a) because renunciation is perfected and purified by wisdom; (b) to show that there is no wisdom in the absence of meditation, since concentration is the proximate cause of wisdom and wisdom the manifestation of concentration; (c) in order to list the causal basis for equanimity immediately after the causal basis for serenity; and (d) to show that skillful means in working for the welfare of others springs from meditation directed to their welfare.

(5) *Energy* is stated immediately after wisdom: (a) because the function of wisdom is perfected by the arousing of energy; (b) to show the miraculous work the bodhisattva undertakes for the welfare of beings after he has reached reflective acquiescence in their emptiness;

---

194. According to the working of the kammic law, the practice of giving brings as its retribution the acquisition of wealth, the observance of precepts the attainment of a happy rebirth either in the heavens or in the human world.

195. "Renunciation" means not only the outward renunciation of material things, but the abandoning of mental defilements as well. Buddhist psychology recognizes three stages in the working of a defilement: (1) the stage of dormancy, where the defilement remains as a latent tendency (*anusaya*) at the base of the mental continuum; (2) the stage of obsession (*pariyuṭṭhāna*), when the defilement comes to the surface as a factor of active consciousness; and (3) the stage of transgression (*vītikkama*), when the defilement motivates some unwholesome action of body or speech. Virtue, as the observance of precepts, inhibits the active expression of defilements through body or speech. Serenity meditation, especially at the level of jhāna or absorption, prevents the rise of mental obsessions. And wisdom or insight brings about the eradication of defilements right down to the most basic level of dormancy.

(c) to state the causal basis for exertion right after the basis for equanimity; and (d) to state the arousing of energy right after the activity of careful consideration, according to the statement: "The activity of those who have carefully considered brings excellent results."

(6) *Patience* is mentioned immediately after energy: (a) because patience is perfected by energy, as it said: "The energetic person, by arousing energy, overcomes the suffering imposed by beings and formations"; (b) because patience is an adornment of energy, as it is said: "The patience of the energetic person shines with splendor"; (c) in order to state the causal basis for serenity immediately after the basis for exertion, for restlessness due to excessive activity is abandoned through reflective acquiescence in the Dhamma (*dhammanijjhānakkhanti*);[196] (d) in order to show the perseverance of an energetic person, since one who is patient and free from restlessness perseveres in his work; (e) in order to show the absence of craving for rewards in a bodhisattva diligently engaged in activity for the welfare of others, for there is no craving when he reflects on the Dhamma in accordance with actuality; and (f) to show that the bodhisattva must patiently endure the suffering created by others even when he is working to the utmost for their welfare.

(7) *Truthfulness* is stated immediately after patience: (a) because the determination to practice patience continues long through truthfulness; (b) having first mentioned the patient endurance of wrongs inflicted by others, to mention next fidelity to one's word to render them help; (c) in order to show that a bodhisattva who through patience does not vacillate in the face of abuse, through truthful speech

---

196. *Dhammanijjhānakkhanti.* The word *khanti,* ordinarily used to mean patience in the sense of the forbearance of the wrongs of others and the endurance of hardships, is sometimes also used to signify the intellectual acceptance of doctrines not yet completely clear to the understanding. Patience thus becomes a virtue not only of the will but of the intellect. It is a "suspension of disbelief" born of trust, a willingness to acquiesce in propositions baffling or even scandalous to the rational understanding in the confidence that the growth of wisdom will transform this acquiescence into clear and certain knowledge. The compound *dhammanijjhānakkhanti* seems to indicate an intermediate stage in this process of transformation, where the understanding can accept by way of reflection the article initially assented to in faith, without fully grasping it by immediate insight.

does not relinquish (his antagonist); and (d) to show the truthfulness of the knowledge developed through reflective acquiescence in the emptiness of beings.

(8) *Determination* is stated immediately after truthfulness; (a) because truthfulness is perfected by determination, since abstinence (from falsehood) becomes perfect in one whose determination is unshakable; (b) having first shown non-deception in speech, to show next unshakable commitment to one's word, for a bodhisattva devoted to truth proceeds to fulfill his vows of giving, etc., without wavering; and (c) to show, right after the veracity of knowledge, the complete accumulation of the requisites of enlightenment (*bodhisambhāra*); for one who knows things as they really are determines upon the requisites of enlightenment and brings them to completion by refusing to vacillate in the face of their opposites.[197]

(9) *Loving kindness* is mentioned immediately after determination: (a) because loving kindness perfects the determination to undertake activity for the welfare of others; (b) in order to list the work of actually providing for the welfare of others right after stating the determination to do so, for "one determined upon the requisites of enlightenment abides in loving kindness"; and (c) because the undertaking (of activity for the welfare of others) proceeds imperturbably only when determination is unshakable.

(10) *Equanimity* is mentioned immediately after loving kindness: (a) because equanimity purifies loving kindness; (b) in order to show the indifference one must maintain towards the wrongs inflicted by others when one is providing for their welfare; (c) having mentioned the development of loving kindness, to state next the development of the quality which evolves from it; and (d) to show the bodhisattva's wonderful virtue of remaining impartial even towards those who wish him well.

Thus the sequence of the pāramīs should be understood as explained.

---

197. The requisites of enlightenment are the pāramīs themselves, divided into two groups: the requisites of merit (*puññasambhāra*) and the requisites of knowledge (*ñāṇasambhāra*).

(v) What are their characteristics, functions, manifestations, and proximate causes?

Firstly, all the pāramīs, without exception, have as their characteristic the benefitting of others; as their function, the rendering of help to others, or not vacillating; as their manifestation, the wish for the welfare of others, or Buddhahood; and as their proximate cause, great compassion, or compassion and skillful means.

Taken separately, the perfection of giving is the volition of relinquishing oneself and one's belongings, accompanied by compassion and skillful means. The perfection of virtue is good conduct of body and speech, accompanied by compassion and skillful means; in denotation, it is the abstinence from what should not be done, the volition to do what should be done, etc. The perfection of renunciation is the act of consciousness that occurs renouncing sense pleasures and existence preceded by the perception of their inherent unsatisfactoriness, and accompanied by compassion and skillful means. The perfection of wisdom is the comprehension of the general and particular characteristics of dhammas, accompanied by compassion and skillful means. The perfection of energy is bodily and mental work for the welfare of others, accompanied by compassion and skillful means. The perfection of patience is the endurance of harm imposed by beings and formations, or the act of consciousness occurring in such a mode, predominated by non-aversion and accompanied by compassion and skillful means. The perfection of truthfulness is non-deceptiveness in speech, analyzed into an abstinence, a volition, etc., accompanied by compassion and skillful means. The perfection of determination is the unshakable determination to undertake (activity for the good of others), accompanied by compassion and skillful means; or it is the act of consciousness occurring in such a mode. The perfection of loving kindness is the wish to provide for the welfare and happiness of the world, accompanied by compassion and skillful means; in denotation, it is benevolence. The perfection of equanimity is the attitude of impartiality towards desirable and undesirable beings and formations, dispelling attraction and repulsion, accompanied by compassion and skillful means.

(On the basis of these definitions, the characteristics, etc., may be stated thus:)

(1) *Giving* has the characteristic of relinquishing; its function is to dispel greed for things that can be given away; its manifestation is non-attachment, or the achievement of prosperity and a favorable state of existence; an object that can he relinquished is its proximate cause.

(2) *Virtue* has the characteristic of composing (*sīlana*); coordinating (*samādhāna*) and establishing (*patiṭṭhana*) are also mentioned as its characteristic. Its function is to dispel moral depravity, or its function is blameless conduct; its manifestation is moral purity; shame and moral dread are its proximate cause.

(3) *Renunciation* has the characteristic of departing from sense pleasures and existence; its function is to verify their inherent unsatisfactoriness; its manifestation is the withdrawal from them; a sense of spiritual urgency is its proximate cause.

(4) *Wisdom* has the characteristic of penetrating the real specific nature (of dhammas), or the characteristic of sure penetration, like the penetration of an arrow shot by a skillful archer; its function is to illuminate the objective field, like a lamp; its manifestation is non-confusion, like a guide in a forest; concentration, or the four (noble) truths, is its proximate cause.

(5) *Energy* has the characteristic of striving; its function is to fortify; its manifestation is indefatigability; an occasion for the arousing of energy, or a sense of spiritual urgency, is its proximate cause.

(6) *Patience* has the characteristic of acceptance; its function is to endure the desirable and undesirable; its manifestation is tolerance or non-opposition; seeing things as they really are is its proximate cause.

(7) *Truthfulness* has the characteristic of non-deceptiveness in speech; its function is to verify in accordance with fact; its manifestation is excellence; honesty is its proximate cause.

(8) *Determination* has the characteristic of determining upon the requisites of enlightenment; its function is to overcome their opposites; its manifestation is unshakeableness in that task; the requisites of enlightenment are its proximate cause.

(9) *Loving kindness* has the characteristic of promoting the welfare (of living beings); its function is to provide for their welfare, or its function is to remove resentment; its manifestation is kindliness; seeing the agreeable side of beings is its proximate cause.

(10) *Equanimity* has the characteristic of promoting the aspect of neutrality; its function is to see things impartially; its manifestation is

the subsiding of attraction and repulsion; reflection upon the fact that all beings inherit the results of their own kamma is its proximate cause.

And here it should be mentioned that accompaniment by compassion and skillful means is the distinguishing feature of the characteristic of each virtue—e.g., of relinquishing in the case of giving, etc. For the virtues such as giving, etc., which occur in the mental continuities of bodhisattvas, are always accompanied by compassion and skillful means. It is this which makes them pāramīs.

(vi) What is their condition?

The condition of the pāramīs is, firstly, the great aspiration (*abhinīhāra*). This is the aspiration supported by the eight qualifications (to be shortly discussed), which occurs thus: "Crossed I would cross, freed I would free, tamed I would tame, calmed I would calm, comforted I would comfort, attained to nibbāna I would lead to nibbāna, purified I would purify, enlightened I would enlighten!" This is the condition for all the pāramīs without exception.

The eight qualifications through which the aspiration succeeds are: the human state, the male sex, the cause, the sight of the Master, the going forth, the achievement of noble qualities, extreme dedication, and strong desire.[198]

(1) The human state (*manussatta*): The aspiration for Buddhahood only succeeds when made by one who has attained to the human state of existence, not when made by one existing as a nāga, supaṇṇa, etc. Why? Because these other states do not correspond with the state of a Buddha (who always arises in the human state).

(2) The male sex (*liṅgasampatti*): For one who has attained to the human state, the aspiration only succeeds when made by a man, not when made by a woman, eunuch, neuter, or hermaphrodite. Why? For the aforesaid reason (i.e., because the Buddha is always of the male sex), and because there is no fulfillment of the required characteristics (in these other cases). As it is said: "This is impossible, bhikkhus, this cannot come to pass, that a woman might become a Holy One, a perfectly enlightened Buddha" (MN 115.15, AN 1:15).

198. See Bv II v. 59.

(3) The cause (*hetu*): the achievement of the necessary supporting conditions. Even for a man, the aspiration only succeeds for one endowed with the necessary supporting conditions, that is, one who has achieved the requisite causal foundation, not for anyone else.

(4) The sight of the Master (*satthāradassana*): the personal presence of the Master. The aspiration only succeeds when made by one aspiring in the presence of a living Buddha. When made after the Exalted One has passed into parinibbāna—before a shrine, at the foot of the Bodhi Tree, in front of an image, or in the presence of paccekabuddhas or the Buddha's disciples—the aspiration does not succeed. Why? Because the recipient lacks the power (necessary to confirm the aspiration). The aspiration only succeeds when made in the presence of the Buddhas, for they alone possess spiritual power adequate to the loftiness of the aspiration.

(5) The going forth (*pabbajjā*): The aspiration succeeds only when made in the presence of the Exalted Buddha by one who has gone forth (into the homeless state of a monk), either as a bhikkhu or as an ascetic who maintains the doctrine of kamma and the moral efficacy of action; it does not succeed for one living in the household state. Why? Because the household state does not correspond with that of a Buddha (who has himself gone forth). The great bodhisattvas (in their last existence) attain the supreme enlightenment only after they have gone forth into homelessness, not while they are still householders. Therefore, at the time of making the resolution, it is only one who has gone forth, endowed with the appropriate qualities and determination, who can succeed.

(6) The achievement of noble qualities (*guṇasampatti*): the achievement of such noble qualities as the direct knowledges, etc. For the aspiration only succeeds when made by one who has gone forth and gained the eight meditative attainments (*samāpatti*) and the five mundane kinds of direct knowledge;[199] it does not succeed for one devoid of these qualities. Why? Because one devoid of them is incapable of investigating the pāramīs. It is because he possesses the necessary supporting conditions and the direct knowledges that the

---

199. The eight meditative attainments are the four jhānas and the four immaterial attainments. The five mundane kinds of direct knowledge are discussed briefly below, in the section on the practice of the perfection of wisdom.

Great Man, after he has made the aspiration, is able to investigate the pāramīs by himself.

(7) Extreme dedication (*adhikāra*): extreme devotion. The aspiration only succeeds for one endowed with the aforesaid qualities who at the time has such strong devotion for the Buddhas that he is prepared to relinquish his very life for them.

(8) Strong desire (*chandatā*): wholesome desire, the wish for accomplishment. One possessed of the aforesaid qualities must have strong desire, yearning, and longing to practice the dhammas culminating in Buddhahood. Only then does his aspiration succeed, not otherwise.

The following similes illustrate the magnitude of the desire required. If he were to hear: "He alone can attain Buddhahood who can cross a whole world system filled with water and reach the farther shore by the bare strength of his arms"—he would not deem that difficult to do, but would be filled with desire for the task and would not shrink away. If he were to hear: "He alone can attain Buddhahood who can tread across a whole world system filled with flameless, smokeless red-hot coals, cross over, and reach the other side," etc.... If he were to hear: "He alone can attain Buddhahood who can tread across a whole world system that has become a solid mass of sharp pointed sword-stakes, cross over, and reach the other side," etc.... If he were to hear: "He alone can attain Buddhahood who can cut through a whole world system that has become a jungle of thorny creepers covered by a solid thicket of bamboo, cross over, and reach the other side," etc.... If he were to hear: "Buddhahood can only be attained after being tortured in hell for four incalculables and a 100,000 aeons"—he would not deem that difficult to do, but would be filled with desire for the task and would not shrink away. Such is the magnitude of the desire required.

The aspiration, made by one endowed with these eight factors, is in denotation the act of consciousness occurring together with the collection of these eight factors. Its characteristic is rightly resolving to attain the supreme enlightenment. Its function is to yearn, "Oh, may I awaken to the supreme perfect enlightenment, and bring well-being and happiness to all beings!" It is manifest as the root cause for the requisites of enlightenment. Its proximate cause is great compassion, or the achievement of the necessary supporting conditions. Since it has as its object the inconceivable plane of the Buddhas and the welfare of the whole immeasurable world of beings, it should be seen as the loftiest, most sublime, and most exalted distinction of merit, endowed with immeasurable potency, the root cause of all the dhammas culminating in Buddhahood.

Simultaneous with its arising, the Great Man enters upon the practice of the vehicle to great enlightenment. He becomes fixed in his destiny, irreversible, and therefore properly gains the designation "bodhisattva." His mind becomes fully devoted to the supreme enlightenment in its completeness, and his capacity to fulfill the training in the requisites of enlightenment is established. For when their aspiration succeeds, the Great Men correctly investigate all the pāramīs with their self-evolved knowledge which prefigures their future attainment of omniscience. Then they undertake their practice, and fulfill them in due order, as was done by the wise Sumedha when he made his great aspiration.

The aspiration has four conditions (*paccaya*), four causes (*hetu*), and four powers (*bala*).

Therein, what are the four conditions? (1) First, the Great Man sees a Tathāgata performing a miracle, replete with wonders and marvels, through the great spiritual power of a Buddha. His mind, taking this display as its object and support, becomes fixed upon the great enlightenment, and he thinks: "This Dhamma-element is indeed endowed with tremendous spiritual power, since by penetrating it the Exalted One has acquired such a wonderful and marvelous nature and such inconceivable spiritual power." Taking this display of the Buddha's spiritual power as condition and support, he resolves upon the supreme enlightenment and fixes his mind on this goal. (2) In the second case he does not see the great spiritual power of the Tathāgata, but he hears: "The Exalted One is of such and such a nature." Taking this as condition and support, he resolves upon the supreme enlightenment and fixes his mind on this goal. (3) In the third, he neither sees the great spiritual power of the Tathāgata, nor hears about it from another, but he hears someone expounding the Tathāgata's Dhamma with a discourse concerning the spiritual power of a Buddha, such as a discourse on the ten powers of a Tathāgata (MN 12.9–20). Taking this as condition and support, he resolves upon the supreme enlightenment and fixes his mind on this goal. (4) In the fourth case, he neither sees the great spiritual power of the Tathāgata, nor hears about it from another, nor hears the Dhamma of the Tathāgata. But he is a man of lofty temperament and a noble disposition, and he thinks: "I will protect the heritage, lineage, tradition, and law of the Buddhas." To this end he honors, reveres, esteems, worships, and venerates the Dhamma. Taking this as condition and support, he resolves upon the supreme enlightenment and fixes his mind on this goal.

What are the four causes for the great aspiration? (1) First, the Great Man is naturally endowed with the necessary supporting conditions (*upanissaya*), having observed his course of duties under former Buddhas. (2) The Great Man is naturally endowed with a compassionate temperament and disposition. He desires to alleviate the suffering of beings and is even ready to relinquish his own body and life to do so. (3) Until he reaches his goal, the Great Man is willing to struggle and strive for an extremely long time along a course involving great hardship, without fear and without becoming disenchanted with all the suffering of the round, all for the sake of the welfare of other beings. (4) The Great Man relies upon good friends, who restrain him from evil and establish him in what is good.

These are the necessary supporting conditions with which the Great Man is endowed: Just as his temperament slants, slopes, and slides without deviation to full enlightenment, so too it inclines to conduct for the welfare of beings; for in the presence of former Buddhas he has made the resolution for full enlightenment, declaring mentally or verbally: "I too would become a perfectly enlightened Buddha and promote the welfare and happiness of all beings." Because he is endowed with such supporting conditions, the following traits appear in him, creating a sharp distinction between himself and beings bound for the enlightenment of a disciple (*sāvakabodhisatta*) or the enlightenment of a paccekabuddha (*paccekabodhisatta*), with regard to their faculties (*indriyato*), ways of practice (*paṭipattito*), and skillfulness (*kosallato*). First, the Great Man, endowed with the necessary supporting conditions, possesses lucid faculties and lucid knowledge, but not so the others. Second, the Great Man practices not for his own welfare but for the welfare of others—for the welfare and happiness of the many, out of compassion for the world, for the good, welfare, and happiness of gods and men, but not so the others. And third, he applies skillfulness to his practice through his ingenuity in creating opportunities (to benefit others) and his skill in distinguishing what is possible from what is not possible.

Thus the Great Man is naturally inclined to giving and delights in giving. Whenever he has anything that may be given away he gives it away and does not feel any annoyance on account of giving. He is constantly and continually in the habit of sharing. He gives joyfully, full of solicitude, not with an apathetic mind. Even after giving a large gift he does not become complacent, much less after giving a small gift. To generate zeal in others, he speaks in praise of giving; he delivers discourses concerned with giving; he is elated when he sees others practicing giving; and he gives fearlessness to others in fearful situations. These are some of the Great Man's traits, indicating the perfection of giving, due to his inclination towards giving.

Again, the Great Man feels shame and moral dread over evil deeds such as taking life, etc. He is benevolent towards living beings. He is meek, good-natured, free from craftiness and hypocrisy, upright, easy to admonish and endowed with qualities which make him easy to admonish, gentle, compliant, and humble. He never takes an article belonging to someone else, not even a blade of grass. If he offers to cover another's expenses himself, he does not break his word. If someone, through forgetfulness or negligence, leaves some article behind, he reminds him and endeavors to prevent it from falling into another's hands. He is not lustful, does not arouse even an evil thought over women bound to other men, and avoids misconduct with women from afar. He is a speaker of truth, devoted to truth; one who reconciles those who are at variance and promotes friendships; his speech is endearing, preceded by a smile, congenial; he speaks on the good, speaks on the Dhamma. He is free from covetousness, ill will, and inverted views, possessing the knowledge of the ownership of action and the knowledge in conformity with the Four Noble Truths. He is grateful and thankful, venerates his elders, is completely pure in his livelihood, and a lover of the Dhamma. He exhorts others to undertake the Dhamma, restrains beings in every possible way from doing what is improper, and establishes them in the fulfillment of their duties. He himself endeavors to fulfil his own duties, and if he finds that he has done something he should not have done he immediately desists. These are some of the Great Man's traits, indicating the perfection of virtue, due to his inclination towards virtue.

Again, his defilements and hindrances are feeble. He inclines towards solitude and is generally free from distraction. Evil thoughts do not invade his mind. When he has gone into solitude he can concentrate his mind with little trouble. Thoughts of loving kindness readily flow from him even towards those who are hostile towards him; how much more then towards others? He is mindful, remembering and recollecting what was done and said long ago, and intelligent, being endowed with wisdom nourished by the Dhamma. He is adroit in the fulfilment of his various duties and energetic in working for the welfare of beings. Through the power of his patience he can endure anything. His determination is unshakable, and he stands firm in his undertakings (to promote the welfare of beings). And he remains equanimous in all situations requiring equanimity. These are some of the Great Man's traits, indicating the remaining pāramīs, due to his inclination towards the qualities for which they stand.

When it is said of the Great Man, endowed with these traits indicating the requisites of enlightenment, that "reliance upon good friends is a cause for the great aspiration"—this, in brief, is the characteristic of the good friend. The good friend possesses faith, virtue, learning, renunciation, energy, mindfulness, concentration, and wisdom. Through his accomplishment in faith he has faith in the enlightenment of the Tathāgata and in kamma and its fruits; thus he does not abandon his wish for the welfare of beings, the root cause for the supreme enlightenment. Through his accomplishment in virtue he is dear and agreeable to beings, revered and esteemed, an exhorter, a censor of evil, a teacher patient in speech. Through his accomplishment in learning he gives profound discourses, leading to the welfare and happiness of beings. Through his accomplishment in renunciation he is of few wishes, content, secluded, and aloof. Through his accomplishment in energy he is energetic in promoting the welfare of beings. Through his accomplishment in mindfulness his mindfulness is established in blameless states. Through his accomplishment in concentration he is undistracted and concentrated in mind. Through his accomplishment in wisdom he understands things in their undistorted nature. Through mindfulness he examines the consequences of wholesome and unwholesome actions; through wisdom he understands as they really are what is beneficial and harmful for beings; through concentration he unifies his mind on that matter; and through energy he restrains beings from what is harmful and enjoins them in what is beneficial. Hence it is said:

He is dear, revered, and esteemed,
A teacher patient in speech.
The talks he gives are deep and profound,
He does not enjoin one in improper ways. (AN 7:36)

Relying on a good friend possessed of these qualities, the Great Man brings to perfection his own achievement of the necessary supporting conditions. Having fully purified his end and means and come into possession of the four powers, it is not long before he acquires the eight factors, makes the great aspiration, and becomes established in the state of a bodhisattva—irreversible, fixed in destination, bound for full enlightenment.

These are his *four powers:* (1) The "internal power" (*ajjhattikabala*) is the longing or undeviating inclination for the supreme enlightenment which is grounded upon personal ideals (*attasannissaya*) and in reverence for the Dhamma; through this power the Great Man, dominated by his personal ideals (*attādhipati*) and upheld by a sense of shame, forms the aspiration, fulfills the pāramīs, and attains the supreme enlightenment. (2) The "external power" (*bāhirabala*) is the longing or undeviating inclination for the supreme enlightenment, which is grounded upon consideration for others; through this power the Great Man, dominated by a consideration for the world (*lokādhipati*) and upheld by a sense of moral dread,[200] forms the aspiration, fulfills the pāramīs, and attains the supreme enlightenment. (3) The "power of the supporting conditions" (*upanissayabala*) is the longing or undeviating inclination for the supreme enlightenment based on the achievement of the necessary supporting conditions; through this power the Great Man, endowed with sharp faculties and a lucid constitution and upheld by mindfulness, forms the aspiration, fulfills the pāramīs, and attains the supreme enlightenment. (4) The "power of effort" (*payogabala*) is the Great Man's endowment with the appropriate effort for supreme enlightenment, that is, his thoroughness and perseverance in his work; through this power the Great Man, with purified effort and uninterrupted work, forms the aspiration, fulfills the pāramīs, and attains the supreme enlightenment.

---

200. Preferring here the reading in N.Sub.Cy., *ottappasannissaya.* Cp-a has *mānāpassaya*, "upheld by conceit," which seems out of place.

The aspiration originating by means of the four conditions, the four causes, and the four powers, and succeeding when it becomes endowed with the collection of eight factors, is the condition—the root cause—for the pāramīs. When it arises, four wonderful and marvellous qualities establish themselves in the Great Man: (1) He develops a heart of love for all living beings in every realm of existence, just as if they were his own dear children; yet his mind does not become defiled by worldly affection for children. (2) His inclination and efforts turn towards promoting the welfare and happiness of beings. (3) The potential Buddha-qualities within himself grow more and more prominent and come to maturity. (4) Since the Great Man possesses the condition for the loftiest flood of merit and goodness, the very nutriment of happiness, he becomes worthy of gifts, the ultimate receptacle for the reverence of beings, an unequalled field of merit for the world. It is in this way that the great aspiration, with its numerous noble qualities and benefits, functions as the condition for the pāramīs.

Like the aspiration, great compassion (*mahākaruṇā*) and skillful means (*upāyakosalla*) are also conditions for the pāramīs. Therein, "skillful means" is the wisdom which transforms giving (and the other nine virtues) into requisites of enlightenment. Through their great compassion and skillful means, the Great Men devote themselves to working uninterruptedly for the welfare of others without any concern for their own happiness and without any fear of the extremely difficult course of conduct that great bodhisattvas must follow. And their nature is such that they are able to promote the welfare and happiness of beings even on occasions when they are merely seen, heard of, or recollected, (since even the sight, report, or thought of them) inspires confidence. Through his wisdom, the bodhisattva perfects within himself the character of a Buddha, and through his compassion, the ability to perform the work of a Buddha. Through wisdom he brings himself across (the stream of becoming), through compassion he leads others across. Through wisdom he understands the suffering of others, through compassion he strives to alleviate their suffering. Through wisdom he becomes disenchanted with suffering, through compassion he accepts suffering. Through wisdom he aspires for nibbāna, through compassion he remains in the round of existence. Through compassion he enters saṃsāra, through wisdom he does not delight in it. Through wisdom he destroys all attachments, but because his wisdom is accompanied by compassion he never desists from activity that benefits others. Through compassion he shakes with sympathy for all, but because his compassion is accompanied by wisdom his mind is unattached. Through wisdom he is free from "I-making" and "my-making," through compassion he is free from lethargy and depression.

So too, through wisdom and compassion respectively, he becomes his own protector and the protector of others, a sage and a hero, one who does not torment himself and one who does not torment others, one who promotes his own welfare and the welfare of others, fearless and a giver of fearlessness, dominated by consideration for the Dhamma and by consideration for the world, grateful for favors done and forward in doing favors for others, devoid of delusion and devoid of craving, accomplished in knowledge and accomplished in conduct, possessed of the powers and possessed of the grounds of self-confidence. Thus wisdom and compassion, as the means for attaining each of the specific fruits of the pāramitās, is the condition for the pāramīs. And the same pair is a condition for the resolution as well.

The four factors—zeal, intelligence, stability, and beneficent conduct—are likewise conditions for the pāramīs. Because they serve as the basis for the arising of Buddhahood, these factors are called "grounds for Buddhahood" (*buddhabhūmiyo*). Herein, "zeal" (*ussāha*) means energy in striving for the requisites of enlightenment. "Intelligence" (*ummaṅga*) is wisdom in applying skillful means to the requisites of enlightenment. "Stability" (*avatthāna*) is determination, an unshakable determination of the will. "Beneficent conduct" (*hitacariyā*) is the development of loving kindness and compassion.[201]

Another set of conditions is the six inclinations—the inclinations towards renunciation, solitude, non-greed, non-hatred, non-delusion, and escape. For bodhisattvas, seeing the fault in sense pleasures and in household life, incline to renunciation. Seeing the fault in company, they incline to solitude. Seeing the faults in greed, hatred, and delusion, they incline to non-greed, non-hatred, and non-delusion. Seeing the fault in all the realms of existence, bodhisattvas incline to escape. Therefore these six inclinations of bodhisattvas are conditions for the pāramīs. For the pāramīs do not arise without seeing the danger in greed, etc., and the superiority of non-greed, etc. The inclination to non-greed, etc., is the slanting of the mind towards relinquishing, etc., because of the superiority of non-greed, etc.[202]

---

201. Sn-a I 50

So too, for bodhisattvas striving for enlightenment, the inclination towards each of the ten pāramīs is a condition for the practice of each. For bodhisattvas, through their inclination towards giving, see the fault in its opposite, i.e., in stinginess, and therefore fulfill the perfection of giving. Through their inclination towards virtue, they see the fault in moral depravity, and therefore fulfill the perfection of virtue. Through their inclination towards renunciation, they see the fault in sense pleasures and in household life; through their inclination towards knowing things as they really are, they see the faults in ignorance and perplexity; through their inclination towards energy, they see the fault in laziness; through their inclination towards patience, they see the fault in impatience; through their inclination towards truthfulness, they see the fault in deceptive speech; through their inclination towards determination, they see the fault in lack of determination; through their inclination towards loving kindness, they see the fault in ill will; and through their inclination towards equanimity, they see the danger in the vicissitudes of the world. Thus they fulfill the perfection of renunciation, and the other perfections down to equanimity. In this way, the inclination towards giving, and towards the other nine virtues, by bringing about the achievement of all the pāramīs, serve as their condition.

Reviewing the danger in their opposites and the benefits in their practice is another condition for the pāramīs; e.g., in the case of the perfection of giving, the danger in non-relinquishing and the benefit in relinquishing. This is the method of reviewing:

(1) The *perfection of giving* should be reflected upon thus: "Possessions such as fields, land, bullion, gold, cattle, buffaloes, slaves, children, wives, etc., bring immense harm to those attached to them. Because they stimulate desire they are wanted by many people; they can be confiscated by kings and thieves; they spark off disputes and create enemies; they are basically insubstantial; to acquire and protect them one has to harass others; when they are destroyed, many kinds of calamities, such as sorrow, etc., follow; and because of attachment to these things, the mind becomes obsessed with the stain of stinginess, and as a result one is reborn in the plane of misery. On the other hand, one act of relinquishing these things is one step to safety. Therefore one should diligently relinquish them."

---

202. Ibid.

Further, when a suppliant asks for something, a bodhisattva should reflect: "He is my intimate friend, for he divulges his own secret to me. He is my teacher, for he teaches me: 'When you go, you have to abandon all. Going to the world beyond, you cannot even take your own possessions!' He is a companion helping me to remove my belongings from this world which, like a blazing house, is blazing with the fire of death. In removing this he helps me to get rid of the worry it costs me. He is my best friend, for by enabling me to perform this noble act of giving, he helps me to accomplish the most eminent and difficult of all achievements, the attainment of the plane of the Buddhas."

He should further reflect: "He honors me with a lofty task; therefore I should acknowledge that honor faithfully." And: "Since life is bound to end I should give even when not asked, much more when asked." And: "Those with a lofty temperament search for someone to give to, but he has come to me on his own accord because of my merit." And: "Bestowing a gift upon a suppliant will be beneficial to me as well as to him." And: "Just as I would benefit myself, so should I benefit all the world." And: "If there were no suppliants, how would I fulfill the perfection of giving?" And: "Everything I acquire should be obtained only to give to others." And: "When will beggars feel free to take my belongings on their own accord, without asking?" And: "How can I be dear and agreeable to beggars, and how can they be dear and agreeable to me? How can I give, and after giving be elated, exultant, filled with rapture and joy? And how can beggars be so on my account? How can my inclination to giving be lofty? How can I give to beggars even without beings asked, knowing their hearts' desire?" And: "Since there are goods, and beggars have come, not to give them something would be a great deception on my part." And: "How can I relinquish my own life and limbs to those who ask for them?"

He should arouse a desire to give things away without concern by reflecting: "Good returns to the one who gives without his concern, just as the boomerang[203] returns to the one who threw it without his concern." If a dear person asks for something, he should arouse joy by reflecting: "One who is dear is asking me for something." If an

---

203. *Kiṭṭaka.* None of the meanings in the standard dictionaries are relevant to the context. This guess at its meaning seems to be what the context requires.

indifferent person asks for something, he should arouse joy by reflecting: "Surely, if I give him something he will become my friend, since giving to those who ask wins their affection." And if a hostile person asks for something he should be especially happy, thinking: "My foe is asking me for something; though he is hostile towards me, by means of this gift he will surely become my dear friend." Thus he should give to neutral and hostile people in the same way he gives to dear people, having first aroused loving kindness and compassion.

If, due to their cumulative force, states of greed should arise for things that can be given away, the bodhisattva-aspirant should reflect: "Well now, good man, when you made the aspiration for full enlightenment, did you not surrender this body as well as the merit gained in relinquishing it for the sake of helping all beings? Attachment to external objects is like the bathing of an elephant; therefore you should not be attached to anything. Suppose there is a great medicine-tree, and someone in need of its roots, takes away its roots; someone in need of its shoots, bark, trunk, limbs, heartwood, branches, foliage, flowers, or fruits, takes away its shoots, bark, trunk, etc. The tree would not be assailed by such thoughts as: 'They are taking away my belongings.' In the same way, when I have undertaken to exert myself for the welfare of all the world, I should not arouse even the subtlest wrong thought over this wretched, ungrateful, impure body, which I have entrusted to the service of others. And besides, what distinction can be made between the internal material elements (of the body) and the external material elements (of the world)? They are both subject to inevitable breaking up, dispersal, and dissolution. This is only confused prattle, the adherence to this body as 'This is mine, this am I, this is my self.' I should have no more concern over my own hands, feet, eyes, and flesh, than over external things. Instead I should arouse the thought to surrender them to others: 'Let those who need them take them away.'"

As he reflects in this way, resolved upon full enlightenment, without concern for his body or life, his bodily, vocal, and mental actions will easily become fully purified. When his bodily, vocal, and mental actions, along with his livelihood, become purified, he abides in the practice of the true way, and through his skillful means in regard to gain and loss, he is able to benefit all beings to an even greater extent by relinquishing material gifts and by giving the gift of fearlessness and the gift of the true Dhamma.

This is the method of reflecting on the perfection of giving.

(2) The *perfection of virtue* should be reflected upon as follows: "Even the waters of the Ganges cannot wash away the stain of hatred, yet the water of virtue is able to do so. Even yellow sandalwood cannot cool the fever of lust, yet virtue is able to remove it. Virtue is the unique adornment of the good, surpassing the adornments cherished by ordinary people, such as necklaces, diadems, and earrings. It is a sweet-scented fragrance superior to incense as it pervades all directions and is always in place; a supreme magical spell which wins the homage of deities and of powerful khattiyas, etc.; a staircase ascending to the world of the gods, to the heaven of the Four Great Kings,[204] etc.; a means for achieving the jhānas and the direct knowledges; a highway leading to the great city of nibbāna; the foundation for the enlightenment of disciples, paccekabuddhas, and perfectly enlightened Buddhas. And as a means for the fulfilment of all one's wishes and desires, it surpasses the tree of plenty and the wish-fulfilling gem.

And the Exalted One has said: "The heart's resolution of the virtuous, bhikkhus, succeeds on account of his purity" (AN 8:35). And: "If, bhikkhus, a bhikkhu should wish: 'May I be dear and agreeable to my companions in the Holy Life, revered and esteemed,' he should be perfect in fulfilling the rules of conduct" (MN 6.3). And: "Wholesome virtues, Ānanda, lead to freedom from remorse" (AN 10:1). And: "These, householders, are the five benefits of the virtuous man's endowment with virtue" (DN 16.1.24). Thus the noble qualities of virtue should be reflected upon by way of these suttas, and the danger in moral depravity by way of such suttas as "The Simile of the Mass of Fire" (AN 7:68).

Virtue should be reflected upon as the basis for rapture and joy; as giving immunity from fear of self-reproach, the reproach of others, temporal punishment, and an evil destination after death; as praised by the wise; as the root cause for freedom from remorse; as the basis for security; and as surpassing the achievements of high birth, wealth, sovereignty, long life, beauty, status, kinsmen, and friends. For great

---

204. The first and lowest of the six sense-sphere heavens of Buddhist cosmology. The "etc." indicates that the observance of virtue of a superior grade and intensity will give access to the five higher heavens of the sensuous realm, or to the Brahma-world if coupled with the attainment of the meditative absorptions.

rapture and joy arise in the virtuous man when he reflects on his own accomplishment in virtue: "I have done what is wholesome, I have done what is good, I have built myself a shelter from fear." The virtuous man does not blame himself, and other wise men do not blame him, and he does not encounter the dangers of temporal punishment or an evil destination after death. To the contrary, the wise praise the noble character of the virtuous man, and the virtuous man is not subject to the remorse which arises in the immoral man when he thinks: "I have committed evil, wicked, sinful deeds." And virtue is the supreme basis for security, since it is the foundation for diligence, a blessing and a means for achieving great benefits, such as preventing the loss of wealth, etc. Accomplishment in virtue surpasses birth in a good family, since a virtuous man of low birth deserves to be worshipped even by great, powerful khattiyas. Virtue surpasses material wealth, for it cannot be confiscated by thieves, follows one to the world beyond, produces great fruit, and acts as the foundation for such qualities as serenity, etc. Because it enables one to achieve supreme sovereignty over one's own mind, virtue surpasses the sovereignty of khattiyas, etc. And because of their virtue, beings attain sovereignty in their respective orders. Virtue is superior even to life, for it is said that a single day in the life of the virtuous is better than a hundred years of life devoid of virtue (Dhp 110); and there being life, the disavowal of the training (in the Holy Life) is called (spiritual) death (MN 105.22). Virtue surpasses the achievement of beauty, for it makes one beautiful even to one's enemies, and it cannot be vanquished by the adversities of aging and sickness. As the foundation for distinguished states of happiness, virtue surpasses such distinguished dwellings as palaces, mansions, etc., and such distinguished social positions as that of a king, prince, or general. Because it promotes one's highest welfare and follows one to the world beyond, virtue surpasses kinsmen and friends, even those who are close and affectionate. Again, in accomplishing the difficult task of self-protection, virtue is superior to troops of elephants, horses, chariots, and infantry, as well as to such devices as mantras, spells, and blessings, for it depends on oneself, does not depend on others, and has a great sphere of influence. Thus it is said: "The Dhamma protects the one who lives by the Dhamma" (Th 303).

When one reflects in this way upon the numerous noble qualities of virtue, one's unfulfilled achievement of virtue will become fulfilled, and one's unpurified virtue will become purified.

If, due to their cumulative force, states antithetical to virtue, such as aversion, should arise from time to time, the aspirant should reflect: "Did you not make the resolution to win full enlightenment? One defective in virtue cannot even succeed in mundane affairs, much less in supramundane matters. You should reach the peak of virtue, for virtue is the foundation for supreme enlightenment, the foremost of all achievements. You should always be well behaved, safeguarding your virtue perfectly, more carefully than a hen safeguarding its eggs. Further, by teaching the Dhamma you should help beings to enter and reach maturity in the three vehicles.[205] But the word of a morally dubious man is no more reliable than the remedy of a doctor who does not consider what is suitable for his patients. How can I be trustworthy, so that I can help beings to enter and reach maturity in the three vehicles? I must be pure in character and in virtue. How can I acquire the distinguished attainments such as the jhānas, etc., so that I will be capable of helping others and of fulfilling the perfection of wisdom, etc? The distinguished attainments such as the jhānas, etc., are not possible without purification of virtue. Therefore virtue should be made perfectly pure."

(3) The *perfection of renunciation* should be reflected upon by first discerning the dangers in household life, according to the text "Household life is constricting, a path for the dust of passions," etc. (DN 2.41); in sense pleasures, according to the text, "Sense pleasures are like a skeleton," etc. (MN 54.15); and in sensual desire, according to the text "Suppose a man borrowed a loan and undertook work," etc. (DN 2.69). Then, in the opposite way, one should reflect upon the benefits in going forth,[206] according to the text "Going forth is like open space," etc. (DN 2.41). This is a brief statement. For details one should consult such suttas as "The Great Mass of Suffering" (MN 13) or "The Simile of the Venomous Snakes" (SN 35:238).

205. See discussion of the "three vehicles," in Introduction, p. 41.

206. *Pabbajjā*. The going forth from household life into the homeless life of a monk; specifically, the first stage of ordination into the Buddhist monastic order.

(4) For the *perfection of wisdom*, the noble qualities of wisdom should be considered, as follows: "Without wisdom, the virtues such as giving do not become purified and cannot perform their respective functions. Just as, without life, the bodily organism loses its luster and cannot perform its proper activities, and as without consciousness, the sense faculties cannot exercise their functions in their respective spheres, just so, without wisdom, the faculties such as faith, etc., cannot perform their functions. Wisdom is the chief cause for the practice of the other pāramīs. For when their wisdom-eyes open up, the great bodhisattvas give even their own limbs and organs without extolling themselves and disparaging others. Like medicine-trees, they give devoid of discrimination, filled with joy throughout the three times. By means of wisdom, the act of relinquishing, exercised with skillful means and practiced for the welfare of others, attains the status of a pāramī; but giving for one's own benefit is like an investment. Again, without wisdom, virtue cannot be severed from the defilements of craving, etc., and therefore cannot even reach purification, much less serve as the foundation for the qualities of an omniscient Buddha. Only the man of wisdom clearly recognizes the dangers in household life, in the strands of sense pleasure, and in saṃsāra, and sees the benefits in going forth, in attaining the jhānas, and in realizing nibbāna; and he alone goes forth into homelessness, develops the jhānic attainments, and directed towards nibbāna, establishes others therein.

"Energy devoid of wisdom does not accomplish the purpose desired since it is wrongly aroused, and it is better not to arouse energy at all than to arouse it in the wrong way. But when energy is conjoined with wisdom, there is nothing it cannot accomplish, if equipped with the proper means. Again, only the man of wisdom can patiently tolerate the wrongs of others, not the dull-witted man. In the man lacking wisdom, the wrongs of others only provoke impatience; but for the wise, they call his patience into play and make it grow even stronger. The wise man, having understood as they really are three noble truths,[207] their causes and opposites, never speaks deceptively to others. So too, having fortified himself with the power of wisdom, the wise man in his fortitude forms an unshakable determination to undertake all the pāramīs. Only the man of wisdom is skillful in

---

207. Excluding the third noble truth, the cessation of suffering, which the bodhisattva will only realize directly upon his attainment to Buddhahood.

providing for the welfare of all beings, without discriminating between dear people, neutrals, and enemies. And only by means of wisdom can he remain indifferent to the vicissitudes of the world, such as gain and loss, without being affected by them."

In this way one should reflect upon the noble qualities of wisdom, recognizing it to be the cause for the purification of all the pāramīs.

Furthermore, without wisdom there is no achievement of vision, and without the achievement of vision there can be no accomplishment in virtue. One lacking virtue and vision cannot achieve concentration, and without concentration one cannot even secure one's own welfare, much less the lofty goal of providing for the welfare of others. Therefore a bodhisattva, practicing for the welfare of others, should admonish himself: "Have you made a thorough effort to purify your wisdom?" For it is by the spiritual power of wisdom that the Great Beings, established in the four foundations, benefit the world with the four bases of beneficence, help beings enter the path to emancipation, and bring their faculties to maturity.[208] Through the power of wisdom, again, they are devoted to the investigation of the aggregates, sense bases, etc., fully comprehend the processes of origination and cessation in accordance with actuality, develop the qualities of giving, etc., to the stages of distinction and penetration, and perfect the training of bodhisattvas. Thus the perfection of wisdom should be reinforced by determining the noble qualities of wisdom with their numerous modes and constituents.

(5) The *perfection of energy* should be reflected upon thus: "Without energy a man cannot even achieve success in worldly works directed to visible ends. But there is nothing the energetic, indefatigable man cannot achieve. One lacking energy cannot undertake to rescue all beings from the great flood of saṃsāra; even if his energy is only moderate he will give up in the middle. But one bristling with energy can achieve perfection in all he undertakes."

The noble qualities of energy should be further reviewed as follows: "One intent on rescuing himself alone from the mire of saṃsāra cannot fulfil his ideal if he relaxes his energy; how much less one who aspires to rescue the entire world?" And: "Through the power of energy such wrong thoughts as the following are kept away: 'It is quite right for you to escape from the suffering of saṃsāra by yourself alone; for so long as

---

208. For the four foundations, see p. 302; for the four bases, p. 310.

you are a foolish worldling the host of defilements is as difficult to restrain as a herd of mad elephants, the kamma caused by them is like a murderer with drawn sword, the evil destinations based on these actions stand constantly before you with open doors, and evil friends are always around to enjoin you in those actions and admonish you to practice them.'" And: "If even full enlightenment can be achieved by one's own energy, what can be difficult?"

(6) The *perfection of patience* should be considered next: "Patience is the unimpeded weapon of the good in the development of noble qualities, for it dispels anger, the opposite of all such qualities, without residue. It is the adornment of those capable of vanquishing the foe; the strength of recluses and brahmins; a stream of water extinguishing the fire of anger; the basis for acquiring a good reputation; a mantra for quelling the poisonous speech of evil people; the supreme source of constancy in those established in restraint. Patience is an ocean on account of its depth; a shore bounding the great ocean of hatred; a panel closing off the door to the plane of misery; a staircase ascending to the worlds of the gods and Brahmās; the ground for the habitation of all noble qualities; the supreme purification of body, speech, and mind."

Patience should be further strengthened by reflecting: "Those who lack patience are afflicted in this world and apply themselves to actions that will lead to their affliction in the life to come." And: "Although this suffering arises through the wrong deeds of others, this body of mine is the field for that suffering, and the action which is its seed was sown by me alone." And: "This suffering will release me from the debt of that kamma." And: "If there were no wrongdoers, how could I accomplish the perfection of patience?" And: "Although he is a wrongdoer now, in the past he was my benefactor." And: "A wrongdoer is also a benefactor, for he is the basis for the developing of patience." And: "All beings are like my own children. Who becomes angry over the misdeeds of his own children?" And: "He wrongs me because of some residue of anger in myself; I should remove this residue." And: "I am just as much the cause as he is for the wrong on account of which this suffering has arisen." And: "All those dhammas by which wrong was done, and those to whom it was done—all those, at this very moment, have ceased. With whom, then, should you now be angry, and by whom should anger be aroused? When all dhammas are non-self, who can do wrong to whom?"

If, due to its cumulative force, anger caused by the wrongs of others should continue to overpower the mind, one should reflect: "Patience is the contributive cause for rendering help to others in return for their wrongs." And: "This wrong, by causing me suffering, is a condition for faith, since suffering is said to be the decisive support for faith, and it is also a condition for the perception of discontent with all the world."[209] And: "This is the nature of the sense faculties—to encounter desirable and undesirable objects. How, then, is it possible not to encounter undesirable objects?" And: "Under the control of anger, a person becomes mad and distraught, so why retaliate?" And: "All these beings are watched over by the Buddha as if they were his own dear children. Therefore I should not be angry with them." And: "When the wrongdoer is endowed with noble qualities, I should not be angry with him. And when he does not have any noble qualities, then I should regard him with compassion." And: "Because of anger my fame and noble qualities diminish, and to the pleasure of my enemies I become ugly, sleep in discomfort, etc." And: "Anger is the only real enemy, for it is the agent of all harm and the destroyer of all good." And: "When one has patience one has no enemies." And "Because of his wrong, the wrongdoer will meet suffering in the future, but so long as I remain patient I will not." And: "Enemies are the consequence of my angry thought. When I vanquish anger by patience, my foe, who is the by-product of my anger, will also be vanquished." And: "I should not relinquish the noble quality of patience because of a little anger. Anger is the antithesis and obstruction to all noble qualities, so if I become angry, how can my virtue, etc., reach fulfilment? And when those qualities are absent, how can I devote myself to helping other beings and attain the ultimate goal in accordance with my vows." And: "When there is patience, the mind becomes concentrated, free from external distraction. With the mind concentrated, all formations appear to reflection as impermanent and suffering, all dhammas as non-self, nibbāna as unconditioned, deathless, peaceful, and sublime, and the Buddha-qualities as endowed with inconceivable and immeasurable potency. Then, established in acquiescence in conformity,[210] the groundlessness of all 'I-making'

---

209. Suffering is said to be the decisive support for faith in the Upanisa Sutta, SN 12:23. The "perception of discontent with all the world" is one of the subjects of meditation mentioned in the Girimānanda Sutta (AN 10:60).

and 'mine-making' becomes evident to reflection thus: 'Mere dhammas alone exist, devoid of a self or of anything pertaining to a self. They arise and pass away in accordance with their conditions. They do not come from anywhere; they do not go anywhere; they are not established anywhere. There is no agency in anything whatsoever.' In this way a bodhisattva becomes fixed in his destiny, bound for enlightenment, irreversible."

This is the method of reflecting upon the perfection of patience.

(7) The *perfection of truthfulness* should be reviewed thus: "Without truthfulness, virtue, etc., is impossible, and there can be no practice in accordance with one's vows. All evil states converge upon the transgression of truth. One who is not devoted to truth is unreliable and his word cannot be accepted in the future. On the other hand, one devoted to truth secures the foundation of all noble qualities. With truthfulness as the foundation, he is capable of purifying and fulfilling all the requisites of enlightenment. Not deceived about the true nature of dhammas, he performs the functions of all the requisites of enlightenment and completes the practice of the bodhisattva path."

(8) The *perfection of determination* should be reviewed thus: "Without firmly undertaking the practice of giving (and the other pāramīs), maintaining an unshakable determination in the encounter with their opposites, and practicing them with constancy and vigor, the bases of enlightenment—i.e., the requisites such as giving, etc.—do not arise."

(9) The *noble qualities of loving kindness* should be reflected upon as follows: "One resolved only upon his own welfare cannot achieve success in this world or a happy rebirth in the life to come without some concern for the welfare of others; how, then, can one wishing to establish all beings in the attainment of nibbāna succeed without loving kindness? And if you wish to ultimately lead all beings to the supramundane achievement of nibbāna, you should begin by wishing for their mundane success here and now." And: "I cannot provide for the welfare and happiness of others merely by wishing for

---

210. *Anulomiyam khantiyam ṭhito.* "Acquiescence in conformity" is the stage in the development of insight where the meditator can accept the basic truths revealed by contemplation without yet having fully apprehended them by wisdom. *Khanti* here signifies the acceptance of recondite doctrines rather than patience in the ordinary sense. See p. 247, n. 196.

it. Let me put forth effort to accomplish it." And: "Now I support them by promoting their welfare and happiness; afterwards they will be my companions in sharing the Dhamma." And: "Without these beings, I could not acquire the requisites of enlightenment. Since they are the cause for the manifestation and perfecting of all the Buddha-qualities, these beings are for me a supreme field of merit, the incomparable basis for planting wholesome roots, the ultimate object of reverence."

Thus one should arouse an especially strong inclination towards promoting the welfare of all beings. And why should loving kindness be developed towards all beings? Because it is the foundation for compassion. For when one delights in providing for the welfare and happiness of other beings with an unbounded heart, the desire to remove their affliction and suffering becomes powerful and firmly rooted. And compassion is the first of all the dhammas culminating in Buddhahood—their footing, foundation, root, head, and chief.

(10) The *perfection of equanimity* should be considered thus: "When there is no equanimity, the offensive actions performed by beings cause oscillation in the mind. And when the mind oscillates, it is impossible to practice the requisites of enlightenment." And: "Even though the mind has been softened with the moisture of loving kindness, without equanimity one cannot purify the requisites of enlightenment and cannot dedicate one's requisites of merit along with their results to furthering the welfare of beings."

Moreover, the undertaking, determination, fulfilment, and completion[211] of all the requisites of enlightenment succeed through the power of equanimity. For without equanimity, the aspirant cannot relinquish something without making false discriminations over gifts and recipients. Without equanimity, he cannot purify his virtue without always thinking about the obstacles to his life and to his vital needs. Equanimity perfects the power of renunciation, for by its means he overcomes discontent and delight. It perfects the functions of all the requisites (by enabling wisdom) to examine them according to their origin. When energy is aroused to excess because it hasn't been examined with equanimity, it cannot perform its proper function of striving. Forbearance and reflective acquiescence (the modes of patience) are possible only in one possessed of equanimity. Because of this quality, he does not speak deceptively about beings or formations.

211. *Samādānādhiṭṭhānapāripūrinipphattiyo.*

By looking upon the vicissitudes of worldly events with an equal mind, his determination to fulfil the practices he has undertaken becomes completely unshakable. And because he is unconcerned over the wrongs done by others, he perfects the abiding in loving kindness. Thus equanimity is indispensable to the practice of all the other pāramīs.

Such is the reflection on the perfection of equanimity.

Thus reviewing the danger in their opposites and the benefits in their practice is a condition for the pāramīs.

Another condition for the pāramīs consists in the fifteen dhammas comprising right conduct (*caraṇa*) and the five mundane kinds of direct knowledge, together with their requisites.[212] Herein, the dhammas comprising right conduct are: restraint by virtue, guarding the doors of the sense faculties, moderation in eating, application to wakefulness, the seven good dhammas,[213] and the four jhānas. The thirteen ascetic practices[214] and the qualities such as fewness of wishes are the requisites for the four states beginning with restraint by virtue. Among the seven good dhammas, the requisites for faith are: the seven recollections—of the Buddha, the Dhamma, and the Saṅgha, of virtue, generosity, the deities, and peace; the avoidance of mean people and association with affectionate people; reflection upon things inspiring confidence; and the disposition towards faith. The requisites for shame and moral dread are: reflection upon the danger in immoral conduct; reflection upon the danger (of rebirth) in the plane of misery; reflection on the fortifying character of wholesome states; the avoidance of people devoid of shame and moral dread and association with people endowed with these qualities; and the disposition towards shame and moral dread. The requisites for learning are: previous effort; interrogation; application to the true Dhamma; the study of blameless branches of knowledge; maturity of the faculties; remoteness from the defilements; the avoidance of ignorant people and association with learned people; and the disposition towards erudition. The requisites for energy are: reflection upon the fearfulness in the

212. These two sets are the foundation for the bodhisattva's endowment with knowledge and conduct, which comes to maturity as one of the nine distinctive attributes of a Buddha indicated in the epithet *vijjācaraṇasampanno*.

213. Faith, shame, moral dread, learning, energy, mindfulness and wisdom.

214. *Dhutadhammā:* the thirteen ascetic practices are discussed in Vism 2.

plane of misery; reflection upon the course to be followed; reflection upon the greatness of the Dhamma; the dispelling of sloth and torpor; the avoidance of lazy people and association with energetic people; reflection upon right endeavor; and the disposition towards energy. The requisites for mindfulness are: mindfulness and clear comprehension; the avoidance of people with confused mindfulness and association with people with established mindfulness; and the disposition towards mindfulness. And the requisites for wisdom are: interrogation; the cleansing of the bases (i.e., maintaining a clean body and dwelling-place); the harmonization of the faculties;[215] the avoidance of dull-witted people and association with wise people; reflection upon the profound course of knowledge; and the inclination towards wisdom.

The requisites for the four jhānas are: the four factors beginning with restraint by virtue; the development of meditation in the preliminary portion with a certain object among the thirty-eight objects of meditation; and the five achievements of mastery.[216] The way the factors of right conduct, etc., serve as conditions for the requisites of enlightenment (i.e., for the pāramīs), can be adduced as follows: "He is capable of offering the gift of fearlessness to beings through the purification of his means (*payoga*) by virtue, etc.; of offering material gifts through the purification of his end (*āsaya*); and of offering the gift of the Dhamma through the purification of both," and so on, as is appropriate in each case. But we do not adduce it at length for fear of getting caught up in excessive details. So too, the "wheels of achievement," etc., are also conditions for the pāramīs.

---

215. The "harmonization of the faculties" requires the balancing of faith with wisdom, and of energy with concentration, since an excess of one member of each pair over its counterpart leads to a deviation from the correct path of practice.

216. The thirty-eight objects are the forty traditional subjects of serenity meditation given in the standard meditation manuals, minus two kasiṇas. See Vism 3.104–105. The preliminary portion of development is the practice preceding and leading up to the jhānas. "The five types of mastery" are mastery in adverting to the jhāna, in attaining it, in resolving, in emerging, and in reviewing. See Vism 3.131–136.

(vii) What is their defilement (*saṅkilesa*)?

In general, being misapprehended by craving, etc., is the defilement of all the pāramīs. Taken separately, discriminating thoughts (*vikappa*) over gifts and recipients are the defilement of the perfection of giving. Discriminating thoughts over beings and times are the defilement of the perfection of virtue. Discriminating thoughts of delight in sense pleasures and existence, and of discontent with their pacification, are the defilement of the perfection of renunciation. Discriminating thoughts of "I" and "mine" are the defilement of the perfection of wisdom; discriminating thoughts leaning to listlessness and restlessness, of the perfection of energy; discriminating thoughts of oneself and others, of the perfection of patience; discriminating thoughts of avowing to have seen what was not seen, etc., of the perfection of truthfulness; discriminating thoughts perceiving flaws in the requisites of enlightenment and virtues in their opposites, of the perfection of determination; discriminating thoughts confusing what is harmful with what is beneficial, of the perfection of loving kindness; and discriminating thoughts over the desirable and undesirable, of the perfection of equanimity. Thus the defilements should be understood.

(viii) What is their cleansing (*vodāna*)?

Their cleansing is the removal of the taints of craving, etc., and the absence of the aforementioned discriminations. For the pāramīs become pure and luminous when untainted by such defilements as craving, conceit, views, anger, malice, denigration, domineering, envy, stinginess, craftiness, hypocrisy, obstinacy, presumption, vanity, and negligence, and when devoid of the discriminating thoughts over gifts and recipients, etc.

(ix) What are their opposites (*paṭipakkha*)?

In general, all the defilements and all unwholesome dhammas are their opposites. Taken separately, stinginess is the opposite of giving, and so on, as mentioned earlier.[217] Further, giving is opposed to greed,

217. See p. 261

hatred, and delusion, since it applies the qualities of non-greed, non-hatred, and non-delusion, to gifts, recipients, and the fruits of giving, respectively. Virtue is opposed to greed, hatred, and delusion, since it removes crookedness and corruption in bodily conduct, etc. Renunciation is opposed to these three corruptions since it avoids indulgence in sense pleasures, the affliction of others, and self-mortification. Wisdom opposes them in so far as greed, etc., create blindness, while knowledge restores sight. Energy opposes them by arousing the true way free from both listlessness and restlessness. Patience opposes them by accepting the desirable, the undesirable, and emptiness. Truthfulness is their opposite because it proceeds in accordance with fact whether others render help or inflict harm. Determination is the opposite of these three defilements since, after vanquishing the vicissitudes of the world, it remains unshakable in fulfilling the requisites of enlightenment in the way they have been undertaken. Loving kindness is the opposite of greed, hatred, and delusion, through its seclusion from the hindrances. And equanimity is their opposite by dispelling attraction and repulsion towards desirable and undesirable objects, respectively, and by proceeding evenly under varying circumstances.

(x) How are they to be practiced?

(1) The *perfection of giving*, firstly, is to be practiced by benefitting beings in many ways—by relinquishing one's happiness, belongings, body, and life to others, by dispelling their fear, and by instructing them in the Dhamma. Herein, giving is threefold by way of the object to be given: the giving of material things (*āmisadāna*), the giving of fearlessness (*abhayadāna*), and the giving of the Dhamma (*dhammadāna*). Among these, the object to be given can be twofold: internal and external. The external gift is tenfold: food, drink, garments, vehicles, garlands, scents, unguents, bedding, dwellings, and lamps. These gifts, again, become manifold by analyzing each into its constituents, e.g., food into hard food, soft food, etc. The external gift can also become sixfold when analyzed by way of sense object (*ārammaṇato*): visible forms, sounds, smells, tastes, tangibles, and non-sensory objects. The sense objects, such as visible forms, become manifold when analyzed into blue, etc. So too, the external gift is manifold by way of the divers valuables and belongings, such as gems,

gold, silver, pearls, coral, etc.; fields, lands, parks, etc.; slaves, cows, buffaloes, etc.

When the Great Man gives an external object, he gives whatever is needed to whomever stands in need of it; and knowing by himself that someone is in need of something, he gives it even unasked, much more when asked. He gives generously, not ungenerously. He gives sufficiently, not insufficiently, when there is something to be given. He does not give because he expects something in return. And when there is not enough to give sufficiently to all, he distributes evenly whatever can be shared. But he does not give things that bring affliction to others, such as weapons, poisons, and intoxicants. Nor does he give amusements that are harmful and lead to negligence. And he does not give unsuitable food or drink to a person who is sick, even though he might ask for it, and he does not give what is suitable beyond the proper measure.

Again, when asked, he gives to householders things appropriate for householders, and to monks things appropriate for monks. He gives to his mother and father, kinsmen and relatives, friends and colleagues, children, wife, slaves, and workers, without causing pain to anyone. Having promised an excellent gift, he does not give something mean. He does not give because he desires gain, honor, or fame, or because he expects something in return, or out of expectation of some fruit other than the supreme enlightenment. He does not give detesting the gift or those who ask. He does not give a discarded object as a gift, not even to unrestrained beggars who revile and abuse him. Invariably he gives with care, with a serene mind, full of compassion. He does not give through belief in superstitious omens; but he gives believing in kamma and its fruit. When he gives he does not afflict those who ask by making them do homage to him, etc.; but he gives without afflicting others. He does not give a gift with the intention of deceiving others or with the intention of injuring; he gives only with an undefiled mind. He does not give a gift with harsh words or a frown, but with words of endearment, congenial speech, and a smile on his face. Whenever greed for a particular object becomes excessive, due to its high value and beauty, its antiquity, or personal attachment, the bodhisattva recognizes his greed, quickly dispels it, seeks out some recipients, and gives it away. And if there should be an object of limited value that can be given and a suppliant expecting it, without a second thought he bestirs himself and gives it to him, honoring him as though he were an uncelebrated sage. Asked for his own children, wife, slaves, workers, and servants, the Great Man does not give them while they are as yet unwilling to go, afflicted with grief. But when they are willing and joyful, then he gives them. But if he knows that those who ask for them are demonic beings—ogres, demons, or goblins—or men of cruel disposition, then he does not give them away. So too, he will not give his kingdom to those intent on the harm, suffering, and affliction of the world, but he would give it away to righteous men who protect the world with Dhamma.

This, firstly, is the way to practice the giving of external gifts.

The internal gift should be understood in two ways. How? Just as a man, for the sake of food and clothing, surrenders himself to another and enters into servitude and slavery, in the same way the Great Man, wishing for the supreme welfare and happiness of all beings, desiring to fulfil his own perfection of giving, with a spiritually oriented mind, for the sake of enlightenment, surrenders himself to another and enters into servitude, placing himself at the disposal of others. Whatever limbs or organs of his might be needed by others— hands, feet, eyes, etc.—he gives them away to those who need them, without trembling and without cowering. He is no more attached to them, and no more shrinks away (from giving them to others) than if they were external objects. Thus the Great Man relinquishes an internal object in two ways: for the enjoyment of others according to their pleasure; or, while fulfilling the wishes of those who ask, for his own self-mastery. In this matter he is completely generous, and thinks: "I will attain enlightenment through non-attachment." Thus the giving of the internal gift should be understood.

Herein, giving an internal gift, he gives only what leads to the welfare of the recipient, and nothing else. The Great Man does not knowingly give his own body, limbs, and organs to Māra or to the malevolent deities in Māra's company, thinking: "Let this not lead to their harm." And likewise, he does not give to those possessed by Māra or his deities, or to madmen. But when asked for these things by others, he gives immediately, because of the rarity of such a request and the difficulty of making such a gift.

The giving of fearlessness is the giving of protection to beings when they have become frightened on account of kings, thieves, fire, water, enemies, lions, tigers, other wild beasts, dragons, ogres, demons, goblins, etc.

The giving of the Dhamma is an undistorted discourse on the Dhamma given with an undefiled mind; that is, methodical instruction conducive to good in the present life, to good in the life to come, and to the ultimate good. By means of such discourses, those who have not entered the Buddha's Dispensation enter it, while those who have entered it reach maturity therein. This is the method: In brief, he gives a talk on giving, on virtue, and on heaven, on the unsatisfactoriness and defilement in sense pleasures, and on the benefit in renouncing them. In detail, to those whose minds are disposed towards the enlightenment of disciples, he gives a discourse establishing and purifying them (in progress towards their goal) by elaborating upon the noble qualities of whichever among the following topics is appropriate: going for refuge, restraint by virtue, guarding the doors of the sense faculties, moderation in eating, application to wakefulness, the seven good dhammas; application to serenity by practicing meditation on one of the thirty-eight objects (of serenity meditation); application to insight by contemplating the objects of insight-interpretation such as the material body; the progressive stages of purification, the apprehension of the course of rightness, the three kinds of clear knowledge, the six direct knowledges, the four discriminations, and the enlightenment of a disciple.[218] So too, for beings whose minds are disposed towards the enlightenment of paccekabuddhas and of perfectly enlightened Buddhas, he gives a discourse establishing and purifying them in the two vehicles (leading to these two types of enlightenment) by elaborating upon the greatness of the spiritual power of those Buddhas, and by explaining the specific nature, characteristic, function, etc., of the ten pāramīs in their three stages. Thus the Great Man gives the gift of the Dhamma to beings.

---

218. The seven stages of purification (*satta visuddhi*) are given in brief in the Rathavinīta Sutta (MN 24), and in full detail in the *Visuddhimagga*. The "course of rightness" (*samatta-niyāma*) is the supramundane path leading to nibbāna, which opens up to the contemplative disciple when he has reached the peak of insight; upon entering this course he becomes irreversibly bound for enlightenment and final deliverance. The three kinds of clear knowledge (*vijjā*) are the recollection of past lives, knowledge of the passing away and rebirth of beings, and knowledge of the destruction of the cankers. The six direct knowledges (*abhiññā*) are given above. The four discriminations (*paṭisambhidā*) are the discrimination of meaning, of dhammas, of etymology, and of ingenuity.

When he gives a material gift, the Great Man gives food thinking: "May I, by this gift, enable beings to achieve long life, beauty, happiness, strength, intelligence, and the supreme fruit of unsullied bliss." He gives drink wishing to allay the thirst of sensual defilements; garments to gain the adornments of shame and moral dread and the golden complexion (of a Buddha); vehicles for attaining the modes of psychic potency and the bliss of nibbāna; scents for producing the sweet scent of virtue; garlands and unguents for producing the beauty of the Buddha-qualities; seats for producing the seat on the terrace of enlightenment; bedding for producing the bed of a Tathāgata's rest; dwellings so he might become a refuge for beings; lamps so he might obtain the five eyes.[219] He gives visible forms for producing the fathom-wide aura (surrounding a Buddha); sounds for producing the Brahmā-like voice (of a Buddha); tastes for endearing himself to all the world; and tangibles for acquiring a Buddha's elegance.

He gives medicines so he might later give the ageless and deathless state of nibbāna. He gives slaves the gift of freedom so he might later emancipate beings from the slavery of the defilements. He gives blameless amusements and enjoyments in order to produce delight in the true Dhamma. He gives his own children as a gift in order that he might adopt all beings as his children by granting them an ariyan birth. He gives his wife as a gift in order that he might become master over the entire world. He gives gifts of gold, gems, pearls, coral, etc., in order to achieve the major marks of physical beauty (characteristic of a Buddha's body), and gifts of the diverse means of beautification in order to achieve the minor features of physical beauty.[220] He gives his treasuries as a gift in order to obtain the treasury of the true Dhamma; the gift of his kingdom in order to

---

219. The five eyes are the fleshly eye (*maṃsaccakkhu*), the organ of physical sight, which for a Buddha is said to be still many times more powerful than the eyes of an ordinary person; the divine eye (*dibbacakkhu*), by which he sees beings pass away and re-arise in accordance with their kamma throughout all the planes of existence; the wisdom eye (*paññācakkhu*), by which he sees all dhammas in their specific and general characteristics and the modes of conditionality; the Buddha-eye (*buddhacakkhu*), by which he sees the propensities and dispositions of beings, as well as the maturity of their faculties; and the universal eye (*samantacakkhu*), his knowledge of omniscience. See Nidd I pp. 356–360.

become the king of the Dhamma; the gift of monasteries, parks, ponds, and groves in order to achieve the jhānas, etc.; the gift of his feet in order that he might approach the terrace of enlightenment with feet marked with the auspicious wheels; the gift of his hands in order that he might give to beings the rescuing hand of the true Dhamma to help them across the four floods[221]; the gift of his ears, nose, etc., in order to obtain the spiritual faculties of faith, etc.; the gift of his eyes in order to obtain the universal eye; the gift of his flesh and blood with the thought: "May my body be the means of life for all the world! May it bring welfare and happiness to all beings at all times, even on occasions of merely seeing, hearing, recollecting, or ministering to me!" And he gives the gift of his head in order to become supreme in all the world.

Giving thus, the Great Man does not give unwillingly, nor by afflicting others, nor out of fear, moral shame, or the scolding of those in need of gifts. When there is something excellent, he does not give what is mean. He does not give extolling himself and disparaging others. He does not give out of desire for the fruit, nor with loathing for those who ask, nor with lack of consideration. Rather, he gives thoroughly, with his own hand, at the proper time, considerately, without discrimination, filled with joy throughout the three times.[222] Having given, he does not become remorseful afterwards. He does not become either conceited or obsequious in relation to the recipients, but behaves amiably towards them. Bountiful and liberal, he gives things together with a bonus. For when he gives food, thinking: "I will give this along with a bonus," he gives garments, etc., as well. And when he gives garments, thinking: "I will give this along with a bonus," he gives food, etc., as well, The same method with gifts of vehicles, etc. And when he gives a gift of one of the sense objects, such as visible forms, he gives the other sense objects also as a bonus.

The gift of visible forms should be understood thus. Having gained something, such as a flower, garment, or relic of a blue, yellow,

---

220. The thirty-two major and eighty minor characteristics of a Great Man's body.

221. The four floods of sensual desire, desire for existence, wrong views, and ignorance.

222. The "three times" are before presenting the gift, while giving it, and after giving it.

red, or white color, etc., considering it in terms of its visible form, thinking to make a gift of a visible form, he offers it to a worthy recipient together with its base.

The gift of sounds should be understood by way of the sounds of drums, etc. It is certainly not possible to give a sound as one gives a cluster of lotuses, tearing it out by its bulb and roots and placing it in the hands. But one gives a gift of sound by giving its base. Thus he makes a gift of sound by presenting a musical instrument, such as drums or tom toms, to the Triple Gem; or by giving medicine for the voice, such as oil and molasses, to preachers of the Dhamma; or by announcing a lecture on the Dhamma, chanting the scriptures, giving a discourse on the Dhamma, holding a discussion, or expressing appreciation for the good deeds of others.

The gift of scents is made when, after getting a delightfully scented object, such as scented roots, powdered scent, etc., considering it in terms of its scent, thinking to make a gift of scent, he offers it to the Triple Gem. He relinquishes a scented object such as *agaru* or sandalwood, for the purpose of making an offering of scent.

The gift of tastes is made when, after getting a delightfully flavored object, such as flavored roots, etc., considering it in terms of its taste, thinking to make a gift of taste, he gives it to worthy recipients. Or he relinquishes a flavorful object, such as grain, cows, etc.[223]

The gift of tangibles should be understood by way of beds, chairs, etc., and by way of coverlets and mantels, etc. For having gained some soft, delightful, blameless tangible object, such as a bed, chair, cushion, pillow, undergarment, or upper garment, considering it in terms of its tangible qualities, thinking to make a gift of a tangible item, he gives it to worthy recipients; having gained the aforesaid tangible objects, he relinquishes them.

The gift of mental objects (*dhammadāna*)[224] should be understood by way of nutriment, drink, and life, since it is the mental-object base (*dhammārammaṇa*) that is intended here. Having gained a delightful object such as nutriment, considering it as part of the mental-object base, thinking to make a gift of a non-sensory object, he gives

223. Our Indian commentator is no doubt thinking of cows as a source for the "five delicacies"—milk, curd, butter, ghee, and cream of ghee—not as a source of beefsteak.

nutriment—i.e., ghee, butter, etc; or a drink—i.e., the eight kinds of drink such as mango juice, etc.; or, considering it a gift of life, he gives a ticket-meal or a fortnightly meal, etc., gets doctors to wait upon the sick and afflicted, liberates animals from a net, has a fishing net or bird-cage destroyed, releases prisoners from prison, causes an injunction to be given forbidding the slaughter of animals, or undertakes any action of a similar nature for the sake of protecting the life of beings.

This entire accomplishment in giving he dedicates to the welfare and happiness of the whole world, and to his own unshakable emancipation through supreme enlightenment. He dedicates it to the attainment of inexhaustible desire (for the good),[225] inexhaustible concentration, ingenuity, knowledge, and emancipation. In practicing the perfection of giving the Great Being should apply the perception of impermanence to life and possessions. He should consider them as shared in common with many, and should constantly and continuously arouse great compassion towards beings. Just as, when a house is blazing, the owner removes all his property of essential value and himself as well without leaving anything important behind, so does the Great Man invariably give, without discrimination and without concern.

This is the method of practicing the perfection of giving.

(2) Now comes the method of practicing the perfection of virtue. Since the Great Man desires to adorn beings with the adornment of the virtue of the omniscient, at the beginning he must first purify his own

---

224. The word *dhamma* here, signifying the sixth external sense base, the objective sphere of ideation, imagination, and reflection, and reflective thought, signifies not only ideas, images, and mental properties, but also, according to the Abhidhamma method, a number of material phenomena not accessible to sensory perception, such as the nutritive essence of food, the life faculty, the element of material cohesion, etc., the existence of which is inferred from the patterns of behavior exhibited by sensory phenomena. Thus while these phenomena are material and not ideational, they are still incorporated in the mental-object base because they are accessible to inferential thought rather than to immediate sensation. Needless to say, this *dhammadāna* should be distinguished from the similarly named gift of the Buddha's Teaching.

225. *Chanda*, here signifying not craving or lust, but the morally wholesome application of will power to the practice of the Dhamma.

virtue. Herein, virtue is purified in four modes: (1) by the purification of one's inclinations (*ajjhāsayavisuddhi*); (2) by the undertaking of precepts (*samādāna*); (3) by non-transgression (*avītikkamana*); and (4) by making amends for transgressions (*patipākatikaraṇa*). For someone who is dominated by personal ideals is naturally disgusted with evil through the purity of his own inclinations and purifies his conduct by arousing his inward sense of shame. Someone else, who is dominated by a consideration for the world, afraid of evil, purifies his conduct by receiving precepts from another person and by arousing his sense of moral dread. Both establish themselves in virtue through non-transgression. But if, due to forgetfulness, they sometimes break a precept, through their sense of shame and moral dread, respectively, they quickly make amends for it through the proper means of rehabilitation.

Virtue is twofold as avoidance (*vāritta*) and performance (*cāritta*). Herein, this is the method by which virtue as avoidance should be practiced. A bodhisattva should have such a heart of sympathy for all beings that he does not feel any resentment towards anyone, even in a dream. Because he is dedicated to helping others, he would no more misappropriate the belongings of others than he would take hold of a poisonous water-snake. If he is a monk, he should live remote from unchastity, abstaining from the seven bonds of sexuality, not to speak of adultery.[226] If he is a householder, he should never arouse even an evil thought of lust for the wives of others. When he speaks, his statements should be truthful, beneficial, and endearing, and his talk measured, timely, and concerned with the Dhamma. His mind should always be devoid of covetousness, ill will, and inverted views. He should possess the knowledge of the ownership of kamma, and have settled faith and affection for recluses and brahmins who are faring and practicing rightly.

Because he abstains from unwholesome states and from the unwholesome courses of kamma leading to the four planes of misery and the suffering of the round, and because he is established in the wholesome courses of kamma leading to heaven and liberation, through the purity of his end and the purity of his means the Great Man's wishes for the welfare and happiness of beings succeed immediately, exactly in the way they are formed, and his pāramīs reach fulfilment, for such is his

---

226. On the "seven bonds of sexuality," see p. 116, n. 40.

nature. Since he desists from injuring others, he gives the gift of fearlessness to all beings. He perfects the meditation on loving kindness without trouble, and enjoys the eleven benefits of loving kindness (AN 11:16). He is healthy and robust, attains longevity, abundant happiness, and distinguished characteristics, and eradicates the mental impression of hatred.[227] So too, because he desists from taking what is not given, his possessions cannot be confiscated by thieves, etc. He is unsuspicious to others, dear and agreeable, trustworthy, unattached to prosperity and success, inclined to relinquishing, and he eradicates the mental impression of greed.

By desisting from unchastity he becomes unexcitable, peaceful in body and mind, dear and agreeable, unsuspicious to beings. A good report circulates concerning him. He is without lust or attachment to women, is devoted to renunciation, achieves distinguished characteristics, and eradicates the mental impression of greed.

By desisting from false speech his word comes to be authoritative for others. He is regarded as reliable and trustworthy, one whose statements are always accepted. He is dear and agreeable to deities. His mouth gives off a sweet fragrance and his bodily and vocal conduct are protected. He achieves distinguished characteristics, and eradicates the mental impressions of the defilements.

---

227. On the subject of the *vāsanā* or "mental impressions" the commentary to the Udāna says: "The vāsanā are particular dispositions to actions existing as mere potential forces built up through the defilements that have been brought into play through the course of beginningless time. Found in the mental continuities even of those devoid of defilements (i.e., of arahats), they function as motives for conduct similar to the conduct followed while the defilements were yet unabandoned. In the case of the Exalted Buddhas, who through the fulfilment of their original aspiration abandon the defilements along with the obstruction of the knowable, no *vāsanā* remain in their mental continuities. But in the case of disciple-arahats and paccekabuddhas, who abandon the defilements without removing the obstruction of the knowable, the *vāsanā* remain." The classical example of this is the case of the monk Pilindavaccha who, though an arahat, continued to address other bhikkhus by the word *vasala,* a derogatory term used by brahmins to refer to those of low caste. For this bhikkhu, however, the word was not used due to conceit or contempt for others, but merely through the habitual force of past usage, since he had been a brahmin through many previous lives. See Ud. 3.6 and its commentary.

By desisting from slander he obtains a retinue and following that cannot be divided by the attacks of others. He possesses unbreakable faith in the true Dhamma. He is a firm friend, as exceedingly dear to beings as though they were acquainted with him in the last existence. And he is devoted to non-defilement.

By desisting from harsh speech he becomes dear and agreeable to beings, pleasant in character, sweet in speech, held in esteem. And he develops a voice endowed with eight factors.[228]

By desisting from idle chatter he becomes dear and agreeable to beings, revered, held in esteem. His statements are accepted and his talk is measured. He acquires great influence and power, and becomes skillful in answering the questions of others with the ingenuity that creates opportunities (to benefit others). And when he reaches the plane of Buddhahood, he becomes capable of answering the numerous questions of beings, speaking numerous languages all with a single reply.

Through his freedom from covetousness he gains what he wishes and obtains whatever excellent possessions he needs. He is honored by powerful khattiyas. He can never be vanquished by his adversaries, is never defective in his faculties, and becomes the peerless individual.

Through his freedom from ill will he gains a pleasant appearance. He is esteemed by others, and because he delights in the welfare of beings, he automatically inspires their confidence. He becomes lofty in character, abides in loving kindness, and acquires great influence and power.

Through his freedom from wrong view he gains good companions. Even if he is threatened with the guillotine, he will not perform an evil deed. Because he holds to the ownership of kamma, he does not believe in superstitious omens. His faith in the true Dhamma is established and firmly rooted. He has faith in the enlightenment of the Tathāgatas, and no more delights in the diversity of outside creeds than a royal swan delights in a dung heap. He is skillful in fully understanding the three characteristics (of impermanence, suffering, and non-self), and in the end gains the unobstructed knowledge of omniscience. Until he attains final enlightenment he becomes the

228. The eight qualities of the Buddha's voice: it is frank, clear, melodious, pleasant, full, carrying, deep and resonant, and does not travel beyond his audience.

foremost in whatever order of beings (he happens to be reborn in), and acquires the most excellent achievements.

Thus, esteeming virtue as the foundation for all achievements—as the soil for the origination of all the Buddha-qualities, the beginning, footing, head, and chief of all the dhammas culminating in Buddhahood—and recognizing gain, honor, and fame as a foe in the guise of a friend, a bodhisattva should diligently and thoroughly perfect his virtue as a hen guards its eggs: through the power of mindfulness and clear comprehension in the control of bodily and vocal action, in the taming of the sense faculties, in purification of livelihood, and in the use of the requisites.

This, firstly, is the method of practicing virtue as avoidance.

The practice of virtue as performance should be understood as follows: Herein, at the appropriate time, a bodhisattva practices paying homage, rising up, making reverential salutations, and courteous conduct towards good friends worthy of reverence. At the appropriate time he renders them service, and he waits upon them when they are sick. When he receives well-spoken advice he expresses his appreciation. He praises the noble qualities of the virtuous and patiently endures the abuse of antagonists. He remembers help rendered to him by others, rejoices in their merits, dedicates his own merits to the supreme enlightenment, and always abides diligently in the practice of wholesome dhammas. When he commits a transgression he acknowledges it as such and confesses it to his co-religionists. Afterwards he perfectly fulfils the right practice.

He is adroit and nimble in fulfilling his duties towards beings when these are conducive to their good. He serves as their companion. When beings are afflicted with the suffering of disease, etc., he prepares the appropriate remedy. He dispels the sorrow of those afflicted by the loss of wealth, etc. Of a helpful disposition, he restrains with Dhamma those who need to be restrained, rehabilitates them from unwholesome ways, and establishes them in wholesome courses of conduct. He inspires with Dhamma those in need of inspiration. And when he hears about the loftiest, most difficult, inconceivably powerful deeds of the great bodhisattvas of the past, resulting in the ultimate welfare and happiness of beings, by means of which they reached perfect maturity in the requisites of enlightenment, he does not become agitated and alarmed, but reflects: "Those Great Beings were only human. But by developing themselves through the orderly fulfilment of the training they attained the loftiest spiritual power and the highest perfection in the requisites of enlightenment. I, too, should practice the same training in virtue, etc. In that way I, too, will gradually fulfil the training and in the end attain the same state." Then, with unflagging energy preceded by this faith, he perfectly fulfils the training in virtue, etc.

Again, he conceals his virtues and reveals his faults. He is few in his wishes, content, fond of solitude, aloof, capable of enduring suffering, and free from anxiety. He is not restless, puffed up, fickle, scurrilous, or scattered in speech, but calm in his faculties and mind. Avoiding such wrong means of livelihood as scheming, etc., he is endowed with proper conduct and a suitable resort (for alms). He sees danger in the slightest faults, and having undertaken the rules of training, trains himself in them, energetic and resolute, without regard for body or life. He does not tolerate even the slightest concern for his body or life but abandons and dispels it; how much more, then, excessive concern? He abandons and dispels all the corruptions such as anger, malice, etc., which are the cause for moral depravity. He does not become complacent over some minor achievement of distinction and does not shrink away, but strives for successively higher achievements. In this way the achievements he gains do not partake of diminution or stagnation.

The Great Man serves as a guide for the blind, explaining to them the right path. To the deaf he gives signals with gestures of his hands, and in that way benefits them with good. So too for the dumb. To cripples he gives a chair, or a vehicle, or some other means of conveyance. He strives that the faithless may gain faith, that the lazy may generate zeal, that those of confused mindfulness may develop mindfulness, that those with wandering minds may become accomplished in concentration, and that the dull-witted may acquire wisdom. He strives to dispel sensual desire, ill will, sloth-and-torpor, restlessness-and-worry, and perplexity in those obsessed by these hindrances, and to dispel wrong thoughts of sensuality, ill will, and aggression in those subjugated by these thoughts. Out of gratitude to those who have helped him, he benefits and honors them with a similar or greater benefit in return, congenial in speech and endearing in his words.

He is a companion in misfortune. Understanding the nature and character of beings, he associates with whatever beings need his presence, in whatever way they need it; and he practices together with whatever beings need to practice with him, in whatever way of practice is necessary for them. But he proceeds only by rehabilitating them from the unwholesome and establishing them in the wholesome, not in other ways. For in order to protect the minds of others, bodhisattvas behave only in ways which increase the wholesome.[229] So too, because his inclination is to benefit others, he should never harm them, abuse them, humiliate them, arouse remorse in them, or incite them to act in ways that should be avoided. Nor should he place himself in a higher position than those of inferior conduct. He should be neither altogether inaccessible to others, nor too accessible, and he should not associate with others at the wrong time.[230]

He associates with beings whom it is proper to associate with at the appropriate time and place. He does not criticize those who are dear to others in front of them, nor praise those who are resented by them. He is not intimate with those who are not trustworthy. He does not refuse a proper invitation, or engage in persuasion, or accept excessively. He encourages those endowed with faith with a discourse on the benefits of faith; and he encourages as well those endowed with virtue, learning, generosity, and wisdom with a discourse on the benefits of those qualities. If the bodhisattva has attained to the direct knowledges, he may inspire a sense of spiritual urgency in the negligent by showing them the fate of those in hell, etc., as is fit. Thereby he establishes the faithless (immoral, ignorant, stingy, and dull-witted) in faith (virtue, learning, generosity, and wisdom). He makes them enter the Buddha's Dispensation and brings to maturity those already endowed with these qualities. In this way, through his virtuous conduct, the Great Man's immeasurable flood of merit and goodness ascends to ever increasing heights.

The detailed explanation of virtue is given in diverse ways in the *Visuddhimagga* in the passage beginning: "Virtue is the states beginning with volition, present in one who abstains from the destruction of life, etc. or in one who fulfills the practice of the duties"

---

229. The author introduces this word of caution apparently as a safeguard against the tendency to use the principle of compassion as a pretext for behaving in ways that violate the basic principles of ethics.

230. This may also be translated: "He should not be unserviceable to others, nor too servile, nor should he serve at the wrong time."

(Chapter I). All that should be brought in here. Only there is this distinction: in that work the discussion of virtue has come down for beings who seek the enlightenment of disciples (*sāvakabodhisattavasena*); but here, because the discussion is intended for great bodhisattvas (*mahābodhisattavasena*), it should be explained making compassion and skillful means the forerunners. Just as the Great Man does not dedicate the merits from his practice of virtue to his own release from affliction in the unfortunate destinations, or to his own achievement of kingship in the fortunate destinations, or to becoming a world-ruling monarch, a god, Sakka, Māra, or Brahmā, so too he does not dedicate it to his own attainment of the threefold knowledge, the six direct knowledges, the four discriminations, the enlightenment of a disciple, or the enlightenment of a paccekabuddhas. But rather he dedicates it only for the purpose of becoming an omniscient Buddha in order to enable all beings to acquire the incomparable adornment of virtue.

This is the method of practicing the perfection of virtue.

(3) The perfection of renunciation is the wholesome act of consciousness that occurs renouncing sense pleasures and existence, preceded by the perception of their inherent unsatisfactoriness and accompanied by compassion and skillful means. The bodhisattva should practice the perfection of renunciation by first recognizing the unsatisfactoriness in sense pleasures, etc., according to the following method: "For one dwelling in a home there is no opportunity to enjoy the happiness of renunciation, etc., because the home life is the dwelling place of all the defilements, because a wife and children impose restrictions (on one's freedom), and because the diverse crafts and occupations such as agriculture and trade lead to numerous entanglements. And sense pleasures, like a drop of honey smeared over the blade of a sword, give limited satisfaction and entail abundant harm. They are fleeting like a show perceived in a flash of lightning; enjoyable only through an inversion of perception like the adornments of a madman; a means of vengeance like a camouflaged pit of excrement; unsatisfying like a thin drink or water moistening the fingers; afflictive like food inwardly rotten; a cause for calamity like a baited hook; the cause of suffering in the three times like a burning fire; a basis for bondage like monkey's glue; a camouflage for destruction like a murderer's cloak; a place of danger like a dwelling in an enemy village; food for the Māra of the defilements like the

supporter of one's foes; subject to suffering through change like the enjoyment of a festival; inwardly burning like the fire in the hollow of a tree; fraught with danger like a ball of honey suspended from bīrana grass in an old pit; intensifying thirst like a drink of salt water; resorted to by the vulgar like liquor and wine; and giving little satisfaction like a chain of bones."

Having recognized the unsatisfactoriness in sense pleasures in accordance with this method, he should then, by the reverse method, contemplate the benefits in renunciation, with a mind slanting, sloping, and inclining towards the happiness of renunciation, solitude, and peace.

Since renunciation is rooted in the going forth (i.e., into the homeless life of a monk), the going forth should be undertaken. If the Great Being is living at a time when no Buddha has arisen in the world, he should go forth under ascetics or wanderers who maintain the doctrine of kamma and the moral efficacy of action. But when the perfectly enlightened Buddhas appear in the world, he should go forth only in their Dispensation. Having gone forth, he should establish himself in virtue, as described above, and in order to cleanse his virtue, should undertake the ascetic practices. For Great Men who undertake the ascetic practices and maintain them properly become content and few in their wishes. The stains of their defilements are washed off in the waters of such noble qualities as effacement, solitude, aloofness from society, the arousal of energy, and ease of maintenance, and all their conduct becomes purified through their blameless rules, observances, and noble qualities. Established in three of the ancient traditions of the ariyans,[231] they are able to achieve the fourth of the ariyan traditions, i.e., delight in meditation, entering and abiding in jhāna, both access and absorption, through whichever among the forty subjects of meditation are appropriate. Thus they completely fulfil the perfection of renunciation.

At this point it would be proper to explain in detail the thirteen ascetic practices and the forty meditation subjects for the development of concentration, i.e., the ten kasiṇa-devices, the ten impurities, the ten recollections, the four divine abodes, the four immaterial states, the one perception, and the one analysis. But since all these are explained

231. The four ariyan traditions (*ariyavaṃsa*) are contentment with any kind of robe, almsfood, and dwelling, and delight in meditation.

in complete detail in the *Visuddhimagga*, it should be understood in the way stated there. Only there is this distinction: in that work the subject is explained for beings who seek the enlightenment of disciples. But here, because it is intended for great bodhisattvas, it should be explained making compassion and skillful means the forerunners.

This is the method of practicing the perfection of renunciation.

(4) Just as light cannot co-exist with darkness, wisdom cannot co-exist with delusion. Therefore a bodhisattva wishing to accomplish the perfection of wisdom should avoid the causes of delusion. These are the causes of delusion: discontent, languor, drowsiness, lethargy, delight in company, attachment to sleep, irresoluteness, lack of enthusiasm for knowledge, false over-estimation of oneself, non-interrogation, not maintaining one's body properly, lack of mental concentration, association with dull-witted people, not ministering to those possessed of wisdom, self-contempt, false discrimination, adherence to inverted views, athleticism, lack of a sense of spiritual urgency, and the five hindrances; or, in brief, any states which, when indulged in, prevent the unarisen wisdom from arising and cause the arisen wisdom to diminish. Avoiding these causes of confusion, one should apply effort to learning as well as to the jhānas, etc.

This is an analysis of the sphere of learning: the five aggregates, the twelve sense bases, the eighteen elements, the four truths, the twenty-two faculties, the twelve factors of dependent origination, the foundations of mindfulness, etc., the various classifications of dhammas such as the wholesome, etc., as well as any blameless secular fields of knowledge that may be suitable for promoting the welfare and happiness of beings, particularly grammar.[232] Thus, with wisdom, mindfulness, and energy preceded by skillful means, a bodhisattva should first thoroughly immerse himself in this entire sphere of learning—through study, listening, memorization, learning, and interrogation; then he should establish others in learning. In this way the wisdom born of learning (*sutamayī paññā*) can be developed. So too, out of his wish for the welfare of others, the bodhisattva should

232. The "etc." after the foundations of mindfulness implies the remainder of the thirty-seven constituents of enlightenment. The "etc." after "wholesome" implies the entirety of the Abhidhamma classification of *dhammas*. Grammar is the traditional queen of Indian secular sciences.

develop the wisdom of ingenuity in creating opportunities to fulfil his various duties to his fellow beings, and the skillful means in understanding their happiness and misery.

Then he should develop wisdom born of reflection (*cintāmayī paññā*) by first reflecting upon the specific nature of the dhammas such as the aggregates, and then arousing reflective acquiescence in them. Next, he should perfect the preliminary portion of the wisdom born of meditation (*pubbabhāgabhāvanāpaññā*) by developing the mundane kinds of full understanding through the discernment of the specific and general characteristics of the aggregates, etc.[233] To do so, he should fully understand all internal and external dhammas without exception as follows: "This is mere mentality-materiality (*nāmarūpamatta*), which arises and ceases according to conditions. There is here no agent or actor. It is 'impermanent' in the sense of not being after having been; 'suffering" in the sense of oppression by rise and fall; and 'non-self' in the sense of being insusceptible to the exercise of mastery." Comprehending them in this way, he abandons attachment to them, and helps others to do so as well. Entirely out of compassion, he continues to help his fellow beings enter and reach maturity in the three vehicles, assists them to achieve mastery over the jhānas, deliverances, concentrations, attainments, and mundane direct knowledges, and does not desist until he reaches the very peak of wisdom and all the Buddha-qualities come within his grasp.

The wisdom born of meditation may be divided into two groups. The first comprises the mundane direct knowledges, together with their accessories; namely, the knowledge of the modes of psychic power, the knowledge of the divine ear-element, the knowledge of penetrating other minds, the knowledge of recollecting past lives, the knowledge of the divine eye, the knowledge of kammic retribution, and the knowledge of the future.[234] The second comprises the five

---

233. For the mundane kinds of full understanding (*pariññā*), see Vism 20.3-5. The specific characteristics are the defining marks of each particular type of phenomena, the general characteristics their common marks of impermanence, suffering, and non-self. The preliminary portion of the wisdom born of meditation is comprised under the mundane kinds of full understanding. According to the Theravāda account, a bodhisatta cannot attain supramundane wisdom until the eve of his enlightenment, for he must wait until his pāramīs have reached the level of completeness required for Buddhahood before entering the path to final deliverance.

purifications—purification of view, purification by overcoming doubt, purification by knowledge and vision of what is and what is not the path, purification by knowledge and vision of the way, and purification by knowledge and vision. The first four of these are mundane, the last is supramundane. After acquiring through study and interrogation a knowledge of the dhammas such as the aggregates, etc., constituting the soil of wisdom, he should establish himself in the two purifications constituting its roots, purification of virtue and purification of mind, and then accomplish the five purifications just mentioned which constitute the trunk of wisdom. Since the method for accomplishing these, along with the analysis of their objective sphere, is explained in complete detail in the *Visuddhimagga*, it should be understood in the way given there.[235] Only in that work the explanation of wisdom has come down for beings seeking the enlightenment of disciples. But here, because it is intended for the great bodhisattvas, it should be explained making compassion and skillful means the forerunners. One further distinction must also be made: here insight should be developed only as far as purification by knowledge and vision of the way, without attaining purification by knowledge and vision.[236]

A Great Being who has formed his aspiration for supreme enlightenment should, for the sake of fulfilling his pāramīs, always be devoted to what is proper and intent upon service.[237] Therefore he should be zealous in providing for the welfare of beings, and from time to time, day by day, should reflect: "Have I accumulated any requisites of merit and knowledge today? What have I done for the

---

234. The knowledge of kammic retribution (also called knowledge of the passing away and re-arising of beings) and the knowledge of the future are two accessories of the divine eye; thus, though seven items are listed, only five direct knowledges are involved. The sixth, supramundane direct knowledge is the knowledge of the destruction of the cankers, the attainment of arahatship.

235. For the five direct knowledges, see Vism 12 and 13; for the sphere of wisdom, 14 through 17; for the five purifications of wisdom, 18 through 22.

236. Purification by knowledge and vision is the supramundane wisdom of the four noble truths. Because this purification issues in the realization of nibbāna, the bodhisattva-aspirant must stop short of this attainment so that his realization of nibbāna will coincide with his perfect enlightenment.

237. From this point on the remaining pāramīs are treated piecemeal and synoptically rather than in systematic detail like the first four.

welfare of others?" In order to help all beings he should surrender some possession of his with a mind unconcerned with body or life. Whatever action he does, bodily or vocal, all should be done with a mind slanting towards full enlightenment; all should be dedicated to enlightenment. He should turn his mind away from sense pleasures whether superior or inferior and should apply skillful means to the fulfilment of his various duties.

He should work energetically for the welfare of beings, be capable of enduring everything, whether desirable or undesirable, and should speak without deception.[238] He should suffuse all beings with universal loving kindness and compassion. Whatever causes suffering for beings, all that he should be ready to take upon himself; and he should rejoice in the merits of all beings. He should frequently reflect upon the greatness of the Buddhas and the greatness of their spiritual power. Whatever action he does by body or speech, all should be preceded with a mind slanting towards full enlightenment. In this way, the Great Being, the bodhisattva, devoted to what is proper, endowed with strength, firm in striving, day by day accumulates immeasurable requisites of merit and knowledge through the practice of the pāramīs.

Further, having relinquished his own body and life for the use and protection of beings, the bodhisattva should seek out and apply the antidotes to the various kinds of suffering to which beings are exposed—hunger, thirst, cold, heat, wind, sun, etc. And whatever happiness he himself gains by alleviating these kinds of suffering, and the happiness he gains when his own bodily and mental afflictions subside in delightful parks, gardens, mansions, pools, and forest abodes, and the happiness of the blissful jhānic attainments he hears are experienced by the Buddhas, their enlightened disciples, paccekabuddhas, and great bodhisattvas, established in the practice of renunciation—all that he seeks to procure universally for all beings.

This, firstly, is the method for a bodhisattva not yet established on the plane of concentration. One established on the plane of concentration bestows upon beings the rapture, tranquillity, happiness, concentration, and true knowledge produced in the achievements of distinction as they are experienced by himself. He procures them and dedicates them to all. Such a bodhisattva should contemplate the whole world of sentient beings immersed in the great suffering of

238. An allusion to the pāramīs of energy, patience, and truthfulness.

saṃsāra and in the sufferings of the defilements and kamma-formations at its base. He should see the beings in hell experiencing violent, racking, agonizing pains uninterruptedly over long periods, produced as they are cut up, dismembered, split, pulverized, and roasted in scorching fires; the great suffering of the animals due to their mutual hostility, as they afflict, harass, and kill one another, or fall into captivity at the hands of others; and the suffering of the various classes of ghosts, going about with their bodies aflame, consumed and withered by hunger, thirst, wind, and sun, weeping and wailing as their food turns into vomit and spittle. He should contemplate as well the suffering experienced by men, which is often indistinguishable from the suffering in the plane of misery: the misery and ruin they encounter in their search (for the means of sustenance and enjoyment); the various punishments they may meet, such as the cutting off of their hands, etc.; ugliness, deformity, and poverty; affliction by hunger and thirst; being vanquished by the more powerful, pressed into the service of others, and made dependent upon others; and when they pass away, falling over into the hells, the realm of ghosts, and the animal kingdom. He should see the gods of the sense-sphere being consumed by the fevers of lust as they enjoy their sense objects with scattered minds; living with their fever (of passions) unextinguished like a mass of fire stoked up with blasts of wind and fed with a stock of dry wood; without peace, dejected, and dependent on others. And he should see the gods of the fine-material and immaterial spheres, after so long a life span, in the end succumb to the law of impermanence, plunging from their heights back down into the round of birth, aging, and death, like birds swooping swiftly down from the heights of the sky or like arrows shot by a strong arm descending in the distance. And having seen all his, he should arouse a sense of spiritual urgency and suffuse all beings universally with loving kindness and compassion. Accumulating the requisites of enlightenment in this way by body, speech, and mind without interruption, he should fulfil the perfection of energy, arousing zeal while working thoroughly and perseveringly and acting without cowering, in order that all the pāramīs may reach fulfilment.

While striving for the state of Buddhahood, the store and repository of inconceivable, immeasurable, vast, lofty, stainless, incomparable, undefiled qualities, he should encourage the arising of energy; for such energy is endowed with inconceivable spiritual power, which common people cannot even hear about, much less practice. It is entirely through the spiritual power of energy that the practice of all the requisites of enlightenment succeeds—the threefold arising of the great aspiration, the four grounds for Buddhahood, the four bases of beneficence, the single flavor of compassion, the reflective acquiescence which is the specific condition for the realization of the Buddha-qualities, being untainted amidst all things, the perception of all beings as his own dear children, not being fatigued by all the sufferings of saṃsāra, the relinquishing of everything that may be given away, delight in so giving, the determination upon the higher virtue, etc., unshakeableness therein, rapture and exultation in wholesome actions, the inclination towards seclusion, application to the jhānas, being insatiable in blameless states, teaching the Dhamma to others as he has learned it out of the wish for their welfare, firm initiative in setting beings upon the true path, sagacity and heroism, being imperturbable in face of the abusive speech and wrongs of others, the determination upon truth, mastery over the meditative attainments, the attainment of power through the direct knowledges, the comprehension of the three characteristics, the accumulation of the requisites for the supramundane path by practicing meditation in the foundations of mindfulness, etc., and the descent on to the nine supramundane dhammas[239]. Thus from the time of forming the aspiration until the great enlightenment, a bodhisattva should perfect his energy thoroughly and uninterruptedly, without surrendering, so that it might issue in higher and higher states of distinction. And when this energy succeeds, all the requisites of enlightenment—patience, truthfulness, determination, etc., as well as giving, virtue, etc.—will succeed; for all these occur in dependence on energy.

The practice of patience and the rest should be understood in accordance with the same method.

Thus through giving, relinquishing his own happiness and belongings to others, he practices the benefitting of others in many ways; through virtue, the protection of their lives, property, and wives, the non-breach of his word, endearing and beneficial speech, non-injury, etc.; through renunciation, many kinds of beneficial conduct such as giving the gift of the Dhamma in return for their material gifts;

239. The four paths, the four fruits, and nibbāna.

through wisdom, skillful means in providing for their welfare; through energy, the arousing of zeal in his work without slacking off; through patience, the enduring of the wrongs of others; through truthfulness, not breaking his pledge to help others without deception; through determination, remaining unshakable in rendering them help even when encountering difficulties; through loving kindness, concern for their welfare and happiness; and through equanimity, remaining imperturbable whether others render help or inflict harm.

This is the practice that the great bodhisattva, compassionate for all beings, undertakes for the sake of incalculable beings, by means of which he accumulates immeasurable requisites of merit and knowledge not shared by worldlings. Their condition has been stated. They should be accomplished thoroughly.

(xi) How are they analyzed? (*ko vibhāgo*)

They are analyzed into thirty pāramīs: ten (basic) pāramīs, ten intermediate pāramīs (*upapāramī*), and ten ultimate pāramīs (*paramatthapāramī*).

Herein, some teachers say that the ten basic pāramīs are the intermingled bright and dark dhammas practiced by a bodhisattva who has just formed his aspiration, whose end is the welfare of others, and whose means are directed towards working for this end; the intermediate pāramīs are the bright dhammas untainted by any darkness; and the ultimate pāramīs are the dhammas which are neither dark nor bright.

Others say that the basic pāramīs are being filled at the time of the commencement;[240] the intermediate pāramīs are filled on the plane of bodhisattvahood; and the ultimate pāramīs reach perfect fulfilment in all modes on the plane of Buddhahood. Or alternatively, the basic pāramīs involve working for the welfare of others on the plane of bodhisattvahood; the intermediate pāramīs, working for one's own welfare; and the ultimate pāramīs, the fulfilment of the welfare of both oneself and others with the achievement of the Tathāgata's powers and grounds of self-confidence on the plane of Buddhahood. Thus they analyze the pāramīs according to the beginning, middle, and

240. *Samudāgama*: the commencement of a bodhisattva's career, when the pāramīs arise together in his mind as the potential out of which his ascent to Buddhahood will grow.

consummation (of the bodhisattva's career) by way of the resolution (to fulfil them), the undertaking (of their practice), and their completion, respectively.

Still others analyze them according to the division in the accumulation of merit of those who are by nature compassionate and free from hate, according to whether they have attained to the happiness (of a favorable state) of existence, the happiness of emancipation, or the ultimate happiness.

Again, some say that among those upheld by a sense of shame, mindfulness, and self-esteem, who give predominance to the supramundane Dhamma and revere virtue, concentration, and wisdom, the pāramīs are analyzed according to their ability to facilitate the attainment of the three types of enlightenment—the basic pāramīs issuing in the enlightenment of a disciple who requires the help (of a Buddha) to cross (the current of saṃsāra), the intermediate pāramīs in the enlightenment of a paccekabuddha who crosses over himself (but cannot help others to cross), and the ultimate pāramīs in the enlightenment of a supreme Buddha who helps others across.

Others hold that the basic pāramīs are the requisites occurring from the time of the mental resolution until the resolution by speech; the intermediate, those which occur from the time of the spoken resolution until the resolution by body; and the ultimate, those which occur following the resolution by body. But still others explain that the basic pāramīs are the requisites which occur by rejoicing in the merits of others; the intermediate, those which occur by exhorting others to practice; and the ultimate, those which occur through one's own practice. So too, some say the basic pāramīs are the requisites of merit and knowledge issuing in a happy state of existence; the intermediate, those issuing in the happiness of nibbāna for oneself; and the ultimate, those issuing in both kinds of happiness for others.

The basic perfection of giving (*dānapāramī*) is the relinquishing of one's children, wife, and belongings, such as wealth; the intermediate perfection of giving (*dāna-upapāramī*), the relinquishing of one's own limbs; and the ultimate perfection of giving (*dānaparamatthapāramī*), the relinquishing of one's own life. The three stages in the perfection of virtue should be understood as the non-transgression (of moral conduct) on account of the three—children and wife, limbs, and life; the three stages in the perfection of renunciation, as the renunciation of those three bases after cutting off attachment to them; the three stages in the perfection of wisdom, as the discrimination between what is beneficial and harmful to beings, after rooting out craving for one's belongings, limbs, and life; the three stages in the perfection of energy, as striving for the relinquishing of the aforementioned things; the three stages in the perfection of patience, as the endurance of obstacles to one's belongings, limbs, and life; the three stages in the perfection of truthfulness, as the non-abandoning of truthfulness on account of one's belongings, limbs, and life; the three stages in the perfection of determination, as unshakable determination despite the destruction of one's belongings, limbs, and life, bearing in mind that the pāramīs ultimately succeed through unflinching determination; the three stages in the perfection of loving kindness, as maintaining loving kindness towards beings who destroy one's belongings, etc; and the three stages in the perfection of equanimity, as maintaining an attitude of impartial neutrality towards beings and formations whether they are helpful or harmful in regard to the aforementioned three bases (i.e., belongings, limbs, and life).

In this way the analysis of the pāramīs should be understood

(xii) How are they synthesized? (*ko saṅgaho*)

Just as the ten pāramīs become thirtyfold through analysis, so they become sixfold through their specific nature: as giving, virtue, patience, energy, meditation, and wisdom.[241]

When this set is considered, the perfection of renunciation, as the going forth into homelessness, is included in the perfection of virtue; as seclusion from the hindrances, in the perfection of meditation; and as a generally wholesome dhamma, in all six pāramitās. One part of the perfection of truthfulness, i.e., its aspect of truthful speech or abstinence from falsehood, is included in the perfection of virtue, and one part, i.e., its aspect of truthful knowledge, in the perfection of wisdom. The perfection of loving kindness is included in the perfection of meditation, and the perfection of equanimity in the perfections of meditation and of wisdom. The perfection of determination is included by all.

---

241. This is the standard enumeration of the pāramitās in the Mahāyāna literature, though the list itself probably goes back to the pre-Mahāyāna schools.

These six pāramīs fall into at least fifteen pairs of complementary qualities which perfect fifteen other pairs of qualities. How?

(1) The pair—giving and virtue—perfects the pair of doing what is beneficial for others and abstaining from what is harmful to them.

(2) The pair—giving and patience—perfects the pair of non-greed and non-hatred.

(3) The pair—giving and energy—perfects the pair of generosity and learning.

(4) The pair—giving and meditation—perfects the abandoning of sensual desire and hatred.

(5) The pair giving and wisdom, the ariyan vehicle and burden.

(6) The dyad of virtue and patience, the purification of means and the purification of the end.

(7) The dyad of virtue and energy, the dyad of meditative development (i.e., serenity and insight).

(8) The dyad of virtue and meditation, the abandoning of moral depravity and of mental obsession.

(9) The dyad of virtue and wisdom, the dyad of giving.[242]

(10) The dyad of patience and energy, the dyad of acceptance and heat.[243]

(11) The dyad of patience and meditation, the abandoning of opposing and favoring.

(12) The dyad of patience and wisdom, the acceptance and penetration of emptiness.

(13) The dyad of energy and meditation, the dyad of exertion and non-distraction.

(14) The dyad of energy and wisdom, the dyad of refuges.

(15) The dyad of meditation and wisdom perfects the dyad of vehicles (i.e., the vehicles of serenity and insight).

The triad of giving, virtue, and patience perfects the abandoning of greed, hatred, and delusion. The triad of giving, virtue, and energy perfects the giving of wealth, life, and bodily vitality. The triad of giving, virtue, and meditation perfects the three bases of meritorious

---

242. Perhaps giving fearlessness through observing the precepts, and giving the Dhamma through wisdom.

243. The heat of meditative endeavor; as this is a technical term of the Sarvāstivāda school, it seems the six pāramitās were formulated by its adherents, who flourished in northwest India.

deeds. The triad of giving, virtue, and wisdom perfects the triad of giving material gifts, fearlessness, and the Dhamma. In the same way, the other triads and tetrads may be applied to one another as is appropriate in each case.

These six pāramīs are also included in the four foundations, which provide a synthesis of all the pāramīs.[244] What are they? The foundations of truth, the foundation of relinquishment, the foundation of peace, and the foundation of wisdom. Here is the word explanation: it is a foundation because it is founded by this, or it is founded upon this, or it itself is a foundation. It is truth and it is a foundation, or it is the foundation for truth, or truth is the foundation for this—thus it is the foundation of truth. The same with the rest.

Therein, taking them first without distinction: after making his aspiration for the supramundane qualities, the Great Being, filled with compassion for all beings, establishes the foundation of truth by acquiring all the pāramīs in conformity with his vow; the foundation of relinquishment by relinquishing their opposites; the foundation of peace by pacifying their opposites with all the qualities of the pāramīs; and the foundation of wisdom by skillful means in promoting the welfare of others through those same qualities.

Taken separately, giving is a proximate cause for the four foundations of wholesome dhammas as follows: (1) (for the foundation of truth) since one vows to give to those who ask without deceiving them, gives without violating one's vows, and rejoices without deceiving them about the gift; (2) (for the foundation of relinquishment) through the relinquishing of the opposite qualities such as stinginess, etc.; (3) (for the foundation of peace) through the pacification of greed, hatred, delusion, and fear, in regard to the objects to be given, the recipients, the act of giving, and the loss of the objects to be given, respectively; (4) (and for the foundation of wisdom) through giving according to desert, at the proper time, in the appropriate manner, and through the pre-eminence of wisdom. Virtue is a proximate cause for the four foundations, thus: (1) through non-transgression of the restraint undertaken; (2) through the relinquishing of moral depravity; (3) through the pacification of misconduct; and

---

244. The suttanta basis for these four foundations (*cattāri adhiṭṭhānāni*) is the Dhātuvibhaṅga Sutta, MN 140, though there the foundations are given not in relation to the pāramīs but as qualities of the arahat.

(4) through the pre-eminence of wisdom. Patience is a proximate cause for the four foundations, thus: (1) through patient acceptance in accordance with one's vow; (2) through the relinquishing of discrimination against others on account of their wrongs; (3) through the pacification of the obsession of anger; and (4) through the pre-eminence of wisdom.

Energy is a proximate cause for the four foundations: (1) through working for the welfare of others in accordance with one's vows; (2) through the relinquishing of dejection; (3) through the pacification of unwholesome dhammas; and (4) through the pre-eminence of wisdom. Meditation is a proximate cause for the four foundations: (1) through concern for the welfare of the world in accordance with one's vow; (2) through the relinquishing of the hindrances; (3) through the pacification of the mind; and (4) through the pre-eminence of wisdom. And wisdom is a proximate cause for the four foundations: (1) through skillful means in promoting the welfare of others in accordance with one's vow; (2) through the relinquishing of unskillful activity; (3) through the pacification of the fevers springing from delusion; and (4) through the attainment of omniscience.

The foundation of truth is practiced by acting in accordance with one's vow and understanding;[245] the foundation of relinquishment by relinquishing (outer) objects of sense enjoyment and the (inner) defilement of sensuality; the foundation of peace by the pacification of hatred and suffering; and the foundation of wisdom by understanding and penetration. The foundation of truth is embraced by the threefold truth and opposed to the three corruptions (of greed, hatred, and delusion). The foundation of relinquishing is embraced by the threefold relinquishment and opposed to the three corruptions. The foundation of peace is embraced by the threefold pacification and opposed to the three corruptions. And the foundation of wisdom is embraced by the threefold knowledge and opposed to the three corruptions.

The foundation of truth embraces the foundations of relinquishment, peace, and wisdom through non-deceptiveness and through acting in accordance with one's vow. The foundation of relinquishment embraces the foundations of truth, peace, and wisdom

245. *Neyya*: literally, "the knowable," but it here seems that the understanding of the knowable rather than the object of knowledge is meant.

through the relinquishing of their opposites and as the fruit of relinquishing everything. The foundation of peace embraces the foundations of truth, relinquishment, and wisdom, through the pacification of the fever of defilement and the fever of kamma.[246] And the foundation of wisdom embraces the foundations of truth, relinquishment, and peace, since they are all preceded and accompanied by knowledge. Thus all the pāramīs are grounded in truth, clarified by relinquishment, intensified by peace, and purified by wisdom. For truth is the cause for their genesis, relinquishment the cause for their acquisition, peace the cause for their growth, and wisdom the cause for their purification.

In the beginning (of the bodhisattva's career) truth is the foundation, since his vow is made in accordance with truth. In the middle, relinquishment is the foundation, since after forming his aspiration the bodhisattva relinquishes himself for the welfare of others. In the end, peace is the foundation, since the consummation (of the career) is the attainment of perfect peace. And in every phase—the beginning, the middle, and the end—wisdom is the foundation, since the entire career originates when wisdom is present, does not exist when it is absent, and because the nature (of wisdom) accords with the vow.

Through the foundations of truth and relinquishment, which promote one's own and others' welfare and create reverence and love, the Great Men, as laymen, benefit others with material gifts. And through the foundations of peace and wisdom, which likewise promote one's own and others' welfare and create reverence and love, the Great Men, as monks, benefit others with the gift of the Dhamma.

The fulfilment of the four foundations takes place in the bodhisattva's last existence. Some say that rebirth into the final existence takes place when the four foundations are fulfilled. (On this interpretation) the bodhisattva descends into his mother's womb, remains there, and emerges mindfully and clearly comprehending through his commencement of the foundation of wisdom. Through his fulfilment of the foundations of truth,[247] as soon as he is born he goes forward with a stride of seven steps facing north, surveys all the directions, and with a voice encompassed by truth, roars his lion's roar three times: "I am the foremost in the world, I am pre-eminent in the

246. Preferring reading in N.Sub.Cy. to Cp-a.

world, I am supreme in the world." Through the commencement of the foundation of peace, when he sees the old man, the sick man, the corpse, and the monk, skilled in a section of the four truths, his intoxication with youth, health, and life becomes pacified. And through the commencement of the foundation of relinquishment, he is able to relinquish without concern a great circle of relatives and the sovereignty of a world-ruling monarch that lay within his grasp.

Others hold, as a second position, that the four foundations are fulfilled with the enlightenment. For through the commencement of the foundation of truth in accordance with his vow, he penetrates the Four Noble Truths; thus the foundation of truth is fulfilled. Through the commencement of the foundation of relinquishment, he relinquishes all the defilements and corruptions; thus the foundation of relinquishment is fulfilled. Through the commencement of the foundation of peace, he attains the supreme peace; thus the foundation of peace is fulfilled. And through the commencement of the foundation of wisdom, he obtains the unobstructed knowledge; thus the foundation of wisdom is fulfilled. But despite the ultimacy of the enlightenment, this position is untenable.

Others hold, as a third position, that the four foundations are fulfilled with the setting in motion of the Wheel of the Dhamma. For having commenced the foundation of truth, he fulfils the foundation of truth by teaching the Four Noble Truths in their twelve modes. Having commenced the foundation of relinquishment, he fulfils the foundation of relinquishment by making the great offering of the true Dhamma. Having himself attained the supreme peace through his commencement of the foundation of peace, he fulfils the foundation of peace by (bringing peace) to others. And having commenced the foundation of wisdom, he fulfils the foundation of wisdom by understanding the propensities, etc., of the people to be trained. This

---

247. Should this be commencement (*samudāgama*) rather than fulfilment (*pāripūri*)? All the texts read pāripūri, though the context seems to require *samudāgama*. Technically, the commencement signifies the arising of the particular virtues at the beginning of the bodhisattva's career and their gradual maturation over many lives, the fulfilment the full flowering of those same virtues. This first position places the fulfilment of the foundations all before the enlightenment.

position, too, is not tenable, for even at this point the function of a Buddha has not yet been concluded.

Still others hold, as a fourth position, that the four foundations are fulfilled with the parinibbāna. For with the parinibbāna, the foundation of truth is fulfilled by the attainment of the ultimate truth; the foundation of relinquishment, by the relinquishing of all the strata of existence; the foundation of peace, by the pacification of all formations; and the foundation of wisdom, by the completion of the purpose of wisdom.[248]

Herein, after he has commenced the foundation of truth, the Great Man's fulfilment of the foundation of truth is particularly evident at his birth, which is the field for his loving kindness. After he has commenced the foundation of wisdom, his fulfilment of the foundation of wisdom is particularly evident at his enlightenment, which is the field for his compassion. After he has commenced the foundation of relinquishment, his fulfilment of the foundation of relinquishment is particularly evident when he sets in motion the Wheel of the Dhamma, which is the field for his sympathetic joy. And after he has commenced the foundation of peace, his fulfilment of the foundation of peace is particularly evident at his parinibbāna, which is the field for his equanimity.

The virtue of one who has commenced the foundation of truth is to be known by living together with him. The honesty of one who has commenced the foundation of relinquishment is to be known through intercourse with him. The fortitude of one who has commenced the foundation of peace is to be known on occasions of misfortune. And the wisdom of one who has commenced the foundation of wisdom is to be known through discussion with him. Thus his purification of virtue, livelihood, mind, and view should be known.

Again, through his commencement of the foundation of truth, he does not follow a wrong course out of hatred, since he is free from deceptiveness. Through his commencement of the foundation of relinquishment, he does not follow a wrong course out of greed, since he is without attachment. Through his commencement of the foundation of peace, he does not follow a wrong course out of fear, since he is without obstruction. And through his commencement of the

248. For the ultimate purpose of wisdom is the attainment of the nibbāna-element without residue, the ending of the round of birth and death.

foundation of wisdom, he does not follow a wrong course out of delusion, since he comprehends things as they really are.

Thus through the first foundation he tolerates without hatred: through the second he uses without greed: through the third he avoids without fear; and through the fourth he dispels without delusion. Through the first he attains the happiness of renunciation, and through the others, the happiness of solitude, of peace, and of enlightenment, respectively. So too, through the four foundations he attains, respectively, the rapture and happiness born of seclusion, the rapture and happiness born of concentration, the bodily happiness unaccompanied by rapture, and the happiness of equanimity born of the purification of mindfulness.

Thus it should be understood how the body of the pāramīs is included in the four foundations, which are adorned with numerous noble qualities. And just as the pāramīs are all included in the four foundations, they are also included in wisdom and compassion. For all the requisites of enlightenment can be included in wisdom and compassion, and the noble qualities such as giving (and the other pāramīs), accompanied by wisdom and compassion, are the requisites for the great enlightenment culminating in the perfection of Buddhahood.

(xiii) By what means are they accomplished?

The means by which the pāramīs are accomplished is the four-factored method: (1) the accumulation without omission of all the requisites of merit, etc., for the sake of supreme enlightenment, by performing them without deficiency; (2) performing them thoroughly with respect and high esteem; (3) performing them perseveringly without interruption; and (4) enduring effort over a long period without coming to a halt half-way. We will explain the length of time later.

For the sake of the supreme enlightenment, the Great Being, striving for enlightenment, should first of all surrender himself to the Buddhas, thus: "I offer myself up to the Buddhas." And whenever he obtains any possession, he should first of all resolve upon it as a potential gift: "Whatever requisite of life comes my way, that I will give to those who need it, and I myself will only use what remains over from this gift."

When he has made a mental determination to completely relinquish whatever possessions come his way, whether animate or inanimate, there are four shackles to giving (which he must overcome), namely: not being accustomed to giving in the past, the inferiority of the object to be given, the excellence and beauty of the object, and worry over the loss of the object.

(1) When the bodhisattva possesses objects that can be given and suppliants are present, but his mind does not leap up at the thought of giving and he does not want to give, he should conclude: "Surely, I have not been accustomed to giving in the past, therefore a desire to give does not arise now in my mind. So that my mind will delight in giving in the future, I will give a gift. With an eye for the future let me now relinquish what I have to those in need." Thus he gives a gift—generous, open-handed, delighting in relinquishing, one who gives when asked, delighting in giving and in sharing. In this way the Great Being destroys, shatters, and eradicates the first shackle to giving.

(2) Again, when the object to be given is inferior or defective, the Great Being reflects: "Because I was not inclined to giving in the past, at present my requisites are defective. Therefore, though it pains me, let me give whatever I have as a gift even if the object is low and inferior. In that way I will, in the future, reach the peak in the perfection of giving." Thus he gives whatever kind of gift he can—generous, open-handed, delighting in relinquishing, one who gives when asked, delighting in giving and in sharing. In this way the Great Being destroys, shatters, and eradicates the second shackle to giving.

(3) When a reluctance to give arises due to the excellence or beauty of the object to be given, the Great Being admonishes himself: "Good man, haven't you made the aspiration for the supreme enlightenment, the loftiest and most superior of all states? Well then, for the sake of enlightenment, it is proper for you to give excellent and beautiful objects as gifts." Thus he gives what is excellent and beautiful—generous, open-handed, delighting in relinquishing, one who gives when asked, delighting in giving and in sharing. In this way the Great Man destroys, shatters, and eradicates the third shackle to giving.

(4) When the Great Being is giving a gift, and he sees the loss of the object being given, he reflects thus: "This is the nature of material possessions, that they are subject to loss and to passing away. Moreover, it is because I did not give such gifts in the past that my

possessions are now depleted. Let me then give whatever I have as a gift, whether it be limited or abundant. In that way I will, in the future, reach the peak in the perfection of giving." Thus he gives whatever he has as a gift—generous, open-handed, delighting in relinquishing, one who gives when asked, delighting in giving and in sharing. In this way the Great Being destroys, shatters, and eradicates the fourth shackle to giving.

Reflecting upon them thus in whatever way is appropriate is the means for dispelling the harmful shackles to the perfection of giving. The same method used for the perfection of giving also applies to the perfection of virtue and the other perfections.

Further, self-surrender to the Buddhas is also a means for the complete accomplishment of the pāramīs. For when the Great Man, straining and striving for the fulfilment of the requisites of enlightenment, encounters troubles difficult to endure, depriving him of happiness and his means of support, or when he encounters injuries imposed by beings and formations—difficult to overcome, violent, sapping the vitality—then, since he has surrendered himself to the Buddhas, he reflects: "I have relinquished my very self to the Buddhas. Whatever comes, let it come." For this reason he does not waver, does not quake, does not undergo the least vacillation, but remains absolutely unshaken in his determination to undertake the good.

In brief, the destruction of self-love and the development of love for others are the means for the accomplishing of the pāramīs. For by fully understanding all dhammas in accordance with their nature, the Great Being who has formed the resolution to attain the supreme enlightenment remains untainted by them, and his self-love thereby becomes eliminated and exhausted. Then, since through the repeated practice of great compassion he has come to regard all beings as his dear children, his loving kindness, compassion, and affection for them increase. In conformity with this stage the Great Man, having expelled the defilements such as stinginess, etc., opposed to the requisites of enlightenment, and dispelled greed, hatred, and delusion in regard to himself and others, further causes people to enter and reach maturity in the three vehicles by benefitting them to the utmost with the four bases of beneficence which accompany the four foundations, namely: giving, loving speech, beneficent conduct, and equality of treatment.

For the great compassion and the great wisdom of the Great Beings are adorned by giving. Their giving is adorned and accompanied by loving speech, loving speech by beneficent conduct, and beneficent conduct by equality of treatment. When the bodhisattvas are practicing the requisites of enlightenment, they treat all beings without exception as equal with themselves, and perfect their sense of equality by remaining the same under all circumstances, pleasant or painful. And when they become Buddhas, their ability to train people is perfected by benefitting them to the utmost with these same four bases of beneficence brought to fulfilment by the four foundations. For the perfectly enlightened Buddhas, the base of giving is brought to fulfilment by the foundation of relinquishment, the base of loving speech by the foundation of truth, the base of beneficent conduct by the foundation of wisdom, and the base of equal treatment by the foundation of peace. For in regard to parinibbāna, all the disciples and paccekabuddhas are completely equal to the Tathāgatas; they are identical, without any distinction. Thus it is said: "There is no diversity among them in regard to emancipation" (see SN 22:58).

He is truthful, generous, and peaceful,
Endowed with wisdom and sympathy,
Complete in all the requisites,
What good can he not achieve?

He is the great compassionate Teacher,
Equanimous yet seeking the welfare of all,
Free from concern on all occasions,
Oh, how wonderful is the Conqueror!

Dispassionate towards all dhammas,
And towards all beings of equal mind,
Still he abides devoted to their welfare,
Oh, how wonderful is the Conqueror!

Always engaged in work promoting
The welfare and happiness of all living beings,
He never ceases on account of the trouble—
Oh, how wonderful is the Conqueror!

(xiv) How much time is required to accomplish them?

As a minimum, four incalculables (*asaṅkheyya*) and a hundred thousand great aeons (*mahākappa*); as a middle figure, eight incalculables and a hundred thousand great aeons; and as a maximum, sixteen incalculables and a hundred thousand great aeons.[249] This threefold division obtains by way of those in whom wisdom is predominant, those in whom faith is predominant, and those in whom energy is predominant, respectively. For those in whom wisdom is predominant, faith is weakest and wisdom keenest; for those in whom faith is predominant, wisdom is middling (and energy weakest); and for those in whom energy is predominant, wisdom is weakest (and faith middling). But supreme enlightenment must be achieved by the power of wisdom; so it is said in the commentary.

But others say that the classification of the time required for bodhisattvas obtains by way of the keen, middling, and tender quality of their energy. Still others say that without distinction the three divisions of time correspond to the time required for their requisites of enlightenment to reach fulfilment, which in turn is determined by the keen, middling, and tender quality of their factors maturing towards emancipation (*vimuttiparipācanīyā dhammā*).

Bodhisattvas also become threefold at the moment they form the aspiration, according to their division into those who comprehend through a condensed teaching (*ugghaṭitaññū*), those who comprehend through an elaborated teaching (*vipañcitaññū*), and those who are capable of training (*neyya*).[250] Among these, he who comprehends through a condensed teaching has such supporting conditions that, if he were disposed towards the enlightenment of a disciple, he could

---

249. The duration of a great aeon is indicated in the text only by means of similes. E.g., if there were a mountain crag of solid granite a *yojana* (i.e., approximately seven miles) high and a *yojana* round, and a man passing it once every hundred years were to stroke it once with a silk handkerchief, by this means it would take less time for him to wear away the mountain than it takes for an aeon to elapse. An "incalculable" means an incalculable number of great aeons; it must be distinguished from the four incalculables which make up each great aeon, the four periods of expansion, evolution, contraction, and dissolution.

250. The Suttanta basis for this classification is found in AN 4:133. For an explanation of these types, see *The Guide*, p. 15, n. 41/1,41/2.

attain arahatship together with the four discriminations and the six direct knowledges while listening to a four-line stanza from the lips of a perfectly enlightened Buddha, even while the third line has not yet been concluded. The second has such supporting conditions that, if he were disposed towards the enlightenment of a disciple, he could attain arahatship together with the six direct knowledges while listening to a four-line stanza from the lips of the Exalted One, even while the fourth line has not yet been concluded. And the third has the supporting conditions to attain arahatship together with the six direct knowledges when the four-line stanza he hears from the Exalted One has been concluded.

These three types, who form their aspirations without any allotted division of time, receive predictions (of their future Buddhahood) directly from the Buddhas. Then they fulfil the pāramīs in order and reach the supreme enlightenment according to the aforementioned time allotted to each type. But that these Great Beings—day by day giving great gifts like those given by Vessantara,[251] accumulating all the other pāramīs in the same way, making the five great relinquishings, reaching the summit in conduct for the good of relatives, conduct for the good of the world, and conduct developing intelligence—should become perfectly enlightened Buddhas before the time allotted to their respective types is fulfilled, this is not possible. Why? Because their knowledge is not yet mature enough and their accumulation of the factors culminating in Buddhahood not yet complete. For just as grain ripens only after the lapse of the time required (for its growth), so too the supreme enlightenment is perfected only after the lapse of the aforementioned periods of time. Before then, even though striving with all his might, the bodhisattva cannot attain enlightenment. The pāramīs are fulfilled according to the aforementioned distinction of time. Thus it should be understood.

(xv) What benefits do they bring?

The benefits obtained by bodhisattvas who have formed their aspirations are explained thus:

---

251. A prince noted for his generosity and selflessness; the last human existence of the bodhisattva who became the Buddha Gotama.

Those men in all factors complete,
Bound for perfect enlightenment,
Though wandering through the round of births
For countless aeons yet to come

Never arise in Avīci hell,
Nor in the intermundane voids.
They never appear as tawny titans
Or ghosts consumed by hunger and thirst.

Though reborn in the plane of woe,
They do not take on minor forms,
And when reborn in the world of men
They never come deprived of sight.

Their hearing is intact from birth,
Nor are they dumb or lame of limb.
They never become of female sex,
Eunuchs or hermaphrodites.

Those men bound for enlightenment
Never commit the five dark deeds.
Always pure in their way of life,
Their conduct's range is free from flaw.

They never hold inverted views
But recognize the law of kamma.
They are born at times in heavenly worlds,
But not in the insentient or pure abodes.

Those true men bent on renunciation,
Detached from all the planes of existence,
Plough their course for the good of the world,
Striving to fulfil the pāramīs.

Some other benefits of the pāramīs are the following: the sixteen wonderful and marvellous qualities that begin: "Mindful and clearly comprehending, Ānanda, the bodhisattva passes away from the Tusita heaven and descends into his mother's womb" (MN 123.6); the thirty-two portents, such as "cold disappears and heat is allayed," and "when the bodhisattva is born, this ten-thousandfold world system shakes, trembles, and quakes," etc. (ibid.); and the other qualities shown here and there in the Jātakas, the Buddhavaṃsa, etc., such as the fulfilment of the bodhisattva's wishes, his mastery over kamma, and so forth. Other benefits are the pairs of complementary qualities such as non-greed and non-hatred already discussed.

Moreover, from the time that he makes the aspiration, the bodhisattva becomes like a father to all beings, wishing for their welfare. By reason of his distinguished qualities he is worthy of offerings, worthy of reverence, worthy of esteem, a supreme field of merit. He is generally dear to humans and to non-humans alike, and is protected by deities. Because his mind is grounded in loving kindness and compassion, he cannot be harmed by wild beasts, etc. Whatever order of beings he is reborn in, on account of his distinguished merit, he surpasses the other beings there in his superior beauty, fame, happiness, strength, and dominion.

He is healthy and robust. His faith is very pure and lucid. His energy, mindfulness, concentration, and wisdom are also very pure and lucid. His defilements, disturbances, and passions are weak. Because his defilements are weak, he is easy to admonish, adroit, patient, meek, congenial, and hospitable. He is free from anger, malice, denigration, domineering, envy, stinginess, craftiness, hypocrisy, obstinacy, pride, presumption, and negligence. He endures torments at the hands of others but never torments anyone himself. Whenever he enters a village area, the unarisen dangers and calamities facing the beings there generally do not arise, and those that have arisen subside. And whenever he is reborn in the planes of misery, unlike the common inhabitants there, he is not oppressed by excessive suffering but acquires an even greater sense of spiritual urgency.

Therefore these distinguished qualities of the Great Man—such as being like a father to beings, being worthy of offerings, etc.—found in this or that state of existence, are the benefits of the pāramīs.

Further, the accomplishment of life span, the accomplishment of form, the accomplishment of family, the accomplishment of sovereignty, credibility, and greatness of spiritual power are also benefits of the Great Man's pāramīs. Therein, the "accomplishment of life span" (*āyusampadā*) is length of life or longevity in whatever state of existence he takes rebirth in; by this means he concludes whatever wholesome undertakings he began and accumulates many wholesome qualities. The "accomplishment of form" (*rūpasampadā*) is beauty of form, comeliness, or loveliness; by this means he inspires confidence and esteem in beings who take physical form as their standard. The "accomplishment of family" (*kulasampadā*) is rebirth in excellent families; by this means he is (judged) to be worth approaching and ministering to by beings who are intoxicated with the vanity of birth, etc. The "accomplishment of sovereignty" (*issariyasampadā*) is greatness of power, greatness of influence, and greatness of retinue; by means of these he is able to benefit with the four bases of beneficence those who need to be benefited and to restrain with Dhamma those who need to be restrained. "Credibility" (*ādeyyavacanatā*) means trustworthiness, reliability; by this means he becomes an authority for beings, and his command cannot be disregarded. "Greatness of spiritual power" (*mahānubhāvatā*) means magnitude of spiritual power; by this means he cannot be vanquished by others, but he himself invariably vanquishes them—by Dhamma, by righteousness, and by his genuine noble qualities.

Thus the accomplishment of life span and the rest are benefits of the Great Man's pāramīs. These are the cause for the growth of his own boundless requisites of merit, and the means by which he leads other beings to enter and reach maturity in the three vehicles.

(xvi) What is their fruit?

Their fruit is, in brief, the state of perfect Buddhahood. In detail, it is the acquisition of the form-body (*rūpakāya*) resplendent with the multitude of meritorious qualities such as the thirty-two characteristics of a Great Man, the eighty minor marks of physical beauty, the fathom-wide aura, etc.; and, founded upon this, the glorious Dhamma-body (*dhammakāya*) radiant with its collection of infinite and boundless meritorious qualities—the ten powers, the four grounds of self-confidence, the six kinds of knowledge not held in common with others, the eighteen unique Buddha-dhammas, and so forth.[252] And so numerous are the Buddha-qualities that even a perfectly enlightened Buddha could not finish describing them, even after many aeons. This is their fruit.

---

252. Although in late Mahāyāna Buddhism, the concept of the *dharmakāya* came to express the identity of the Buddha's essential nature with the essential nature of all particular existents, here the term *dhammakāya* is used simply to signify the collection of spiritual qualities that define a Buddha as such, without any ontological implications.

And it is said:

> If a Buddha were to speak in praise of a Buddha,
> Speaking nothing else through the duration of an aeon,
> Sooner would the long-standing aeon reach its end,
> But the praise of the Tathāgata would not reach its end.

Part Five

THE MEANING OF THE WORD "TATHĀGATA"

CY. The Exalted One is called "the Tathāgata" for eight reasons:

(i) because he has "thus come" (*tathā āgato*);
(ii) because he has "thus gone" (*tathā gato*);
(iii) because he has come to the real characteristic (of dhammas) (*tathalakkhaṇaṃ āgato*);
(iv) because he has awakened to real dhammas in accordance with actuality (*tathadhamme yāthāvato abhisambuddho*);
(v) because he is a seer of the real (*tathadassitāya*);
(vi) because he is a speaker of the real (*tathavāditāya*);
(vii) because he practices what he teaches (*tathakāritāya*);
(viii) and in the sense of vanquishing or surpassing (*abhibhavanaṭṭhena*).

(i) Why is the Exalted One called the Tathāgata because he has "thus come"?

Because he has come in the same way that the previous perfectly enlightened Buddhas came, engaged in exertion for the welfare of the whole world, came—that is, as the Exalted Vipassī, Sikhī, Vessabhū, Kakusandha, Koṇāgamana, and Kassapa (came).[253] What is meant? Our Exalted One (the Buddha Gotama) has come through the very same aspiration (*abhinīhāra*) that these Exalted Ones came through. Or just as the Exalted Vipassī ... the Exalted Kassapa came after they had fulfilled the full thirty pāramīs—i.e., the ten basic, ten intermediate, and ten ultimate pāramīs of giving, virtue, renunciation, wisdom, energy, patience, truthfulness, determination, loving kindness, and equanimity; made the five great relinquishings—i.e., the relinquishing of limbs, eyes, wealth, kingdom, and children and wife; fulfilled the preliminary effort, the preliminary conduct, the preaching of the Dhamma, conduct for the good of relatives, etc.; and reached the summit in conduct developing intelligence—exactly thus has our Exalted One come (*tathā amhākam pi Bhagavā āgato*). Or else, just as the Exalted Vipassī ... Kassapa came by developing and cultivating the four foundations of mindfulness, the four right endeavors, the four bases of spiritual success, the five faculties, the five powers, the seven factors of enlightenment, and the Noble Eightfold Path—exactly thus has our Exalted One come. Hence he is the Tathāgata because he has "thus come."

> As Vipassī and the other great sages of the past
> Came to the state of omniscience in the world,
> In that very same way the Sakyan sage came.
> Thus he, the all-seeing, is called "Tathāgata."

Sub.Cy. Though the five great relinquishings belong to the perfection of giving, they are mentioned separately in order to show that they are distinct forms of relinquishing, that they are extremely difficult to practice, [and that they are distinct requisites for enlightenment]. For the same reasons, the relinquishing of the eyes is mentioned separately from the relinquishing of the limbs. And though they all involve possessions, the relinquishing of children and wife is mentioned separately from the relinquishing of wealth and kingdom. The "preliminary effort" is the achievement of the meditative attainments and the (five) direct knowledges, together with the preliminary portion of practice for these consisting in the duties of advancing and retreating (to and from the village for alms). The "preliminary conduct" is the achievement of extraordinary practice in giving, etc., included in the Cariyāpiṭaka. But some say the preliminary effort is the aspiration, and the preliminary conduct either the practice of giving, etc., or solitary wandering by way of bodily seclusion.

---

253. These are the six Buddhas mentioned in the most ancient canonical texts as the immediate predecessors of the Buddha Gotama. See Mahāpadāna Sutta, DN 14. Later canonical works mention twenty-seven preceding Buddhas, and trace the original aspiration of our present Buddha back to the twenty-fourth, the Buddha Dīpaṅkara.

The "preaching of the Dhamma" is talk that establishes and matures beings in the three types of enlightenment by explaining to them the practice of giving, etc., fewness of wishes, etc., the unsatisfactoriness of saṃsāra and the benefit of nibbāna. "Conduct developing intelligence" is the widening of knowledge by means of the knowledge of the ownership of action (*kammasakatāñāṇa*), the study of blameless occupations and blameless fields of knowledge, the study of the aggregates, bases, etc., and the scrutinization of the three characteristics. In denotation it is the same as the perfection of wisdom but is mentioned separately in order to show the requisite of knowledge.[254] By mentioning the foundations of mindfulness (and the other constituents of enlightenment), he shows the way of arrival that has been brought to its climax, [for those states can be understood as the constituents of the supramundane paths and fruits]. Or the foundations of mindfulness, etc., can be considered only as the accompaniments of insight [by taking them as the preliminary (mundane) portion of practice].[255] And here it should be understood that by mentioning the aspiration he shows the beginning of the way of arrival, by mentioning the pāramīs he shows the middle, and by mentioning the four foundations of mindfulness, etc., he shows the consummation.

CY. (ii) Why is he called the Tathāgata because he has "thus gone"?

Because as soon as he was born, he went in the same way that the Exalted Vipassī... Kassapa went as soon as they were born. And how

254. That is, among the two sets of requisites (*sambhāra*) for enlightenment, the requisites of merit and the requisites of knowledge.

255. The thirty-seven constituents of enlightenment (*bodhipakkhiyadhammā*) are developed in two distinct stages. The first, the preliminary portion, consists in their development at the time of practicing insight on the five aggregates as impermanent, suffering, and not-self. This portion is mundane since its object, the aggregates, is mundane. The second portion of development consists in their maturation in the four supramundane paths. Here the factors come to prominence as components of these momentary, climactic acts of path-consciousness which realize nibbāna and break the fetters of the round. On these occasions, and in the subsequent fruits, they are supramundane, since their object, nibbāna, is a supramundane dhamma.

did the Exalted One go? As soon as he was born he stood with his feet planted evenly on the ground, and then, facing north, went (*gata*) forward with a stride of seven steps. As it is said: "As soon as the bodhisattva was born, Ānanda, he stood with his feet planted evenly on the ground; then, while a white parasol was held over him, facing north, he went forward with a stride of seven steps. Having surveyed all the directions, he then uttered the roar of the Leader of the Herd: 'I am the foremost in the world. I am pre-eminent in the world. I am supreme in the world. This is my last birth. There is now no renewal of existence.'" (MN 123.20)

His way of going was real (*tatha*), not unreal (*avitatha*), for it foretokened his numerous achievements of spiritual distinction, as follows. When, as soon as he was born, he stood with his feet (*pāda*) planted evenly on the ground, that was the foretoken of his obtaining the four bases of spiritual success (*iddhipāda*). When he walked facing north (*uttara*), that was the foretoken of his supremacy in all the world (*sabbalokuttarabhāva*).[256] His stride of seven steps foretokened his obtaining the gems of the seven factors of enlightenment; the golden-staffed chowries that appeared, his defeat of all the sectarian teachers; the white parasol, his obtaining the stainless white parasol of the supreme deliverance of arahatship. When he stood surveying all the directions after completing the seventh step, that foretokened his obtaining the unobstructed knowledge of omniscience. And his uttering the roar of the Leader of the Herd was the foretoken of his setting in motion the supreme, irreversible Wheel of the Dhamma.

Just as the previous Exalted Ones went thus, exactly thus did the present Exalted One go (*tathā ayaṃ Bhagavā pi gato*). And his way of going was real, not unreal, for it foretokened the above achievements of spiritual distinction. Hence the ancients have said:

The very moment the master bull was born,
He stood upon the earth with even feet.
Beneath the parasol the Maruts held,
Gotama took a stride of seven steps.
When he finished taking seven steps,
He surveyed all directions with his gaze,

256. N.Sub.Cy. "Either his supremacy within all the world, or his transcendence over the entire world."

And like a lion poised on a mountain top,
Uttered his roar complete in factors eight.
Hence he is the Tathāgata because he has "thus gone."

Or alternatively, as the Exalted Vipassī ... Kassapa went, exactly thus did the present Exalted One go. That is, abandoning sensual desire by renunciation, ill will by benevolence, sloth-and-torpor by the perception of light, restlessness-and-remorse by non-distraction, and perplexity by the defining of dhammas; shattering ignorance with knowledge, dispelling discontent with joy; (1) knocking away the panel of the (five) hindrances with the first jhāna, (2) making applied and sustained thought subside with the second jhāna, (3) making rapture fade away with the third jhāna, and (4) abandoning pleasure and pain with the fourth jhāna; (5) surmounting perceptions of material forms, impingement, and diversity with the attainment of the base of infinite space, (6) the perception of the base of infinite space with the attainment of the base of infinite consciousness, (7) the perception of the base of infinite consciousness with the attainment of the base of nothingness, and (8) the perception of the base of nothingness with the attainment of the base of neither perception nor non-perception.[257]

Then he went abandoning (1) the perception of permanence with the contemplation of impermanence, (2) the perception of pleasure with the contemplation of suffering, (3) the perception of self with the contemplation of non-self, (4) delight with the contemplation of disenchantment, (5) lust with the contemplation of fading away, (6) origination with the contemplation of cessation, (7) grasping with the contemplation of relinquishment, (8) the perception of compactness with the contemplation of destruction, (9) accumulation with the contemplation of fall, (10) the perception of stability with the contemplation of change, (11) the sign with the contemplation of the signless, (12) wish with the contemplation of the wishless, (13) adherence with the contemplation of emptiness, (14) adherence due to grasping at substance with the higher wisdom of insight into dhammas, (15) adherence due to confusion with the knowledge and vision of things as they really are, (16) the adherence due to reliance

257. These are the eight attainments of serenity meditation, four pertaining to the fine-material and four to the immaterial plane.

with the contemplation of danger, (17) non-reflection with the contemplation of reflection, and (18) adherence due to bondage with the contemplation of the round's end.[258]

Then he went demolishing the defilements co-existing with wrong view with the path of stream-entry, abandoning the gross defilements (of lust, hate, and delusion) with the path of the once-returner, extirpating the defilements accompanied by subtle (sensual lust and ill will) with the path of the non-returner, and eradicating all defilements with the path of arahatship.[259] Thus he is the Tathāgata because he has "thus gone."

Sub.Cy. In the first case, the participle "gone" (*gata*) in the word Tathāgata is explained in the sense of bodily movement. In the second case it is explained in the sense of the movement of knowledge. Here he first shows the Exalted One's state of Tathāgatahood distinguished by its movement of knowledge by way of the preliminary practice for the first jhāna, stated as the abandoning of the five hindrances, sensual desire and the rest; next by the eight meditative attainments together with their means; and then by the eighteen principal insights. Since the perception of impermanence and the rest come to perfection for one established in the full understanding of the known, which drives away the delusion obstructing the discernment of mentality-materiality and the overcoming of doubt, the "shattering of ignorance" is the means for insight. So too, since the jhānas, etc., are easily achieved when discontent is dispelled by joy based on delight in the attainments, the dispelling of discontent is the means for the meditative attainments.

The "contemplation of impermanence" is a name for the insight apprehending the impermanence of the dhammas pertaining to the three planes. The "perception of permanence" is the wrong perception of conditioned dhammas as permanent or eternal. Under the heading of perception, (wrong) views and (wrong) cognition should also be included. The same method applies to the cases that follow. The

---

258. These are the eighteen principal insights (*mahāvipassanā*), shown in contrast to the deluded perceptions and defilements they eliminate.

259. It is of interest to note that according to the commentary here, the Buddha, on the night of his enlightenment, must pass through all the four paths crossed by his disciples: the paths of stream-entry, once-returner, non-returner, and arahatship. These paths are thus not a particularity of the disciples' course, but a necessity for all who attain liberation, since it is the wisdom in these four path attainments that cuts off the fetters.

"contemplation of disenchantment" is the contemplation that occurs in the mode of becoming disenchanted with formations. "Delight" is craving accompanied by rapture. The "contemplation of fading away" is contemplation that occurs in the mode of fading away. "Contemplation of cessation" is either the contemplation of the cessation of formations, or the contemplation that "formations cease only, and do not arise again by way of a future re-origination"; thus it is said, "by the contemplation of cessation he makes (formations) cease and does not originate them." This is powerful desire for liberation. The "contemplation of relinquishment" is contemplation that occurs in the mode of relinquishing; this is the establishing of reflection. "Grasping" is the apprehension (of formations) as permanent, etc. The "perception of compactness" is the apprehension of identity (in a complex of factors) because of continuity, aggregation, (sameness of) function, or (sameness of) object. "Accumulation" is the forming (of kamma). "Change" is the attainment of distinct stages. The "perception of stability" is the apprehension of lastingness. The "sign" is the apprehension of formations as graspable entities, due to the compactness of their aggregation, etc., and to the delimitation of their individual functions. "Wish" is the wishing of lust, etc.; in denotation it is the inclination towards formations because of craving. "Adherence" is the settled view of a self. "Higher wisdom of insight into dhammas" is the scrutinization of all dhammas as impermanent, suffering, etc. "Adherence due to grasping at substance" is the inversion of apprehending a substance in the insubstantial. "Adherence due to confusion" is the adherence (to the view that) the world originated through the creative play of God, etc. "Adherence due to reliance" is the apprehension of formations as a shelter and a haven; the reliance is craving. The "contemplation of reflection" is the knowledge that "formations of such and such a kind are being relinquished." The "ending of the round" is nibbāna, the departure from the round. The "contemplation of the ending of the round" is "change-of-lineage" (*gotrabhū*), the contemplation which occurs taking nibbāna as its object.[260] The "adherence due to bondage" is the adherence to formations due to being bound.

260. Vism 22.1–14.

CY. (iii) Why is he called the Tathāgata because he has come to the real characteristics (of dhammas)?

(The six elements): The earth element has the characteristic of hardness—that is real, not unreal (*thatham avitatham*); the water element, of flowing; the fire element, of heat; the wind element, of distending; the space element, of intangibility; the consciousness element, of cognizing.

(The five aggregates): Material form has the characteristic of deformation; feeling, of being felt; perception, of perceiving; the mental formations, of forming; consciousness, of cognizing.

(The jhāna factors): Applied thought has the characteristic of application of mind; sustained thought, of continued pressure; rapture, of pervading; happiness, of gratification; one-pointedness of mind, of non-distraction; contact, of touching.[261]

(The five faculties): The faculty of faith has the characteristic of resolution; the faculty of energy, of exertion; the faculty of mindfulness, of awareness; the faculty of concentration, of non-distraction; the faculty of wisdom, of understanding.

(The five powers): The power of faith has the characteristic of not wavering because of faithlessness; the power of energy, of not wavering because of laziness; the power of mindfulness, of not wavering because of forgetfulness; the power of concentration, of not wavering because of restlessness; the power of wisdom, of not wavering because of ignorance.

(The seven factors of enlightenment): The enlightenment factor of mindfulness has the characteristic of awareness; the factor of investigation of dhammas, of investigating; the factor of energy, of exertion; the factor of rapture, of pervading; the factor of tranquillity, of subsiding; the factor of concentration, of non-distraction; the factor of equanimity, of detached observation.

(The eight factors of the noble path): right view has the characteristic of seeing; right intention, of application of mind; right speech, of embracing; right action, of originating; right livelihood, of cleansing; right effort, of exertion; right mindfulness, of awareness; right concentration, of non-distraction.

261. Contact (*phassa*), though included in the jhānic consciousness, is not a specific jhāna factor. It is puzzling that it is included here.

(The twelve factors of dependent origination): ignorance has the characteristic of unknowing; kamma-formations, of volition; consciousness, of cognizing; mentality, of inclining, and materiality, of deformation; the six sense bases, of actuating; contact, of touching; feeling, of being felt; craving, of causing; clinging, of holding; existence, of accumulating; birth, of production; aging, of decaying, and death, of passing away.

The elements have the characteristics of emptiness; the sense bases, of actuating; the foundations of mindfulness, of awareness; the right endeavors, of endeavoring; the bases of spiritual success, of succeeding; the faculties, of predominance; the powers, of unwavering; the enlightenment factors, of emancipating; the path, of being a cause.

The truths have the characteristic of reality; serenity, of non-distraction; insight, of contemplation; serenity and insight, of having a single flavor; the pairs of complementary opposites,[262] of not exceeding one another.

The purification of virtue has the characteristic of restraint; purification of mind, of non-distraction; purification of view, of seeing.

The knowledge of destruction has the characteristic of eradication; the knowledge of non-arising has the characteristic of tranquillity.[263]

Desire has the characteristics of being the root; attention, of being the originator; contact, of collecting together; feeling, of convergence; concentration, of eminence; mindfulness, of predominance; wisdom, of supremacy; emancipation, of being the essence; and nibbāna, the plunge into the deathless, of being the consummation.

All these characteristics are real, not unreal. Through the movement of his faculty of knowledge he has come to the real characteristic (of all dhammas); he has reached it without falling away from it, fully arrived at it—therefore he is the Tathāgata.

Thus he is the Tathāgata because he has come to the real characteristic.

---

262. Sub.Cy. "Serenity and insight. Some say faith and wisdom, and exertion and non-distraction."

263. Sub.Cy. "Destruction is the path, for it destroys the defilements; non-arising is the fruit, for it is the conclusion with no further arising."

(iv) Why is he called the Tathāgata because he awakened to real dhammas in accordance with actuality?

It is the Four Noble Truths that are called "real dhammas." As it is said: "These Four Noble Truths, bhikkhus, are real, not unreal, not otherwise (*tathāni avitathāni anaññathāni*). What four? 'This is suffering,' bhikkhus—this is real, not unreal, not otherwise," and so on, in detail. The Exalted One awakened to those truths. Therefore, because he awakened to real dhammas, he is called the Tathāgata; for here the word "gone" has the meaning "awakened" (*abhisambuddhattha*).

Further, the fact that aging and death originate and commence with birth as condition is real, not unreal, not otherwise. (And so forth, until): The fact that the kamma-formations originate and commence with ignorance as condition is real, not unreal, not otherwise. The fact that ignorance is the condition for the kamma-formations, the kamma-formations for consciousness ... birth for aging and death, is real, not unreal, not otherwise. All that the Exalted One awakened to. Because he awakened to real dhammas, he is called the Tathāgata.

Hence he is the Tathāgata because he awakened to real dhammas in accordance with actuality.

Sub.Cy. The four truths are "real" because their specific nature is undistorted (*aviparītasabhāvattā*); "not unreal" because their specific nature is not false (*amusāsabhāvattā*); "not otherwise" because they do not admit of any alteration (*aññākārarahitattā*).

N.Sub.Cy. Having first shown the fourth reason by way of the truths, he next shows it by way of the factors of dependent origination functioning as conditions and conditionally arisen phenomena, which are "real" because of the non-distortion of their specific nature. "Awakened" is said because the root "go" (*gamu*) has the meaning of understanding (*buddhi*).[264]

264. In Pāḷi, words deriving from the root *gam:* "go" and words deriving from the root *budh:* "understand" are often treated as interchangeable in meaning. "For words signifying movement convey the meaning of understanding, and words signifying understanding convey the meaning of movement." (*Yo hi gatyattho so buddhyattho, yo ca buddhyattho so gatyattho,* N.Sub.Cy.)

CY. (v) Why is he called the Tathāgata because he is a seer of the real?

In this world together with its gods, etc., in this generation with its rulers and its men, whatever visible-form object there is that enters the threshold of the eye-door of the innumerable beings throughout the innumerable world systems—that the Exalted One knows and sees in all its modes. And knowing and seeing it thus, he has analyzed it under numerous names, in thirteen sections, and by fifty-two methods, as desirable or undesirable, etc., and as found under the applicable term among the seen, heard, sensed, and cognized, according to the method given thus: "What is the material form that is the visible-form base? The material form derivative upon the four primary elements that is of colored appearance, visible, impinging, blue, yellow," etc. (Dhs 616). This is real, not unreal. The same method applies to sounds entering the threshold of the ear-door (and the other sense objects in their respective sense doors). For the Exalted One has said: "In this world, bhikkhus, together with its gods, etc., in this generation with its rulers and its men, whatever is seen, heard, sensed, cognized, reached, sought after, or examined by the mind—that I know, that I have directly known. That the Tathāgata has understood. But the Tathāgata does not take a stand upon it" (AN 4:24). Hence he is the Tathāgata because he is a seer of the real. Here the term "Tathāgata" should be understood to mean a seer of the real.

Sub.Cy. "Under numerous names": the visible form object is described as desirable, undesirable, neutral, inferior, past, future, present, internal, external, seen, cognized, visible form, visible-form base, visible-form element, a colored appearance, visible, impingent, blue, yellow, etc. "In thirteen sections": this is said in reference to the thirteen expository sections which have come down in the chapter on material form (in the Dhammasaṅgaṇī). "By fifty-two methods": this is said in reference to the four methods of defining contained in each of the thirteen sections.[265] "This is real": because of the undistortedness of his vision and the incontrovertible character of his

265. The thirteen sections are expounded according to the various mental factors, such as feeling, contact, consciousness, etc., which originate with each sense object as their objective basis. The four methods obtain from the differentiation of the cognitive act into past, present, future, and future possibility.

teaching. The analytical derivation of the word "Tathāgata" should be understood thus: he goes to (*gacchati*)—i.e., he sees and knows—these dhammas beginning with the visible-form object, in the very way (*tathā*) they exist in their specific nature and mode.

(vi) Why is he called the Tathāgata because he is a speaker of the real?

In the forty-five year interval between the night when the Exalted One, sitting in the invincible posture on the terrace of enlightenment, crushed the heads of the three Māras[266] and awakened to the supreme perfect enlightenment, and the night when he attained parinibbāna in the nibbāna-element without residue while lying between the twin Sāl trees, whatever the Exalted One spoke, whether in the first, middle, or final periods following the enlightenment—the discourses, mixed prose and verse, expositions, stanzas, joyous exclamations, sayings, birth stories, wonders, and miscellanies[267]—all this is irreproachable in meaning and in phrasing, free from excess and deficiency, perfect in all its modes, crushing the vanity of lust, hatred, and delusion. There is not even as much as a hair's tip in this that is defective. It all appears as though it had been stamped with a single seal, measured with a single ruler, or weighed upon a single pair of scales. It is all real, not unreal, not otherwise. As it is said: "Between the night when the Tathāgata awakens to the supreme perfect enlightenment and the night when he attains parinibbāna in the nibbāna-element without residue, whatever he speaks, utters, or expounds—all that is real, not otherwise. Therefore he is called the Tathāgata" (AN 4:23). For here the word gata has the meaning of enunciation (*gada*).

Hence he is the Tathāgata because he is a speaker of the real.

Further, the word *āgada* or *āgadana* means "pronouncement"; that is, a statement (*vacana*). His pronouncement is real and undistorted. Thus, changing the letter *d* to a *t;* the derivation of the word "Tathāgata" may be understood in this sense.

---

266. The "three Māras" are the defilements, kamma-formations, and the malign deity. The other two Māras—of the aggregates and of death—are only defeated with the attainment of parinibbāna.

267. This is the traditional ninefold classification of the Word of the Buddha.

(vii) Why is he called the Tathāgata because he practices what he teaches?

The bodily action of the Exalted One conforms to his speech, and his speech conforms to his bodily action; therefore he is one who practices what he teaches and teaches what he practices. Since he is of such a nature, his bodily action has "gone thus" (*tathā gata*), proceeding in accordance with his speech, and his speech has "gone thus," proceeding in accordance with his bodily action; thus he is the Tathāgata. As it is said: "As the Tathāgata says, so he does; as he does, so he says. Therefore he is called the Tathāgata" (AN 4:23).

Hence he is the Tathāgata because he practices what he teaches.

(viii) Why is he called the Tathāgata in the sense of vanquishing or surpassing (*abhibhavana*)?

From the pinnacle of existence[268] downwards, and from the Avīci hell upwards, throughout the innumerable world systems, the Tathāgata surpasses (*abhibhavati*) all beings in regard to virtue, concentration, wisdom, emancipation, and knowledge-and-vision of emancipation. There is none his equal or measure. He is unequalled, immeasurable, incomparable—the king of kings, the god of gods, the Sakka above all Sakkas, the Brahmā above all Brahmās. Thus it is said: "In this world, bhikkhus, together with its gods, etc., in this generation with its rulers and its men, the Tathāgata is the vanquisher, the unvanquished, the universal seer, the wielder of power. Therefore he is called the Tathāgata."

Here the word-derivation should be understood as follows: Agada is, as it were, a kind of medicine. What kind? His elegance of teaching and his accumulation of merit. For by means of these, he vanquishes all the rival teachers as well as this world together with its gods in the same way that a powerful physician vanquishes snakes with a divine medicine. Thus his medicine (*agada*) for vanquishing all the world is his real, undistorted elegance of teaching and his accumulations of merit. Changing the letter *d* to a *t*, the derivation of the word "Tathāgata" may be understood thus: he is the Tathāgata in the sense of vanquishing.

---

268. *Bhavagga*: the base of neither perception nor non-perception, the highest plane of existence, the ontological equivalent and kammic consequence of the fourth immaterial meditative attainment.

Furthermore,[269] he is the Tathāgata because he has "gone through reality" (*tathāya gata*) and because he has "really gone" (*tathaṃ gato*). Here "gone" (*gata*) has the meanings of undergone (*avagata*), gone beyond (*atīta*), attained (*patta*), and practiced (*paṭipanna*). Thus he is the Tathāgata because he has gone through—i.e., undergone—reality by fully understanding the entire world[270] through the scrutinization (of its essential characteristics, as impermanent, suffering, and non-self). He is the Tathāgata because he has gone through—i.e., gone beyond—reality by fully understanding the world through the abandonment of its origin. He is the Tathāgata because he has gone through—i.e., attained—reality by realizing the cessation of the world. And he is the Tathāgata because he has really gone along—i.e., practiced—the way leading to the cessation of the world. Thus the Exalted One has said: "The world, bhikkhus, has been awakened to by the Tathāgata; the Tathāgata is detached from the world. The origin of the world has been awakened to by the Tathāgata; the Tathāgata has abandoned the origin of the world. The cessation of the world has been awakened to by the Tathāgata; the Tathāgata has realized the cessation of the world. The way leading to the cessation of the world has been awakened to by the Tathāgata; the Tathāgata has developed the way leading to the cessation of the world. Whatever there is in this world together with its gods, etc., all that has been awakened to by the Tathāgata. Therefore he is called the Tathāgata" (AN 4:23).

The meaning of the word "Tathāgata" should be understood as given. But this is the mere introduction to the explanation of the nature of a Tathāgata. For only a Tathāgata himself can explain the nature of a Tathāgata in its completeness.

Sub.Cy. Why is this the mere introduction? Because the word "Tathāgata," like the word "diligence",[271] contains the entire practice of the Dhamma as well as all the qualities of a Buddha.

---

269. This derivation, though perhaps the deepest and most suggestive of all those given, is not separately enumerated in the text.

270. N.Sub.Cy. "The 'world' here is the noble truth of suffering." The following items should likewise be connected with the remaining three noble truths, in their respective sequence.

271. *Appamāda*: the reference is to the Buddha's last words.

Appendix One

A SUMMARY OF THE NET OF VIEWS

A. Speculations about the Past (18 Views)

1. Eternalism (*Sassatavāda*)
   - (i) Based on recollection of up to 100,000 past lives
   - (ii) Based on recollection of up to ten aeons of world contraction and expansion.
   - (iii) Based on recollection of up to forty such aeons
   - (iv) Based on reasoning
2. Partial-Eternalism (*Ekaccasassatavāda*)
   - (i) Theism
   - (ii) Polytheism held by beings who were gods corrupted by play
   - (iii) Polytheism held by beings who were gods corrupted by mind
   - (iv) Rationalist dualism of an impermanent body and an eternal mind
3. Extensionism (*Antānantavāda*)
   - (i) View that the world is finite
   - (ii) View that the world is infinite
   - (iii) View that the world is finite in vertical direction but infinite across
   - (iv) View that the world is neither finite nor infinite
4. Doctrines of Endless Equivocation (*Amarāvikkhepavāda*)
   - (i) Held by one fearful of making a false statement
   - (ii) Held by one fearful of clinging
   - (iii) Held by one fearful of being cross-examined

(iv) Held by one who is dull and stupid

5. Doctrines of Fortuitous Origination (*Adhiccasamuppanna-vāda*)
   (i) Based on the recollection of the arising of perception after passing away from the plane of non-percipient beings
   (ii) Based on reasoning

B. Speculations about the Future (44 Views)

1. Doctrines of Percipient Immortality (*Saññīvāda*): The self is immutable after death, percipient, and:
   (i) material
   (ii) immaterial
   (iii) both material and immaterial
   (iv) neither material nor immaterial
   (v) finite
   (vi) infinite
   (vii) both finite and infinite
   (vii) neither finite nor infinite
   (ix) of uniform perception
   (x) of diversified perception
   (xi) of limited perception
   (xii) of boundless perception
   (xiii) exclusively happy
   (xiv) exclusively miserable
   (xv) both happy and miserable
   (xvi) neither happy nor miserable

2. Doctrines of Non-percipient Immortality (*Asaññivāda*): The self is immutable after death, non-percipient, and:
   (i) material
   (ii) immaterial
   (iii) both material and immaterial
   (iv) neither material nor immaterial
   (v) finite
   (vi) infinite
   (vii) both finite and infinite
   (viii) neither finite nor infinite

3. Doctrines of Neither Percipient Nor Non-percipient Immortality (*N'evasaññīnāsaññīvāda*):
   The self is immutable after death, neither percipient nor non-percipient, and:
   - (i) material
   - (ii) immaterial
   - (iii) both material and immaterial
   - (iv) neither material nor immaterial
   - (v) finite
   - (vi) infinite
   - (vii) both finite and infinite
   - (viii) neither finite nor infinite
4. Annihilationism (*Ucchedavāda*)
   - (i) annihilation of the self composed of the four elements
   - (ii) annihilation of the divine, sense-sphere self
   - (iii) annihilation of the divine, fine-material-sphere self
   - (iv) annihilation of the self belonging to the base of infinite space
   - (v) annihilation of the self belonging to the base of infinite consciousness
   - (vi) annihilation of the self belonging to the base of nothingness
   - (vii) annihilation of the self belonging to the base of neither perception nor non-perception
5. Doctrines of Nibbāna Here and Now (*Diṭṭhadhammanibbānavāda*)
   - (i) Nibbāna here and now in the enjoyment of the five strands of sense pleasure
   - (ii) Nibbāna here and now in the first jhāna
   - (iii) Nibbāna here and now in the second jhāna
   - (iv) Nibbāna here and now in the third jhāna
   - (v) Nibbāna here and now in the fourth jhāna

Appendix Two

SOME PĀLI PASSAGES FROM THE SUBCOMMENTARIES

(**N.Sub.Cy.** Interpolations in brackets)

1. The act of killing in terms of the doctrine of non-self

Etth'āha: Khaṇe khaṇe nirujjhanasabhāvesu saṅkhāresu ko hanti, ko vā haññati? Yadi cittacetasikasantāno so arūpatāya na chedanabhedanādivasena vikopanasamattho, nāpi vikopanīyo. Atha rūpasantāno so acetanatāya kaṭṭhakaliṅgarūpamo ti na tattha chedanādinā pāṇātipāto labbhati yathā matasarīre. Payogo pi pāṇātipātassa paharaṇappakārādi atītesu vā saṅkhāresu bhaveyya anāgatesu vā paccuppannesu vā, tattha na tāva atītānāgatesu sambhavati tesaṃ abhāvato; paccuppannesu ca saṅkhārāṇaṃ khaṇikattā sarasen'eva nirujjhanasabhāvatāya vināsābhimukhesu nippayojano payogo siyā, vināsassa ca kāraṇarahitattā no paharaṇappakārādipayogahetukaṃ maraṇaṃ, nirīhakatāya ca saṅkhārānaṃ kassa so payogo, khaṇikattā vadhādhippāyasamakālabhijjanakassa kiriyāpariyosānakālānavaṭṭhānato kassa vā pāṇātipātakammabaddho it?

Vuccate: Yathāvuttavadhakacetanāsahito saṅkhārānaṃ puñjo sattasaṅkhāto hantā; tena pavattitavadhakapayoganimittaṃ apagatusmā viññāṇajīvitindriyo matavohārappavattinibandho yathāvuttavadhappayogākaraṇe uppajjanāraho rūpārūpadham masamūho haññati, kevalo vā cittacetasikasantāno. Vadhappayogā-visayabhāve pi tassa pañcavokārabhave rūpasantānādhī-navuttitāya rūpasantāne parena payojitajīvitindriyupacchedakapayogavasena tannibbatti-

vibandhakavisadisarūpuppattiyā vihate vicchedo hotī ti na pāṇātipātassa asambhavo. Nāpi ahetuko pāṇātipāto, na ca payogo nippayojano paccuppannesu saṅkhāresu katapayogavasena tadanantaraṃ uppajjanārahassa saṅkhārakalāpassa tathā anuppattito, khaṇikānaṃ saṅkhārānaṃ khaṇikamaraṇassa idha maraṇabhāvena anadhippetattā, santatimaraṇassa ca yathā-vuttanayena sahetukabhā-vato na ahetukaṃ maraṇaṃ, na ca katturahito pāṇātipātappayogo nirīhakesu pi saṅkhāresu sannihitatā-mattena upakārakesu attano anurūpaphaluppādananiyatesu kāraṇesu kattuvohārasiddhito yathā "padīpo pakāseti, nisākaro candimā" ti ca. Na ca kevalassa vadhādhip-pāyasahabhuno cittacetasikakalāpassa pāṇātipāto icchito santānavasena avaṭṭhitass'eva paṭijānanato; santānavasena pavat-tamānānañca padīpādīnaṃ atthakiriyāsiddhi dissatī ti atth' eva pāṇātipātena kammabaddho. Ayañ ca vicāro adinnādānādīsu pi yathāsambhavaṃ vibhāvetabbo.

2. The Doctrine of Emergent Manifestation: Analogy of the Jar and the Lamp

Kathaṃ pana [sattirūpavasena] vijjamāno yeva pubbe anabhibyatto [byattirūpavasena] abhibyattiṃ gacchatīti? Yathā andhakārena paṭicchanno ghaṭo ālokena abhibyattiṃ gacchati.

Idam ettha vicāretabbaṃ: –Kiṃ karonto āloko ghaṭaṃ pakāsetī ti vuccate? Yadi ghaṭavisayaṃ buddhiṃ karonto [pakāseti], buddhiyā anuppannāya uppattidīpanato abhibyattivādo hāyati. Atha ghaṭabuddhiyā āvaraṇabhūtaṃ andhakāraṃ vidhamanto, evampi abhibyattivādo hāyatyeva. Satihighaṭabuddhiyā andhakāro kathaṃ tassā āvaraṇaṃ hotī ti? Yathā ghaṭassa abhibyatti na yujjati, evaṃ [diṭṭhigatikaparikappitassa] attano pi [abhibyatti na yujjati yeva]. Tatthāpi hi yadi indriyavisayādisannipātena anuppannāya buddhiyā uppatti, uppattivacanen' eva abhibyattivādo hāyati, [abhibyattimat-tam atikkamma anuppannāya eva buddhiyā uppattidīpanato]; tathā sassatavādo pi [ten' eva kāraṇena].

(For the following the more elaborate version of N.Sub.Cy. is given): *Atha buddhippavattiyā āvaraṇabhūtassa andhakāraṭṭhā niyassa mohassa vidhamanena buddhi uppannā. Evampi sati atthavisayāya buddhiyā kathaṃ moho tassā āvaraṇaṃ hotī ti? Hāyat'eva abhibyattivādo. Kiñ ca bhiyyo:-bhedasabbhāvato pi abhi-byattivādo hāyati. Na hi abhibyañjanakānaṃ candima-sūriyamaṇipadīpādīnaṃ bhedena abhibyañjitabbānaṃ ghaṭādīnam bhedo hoti, hoti ca visayabhedena buddhibhedo yathāvisayaṃ buddhiyā sambhavato ti bhiyyo pi abhibyatti na yujjati yeva; na c'ettha vijjamānatābhibyattivasena vuttikappanā yuttā vijjamānatābhibyattikiriyāsaṅkhātāya vuttiyā vuttimato ca anaññathānu jānanto. Anaññā yeva hi tathā vuttisaṅkhātā kiriyā tabbantavatthuto, yathā phassādīhi phusanādibhāvo, tasmā vuttimato anaññāya eva vijjamānatābhibyattisaṅkhātāya vuttiyā parikappito kesañci abhibyattivādo na yutto yevā ti.*

3. An examination of eternalism

Tatth'ayaṃ anuyuñjane saṅkhepakathā: –Yadi hi parena parikappito attā loko vā sassato siyā, tassa nibbikāratāya purimarūpāvijahanato kassaci visesādhānassa kātuṃ asakkuṇeyyatāya ahitato nivattanatthaṃ, hite ca paṭṭipattiatthaṃ upadeso eva nippayojano siyā sassatavādino, kathaṃ vā so upadeso pavattīyati vikārābhāvato? Evañ ca attano ajaṭākāsassa viya dānādikiriyā hiṃsādikiriyā ca na sambhavati. Tathā sukhassa dukkhassa anubhavananibandho eva sassatvādino na yujjati kammabaddhā bhāvato, jātiādīnañ ca asambhavato kuto vimokkho?

Atha pana dhammamattaṃ tassa uppajjati c'eva vinassati ca, yassa vasen'āyaṃ kiriyādivohāro ti vadeyya, evampi purimarū pāvijahanena avaṭṭhitassa attano dhammamattanti na sakkā sambhāvetuṃ. Te vā pan'assa dhammā avatthābhūtā aññe vā siyuṃ anaññe vā. Yadi aññe, na tāhi tassa uppannāhi pi koci viseso atthi, yāhi karoti paṭisaṃvedeti cavati upapajjati cāti icchitaṃ, tasmā tadavattho eva yathāvuttadoso. Kiñca dhammakappanā pi niratthikā siyā, ath'anaññe uppādavināsavantīhi avatthāhi anaññassa attano tāsaṃ viya uppādavināsasabbhāvato kuto niccatāvakāso? Tāsampi vā attano viya niccatāti bandhavimokkhānaṃ asambhavo evā ti na yujjati yeva sassatavādo. Na c'ettha koci vādī dhammānaṃ sassatabhāve parisuddhaṃ yuttiṃ vattuṃ samattho, yuttirahitañ ca vacanaṃ na paṇḍitānaṃ cittaṃ ārādhetīti. Tena vuttaṃ yāva paṇḍitā na samanuyuñjanti, tāva gacchanti, pavattantīti.

4. The origin of annihilationism

Yathā hetuphalabhāvena pavattamānānaṃ sabhāvadhammānaṃ satipi ekasantānapariyāpannānaṃ bhinnasantatipatitehi visese hetuphalānaṃ paramatthato bhinnasabhāvattā bhinnasantā- napatitānaṃ viya accantabhedasanniṭṭhānena nānattanayassa micchāgahaṇaṃ ucchedābhinivesassa kāraṇaṃ; evaṃ hetuphala-bhūtānaṃ dhammānaṃ vijjamāne pi sabhāvabhede ekasantatipari yāpannatāya ekattanayena accantam abhedaggahaṇampi kāraṇam evā ti dassetuṃ "sattassā" ti vuttaṃ pāliyaṃ. Santānavasena hi vattamānesu khandhesu ghanavinibbhogābhāvena sattagāho, sattassa ca atthibhāvagāhanibandhano ucchedagāho yāv'āyaṃ attā na ucchijjati, tāv'āyaṃ vijjati yevāti gahaṇato.

Index

THE BUDDHIST PUBLICATION SOCIETY

The BPS is an approved charity dedicated to making known the Teaching of the Buddha, which has a vital message for all people. Founded in 1958, the BPS has published a wide variety of books and booklets covering a great range of topics. Its publications include accurate annotated translations of the Buddha's discourses, standard reference works, as well as original contemporary expositions of Buddhist thought and practice. These works present Buddhism as it truly is—a dynamic force which has influenced receptive minds for the past 2500 years and is still as relevant today as it was when it first arose.

For more information about the BPS and our publications, please visit our website, or write an e-mail, or a letter to the:

Administrative Secretary
Buddhist Publication Society
P.O. Box 61
54 Sangharaja Mawatha
Kandy • Sri Lanka

E-mail: bps@bps.lk
web site: http://www.bps.lk
Tel: 0094 81 223 7283 • Fax: 0094 81 222 3679

